PARTY AND
PROCEDURE IN THE
UNITED STATES CONGRESS

PARTY AND PROCEDURE IN THE UNITED STATES CONGRESS

Second Edition

Edited by
Jacob R. Straus
Congressional Research Service

Matthew E. Glassman
Congressional Research Service

ROWMAN & LITTLEFIELD
Lanham • Boulder • New York • London

Executive Editor: Traci Crowell
Associate Editor: Molly White
Senior Marketing Manager: Karin Cholak
Marketing Manager: Deborah Hudson
Cover Art: © Sandra Baker / Alamy Stock Photo

Credits and acknowledgments borrowed from other sources and reproduced, with permission, in this textbook appear on appropriate page within the text.

Published by Rowman & Littlefield
A wholly owned subsidiary of The Rowman & Littlefield Publishing Group, Inc.
4501 Forbes Boulevard, Suite 200, Lanham, Maryland 20706
www.rowman.com

Unit A, Whitacre Mews, 26-34 Stannary Street, London SE11 4AB, United Kingdom

Copyright © 2017 by Rowman & Littlefield
First edition 2012.

British Library Cataloguing in Publication Information Available

Library of Congress Cataloging-in-Publication Data

Names: Straus, Jacob R., editor. | Glassman, Matthew, editor.
Title: Party and procedure in the United States Congress / Edited by Jacob R. Straus, Matthew Glassman.
Description: Second edition. | Lanham, Maryland : Rowman & Littlefield, 2016. | Includes bibliographical references and index.
Identifiers: LCCN 2016015417 (print) | LCCN 2016016186 (ebook) | ISBN 9781442258723 (cloth : alk. paper) | ISBN 9781442258730 (pbk. : alk. paper) | ISBN 9781442258747 (electronic)
Subjects: LCSH: United States. Congress—Rules and practice. | Legislation—United States.
Classification: LCC KF4937 .P37 2016 (print) | LCC KF4937 (ebook) | DDC 328.73/05—dc23
LC record available at https://lccn.loc.gov/2016015417

♾™ The paper used in this publication meets the minimum requirements of American National Standard for Information Sciences—Permanence of Paper for Printed Library Materials, ANSI/NISO Z39.48-1992.

Printed in the United States of America

Contents

Section III: Senate

Section IV: Interchamber Analysis and Negotiation

Preface

IN 2012, THE FIRST EDITION of *Party and Procedure in the United States Congress* was published. Since that time, numerous changes have occurred in both the House and the Senate—from a midsession shift to a new Speaker of the House to adoption of the "nuclear option" in the Senate. This book builds on the knowledge that political parties in Congress matter and that procedure is the primary key to influencing the legislative process. Examination of political parties and how they use procedure invites the use of numerous social science methods. The second edition of *Party and Procedure in the United States Congress* highlights these varied approaches to answer questions about agenda setting, decision-making strategy, and compromise.

The modern Congress operates with significant similarities to and growing differences from its historic iterations. In some eras, elected chamber leaders wield the most power (i.e., Speakers Joe Cannon and Newt Gingrich), and at other moments congressional committees utilize their place in the legislative process and the power of procedure to dictate the agenda (i.e., the conservative coalitions between southern Democrats and northern Republicans in the 1960s and 1970s). Recent congresses, however, have also shown the power of the individual, rank-and-file, majority-party member to dictate the congressional agenda. Tea Party and House Freedom Caucus members have demonstrated that the power of procedure can reside not only with party leaders and committee chairs but also with well-placed internal party votes and House and Senate resolutions.

Even with the disbursement of power in the modern Congress, for a bill to be presented to the president both the House of Representatives and the

Senate must pass and present identical language in identical vehicles. The process of going from idea, to introduction, to passage in each chamber is ultimately governed by rules and procedures unique to each body. This volume further examines how parties, elected chamber leadership, and the chambers of Congress use procedure to advance their agendas.

This book would not have been possible without the support of the editorial team at Rowman & Littlefield. The assistance provided by our editor, Traci Crowell, and our associate editor, Molly White, has been invaluable and much appreciated. We are thankful to those colleagues who reviewed this book and offered their invaluable feedback, including Jamie Carson, University of Georgia; John J. Pitney, Claremont McKenna College; and Wendy Schiller, Brown University. Additionally, we are grateful to our colleagues and coauthors who contributed their expertise and dedication to this publication.

This book is clearly a collective effort. We thank all of the contributors who have provided original and important scholarship in each chapter. As editors and authors, we take full responsibility for any omissions or errors of fact and interpretation.

We also want to remember two contributors from the first edition, Representative Major Owens and Barbara Sinclair. Barbara's insight into Congress was an inspiration for a generation of congressional scholars. Congressman Owens was a tireless advocate for his constituents and a founding member of the Congressional Black Caucus. They will both be missed.

Jacob dedicates this book to his family. Thank you Sarah, Lily, and Ben for your love, inspiration, and continued support.

Matt dedicates this book to his three little girls—Anna, Abigail, and Elizabeth—and his one big girl, Sarahjane. Thank you for your endless love and patience with my congressional storytelling.

Jacob R. Straus and Matthew E. Glassman

1

Navigating Congress
in the Age of Partisanship

Jacob R. Straus and Matthew E. Glassman

O N SEPTEMBER 25, 2015, John Boehner announced his resignation as
Speaker of the House and from Congress, effective upon the election of
a new Speaker (DeBonis and Kane 2015; Steinhauer 2015). In announcing
his resignation, the *Washington Times* quoted Boehner as saying that it has
"become clear to me the prolonged leadership turmoil would do irreparable
harm to the institution" (Dinan and Shastry 2015).

The voluntary resignation by a sitting Speaker not under charges of ethical
impropriety is almost unheard of in congressional history (Bomboy 2015).
To understand how the House arrived at this juncture, a brief look at the
historical record is in order. Speaker Boehner, over his last two elections as
Speaker—in 2013 and 2015—had more Republican members vote for other
Speaker candidates than is traditional (Blake 2015; Kasperowicz 2013). In
fact, as chapter 3 by Matthew Green and Briana Bee discusses, most Speaker
elections have featured few dissenting votes by the majority party against its
nominated candidate.

This public dissent by Republican members may have emboldened some to
attempt to exert influence over legislative scheduling and other party-based
political decisions, such as the selection of committee chairs (Ball 2013; Russert 2013). For example, on July 28, 2015, Representative Mark Meadows
(R-NC) introduced a resolution (H. Res. 385) to vacate the chair—which
would have essentially removed Speaker Boehner from office and forced a
new election for Speaker (Feehery 2015). The resolution was, at least in part,
a reaction to Meadows being removed as chairman of a subcommittee for
voting against a procedural matter on the House floor (Wong and Marcos

2015). In the resolution (see box 1.1),[1] Meadows listed many of the grievances shared by more conservative members of the House Republican Conference, including members of the House Freedom Caucus.

In comments to the *Washington Post* after the resolution's introduction, Representative Meadows stated that he did not necessarily expect the resolution to be considered by the House. Instead, he stated, "It's really more about trying to have a conversation on making this place work, where everybody's voice matters, where there's not a punitive culture. . . . Hopefully, we'll have some discussion about that in the days and weeks to come" (DeBonis 2015). While no immediate action was taken following the introduction of Meadows's resolution (Fox and Newhauser 2015), its introduction and the subsequent discussion it facilitated arguably contributed to Speaker Boehner's resignation and the difficulty in finding a suitable candidate for Speaker to replace Boehner. Some journalists have suggested that Speaker Boehner was plenty conservative to meet the Freedom Caucus's policy goals, but it was the way he attempted to move legislation in the House that led to his downfall (Cillizza 2015; Lizza 2015).

Speaker Boehner's presumptive successor—Majority Leader Kevin McCarthy—withdrew as a candidate in early October (DeBonis, Costa, and Helderman 2015). In media reports about his announcement withdrawing as a candidate, McCarthy was quoted as saying, "Over the last week it has become clear to me that our conference is deeply divided and needs to unite behind one leader. I have always put this conference ahead of myself. Therefore I am withdrawing my candidacy for Speaker of the House. I look forward to working alongside my colleagues to help move our conference's agenda and our country forward" (Singer 2015). McCarthy's withdrawal blindsided House Republicans and threw "their already tumultuous chamber into deeper chaos with no clear leader in sight just weeks before a series of high-stakes battles" (Steinhauer and Herszenhorn 2015). Emerging from the "chaos" was former vice presidential candidate and then Ways and Means chairman Representative Paul Ryan, who was elected Speaker on October 29 ("Election of Speaker" 2015).

Ryan's rise to the Speakership was not, however, without tribulations. Before he was able to win the support of House Republicans, he had to negotiate with the House Freedom Caucus—a minority group of conservative Republicans (Lizza 2015)—to prevent them from blocking his nomination on the floor (Berman 2015). While internal party negotiations over candidates are common, the demands and, in particular, the tactics of the Freedom Caucus were unusual. Instead of demanding the next Speaker meet policy standards, the Freedom Caucus instead set procedural and strategic ideals as its primary basis for negotiations and openly threatened to withhold the necessary support on the floor for the conference-nominated candidate (Cillizza

Box 1.1. H. RES. 385 (114th Congress)

Declaring the office of Speaker of the House of Representatives vacant.

IN THE HOUSE OF REPRESENTATIVES

JULY 28, 2015

Mr. MEADOWS submitted the following resolution; which was referred to the Committee on Rules

RESOLUTION

Declaring the office of Speaker of the House of Representatives vacant.

Whereas the Speaker of the House of Representatives for the 114th Congress has endeavored to consolidate power and centralize decision-making, bypassing the majority of the 435 Members of Congress and the people they represent;

Whereas the Speaker has, through inaction, caused the power of Congress to atrophy, thereby making Congress subservient to the executive and judicial branches, diminishing the voice of the American people;

Whereas the Speaker uses the power of the office to punish Members who vote according to their conscience instead of the will of the Speaker;

Whereas the Speaker has intentionally provided for voice votes on consequential and controversial legislation to be taken without notice and with few Members present;

Whereas the Speaker uses the legislative calendar to create crises for the American people, in order to compel Members to vote for legislation;

Whereas the Speaker does not comply with the spirit of the rules of the House of Representatives, which provide that Members shall have three days to review legislation before voting;

Whereas the Speaker continues to direct the Rules Committee to limit meaningful amendments, to limit debate on the House floor, and to subvert a straightforward legislative process; and

Whereas the House of Representatives, to function effectively in the service of all citizens of this country, requires the service of a Speaker who will endeavor to follow an orderly and inclusive process without imposing his or her will upon any Member thereof: Now, therefore, be it

Resolved, That the office of Speaker of the House of Representatives is hereby declared to be vacant.

2015). After several tense days of negotiation, Ryan won the support of most Freedom Caucus members and was nominated by the Republican Conference and subsequently elected Speaker by the House. Many of the procedural issues raised during the previous month, however, remained unaddressed (Herszenhorn and Huetteman 2015).

Shifting Centers of Congressional Power

As the first edition of *Party and Procedure in the United States Congress* reminded us, Congress is a dynamic institution that has seen the center of power shift between political parties, elected chamber leadership, committees, and rank-and-file members at different points in history (Straus 2012). This volume continues to explore the relationship between party and floor procedure. At different times, House and Senate rules have empowered both elected leaders and committee chairs with the ability to direct the chambers' legislative outcomes. While controlling the floor is an art rather than a science, each congressional era has had different ideas about which groups and what processes will best accomplish the goals of Congress. Historically, three main groups have come to share power: political parties, committees, and elected leaders. In the House of Representatives, this is especially true as parties—especially party leadership—and committees dominate. Individual members cannot do much without their party's support. In the Senate, individuals have more power but are still very much constrained by the institutional assignment of power to leaders, parties, and committees.

As the events of September and October 2015 show, however, divisions within the majority over the relative balance of power between leadership, committees, and rank-and-file members, as well the role they should play in setting the House's agenda, create opportunities for entrepreneurial members to use procedural tools to advance their own policy ideas and reshape the balance of power (Richman 2015a, 2015b). An examination of the three centers of power—political parties, committees, and elected leadership—in this context reveals three major themes that appear throughout this volume: the majority party's organizational power, the majority party's legislative power, and the role of the minority of the majority party.

Organizational Power: Control of Committee Assignments

On November 18, 2015, Speaker Ryan facilitated an internal vote within the House Republican Conference to "reconfigure" the party's Steering Committee—the panel charged with assigning Republican members to committees. Prior to the vote, the Steering Committee for the 114th Congress (2015–2016) consisted of thirty-three members, including the elected party leadership, six committee chairs, twelve regional representatives, a small state representative, and four class representatives (House Republicans 2015).[2] Under pressure from Freedom Caucus members, the reconfigured Steering Committee structure replaces the six permanent committee chair slots with six "at-large" appointments in an attempt to broaden the membership to more closely reflect the diversity of the Republican caucus (Phillips 2015). In effect, the change potentially weakens the Speaker's control over committee assignments.

Committees have historically derived their power from both political parties and chamber rules (Rudder 1977; Davidson 1981; Deering and Smith 1997). Since virtually all legislation introduced in the House and Senate is referred to at least one committee, and most controversial legislation must be passed by the committee before floor consideration, committees wield enormous selection power. The policy stances advocated by committee chairs, therefore, can affect legislation's eventual floor success (Unekis and Rieselbach 1983; King 1997). In fact, a committee chair can have so much power that individual members will use political capital to try to become a chair and directly influence public policy (Fenno 1973; Leighton and Lopez 2002). Additionally, committee chairs can also influence how multiply referred legislation is considered by other committees. Baughman (2006, 137–38) argues that when a piece of legislation is multiply referred and the chair of the primary committee sits as a rank-and-file member on the second committee, the chair often exerts his or her influence in an attempt to make the second committee "roll" and defer to the primary committee.

Debate over the organization of Congress and the use of procedural tools to ensure an outcome favorable to the majority has been endemic to the discussion of power in Congress for generations. In this modern context, struggle for congressional control has manifested itself through the way the parties organize and decide to bring legislation to the floor. At different times, House and Senate rules have empowered both elected leaders and committee chairs with the ability to direct legislative outcomes. While the consequences of specific rules changes were not always immediately known, observers knew that how the institution was organized and operated would favor the majority party, regardless of the rhetoric (Sinclair 2012; Dodd and Oppenheimer 2012).

By reconfiguring the Steering Committee, House Republicans were signaling two shifts in power within the caucus. First, by bowing to pressure from the Freedom Caucus to alter the party rules, the leadership conceded a shift in control of the caucus itself away from the existing moderate leaders and toward the conservative rank and file. Speaker Ryan could have fought to maintain stronger leadership control over the Steering Committee, but he did not; by flexing its muscles, the Freedom Caucus showed its ability to drive organizational changes within the conference. Second, the reconfigured Steering Committee will inevitably, albeit indirectly, strengthen the hand of the committee chairs. By reducing the role of the leadership in committee assignment, the caucus not only chose to give the rank and file more say in who was on the committees but also weakened the control of the leadership over the committees *once assigned*. Chairmen who wish to clash with the leadership in the future may have fewer concerns about the ability of the leadership to punish them.

Legislative Power: Control of the Floor Agenda

The challenge of the Freedom Caucus to the Republican House leadership also included complaints about the running of the House floor. Calls from conservative GOP conference members for "regular order"—typically meaning a reduced use of special rules limiting amendments and a reliance on committee drafted legislation rather than airdropped leadership bills—became common during the first session of the 114th Congress. Further, the House Freedom Caucus challenged the power of the Speaker to schedule legislation by insisting that the informal "Hastert Rule"—a policy that only legislation that has the support of a majority of the majority will be scheduled for floor time—would not be violated (Richman 2015a, 2015b).

Control of the floor agenda in both chambers is generally considered the purview of the majority-party leadership (Sinclair 1995; Den Hartog and Monroe 2011). While this power is almost absolute in the House, it is less so in the Senate, where the majority leader only controls the floor agenda through his right of first recognition (i.e., if the majority leader and another senator rise at the same time, the majority leader is recognized first). Further, in the House, the majority leadership is backed up by the Rules Committee—the only supermajoritarian committee in the House that, in the modern age, is considered to be an arm of the leadership (Dion and Huber 1996). With the combined ability of the House and Senate leadership to control the agenda across both chambers, the majority party can usually keep unwanted measures off the House and Senate floor.

Even with the power to control the legislative agenda, the majority-party leadership's power is not absolute. As the House Freedom Caucus has demonstrated in its insistence on the Hastert Rule in the House, legislation supported by the majority leadership and a majority of members does not always receive floor time. In fact, this was one of the chief complaints by the Freedom Caucus against Speaker Boehner—his willingness to occasionally violate the Hastert Rule and use Democratic votes to pass legislation. For example, in January 2013, the House voted to pass a bill to provide relief for victims of Hurricane Sandy with only forty-nine Republicans and all but one Democrat (Binder 2013). The use of less than a majority of Republicans and almost all Democrats to pass the measure was seen by some conservatives as a violation of the Republican Conference's scheduling rules. The passage of the Hurricane Sandy relief bill was not the only time that Speaker Boehner or his predecessors scheduled legislation that did not have support of a majority of the majority party. In fact, the *New York Times* reported that the Hastert Rule has been violated twenty-one times since Speaker Dennis Hastert invented the "rule" in 2003 (*New York Times* 2015).

Leadership Power: Control of the Majority

Finally, and perhaps most fundamentally, the events of fall 2015 raise questions about the ability of the House leadership to maintain its own power. Scholars have long observed that divided majority caucuses tend to weaken leadership, while ideologically homogenous caucuses tend to empower their leaders (Rohde 1991; Theriault 2008). Current divisions with the House GOP, however, may be emblematic of deeper leadership control issues. The willingness of the Freedom Caucus to threaten the leadership with vacancy resolutions and suggestions that it may withhold support for party-nominated Speaker candidates on the floor is virtually unprecedented in modern congressional history. Regardless of whether these maneuvers were in part bluffs, they began to tear at some of the longest-standing norms of majority-party behavior in the House: a united backing of leadership on procedural votes and a basic commitment not to take internal party fights public.

One of Speaker Ryan's goals upon agreeing to run for the office was the elimination of resolutions to vacate the chair as a procedural mechanism. Regardless of whether the procedure is removed from House rules (as of December 31, 2015, it has not been removed), the very need to remove it signals the weakness of the current leadership's control over the conference and the House. When the leadership is strong and has the backing of the vast majority of the conference, members who choose to defect on key procedural votes such as the Speaker election or important special rules could be easily punished by leadership, which would not fear a backlash. Under such conditions, no member would even consider introducing a vacancy resolution, knowing swift and strong retribution would be the result. Under current conditions, however, the leadership is not able to exact such punishments, out of fear of losing control of the caucus. As such, the removal of the vacancy procedure becomes a signal of the leadership's weakness, not its strength.

Such procedural changes, however, can never defang a concerted minority within the majority party. Even if the Speaker cannot be removed directly, any majority-party faction that controls the balance of power in the House can topple the Speaker simply by refusing to agree to special rules brought forward by the Rules Committee under the leadership's direction. If the leadership cannot control the floor agenda, it has ceased, in any real sense, to be in control of the House. This theoretical threat—a general strike by the Freedom Caucus (or any other majority-party faction) against any and all special rules brought up by the majority—is the ultimate question of party and procedure for the House leadership.

Organization of the Book

To address the use of procedure by political parties in Congress, this volume is divided into four parts. Part I focuses on the importance of legislative language for members to express their policy preferences. Part II covers the House of Representatives, part III focuses on the Senate, and part IV discusses intraparty negotiations, the evolving role of women in Congress, and a detailed case study of the October 2013 government shutdown. Each section provides theoretical and practical insights concerning the role that political parties play in using procedure to advance their legislative agendas within Congress. In its own way, each chapter also considers how modern congressional procedure compares to historical trends within Congress.

Part I: Legislative Language

Bills and resolutions are the foundation of the legislature and the legislative process. Before an idea can be implemented, the House and Senate must pass identical language in the same vehicle (i.e., bill or resolution number). In crafting the words in each bill or resolution, representatives and senators must make numerous choices about the measure's content. In chapter 2, "Drafting the Law: Players, Power, and Process," Scott Levy, a former Senate Finance Committee staffer, directly examines the process used to craft legislative language. He begins by outlining the stages of legislative production, with a focus on the parties involved. His analysis then centers on the coordination among both internal and external organizations to draft legislative language.

Part II: House of Representatives

Part II focuses on the House of Representatives. Chapters in this section include an examination of party discipline and dissent, an analysis of the motion to recommit, a study of the use of budget reconciliation for budgetary and nonbudgetary purposes, an evaluation of post–Rules Committee textual adjustments to bills, and an inspection of one-minute speeches.

Chapter 3 begins our discussion of the House of Representatives with an examination of how congressional leadership holds the party together within the chamber. In "Keeping the Team Together: Explaining Party Discipline and Dissent in the U.S. Congress," Matthew Green and Briana Bee discuss the broader context of how party leaders "control" their members to ensure the passage of the party's preferred policy position. Using the recent turmoil within the House Republican Party as a backdrop, the chapter looks at party discipline—including tactics available to punish dissenters—in terms of the theoretical reasons why revolt or dissent may occur. This chapter concludes that dealing with dissent before it occurs, often through a reward system, can be more effective.

In chapter 4, "The Motion to Recommit in the U.S. House," Jennifer Hayes Clark conducts a new analysis of the motion to recommit (MTR) in the House of Representatives. The MTR permits opponents of a measure to offer an alternative for consideration at the end of the legislative process and before the final vote on a measure. Clark places the minority's right to the MTR within the context of political science research on agenda control and the process of drafting special rules. Clark finds that there has been a sharp increase in the number of MTRs offered over the last several congresses but that the number adopted is still relatively low.

In chapter 5, "Evolution of the Reconciliation Process, 1980–2015," James V. Saturno explores the budget reconciliation process—an often misunderstood process that was originally developed to help Congress create and enforce a balanced budget. Saturno begins with a historical analysis of why the reconciliation process began in order to explain the need for a new process to control the federal budget and for congressional committees to set revenue and spending targets. Through a series of case studies spanning 1980 to 2015, Saturno demonstrates how the reconciliation process has changed over time from a tool to set budgetary limits into a tool to pass legislation that is subject to expedited procedures in the Senate that prevent most filibusters. The chapter concludes with an exploration of the limits of reconciliation and discusses the potential impact that infrequent budget resolutions might have on the federal budget and appropriations process.

Chapter 6 continues the focus on setting the rules for debate and making post-committee adjustments to legislation. In "Post-committee Adjustment in the Contemporary House: The Use of Rules Committee Prints," Mark J. Oleszek examines a new trend in making adjustments to the text of legislation in the House. Instead of only offering amendments on the floor, the Rules Committee has begun to use a committee print—a document issued with the text of legislation that has been issued a special rule by the Rules Committee—to make alterations to the bill or resolution's text. In a first-of-its-kind analysis, Oleszek finds that the Rules Committee provides textual clues about the extent of alterations made to the bill's text. He also finds that while the first instance of a post-committee adjustment occurred in 1999, it was not until the 112th Congress (2011–2012) that the practice took off. In the 112th and 113th Congress (2013–2014), the Rules Committee issued seventy-seven prints as compared to five in the previous six congresses combined. Additionally, those prints made changes to 23 percent of bill sections in the 112th Congress and 4 percent in the 113th Congress.

Finally, chapter 7 completes the discussion of the House of Representatives by exploring one-minute speeches in the House. In "Longitudinal Analysis of One-Minute Speeches in the House of Representatives," Colleen J. Shogan and Matthew E. Glassman examine the content and tone of one-minute speeches—daily opportunities for members of the House to talk about virtually any topic in one-minute increments on the House floor. Shogan and Glassman begin with an overview of one-minute speech literature before examining how one-minute speeches help members spread party messages, promote policy priorities, and highlight district activities and concerns. Additionally, the chapter explores these behaviors within the confines of the modern political environment. After coding speeches in 1989, 1999, and 2009, Shogan and Glassman find that there may be a relationship between the frequency of one-minute speeches and political party, a relationship that is likely affected by member ideology. Further, they find support for the categories of incumbent member behavior first observed in 1974 by David Mayhew in *Congress: The Electoral Connection*. Finally, they note that the tone of one-minute speeches has grown increasingly negative over time, with mentions of the opposing party in a negative light increasing from negligible in 1989 to almost routine in 2009.

Part III: Senate

Part III covers the Senate and the specific role that party and procedure play in floor debate. Included in this section are chapters about the evolving "toolbox" available to senators, the electoral politics of Senate procedural votes, the filibuster, the Senate amending process, and exceptions to the filibuster and cloture process. The exploration of the Senate begins with an update to a chapter from the first edition of *Party and Procedure in the United States Congress*. In chapter 8, "A Good Leader Never Blames His Tools: The Evolving Majority-Party Toolkit in the U.S. Senate," Aaron S. King, Frank J. Orlando, and David W. Rohde reexamine the procedural tools available to senators. King, Orlando, and Rohde examine four tools—the motion to table, budgetary points of order, cloture, and filling the amendment tree—within the confines of historic Senate behavior. They find that all types of Senate votes have become more partisan over time, with the three most recent congresses the most partisan of the data set. Further, the use of procedural tools by the majority to wage "partisan warfare" is still greater in the House than in the Senate.

Chapter 9, "The Electoral Politics of Procedural Votes in the U.S. Senate," by Joel Sievert, explores a rarely talked about but important phenomenon: the use of procedural votes by outside interest groups and opponent campaigns to frame a senator's issue positions. While much of this volume discusses procedure from a majority-minority prospective, Sievert examines procedural votes in terms of their impact during campaigns and elections. He finds that while conventional wisdom suggests that procedural votes can provide political cover for senators, in fact these votes can be used to frame votes on more than just narrow internal Senate decision-making. Instead, votes on procedural matters can often be used as stand-ins for votes on final passage and can be used by opponents to paint senators in negative ways. Lastly, the use of procedural votes and the difficulty that both candidates and challengers have in explaining their true purposes can raise questions about the quality of information that voters receive and how voting decisions might be made on Election Day.

In chapter 10, "Partisanship, Filibustering, and Reform in the Senate," Gregory Koger explains the partisan use of obstruction and cloture in the modern Senate and explains the "nuclear option," whereby the Senate reduced the number of votes to a simple majority to invoke cloture on executive branch and non–Supreme Court judicial nominations. Koger explains that both parties try to use the legislative process to improve their brand-name reputations. For the majority party, this means trying to enact landmark legislation, to fulfill the basic tasks of Congress, and to provide benefits for individual majority-party members. In response, the minority-party filibusters to block majority initiatives, to force modifications so that they are acceptable to minority-party members, and to ensure that minority members receive their fair share of spending and other policy benefits. Also, the minority party may filibuster to take legislation "hostage" until the majority party allows votes on its hot-button proposals. This competition has fed a partisan polarization of voting on cloture that resulted in changes during the 113th Congress.

In chapter 11, "Irregular Order: Examining the Changing Congressional Amending Process," Michael S. Lynch, Anthony J. Madonna, and Rachel Surminsky closely examine the process of amending legislation in the Senate. Beginning with a discussion of the Senate's amendment process and continuing with a comparison between the House and the Senate, Lynch, Madonna, and Surminsky use a unique dataset from the University of Georgia Amendments Project to examine the Senate amendment process in new and interesting ways. They find that while the majority party generally controls which issues are scheduled for floor debate, the amendment process provides the minority party an opportunity to alter or adjust majority legislation. Further, the Senate's rules and procedures allow open participation by both the majority and minority in the amendment process, and senators of both parties are increasingly using amendments in an attempt to score political points. The end result of this change in the amendment process is gridlock and a general reduction in lawmaking.

Finally, in chapter 12, "From Base Closings to the Budget: Exceptions to the Filibuster in the U.S. Senate," Molly E. Reynolds explores "majority exceptions" and their impact on future legislative consideration. Reynolds defines a "majority exception" as a provision, included in statutory law, which exempts some future piece of legislation from a filibuster by limiting debate on that measure in the Senate. Two types of "majority exceptions" exist: oversight exemptions, where Congress attempts to protect its right to weigh in on executive branch decisions, and delegate exemptions, where special rules protect a proposal that has been developed by a special agenda setter (e.g., a commission). Including either type of exemption in law for a future bill in effect eliminates the Senate minority's right to block a bill through traditional means. Using several examples, including the Base Realignment and Closing Commission, the Iran nuclear agreement in 2015, and fast-track authority for the Trans-Pacific Partnership (TPP) in the 114th Congress, Reynolds shows that when policies are more unpopular among the public or senators, the majority-party leadership will often attempt to use majority exceptions to push through policy and limit the opportunities for opposition on the Senate floor.

Part IV: Interchamber Analysis and Negotiation

Finally, part IV examines interchamber cooperation, the role of women in the legislative process, and the 2013 government shutdown. Each of these topics brings together research from the House or Senate sections of this volume and utilizes specific examples to demonstrate the importance of party and procedure. In chapter 13, "Intraparty Caucus Formation in the U.S. Congress," James Wallner conducts in-depth case studies of two long-standing

Republican intraparty caucuses: the Republican Study Committee (RSC) in the House and the Senate Steering Committee (SSC). He finds that intraparty caucuses can have a tremendous impact on the party's leadership and policy direction. After examining the lessons that can be learned from the RSC and the SSC, Wallner begins an analysis of the newly formed House Freedom Caucus by applying lessons learned over the years from the RSC and the SSC to understand why the caucus was formed and what impact it might have on the House Republican Party in the future.

Chapter 14, in "Gender and Party Politics in a Polarized Era," Michele L. Swers examines the role that women currently play in congressional party politics. Using hot-button issues including abortion, gay marriage, and the Affordable Care Act (ACA, or ObamaCare), as examples, Swers locates women in the context of both geographic and demographic representatives. Through an easy-to-read examination of the role women have played from the "Year of the Woman" election of 1992 to the present day, she explains how women of both parties have handled the "War on Women" and focused attention on women's issues in the modern context. Swers concludes with a look forward to the 2016 presidential election and discusses the potential role that Hillary Clinton's gender might play in framing issues, should she win the Democratic nomination.

Finally, in chapter 15, "The Government Shutdown of 2013: A Perspective," Walter J. Oleszek provides a comprehensive summation of the book's major themes through an examination of the October 2013 government shutdown. In a detailed analysis of what led to the shutdown and how Congress worked its way to an agreement on appropriations for fiscal year 2014, Oleszek explores the congressional and political landscape of the 113th Congress (2013–2014).

Notes

* This chapter reflects the views of the authors and does not necessarily reflect the view of the Congressional Research Service or the Library of Congress.

1. "H. Res. 385 [114th Congress]—Declaring the Office of Speaker of the House of Representatives Vacant," Congress.gov, July 28, 2015, https://www.congress.gov/bill/114th-congress/house-resolution/385.

2. Included in the House Republican Steering Committee at the beginning of the 114th Congress were the Speaker of the House; the Republican leader; the Republican whip; the chief deputy whip; the Republican Conference chair; the policy chair; the conference vice-chair; the conference secretary; the National Republican Congressional Committee chair and former chair; the Appropriations Committee, Energy and

Commerce Committee, Financial Services Committee, Rules Committee, Ways and Means Committee, and Budget Committee chairs; a representative from Texas; twelve regional representatives; a small state representative (i.e., a state with only one House member); and four class representatives.

References

Ball, Molly. 2013. "Even the Aide Who Coined the Hastert Rule Says the Hastert Rule Isn't Working." *Atlantic*, July 21.

Baughman, John. 2006. *Common Ground: Committee Politics in the U.S. House of Representatives*. Palo Alto, CA: Stanford University Press.

Berman, Russell. 2015. "Paul Ryan's Uneasy Alliance with the House Freedom Caucus." *Atlantic*, October 22.

Binder, Sarah. 2013. "Oh 113th Congress Hastert Rule, We Hardly Knew Ye!" *Brookings Institution Up Front*, http://www.brookings.edu/blogs/up-front/posts/2013/01/17-hastert-rule-binder.

Blake, Aaron. 2015. "John Boehner Just Endured the Biggest Revolt against a House Speaker in More Than 150 Years." *Washington Post*, January 6.

Bomboy, Scott. 2015. "Why Boehner's Resignation Is Truly Historic for House Speakers." *Constitution Daily* (blog), National Constitution Center, September 30, http://blog.constitutioncenter.org/2015/09/why-boehners-resignation-is-truly-historic-for-house-speakers.

Cillizza, Chris. 2015. "How to Negotiate, According to the House Freedom Caucus." *Washington Post*, December 8.

Davidson, Roger H. 1981. "Two Avenues of Change: House and Senate Committee Reorganization." In *Congress Reconsidered*, edited by Lawrence C. Dodd and Bruce I. Oppenheimer, 107–36. 2nd ed. Washington, DC: CQ Press.

DeBonis, Mike. 2015. "GOP Congressman Launches Bid to Oust John Boehner as House Speaker." *Washington Post*, July 28.

DeBonis, Mike, Robert Costa, and Rosaline S. Helderman. 2015. "House Majority Leader Kevin McCarthy Drops out of Race for House Speaker." *Washington Post*, October 8.

DeBonis, Mike, and Paul Kane. 2015. "House Speaker John Boehner to Resign at End of October." *Washington Post*, September 25.

Deering, Christopher J., and Steven S. Smith. 1997. *Committees in Congress*, 3rd ed. New York: Longman.

Den Hartog, Chris, and Nathan W. Monroe. 2011. *Agenda Setting in the U.S. Senate: Costly Consideration and Majority Party Advantage*. New York: Cambridge University Press.

Dinan, Stephen, and Anjali Shastry. 2015. "John Boehner Resigns; Speaker Cites Desire to Avoid 'Prolonged Leadership Turmoil.'" *Washington Times*, September 25.

Dion, Douglas, and John D. Huber. 1996. "Procedural Choice and the House Committee on Rules." *Journal of Politics* 58: 25–53.

Dodd, Lawrence C., and Bruce I. Oppenheimer. 2012. "The House in a Time of Crisis: Economic Turmoil and Partisan Upheaval." In *Congress Reconsidered*, edited by Lawrence C. Dodd and Bruce I. Oppenheimer, 27–58. 10th ed. Washington, DC: CQ Press.

"Election of Speaker." 2015. *Congressional Record*, House of Representatives (daily edition) 161 (October 29): H338–39.

Feehery, John. 2015. "How an Obscure Motion to 'Vacate the Chair' Spoils House GOP's August Vacation." *Christian Science Monitor*, July 31.

Fenno, Richard F. 1973. *Congressmen in Committees*. Boston: Little, Brown, and Company.

Fox, Lauren, and Daniel Newhauser. 2015. "John Boehner's Not Giving Mark Meadows the Chance to Oust Him." *National Journal*, July 29.

Herszenhorn, David M., and Emmarie Huetteman. 2015. "Paul Ryan Wins Backing of Majority in Freedom Caucus for House Speaker." *New York Times*, October 21.

House Republicans. 2015. "House Republican Steering Committee List (114th Congress)." GovDelivery, http://content.govdelivery.com/attachments/USHRC/2014/11/14/file_attachments/341150/114th%2BSteering%2BCommittee%2B114th%2BRoster.pdf.

Kasperowicz, Pete. 2013. "Boehner Reelected as Speaker; Nine Republicans Defect in Vote." *Hill*, January 3.

King, David C. 1997. *Turf Wars: How Congressional Committees Claim Jurisdiction*. Chicago: University of Chicago Press.

Leighton, Wayne A., and Edward J. Lopez. 2002. "Committee Assignments and the Cost of Party Loyalty." *Political Research Quarterly* 55: 59–90.

Lizza, Ryan. 2015. "A House Divided: How a Radical Group of Republicans Pushed Congress to the Right." *New Yorker*, December 14.

New York Times. 2015. "House Votes Violating the 'Hastert Rule.'" *New York Times*, http://politics.nytimes.com/congress/votes/house/hastert-rule.

Phillips, Amber. 2015. "Paul Ryan's Precarious Tight-Rope Walk with House Conservatives." *Washington Post*, December 11.

Richman, Jesse. 2015a. "By Insisting on the 'Hastert Rule,' the House Freedom Caucus Is Endangering the GOP." *Washington Post*, October 20.

———. 2015b. "The Electoral Costs of Party Agenda Setting: Why the Hastert Rule Leads to Defeat." *Journal of Politics* 77: 1129–41.

Rohde, David W. 1991. *Parties and Leaders in the Postreform House*. Chicago: University of Chicago Press.

Rudder, Catherine E. 1977. "Committee Reform and the Revenue Process." In *Congress Reconsidered*, edited by Lawrence C. Dodd and Bruce I. Oppenheimer, 117–39. New York: Praeger.

Russert, Luke. 2013. "Boehner Eschews Hastert Rule for Third Time." NBC News, February 28.

Sinclair, Barbara. 1995. *Legislators, Leaders, and Lawmaking: The U.S. House of Representatives in the Postreform Era*. Baltimore: Johns Hopkins University Press.

———. 2012. "The New World of U.S. Senators." In *Congress Reconsidered*, edited by Lawrence C. Dodd and Bruce I. Oppenheimer, 1–26. 10th ed. Washington, DC: CQ Press.

Singer, Paul. 2015. "Kevin McCarthy Abruptly Quits Speaker Race, Leaving Republicans in Disarray." *USA Today*, October 9.

Steinhauer, Jennifer. 2015. "John Boehner, House Speaker, Will Resign from Congress." *New York Times*, September 25.

Steinhauer, Jennifer, and David M. Herszenhorn. 2015. "Kevin McCarthy Withdraws from Speaker's Race, Putting House in Chaos." *New York Times*, October 8.

Straus, Jacob. 2012. "Navigating Congress." In *Party and Procedure in the United States Congress*, edited by Jacob R. Straus, 1–11. Lanham, MD: Rowman & Littlefield.

Theriault, Sean M. 2008. *Party Polarization in Congress*. New York: Cambridge University Press.

Unekis, Joseph K., and Leroy N. Rieselbach. 1983. "Congressional Committee Leadership, 1971–1978." *Legislative Studies Quarterly* 8: 251–70.

Wong, Scott, and Cristina Marcos. 2015. "Republican Seeks to Oust Boehner." *Hill*, July 28.

I
LEGISLATIVE LANGUAGE

2

Drafting the Law

Players, Power, and Processes

Scott Levy

I N 2013, CONSERVATIVE OPPONENTS to the Affordable Care Act (ACA),
President Barack Obama's crowning legislative achievement, sued to bar
the Internal Revenue Service (IRS) from providing tax credits to Americans
purchasing insurance through Healthcare.gov. This lawsuit was argued before the Supreme Court in March 2015 and turned on the proper interpretation of four words from the ACA: "established by the State." While the Court
ruled 6–3 to uphold the IRS's provision of tax credits, these four words could
have shattered Obama's legislative legacy. Had the Court interpreted those
words differently, millions of previously eligible citizens would have lost the
ability to buy subsidized insurance on the federal ACA exchange.

As the case moved through the federal courts, many writers examined the
legislative history of the ACA and its drafting, exploring the effects of the
legislative process on the legislative drafting of the act. However, political
scientists and, until recently, legal scholars have generally had little to say
about how Congress actually drafts legislation (Katzmann 1989; Nourse and
Schacter 2002; Gluck and Bressman 2013; Bressman and Gluck 2014; Shobe
2014, 2015; Sitaraman 2015; Walker 2015). Too often discussions of the legislative process stop at the policymaking stage without examining how large
policy ideas are fleshed out and translated into legislative language.

Drawing on my experiences drafting legislation as a staffer for the Senate Finance Committee during the 113th Congress (2013–2014) as well as
conversations with current and former staffers, this chapter examines that
process. First, I divide the process of producing legislative language into three
stages and describe each stage. Second, I describe the roles that various politi-

cal actors play in these stages. Third, I provide an overview of the legislative drafting process as performed by congressional staff and the House and Senate Offices of Legislative Counsel and discuss the important roles played by the Congressional Budget Office (CBO), federal agencies, interest groups, and staff negotiations.

Policy Design, Legislative Specifications, and Legislative Drafting

Typically individuals think that the legislative process produces policies, and in large part legislation is important because of its policy changes and the effects it has on people. For instance, the Clean Air Act of 1990 is important because its cap-and-trade scheme limits sulfur dioxide emissions, and the Affordable Care Act is important because it expands access to health-care insurance. At the most literal level, however, Congress does not pass policies. Rather, it passes laws—that is, legislative language. The process of producing legislative language can be divided into three overlapping stages: (1) policy design, (2) legislative specification, and (3) legislative drafting.

The *policy design* stage encompasses all work and processes involved in identifying a problem, considering different potential solutions, selecting a solution, and designing the large moving parts of a policy. Policy design generally stops at the level of detail found in a think tank's policy proposal or white paper.

The *legislative specification* stage refers to the work of preparing bullet points or an outline (referred to colloquially as "leg specs") that will then be used as a guide to draft legislation. Legislative specifications elaborate on the policy design. They can range from a couple of bullet points on the policy's main design elements to a carefully crafted outline, including definitions and cross-references. In order to flesh out a policy design, congressional staff must make many decisions, including ones about policy details. For instance, health-care policy staff might consider questions such as

- What formula should be used to calculate a penalty?
- Should payments be adjusted for varying costs of living around the country?
- Should small businesses be exempted from the policy?

Some of these decisions are operational:

- How much flexibility should the agency have when implementing different parts of the policy?

- What agency in a department should be responsible for implementing this provision?
- By what date must the agency implement this policy?
- Should this policy sunset on a date certain?

Other decisions are procedural and are related to stakeholder participation and congressional oversight:

- Should agency actions and decisions be subject to judicial review?
- How often and in what manner should the agency consult with stakeholders during the rule-making process?
- Should the agency send Congress an annual report on the status of the policy implementation?

The final stage, *legislative drafting*, is the process of converting the legislative specifications into legislative language, and it primarily involves legal questions. Some are mechanical:

- Where in the statute should we place this provision?
- How do we want to define each term?

Others concern the interpretation and implementation of the legislation post-enactment:

- How will the applicable agencies, courts, or states interpret specific language choices?

Still other questions are about optics:

- Will this provision attract bad press if it is kept at this length?
- Should it be shortened?
- How should the headings be labeled?
- Should a cross-reference be used to obscure a controversial decision?

The distinctions between these three processes are hardly strict. In particular, the dividing lines are blurry between policy design and legislative specification and between legislative specification and legislative drafting. While writing legislative specifications, for example, staffers often must reconceptualize or modify their underlying policy designs. Additionally, during the legislative drafting process, legislative counsel often identifies new questions, spots unforeseen problems, and points out secondary effects.

Many substantive decisions are actually made during the legislative drafting phase. Nevertheless, these divisions capture the different levels of analysis and decision-making that staff and other political actors engage in during the legislative process.

The Role of Various Actors in Producing Legislative Language

Members of Congress

Members of Congress (MCs) do not play a direct role in legislative drafting. While they often lead many key parts of the legislative process (e.g., agenda setting, policy design, and negotiation of key issues), they do not draft legislative specifications or legislative language themselves. A member may occasionally review language on issues of personal importance, but for logistical reasons the vast majority of members do not write, read, or even review legislative language.

Legislative language can be extremely time-consuming to read and often obscures more than it elucidates. Instead of reading the bill itself, then, a member generally reads a memo or summary, learning more in less time. If members had to draft every word of every bill proposed or passed, Congress's work would grind to a halt. As former Senate Finance Committee chairman Max Baucus (D-MT) told constituents at a forum in Montana, "I don't think you want me to waste my time to read every page of the healthcare bill. . . . You know why? It's statutory language. . . . We hire experts" (Fabian 2010).

Nevertheless, staffers—keenly aware of their MC's political interests and policy preferences—strive to reflect their boss's preferences. For staffers, then, representing the interests and views of the MC is a professional norm. Because members do not always possess or communicate views on specific issues, however, the task often falls to staff to intuit them. As numerous congressional staffers have told scholars, a staffer who ignores his boss's preferences is quickly out of a job (Romzek 2000; Bressman and Gluck 2014).

Congressional Staff

Two kinds of congressional staff are involved in the legislative drafting process: legislative assistants (LAs) and committee staff. Each MC employs a handful of LAs, who each act as the member's point person on a policy portfolio. For example, a Senate "health LA" would likely handle all federal health-care issues for a senator—Medicare, Medicaid, commercial health insurance, the Food and Drug Administration, the National Institutes of Health, the Centers for Disease Control, and rural health. Given their smaller offices, House LAs tend to cover larger portfolios than Senate LAs. Consequently, a House LA might be responsible for all health, education, and labor issues. Handling so many issues, an LA must be a generalist, developing deep expertise in only a few issues of importance to his member. "On-committee" LAs (i.e., staff handling issues within the jurisdiction of the MC's assigned committees) generally play a more active role in the production of legislative language than "off-committee" LAs.

Each congressional committee also employs staffers to work on the policy areas handled by the committee. Most committees have a set of majority staffers working for the chair and a set of minority staffers working for the committee's ranking member. Although these staff are paid by and work for the committee, in practice majority and minority staff serve at the pleasure of the committee's chair and ranking member, respectively. Committee staff are the policy specialists of Congress. They have narrower portfolios than personal office staff and consequently more expertise about the issues on which they work. For example, a Senate Health, Education, Labor, and Pensions Committee or House Energy and Commerce Committee staffer might be responsible only for Food and Drug Administration issues.[1]

Offices of Legislative Counsel

The House and Senate both have an Office of Legislative Counsel (OLC), a nonpartisan office employing attorneys who are responsible for drafting legislation. OLC attorneys (known as legislative counsel) work with congressional staff to draft legislative language. This work is strictly confidential. In 2014, the House and Senate OLCs employed forty-six and thirty-six legislative counsel, respectively (U.S. Congress 2014). Each of these attorneys specializes in distinct policy areas (e.g., Medicare, campaign finance, unemployment insurance) and develops deep knowledge of the statutes underlying the policies. By virtue of their long tenures at the OLC, legislative counsel possess extensive institutional knowledge and insight into the history of various drafting and policy decisions. The House and Senate OLCs are intimately involved in drafting much, if not most, legislation that passes into law (Gluck and Bressman 2013). While congressional staff certainly draft bills and amendments without legislative counsel, this chapter does not address such drafting.

Party Leadership

Increased consolidation of power in party leadership in Congress over the past thirty years has been extensively documented (Sinclair 1983; Sinclair 2011; Mann and Ornstein 2008). Even so, leadership staffers still handle large portfolios despite the accompanying rise in leadership's staffing budgets (Glassman 2014). In a negotiation, the leadership staff need to make many detailed policy decisions about many different policies. As a former committee staffer observed, "Leadership has lots of moving pieces to balance. They rely on subject matter experts [committee staff] for feedback, opinions, and policy options. If you're doing your job well, you're relied on more." Before or during negotiations, the leadership staff often ask the committee staff to draft different options or to comment on language from the other party's leadership. Leadership also might negotiate a set of parameters and then have the committee staff negotiate the details. These details can have a tremendous impact on the business model or financial viability of a company or the success or failure of a policy. "My clients often say that leadership is running the bill," one lobbyist and former Hill staffer told me. "But I have to remind them, 'Yeah, but who's doing the drafting? Even when leadership is negotiating, the committee staff are often drafting.'"

White House

Staffers consistently report that the White House was directly involved in some major policy items, but they note this involvement occurs at a high level. As one staffer described, "The White House gives us a thumbs up or thumbs down on the big picture, but they don't have enough time to hammer out details. You do that with the agency." An agency official told Shobe (2015, 18), "It is no secret that the President proposes bills to Congress. But where does that language come from? It doesn't appear by magic. Someone in an agency is the one who wrote it."

Academics and Think Tanks

Outside subject matter experts (i.e., researchers, economists, scientists) play a large role in the policy design process but only a small role in legislative drafting. Reading legislative language and understanding its context in existing statutes can prove challenging. The statutes governing federal programs often resemble an intricate web of definitions, formulas, exceptions, and grandfather clauses.

Nonlawyer subject matter experts, like economists and scientists, generally do not have any training or experience in reading or writing legislative language. When they focus their work and research on public policy, they write more frequently about policy design than about operational, technical, and legal concerns. One staffer commented, "These people play almost no role in legislative language. They're great for big ideas, but they offer no granularity."

Interest Groups

Given the highly technical nature of legislative drafting, one might suspect that interest groups would dominate the legislative drafting stage, and many do. Interest groups, however, are not uniformly effective at this stage and are usually more effective at the policy design and legislative specification stages.

Interest groups often pursue different strategies during the legislative process. Some groups focus on cultivating the expertise needed to make detailed comments on policy details and legislative language. Others hire a bevy of lobbyists to pound the pavement and make the rounds on the Hill to rally support or opposition for a bill. These groups typically do not have the same level of sophistication. As one lobbyist said, "I often have to remind my clients, 'He who has the pen wins.' Stakeholders have opinions on the level of policy. On the level of language, they often don't have the insight, and they can't get into the minutia."

Larger groups with greater resources can pursue more strategies and make fewer trade-offs. As a result, they typically have the sophisticated policy shops and the necessary expertise to think about legislative specifications and legislative language. By contrast, most middle- and small-sized groups have the necessary expertise to advocate for policy designs and legislative specifications, but fewer of these groups have the expertise to make sophisticated comments on legislative language.

Producing Legislative Language

Basic Drafting: Staff and Legislative Counsel

At the most basic level, the legislative drafting process is the product of interactions between two people: a legislative drafter from the House or Senate OLC and a staffer for an MC or a congressional committee. Committee staff, in particular, work closely with the OLC. Committee staffers often meet in the OLC's office for thirty minutes to an hour when first discussing legislative specifications.[2] By contrast, the OLC has a much more arm's-length relationship with LAs. Generally, the OLC has a preliminary phone call with LAs, followed by e-mail correspondence. LAs consistently reported that the OLC gave their legislation a more perfunctory treatment and made more judgment calls without consulting them.

Fleshing out a policy requires staff to think through a series of questions. The subsequent act of writing these policy details into precise legal language invariably raises even more questions. The OLC plays a key role in spotting issues, ensuring the legislative language matches the staffer's intent, and devising creative ways to solve problems. As in any profession, there is a distribution of talent and experience among legislative counsel. One committee staffer said, "We often wanted to use Senate Leg Counsel on [this] issue because they were so much more knowledgeable about that part of the statute. They knew that if we modified Section X, there'd be an interaction with Section Y, and we'd need to deal with that."

Similarly, if the Senate legislative counsel is a faster legislative drafter, it can mean that Congress will use the Senate's language instead of the House's as an essential deadline approaches (e.g., a budget deal to avoid a government shutdown). This represents more than a trivial choice of words. As staff told me repeatedly, "The person with the pen wins." A senior House Commerce Committee staffer told David Smith (2002, 78) that the House did better than the Senate on Medicare issues in conference committees in the mid-1990s because it had more staffers than the Senate and a superior legislative counsel.[3]

The legislative drafting process for LAs and committee staff starts the same way:[4]

1. *Staffer prepares materials for OLC.* A staffer will generally write up legislative specifications before e-mailing or calling the OLC. Staffers may send the OLC their own legislative language, an agency's language, or language prepared by an outside group. A staffer can submit legislative language or legislative specifications written by anyone.
2. *Staffer starts discussion with OLC.* The staffer generally starts the discussion with OLC by describing her policy design and the intent behind different elements in the specs. Legislative counsel often has a litany of questions he or she will routinely ask (Katzmann 2014). Even very thorough legislative specifications, however, will leave questions unanswered and details unspecified. Consequently, the legislative counsel also asks a range of policy-specific questions. Legislative counsel wants to be sure he or she understands the intent of the policy design and legislative specifications.
3. *Staffer and OLC discuss additional questions.* Often staff will leave the meeting with a few open questions to investigate and answer for the OLC. The OLC often e-mails or calls staff with additional questions.
4. *OLC drafts the language.* Once most of these questions—particularly those about major points—are answered, legislative counsel completes the draft and e-mails a copy to the staffer.
5. *Staffer and OLC update the draft.* The staffer reviews the legislative language and sends legislative counsel back the draft with tracked changes marking any corrections, additions, or comments. Legislative counsel

incorporates the changes and sends the congressional staffer a new draft of the legislative language.

At this point, LAs are largely finished with drafting their legislative language. They may shop their language around to friends in other offices, Congressional Research Service analysts, or stakeholders with whom they are working and make further modifications. For the most part, however, they are turning their focus away from the details of the legislative language and toward strategic and tactical decisions about how best to advance their policy.

Committee staffers, however, are likely to engage with a wider set of actors as they develop legislative language, also speaking with the Congressional Budget Office and relevant federal agencies and interest groups. They also often participate in negotiations with other staff.[5] A discussion of these engagements will also serve to highlight the difficulty faced by personal office LAs relative to committee staff in drafting legislation.

Working with the Congressional Budget Office

The CBO is a nonpartisan congressional agency that estimates the budgetary impact of pending legislation. It often plays a large role in the legislative process because of its function as scorekeeper. The CBO is responsible for producing budget scores (i.e., an estimate of a bill's effects on federal spending and revenue over the ten-year budget window) for bills reported out of committee. For example, the CBO estimated that the Budget Control Act of 2011 would reduce federal spending by $2.1 trillion over ten years. In general, bills are unlikely to receive consideration on the House or Senate floor without a CBO score. Likewise, a bill would be subject to a point of order if its CBO score states that it will increase the deficit.[6] Therefore, staff routinely work with the CBO during each of the three stages to ensure their language conforms to budget constraints and does not trigger such points of order.

The size of the CBO's role in the legislative process varies by the type of bill. For authorizations to existing discretionary programs not providing or changing appropriations, the CBO plays little to no role in the drafting process because neither the policy design nor the legislative drafting determines the CBO score. For bills with large macroeconomic ramifications—for example, the 2014 immigration bill (S. 744, 113th Congress)—the CBO estimates the score as a function of the bill's policy design, legislative specifications, and legislative drafting. As a result, the CBO is an important participant in the drafting process. The same is true of the CBO's role in scoring direct spending bills, such as Medicare or Social Security legislation.

When CBO scoring is tied to the bill's design and drafting, committee staffers work closely with the CBO throughout the legislative negotiations and drafting. Staffers reach out to the appropriate CBO analysts. For a small- or medium-sized bill, a staffer may e-mail the legislative specifications—often the same ones sent to legislative counsel—to the appropriate CBO analyst and unit chief. Then the staffer and analyst often discuss any preliminary questions or concerns, as well as the priority and urgency of this scoring request relative to the committee's other scoring requests. As committee staff move from policy design to legislative language and then negotiate and refine the language, they periodically send updated versions of the policy and language (accompanied by redlines, showing changes relative to a prior draft) to the CBO. The CBO closely reads these documents and evaluates the impact of language changes on the scoring.

Committee staffers want to understand how the CBO will model a given policy. Because CBO's scoring could render a policy design or legislative specifications unworkable, the staff will want this information before rather than after investing substantial time and resources negotiating each and every policy detail. Staffers face immense uncertainty during negotiations when they do not know how the CBO will score particular policy changes. Consequently, unofficial interim scoring updates from the CBO can represent major turning points in the negotiating process. CBO analysts typically update staff by phone, as the CBO is very conscious about not having an interim score publicized and taken out of context.

Committees work with the CBO to adjust policies carefully to ensure a politically palatable CBO score. This process often requires multiple rounds of changes to policy details and legislative language. Without regular access to the CBO, then, calibrating a complicated policy or bill with budgetary implications can prove very challenging. The CBO generally does not score personal office bills, particularly for off-committee members.[7] One former Senate staffer described the CBO as "massively unresponsive to anyone but committees and leadership."

Because unscored legislation often faces major political challenges, CBO scoring can become a resource for committees to dish out as a political chit. Often member offices will try to pass a small bill with unanimous consent. Although passing a bill this way is always difficult, a bill without a CBO score has even weaker prospects for passage. For this reason, lobbyists regularly ask committee staffers to request scores for a given policy or bill.

Working with Federal Agencies

Like the CBO, committee staffers often work closely with relevant federal agencies throughout the legislative process. Committee staffers receive extensive technical assistance from agencies and—short of an intervention from leadership—receive top priority for their requests for assistance. In contrast, agencies generally provide LAs with less thorough and less timely technical assistance.

An agency legislative affairs office typically acts as the agency's point of contact with committee staff. The legislative affairs office coordinates conversations between the committee staff and the agency's program experts or political appointees. Committee staffers sometimes run policy designs or legislative specifications by the agency early in the process to determine if the agency could implement the policy writ large. Later in the process, they usually send legislative language to the agency for technical assistance.

The agency performs this work on a confidential basis and does not discuss assistance provided to one office with another. However, offices of legislative affairs are often led by political appointees. Additionally, per Office of Management and Budget (OMB) Circular A-19, agencies are required to notify OMB of all technical assistance requests, though agencies routinely ignore this requirement (Walker 2015). As a result, while confidential among congressional offices, senior agency staff (or White House staff) could be made aware of requests for technical assistance absent an explicit request from the congressional staffer.

Different agencies have different internal structures for reviewing legislative language (Shobe 2015; Walker 2015). Agencies almost always provide technical assistance in response to committee staff requests. While agencies are not more responsive to the president's party (Shobe 2015), they are more responsive to majority offices in Congress. Agencies provide most technical assistance through redlines and written comments, while they also provide assistance, particularly on sensitive issues, in person or on the phone (Walker 2015). For a given bill, there might be several rounds of technical assistance as the bill develops and the language changes.

Given its superior size and role in implementing legislation, an agency brings essential expertise to the legislative drafting process. Agencies have a greater number of staff members with more specialized knowledge in a given policy area than Congress does. In the Senate, for example, the Finance Committee has sole jurisdiction over Medicaid and the Children's Health Insurance Program (CHIP). While the committee's Democratic staff had only one full-time employee working on Medicaid and CHIP in 2014, the Centers for Medicare and Medicaid Services (CMS) had over three hundred full-time employees working on these programs (CMS 2015). Agency staffers are responsible for implementing existing statutes and accordingly have a very deep understanding of how the existing language works. They also understand problems in the statute that they have had to work around, as well as issues related to the agency's administrative capacity, operations, and internal politics.

Ultimately, the agency staff members responsible for interpreting and implementing legislation are best able to assess how the agency will interpret and implement the potential legislation.

During the legislative drafting process, agencies spot operational and technical issues and help to create solutions. They carefully review legislative language and often identify more drafting errors than other participants in the drafting process. The line between technical assistance and policy design is blurry. Many committee staffers are solicitous of the agency's viewpoint and welcome far-reaching comments. On the other hand, some committee staffers—typically those opposed to the agency's comments—only want changes that relate to technical, operational, or legal elements. They do not want any commentary on policy design issues. Nevertheless, agency staffers often affect policy design and legislative specifications in the process of reviewing and commenting on legislative drafting.

Because the agency alone is responsible for so much policy implementation, the agency's viewpoint and technical assistance are unique and extremely difficult for an outsider to replicate. As a result, no other actor can fully replace the agency's role in the legislative process. Often, committee staffers have previously worked at agencies, which gives them some independent perspective on agency actions. Despite this, even a former agency staffer likely understands only certain parts of an agency, many of which employ thousands of people. In addition, companies and industry groups often employ former agency staffers and have detailed programmatic knowledge. Committee staffers, however, must closely examine the claims of companies and industry groups, given their financial interest in a preferred outcome. Although staff and agencies do not always agree about policy goals, and agencies surely have their own independent motivations, the committee staffs of both parties generally place significant weight on agency feedback.

An agency's resources are less effective if it does not have extensive experience regulating or overseeing a particular area. A lack of agency expertise in commercial health insurance contributed to some of the drafting errors in Title 1 (commercial health insurance reforms) of the Affordable Care Act.[8] Before the passage of the ACA, the federal government played a very small role in regulating commercial health insurance markets. The CMS—which, along with the IRS, ultimately implemented much of the Title 1 commercial insurance reforms—had no center or office dedicated to commercial insurance issues before 2010. As one committee staffer who worked on the ACA noted, "CMS didn't have experience setting up exchanges and regulating health insurers. So for entirely understandable reasons, the normal safety net that the agency provides us wasn't quite there. The lack of expertise had a large impact on the legislative drafting process."

CBO Enhancing Agency Power

CBO scoring can serve to further agency influence in the legislative drafting process. With staff permission, the CBO often discusses bills confidentially with applicable federal agencies' legislative offices. The CBO's biggest question for an agency's staff is whether it can implement the legislative language as written. This determination is a function not of policy design writ large but rather of the legislative specifications and drafting.

Because CBO analysts generally have neither the time nor expertise to second-guess an agency's assessment, the CBO regularly defers to the agency's view. Consequently, if the agency does not believe that it can meet the legislation's implementation deadlines, the CBO will score the bill on the basis of the agency's anticipated timeline and not the legislation's deadlines. Alternatively, if the agency believes it can implement no part of the policy as written, the CBO will likely give the legislation no score unless the language is modified.

This enhanced voice for the agency is most important when considering deficit-reduction policies. Deficit-reduction policies usually result in some groups receiving fewer funds, services, and so forth. As a result, such policies often prove unpopular. If groups are going to blame MCs for these policies, staff will want to maximize the policy's CBO score (i.e., amount of scored savings). Thus, if an agency tells the CBO that it cannot implement a deficit-reduction policy, the staff will either change the legislative language to satisfy the agency (via the CBO) or drop the policy.[9]

Agencies do not misrepresent legislation to push their own preferred language or policy preferences, but they nonetheless must make quasi-technical, quasi-political determinations when assessing the agency's ability to implement language.[10] Some proposed legislative language is simply too mangled for an agency to implement. Furthermore, some policies simply cannot be implemented given the agency's program infrastructure, manpower, or other limitations. Conversely, some legislative language and policies can be cleanly drafted and easily implemented. Often, however, policies and legislative language occupy the space between these poles, and agency staffers must use their professional judgment to assess the agency's ability to implement the language.

In many cases, the agency's assessment of its ability to implement a provision is inherently a product of the agency's future political decisions.[11] An agency may be able to meet a deadline if it chooses to allocate staff and funds for this new policy (presumably at the expense of other policies).[12] Indeed, an agency's ability to implement a policy is often a function of internal debates and decisions by political appointees. A political appointee may be willing to interpret legislation more "creatively" in order to enable a politically important policy to succeed.

Working with Interest Groups

LAs are typically more receptive than committee staff to an interest group's legislative language. Members (and thus LAs) often focus on district and home-state issues for which they can claim credit (Mayhew 1974). The LAs work very closely with the relevant constituents and associations on legislative language and policy details. Member personal offices are much more likely than committees to introduce language drafted entirely by an outside group.

An LA's increased receptivity to outside language is also driven by necessity. LAs have fewer resources—time, expertise, political information, agenda control, and access to the OLC, CBO, and agency staff—than committee staff. For example, committee staff generally possess (and, when strategic, distribute) key policy and political information (Curry 2015). By contrast, LAs are constantly trying to acquire information and keep abreast of the latest developments. As a result, lobbyists can be crucial sources of political information and policy expertise (Hall and Deardorff 2006). Additionally, interest groups can help build press and momentum for an LA's bill. The assistance provided by outside groups creates strong incentives for LAs to work with these groups in a symbiotic manner.

Many interest groups, large and small, make strategic blunders when pitching legislative language to committee staff. As discussed previously, policy designs leave a number of questions unanswered and details undeveloped. By presenting policy designs, lobbyists leave themselves a lot of room for hand waving. When lobbyists instead present legislative language, they must justify many of their drafting decisions. If lobbyists cannot explain these decisions and walk through all the policy details, they hurt their credibility and the credibility of their policy design. Most groups have lawyers draft their language; however, these lawyers may lack the detailed knowledge of the relevant statute needed to present well-crafted language. Finally, interest groups often overreach by asking for anything and everything imaginable.

Although groups also make this mistake when discussing policies at a conceptual level, they more often find—and rarely overlook—opportunities to overreach in legislative language. One committee staffer said, "Groups give us language. I look at it and if I like something—which is rare—I might show it to leg counsel. But we just don't use their language or even negotiate language with outside groups much."

Negotiating with Other Staff

Staff negotiations are a regular part of the legislative drafting process but are also highly variable and a function of the policy areas, personalities, and politics of the time. During my time with the Senate Finance Committee, I mainly participated in four- or six-way bipartisan, bicameral negotiations.[13] These negotiations were limited to committee staff and were largely kept confidential, with periodic briefings and releases of presentations, white papers, and draft language to on-committee LAs and the public.

However, other processes are more open and inclusive of on-committee LAs. One committee staffer described her committee's frequent use of nested staff-level working groups. The process starts with bipartisan LAs on the committee and committee staff meeting with agency heads, stakeholders, and experts. The committee may also hold hearings depending on the interest in the issue of the MCs, particularly the chair and ranking member. Then, committee staffers meet with on-committee LAs to discuss different policy problems and proposed solutions. LAs often attend the meeting with preferred policies developed with or supported by an LA from the other party.

After committee staffers gauge interest in the various issues, they proceed to hold smaller working group meetings with staff for key offices to develop different provisions. For some provisions, only the staff for the committee chair and ranking member are present. These staffers represent the smallest group, which in turn is included in all larger groups. For a given provision, these staffers would meet with the LAs who put forward a relevant policy proposal. Committee staffers would also include any office that has historically or recently indicated a strong interest in the issue. Next, the group would draft or revise legislative specifications or legislative language and work with the OLC and relevant agencies to develop and refine legislation. Eventually, the committee staff would compile the provisions developed in these several meetings and put forward a bill for the committee to mark up.

Personal Office Staff Drafting versus Committee Staff Drafting

Because of these factors, committee staffers are uniquely situated to design and draft complex policies. Personal offices, on the other hand, often face challenges when drafting complicated bills; even those with a large amount of assistance do not have access to the same resources as committees. As many staffers noted, personal offices thus face challenges in drafting legislation for a workable policy of significant scope.

Although personal offices face institutional disadvantages relative to committee staff in the policy design process, personal offices are better able to overcome these disadvantages than those for the legislative specification and the legislative drafting process. LAs face fewer disadvantages in designing policies than in specifying and drafting legislation. Policy ideas and policy designs often, but not always, originate from outside Congress (Kingdon 1984). Think tanks, academics, innovative companies, and congressional support agencies all develop policy designs and present them in public forums. These outside actors can and often do help staff evaluate and shape the design of a policy. Although these actors generally prefer working with committee staff rather than LAs, they are still eager to work with personal offices, particularly with those members active in the specific policy area. Moreover, experts proposing different policies often abound.

Senator Ron Wyden's (D-OR) efforts during the run-up to the 2009–2010 health reform efforts illustrate this point. In January 2007, Senator Wyden and Senator Bob Bennett (R-UT) introduced the much praised Healthy Americans Act (HAA), an overhaul of commercial health insurance markets and the health-care system more generally. Senator Wyden and his staff worked closely and at great length with the Senate OLC. They also worked tirelessly with analysts at the Congressional Research Service, as well as with technical experts from outside Congress.

Most notably, Senator Wyden even received substantial assistance from the CBO, a rarity for a personal office. In 2009, Senator Wyden told Ezra Klein, "Peter Orszag, who was then the director of the CBO, and I spent 18 months together. It was every week on the sofas in our office going back and forth with various iterations and alternatives for the legislation. . . . You don't get many windows in life where the timing is such that you can really go at it for 18 months with principals like Peter Orszag and the CBO team."

This assistance culminated in the CBO giving the HAA a favorable preliminary score and publicly releasing its analysis on May 1, 2008. The CBO scored the HAA on a conceptual level (i.e., scoring the bill's policy design rather than its legislative language) because the legislative language was not detailed enough for the CBO to score it directly. Legislative drafting for such a complex and ambitious policy proposal required still more specialization and technical assistance than was available to members, such as Senator Wyden, outside a committee process.

Given their robust capacity to present policy ideas and a host of challenges in drafting and specifying legislation, personal offices often resort to proposing three types of bills: (1) messaging bills, (2) agenda-setting legislation, and (3) discrete policy changes. These categories are not mutually exclusive. Indeed, a single bill could fit into all three categories.

Messaging bills are designed to demonstrate the member's support for a constituency or interest group. They may also serve to gin up the base. One staffer pointed out that a well-drafted bill can make for poor messaging: "If the bill says, 'Notwithstanding any other provision of law, the government shall not do whatever,' it's terrible drafting, but it's easy for a member to explain to his constituents and share with his colleagues. A well-drafted bill may be better, but it's probably a lot harder to read."

To raise the profile of a given policy design or issue, MCs propose agenda-setting legislation. An MC hopes such a bill will attract positive media attention, generate interest group support, and draw the interest of colleagues. Furthermore, a bill can put pressure on relevant committees, leading them either to consider the bill or to incorporate it into other legislation. In doing so, committees often rework or refine the legislative specifications and drafting for policies that are complicated or difficult to draft. One LA said, "You quickly realize that [as an LA] you have to give up on the details. If the bill gains traction, everyone will fix it up later." Nevertheless, the members can still (rightfully) claim credit for the legislative win.

Lastly, members may promote bills that would make discrete policy changes. Members might try to pass such bills by unanimous consent in the Senate or on suspension in the House. These bills can have big implications for a given policy area, yet are often fairly simple to draft.

Conclusion

In this chapter, I have explored the process and complexity of legislative drafting as well as the ways different political actors wield influence, affect policy decisions, and help solve problems. Although political scientists have written extensively on the legislative capacity of Congress, most of their works focus primarily on problem solving. Few, if any, have considered legislative drafting as a key process, intermediating variable, or factor in the legislative process. We do not know whether LAs play a larger role in legislative drafting now than in 1996, nor do we know whether agency influence in the drafting process is growing, shrinking, or transforming. Indeed, the entire process is a black box.

As I have argued, the ability of Congress to draw on experts, digest information, and weigh policy alternatives is important, but this tells only the beginning of the story. Congress not only solves problems but also writes legislative language, which (sometimes) becomes law. Although Congress could be a brilliant policy-analyzing machine, its analytic abilities may be for naught if it cannot competently draft legislation. The problem is that we do not know how well Congress can draft legislation and how its skill is (or is not) changing over time. Are the House and Senate equally effective? Are some committees better drafters than others? Why?

These questions are not easy to answer, and, indeed, approaching them proves quite thorny. How does one discern a well-drafted bill from a poorly drafted one? How does one distinguish a drafting error from a questionable policy decision? To be honest, I do not know that we can. One starting point would be to begin periodically surveying agencies and, for some policy areas, the CBO.[14] Even still, such actions will at best reveal only a part of the picture. Nevertheless, as scholars and commentators proffer various reforms to improve the capacity of Congress to pass effective legislation, it is essential that our understanding of congressional capacity incorporate policy analysis *and* legislative drafting.

Notes

* I am grateful to Justin Crowe, Matthew Glassman, Jacob Straus, Sibyl Tilson, and Kristen VanBlargan for their comments on earlier drafts. For helpful discussion, I would also like to thank Abbe Gluck and David Menefee-Libey. Special thanks to the current and former Hill and agency staffers who spoke with me.

1. Committee staffers tend to focus more on "good policy" and less on district- or state-specific issues (Katzmann 2014). Nonetheless, the electoral interests of the chair (ranking member) are never out of mind for majority (minority) staff. Depending on the committee and the chair or ranking member, they may routinely meet with constituents, visit the chair or ranking member's district or state, and work on legislation addressing a specific home district or state issue.

2. Committee staff often will simply call or e-mail OLC for very straightforward policies or when turnaround is urgent.

3. The House Commerce Committee is now known as the House Energy and Commerce Committee.

4. For the sake of simplicity, the process described depicts a policy drafted by a single staffer. If staffers from two member or committee offices are involved, the process is largely the same, though staff may need to negotiate over details. As more offices become involved in the drafting process, negotiations quickly grow more complicated.

5. This chapter only discusses the drafting process through the committee stage; drafting or negotiation processes that occur after the committee markup process (e.g., on the House and Senate floor and in conference committee) are beyond its scope.

6. For a more detailed account of these procedures in the Senate, see Heniff (2015).

7. Per the Congressional Budget Act of 1974, the CBO is responsible for first serving committees then personal offices.

8. These drafting errors are likely far fewer than those resulting from Congress passing the ACA through reconciliation and without a conference committee. Additionally, in many cases, CMS has been able to clarify poor drafting through the regulatory process.

9. On spending bills, an agency telling the CBO that it cannot implement legislation could actually be politically advantageous if the CBO consequently reports that the bill has a smaller cost.

10. Committee staff I interviewed did not think that agencies misrepresent legislation to push their own preferred language or policy preferences. Agency staffers vigorously resisted the idea, stressing their respective offices' emphasis on professionalism and neutrality. However, two staffers reported two instances where they were suspicious of agency personnel manipulating the process.

11. By political, I do not mean partisan. Rather I mean it in the sense of "who gets what, when, [and] how" (Laswell 1936).

12. All agencies operate under resource constraints, and many are overworked, understaffed, and underfunded (DiIulio 2014).

13. For the four-way, Democrat and Republican committee staff from the Senate Finance Committee and House Ways and Means Committee. For the six-way, the same groups plus Democrat and Republican committee staff from the House Energy and Commerce Committee.

14. Shobe (2015) and Walker (2015) both surveyed federal agencies about their roles in the legislative drafting process.

References

Bressman Lisa S., and Abbe R. Gluck. 2014. "Statutory Interpretation from the Inside—An Empirical Study of Congressional Drafting, Delegation, and the Canons: Part II." *Stanford Law Review* 66: 901–1026.

Centers for Medicare and Medicaid Services. 2015. *FY2016 Justification of Estimates for Appropriations Committees*. Department of Health and Human Services. Washington, DC: Government Printing Office, https://www.cms.gov/About-CMS/Agency-Information/PerformanceBudget/Downloads/FY2016-CJ-Final.pdf.

Curry, James M. 2015. *Legislating in the Dark: Information and Power in the House of Representatives*. Chicago: University of Chicago Press.

DiIulio, John J., Jr. 2014. *Bring Back the Bureaucrats: Why More Federal Workers Will Lead to Better (and Smaller!) Government*. West Conshohocken, PA: Templeton Press.

Fabian, Jordan. 2010. "Key Senate Democrat Suggests That He Didn't Read Entire Healthcare Reform Bill." *Hill*, August 25.

Glassman, Matthew. 2014. "Congressional Leadership: A Resource Perspective." In *Party and Procedure in the United States Congress*, edited by Jacob R. Straus, 15–31. Lanham, MD: Rowman & Littlefield.

Gluck, Abbe, and Lisa S. Bressman. 2013. "Statutory Interpretation from the Inside—an Empirical Study of Congressional Drafting, Delegation, and the Canons: Part I." *Stanford Law Review* 65: 725–802.

Hall, Richard L., and Alan V. Deardorff. 2006. "Lobbying as Legislative Subsidy." *American Political Science Review* 100: 69–84.

Heniff, Bill, Jr. 2015. "Budget Enforcement Procedures: The Senate Pay-as-You-Go (PAYGO) Rule." Congressional Research Service. Washington, DC: Library of Congress.

Katzmann, Robert A. 1989. "American Legislative Process as Signal." *Journal of Public Policy* 9: 287–305.

———. 2014. *Judging Statutes.* New York: Oxford University Press.

Kingdon, John W. 1984. *Agendas, Alternatives, and Public Policies.* Boston: Little, Brown.

Klein, Ezra. 2009. "How to Get a Good CBO Score." *Wonkblog* (blog), *Washington Post,* June 19, http://voices.washingtonpost.com/ezra-klein/2009/06/how_to_get_a_good_cbo_score_an.html.

Laswell, Harold. 1936. *Politics: Who Gets What, When, How.* New York: Whittlesey House.

Mann, Thomas F., and Norman J. Ornstein. 2008. *The Broken Branch: How Congress Is Failing America and How to Get It Back on Track.* New York: Oxford University Press.

Mayhew, David. 1974. *Congress: The Electoral Connection.* New Haven, CT: Yale University Press.

Nourse, Victoria F., and Jane S. Schacter. 2002. "The Politics of Legislative Drafting: A Congressional Case Study." *New York University Law Review* 77: 575–624.

Romzek, Barbara S. 2000. "Accountability of Congressional Staff." *Journal of Public Administration Research and Theory* 10: 413–46.

Shobe, Jarrod. 2014. "Intertemporal Statutory Interpretation and the Evolution of Legislative Drafting." *Columbia Law Review* 114: 807–77.

———. 2015. "Agencies as Legislators: The Empirical Study of the Role of Agencies in the Legislative Process." Social Science Research Network, http://papers.ssrn.com/sol3/papers.cfm?abstract_id=2652520.

Sinclair, Barbara. 1983. *Majority Leadership in the U.S. House.* Baltimore: Johns Hopkins University Press.

———. 2011. *Unorthodox Lawmaking: New Legislative Processes in the U.S. Congress,* 4th ed. Washington, DC: CQ Press.

Sitaraman, Ganesh. 2015. "The Origins of Legislation." *Notre Dame Law Review* 91: 79–132.

Smith, David G. 2002. *Entitlement Politics: Medicare and Medicaid, 1995–2001.* New York: Aldine de Gruyter.

U.S. Congress. 2014. *Official Congressional Directory: 113th Congress.* S. Rpt. 113–12. Washington, DC: Government Printing Office.

Walker, Christopher J. 2015. "Federal Agencies in the Administrative Process: Technical Assistance in Statutory Drafting." Administrative Conference of the United States, https://www.acus.gov/sites/default/files/documents/technical-assistance-final-report.pdf.

II

HOUSE OF REPRESENTATIVES

3

Keeping the Team Together

Explaining Party Discipline and Dissent in the U.S. Congress

Matthew Green and Briana Bee

"We should marginalize people that don't know how to govern, who don't want to govern."

—Representative Charles Dent (R-PA)

"I follow the American people. . . . Charlie here wants us to follow, like, a caucus or whatever."

—Representative Dave Brat (R-VA)

WHEN REPUBLICAN CONGRESSMEN Charles Dent and Dave Brat debated each other on an October 2015 episode of NBC's *Meet the Press*, their party was in turmoil. The previous month Speaker of the House John Boehner (R-OH) had unexpectedly announced his resignation from Congress. Then, three days before the Dent-Brat debate, Majority Leader Kevin McCarthy (R-CA)—Boehner's heir apparent—suddenly withdrew his candidacy, leaving no obvious successor to Boehner. Reporters joked that the Speakership had become the most unpopular job in Washington, but its apparently radioactive nature was symptomatic of something far more serious: a deep divide within the GOP that threatened to paralyze the majority party and, by extension, the U.S. House of Representatives.

Dent and Brat represented the two main ideological wings of their party. Dent was a fifth-term moderate who cochaired a group of like-minded Republicans called the Tuesday Group (Dent 2015). Brat, a freshman who had won his seat after a stunning primary election victory against then majority leader Eric Cantor, belonged to a group of independent-minded, largely conservative Republicans called the House Freedom Caucus (Fuller 2015).

But Dent and Brat did not disagree on policy alone. As their statements revealed, they also had contrasting views of the obligations of lawmakers to their parties. In the eyes of Dent, who had often voted for GOP leaders' bills even when a majority of Republicans had not,[1] legislators have a primary responsibility to govern and to do so collectively; parties should "marginalize" those who fail to follow that dictum. Brat, by contrast, believed that lawmakers owe primary allegiance to their constituents, even if it means disobeying their party—as Brat himself had done on a number of occasions, including voting against Boehner for Speaker. That difference underscores an important fact about our national legislature: though lawmakers within political parties tend to vote in unison, there are strong forces that can pull individual members of Congress, like Dave Brat, away from their parties. Furthermore, a representative's reasons for being loyal may depend on his or her views about what is owed to the party as well as his or her constituency or policy principles.

In this chapter we discuss the broader context surrounding recent turmoil within the House Republican Party. We explain the theoretical reasons why revolt and dissent can and do happen in Congress and the ways parties and party leaders try to limit defections and maintain discipline.[2] Though many assume that punishment is the best way to deal with disloyalty, evidence shows that dealing with dissent before it happens—primarily with rewards, not punishments—and developing and maintaining norms of party loyalty (along the lines expressed by Congressman Dent) is far more effective.

Why Members of Congress Dissent from Their Parties

Scholars have identified three major reasons that members of Congress might vote loyally with their party (Carey 2007). The first is that they or their constituents agree with the party ideologically (Krehbiel 1993). The second is that majority-party leaders exercise agenda control, making sure that only bills supported by their fellow partisans are brought to a vote (Cox and McCubbins 1993, 2005; Sinclair 1995, ch. 8).[3] The third is that party leaders impose discipline, making legislators vote in ways they or their constituents would prefer they not (Smith 2007).[4]

Though there is empirical evidence for all three reasons for party loyalty, each is not without limitations. Take first the possibility that party members in Congress vote together because they or their constituents agree ideologically. In fact, American political parties constitute fairly diverse coalitions, and disagreements among their members are not uncommon. Furthermore, some lawmakers represent "swing" districts or states and may feel compelled by constituents to vote against their party (perhaps unsurprisingly, the lowest voting loyalty scores in Congress tend to be held by lawmakers representing such constituencies).[5] Interest groups may also successfully lobby members of Congress to vote against their party. Plus there are always the occasional "mavericks" in Congress, individuals like Senator Ted Cruz (R-TX) or Representative Walter Jones (R-NC), who pride themselves on acting contrary to their partisan brethren (Pathé 2015; Weisman 2013).[6]

Nor is agenda control absolute. Sometimes crises or deadlines force Congress to act on matters that divide the parties. In addition, certain congressional procedures make it possible for rank-and-file legislators to put items on the agenda over the opposition of their leaders. In the Senate, for example, it is usually permitted to offer amendments to legislation even if they are not germane (e.g., proposing an amendment about abortion to a transportation bill). The House minority party is allowed at least one amendment to every bill, known as the motion to recommit (see chapter 4). Bills in the House can be forced out of committees if a majority of representatives sign a so-called discharge petition (Sinclair 1995, 214–16; 2012).

Finally, party leaders have only limited tools to impose discipline. It is exceedingly difficult to expel lawmakers from Congress, and legislators raise money for and manage their own campaigns. The minority party (especially in the House) has fewer resources at its disposal to provide wayward lawmakers the incentive to cooperate (Green 2015). Leaders may also choose not to compel compliance or may not know how.[7] If dissent is not likely to change the outcome of a vote,[8] party leaders will often "let the dogs walk" and permit defections, particularly if lawmakers have good electoral reasons to vote contrary to the party.[9]

It should also be noted that there are many ways lawmakers can dissent from their parties, and some are seen as more disloyal than others. Voting against a party's *policymaking authority*—its power to pass or reject bills and amendments—is generally more acceptable, contingent upon the relative importance of a bill or amendment and how pivotal a lawmaker's vote is. Opposing a party's *procedural authority*,[10] its power to set the agenda, is more problematic. For instance, representatives in the U.S. House are expected to vote with their party on the "rule" of a bill (the terms by which a particular bill is considered, such as which amendments are permitted) and, if they are members of the majority party, are strongly discouraged from signing discharge petitions. Even more objectionable is to rebel against the party's *organizational authority*,[11] its right to choose chamber officers (like the Speaker of the House). Increasingly, lawmakers are expected to help the party raise money, recruit candidates to run for Congress, and support the party's nominees for office, which are all part of its *electoral authority* (Heberlig and Larson 2012).[12]

Recent Dissent in Congress

We live in an era of acute party polarization, with members of each political party in Congress tending to vote together and contrary to members of the other party. In 2014, for instance, 73 percent of all votes in the House of Representatives and 67 percent of all votes in the U.S. Senate were ones in which a majority of one party opposed a majority of the other. On such votes House Democrats voted together 90 percent of the time on average; House Republicans, 91 percent of the time; Senate Democrats, 93 percent of the time; and Senate Republicans, 84 percent of the time (Carney 2015).[13]

Yet one of the paradoxes of today's Congress is that, even as legislators vote along largely partisan lines in the aggregate, lawmakers (especially House Republicans) have shown a greater willingness to buck their party's spheres of authority at key moments. For example, six times in the 113th Congress (2013–2014), bills that had been introduced by Republican leaders passed despite being voted against by a majority of their party—the highest number of "majority rolls" in over a decade (*New York Times* 2015). Even some party leaders themselves have occasionally participated in these defections (Rogers 2015).

Challenges to the majority party's procedural authority have happened as well. In recent years a number of House Republicans have openly opposed the rules governing consideration of legislation, even though doing so is considered a major act of disloyalty (Pearson 2015, 55–56). After thirty-four Republicans voted against a rule for considering a trade bill in June 2015, nearly defeating it, Speaker John Boehner warned, "Voting against rules is not a vote of conscience; it is a vote to hand the floor over to [minority leader] Nancy Pelosi" (Sherman and Palmer 2015). Some House Republicans have also introduced and signed discharge petitions in hopes of forcing bills from committees. In October 2015, Representative Stephen Fincher (R-TN) managed to get the required 218 signatures on his petition to force a vote on the reauthorization of the Export-Import Bank, and an infuriated Representative Jeb Hensarling (R-TX), chairman of the committee that had bottled up the reauthorization bill, warned that Fincher's petition "effectively makes [Democrat] Nancy Pelosi the Speaker of the House" (Ho and Snell 2015).

Even more remarkable is the number of members of both parties willing to break what was once a sacrosanct principle: to always vote for your party's nominee for Speaker on the floor of the House. In nine of the twelve votes for Speaker held between 1995 and 2015 (shown in figure 3.1), at least one member of the House defected from his party and voted "present" or for another candidate (though only once did someone vote for the other party's candidate, the most egregious form of rebellion).[14] In January 2015, twenty-five Republicans and four Democrats did so, the largest number of defections in a vote for Speaker since the nineteenth century (Blake 2015; Jenkins and Stewart 2013).

Some lawmakers have been willing to buck their party's electoral authority too. Between 2008 and 2010, for instance, Senator Jim DeMint (R-SC) directed campaign funds to several candidates in Republican Senate primaries who were unsupported, if not opposed, by his party's campaign committee (Bolton 2009; Overby 2010). More recently, in the 113th Congress a handful of disgruntled House Republicans held back from paying their dues to the party's campaign committee (Isenstadt 2013).

The external causes of this recent dissent are complex and likely a combination of several factors, including ideological differences within the GOP; pressures from activist voters, partisan media outlets, and campaign contributors; and events and conditions that forced Congress to act on divisive

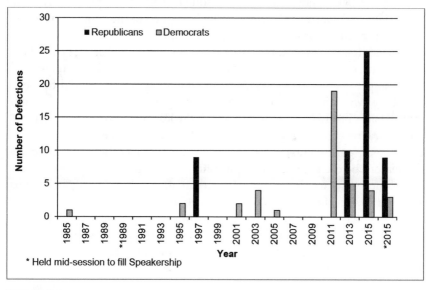

FIGURE 3.1
Number of lawmakers voting against their party's nominee for Speaker.
Source: Beth and Heitshusen 2015.
Note: "Votes against" include ballots cast for the other party's candidate, ballots cast for alternate candidates, and lawmakers voting "present." Ballots cast by the two parties' nominees are excluded.

measures (Draper 2012; Mann and Ornstein 2012; Strong 2013; Woodward 2012). It is worth noting, however, that rebellion and dissent are nothing new for parties in Congress. House Republicans in the early 1900s faced an internal revolt by Progressives that ultimately led to the disempowerment of then Speaker Joe "Czar" Cannon (R-IL); in 1922, the House took nine ballots to choose a Speaker because of the refusal of some Progressive Republicans to go along with their party's nominee; and from the 1930s through the 1970s, House and Senate Democrats were sometimes stymied by a group of south- erners willing to join with minority Republicans in a "conservative coalition" that could defeat Democratic bills. The recurrence of dissent underscores what we previously noted: there are important limitations on the causal forces that keep members of Congress loyal to their parties.

Why Punishment Often Fails

When legislators rebel against their party in ways that jeopardize its ability to govern—whether for personal, electoral, or other reasons and apart from ethical violations[15]—what can party leaders do about it?[16] Many assume that strong parties are those unafraid to punish disloyal members. The success of past leaders like Senator Lyndon Johnson (D-TX) and Representative Tom "The Hammer" DeLay (R-TX) is usually attributed to their tough, even mer- ciless approach to those who dared to cross them. There are some obvious advantages to punishment. For instance, it can rob lawmakers of benefits that help them advance their central goals of reelection, policy enactment, and possessing influence (Fenno 1973, 1), and it may deter other would-be rebels.

Taking away a lawmaker's privileges, status, or assets is, however, uncom- mon. That is probably because it is one of the least effective ways of respond- ing to or preventing dissent.[17] Table 3.1 lists high-profile punishments (or threatened punishments) of members of Congress over the past six decades, the reason for each (threatened) punishment, and the consequences of that punishment (if it was imposed). Note first that, even accounting for the pos- sibility that some instances of retribution go unreported, punishment is quite rare. There have been just twenty-two documented instances in the past fifty years of a lawmaker being punished (and another five punishments have been proposed but not carried out). Second, punishment is far less common in the Senate than in the House. This is not because senators are more loyal but because Senate party leaders have far less control over resources like commit- tee assignments and chairmanships than their House counterparts (Pearson 2015, 175–78). Finally, in over 40 percent of the cases punishment was unsuc- cessful: it was followed by further acts of disloyalty, the punished lawmaker joining the other party, or the punishment being rescinded or mitigated by another reward.

There are several reasons why punishment is uncommon and, when it is imposed, tends not to work. By robbing lawmakers of assets that help them win office, it may increase the likelihood that they will lose reelection (or switch to the other party), shrinking the size of the party and putting its ability to keep or gain majority status at risk (Pearson 2015; Smith 2007, 26–28). Conversely, a legislator's constituents may value rebellion, in which case punishment will not only help the legislator get reelected but tempt him or her to rebel in the future. Nor do dissenters necessarily value the assets they lose. As one Democrat asked sarcastically when a colleague was threatened with removal from the party's whip organization, "What do you need this whip thing for? To put on your résumé?" (Barry 1989, 468).

Finally, because congressional politics resembles a repeated cooperative game, it is critical that legislators not be punished so severely that they become resentful, making it harder to win their support later. Punishments may even "build up a gulag archipelago," with angry dissenters coalescing into an organized threat to party power (Lochhead 2015). Such was the case when Republican rebels, many having been previously punished by the party for disloyalty, formed the House Freedom Caucus in early 2015, defied GOP leaders on a number of high-profile votes, and perhaps even contributed to Speaker John Boehner's decision to resign (French and Sherman 2015; Kackley 2015; T. Lee 2015).

This is not to say that all punishments are ineffective. Punishment "by omission"—not granting favors or scarce goods to lawmakers who seek them—is not only more common but may help encourage greater party loyalty (Pearson 2015). For instance, Representative Jim Leach (R-IA) failed in his bid to win the chairmanship of the International Relations Committee, ostensibly because he had challenged the Speaker's authority and had not done enough fund-raising for the party (Eilperin 2007, 83). As Majority Leader Jim Wright (D-TX) once observed, when someone in your party defects, "you don't take a thing away, but you don't necessarily renew it, either" (Shribman 1981).[18]

Verbal or symbolic reprimands can also work well. Representative Dan Rostenkowski (D-IL), once the powerful chairman of the House Ways and Means Committee, became annoyed with a fellow committee member who had sponsored a major Republican budget bill. In retaliation, he excluded the congressman from a trip to China, had the wheels removed from his chair in the committee room, and on a committee bus trip assigned him a seat next to the lavatory. "He was sending a message," recalled the wayward congressman; "I understood that" (Carlson 1993).

TABLE 3.1.

Punishment Proposed or Imposed by Congressional Parties, 1965–2015

Year	Lawmakers	Punishment	Reason	Consequence
1965	Rep. Albert Watson (D-SC)	Stripped of seniority	Supported Republican candidate for president	Watson resigns, reelected as Republican
1969	Rep. John Bell Williams (D-MS) Rep. Mendel Rivers (D-SC)	Strip of seniority (proposed)	Disloyalty	Not carried out
1969	Rep. John Rarick (D-LA)	Strip of seniority (proposed)	Supported Independent candidate for president	Not carried out
1982*	Rep. Phil Gramm (D-TX)	Removed from committee	Leaked information to Republicans, cosponsored their bill	Resigns, reelected as Republican
1995	Sen. Mark Hatfield (R-OH)	Remove as committee chair (proposed)	Voted against balanced budget amendment	Not carried out
1995	Rep. Charlie Rose (D-NC)	Removed as ranking committee member	Ran against leader	None
1995	Rep. Mark Neumann (R-WI)	Reassigned to different subcommittee	Voted against bills, friction with chairman	Given seat on second committee
2001	Rep. Jim Traficant (D-OH)	Expelled from caucus, removed from all committees	Voted for Republican nominee for Speaker	Expelled from House for felony conviction
2004	Rep. Heather Wilson (R-NM)	Remove from committee (proposed)	Voted for Democratic motion in committee	Not carried out**
2005	Rep. Chris Smith (R-NJ) Rep. Joel Hefley (R-CO)	Removed as committee chair	Disloyalty/failure to protect leader from ethics accusations	None
2010	Sen. Lisa Murkowski (R-AK)	Remove from committee, strip of seniority (proposed)	Lost primary and ran as independent	Not carried out
2011	Rep. Dennis Cardoza (D-CA)	Removed from leadership team	Voted against Pelosi as nominee for Speaker	None

Year		Punishment	Disloyalty	
2012	Rep. Justin Amash (R-MI) Rep. Tim Huelskamp (R-KS) Rep. Walter Jones (R-NC) Rep. David Schweikert (R-AZ)	Removed from committee		Amash, Huelskamp, and Jones vote against Speaker on House floor
2013	Rep. Marlin Stutzman (R-IN)	Removed from whip team	Opposed farm bill	Votes against speaker on House floor
2014	Rep. Bill Cassidy (R-LA) Rep. Gus Bilirakis (R-FL)	Removed from whip team	Opposed his party on flood insurance bill	None
2015	Rep. Rich Nugent (R-FL) Rep. Daniel Webster (R-FL)	Removed from Rules Committee	Voted against Boehner for Speaker	Webster runs for Speaker
2015	Rep. Mark Meadows (R-NC)	Removed as subcommittee chair	Voted against rule, did not contribute to National Republican Campaign Committee	Reinstated; introduces resolution to remove Speaker
2015	Rep. Cynthia Lummis (R-WY) Rep. Trent Franks (R-AZ) Rep. Steve Pearce (R-NM)	Removed from whip team	Voted against rule	None

Sources: Cooper 1994; Deering and Smith 1997, 147; Foerstel 2001; Hunter 2011; Killian 1998, 157–59; Leary 2014; Lyons 1969; Newhauser 2015; Ota 2005; Rohde 1991, 17–18; Strong 2013; Wong and Marcos 2015.

Notes: The table excludes cases involving illegal activity or breaking chamber rules.

* Not included are punishments that were discussed, but not implemented, against other conservative Democrats who had voted against leadership in 1981–1982 (Rohde 1991, 78–81).

** Wilson was, however, forced to leave another committee in 2005 when the same chairman who had wanted her removed from his own committee successfully objected to her serving on two major committees (Marcus 2005).

A Better Approach: Dealing with Dissent before It Happens

Punishments that rob a rebel of an asset or privilege usually fail. But a more customary and effective way that leaders in Congress build support within their party is to do so *before* that support is tested, usually with positive incentives (Smith 2007, 28). Among the most common tactics in this category are lobbying lawmakers, both individually and collectively; bringing likely dissenters into the party's decision-making process; and distributing select benefits to those who are loyal.

Individual Lobbying

Lobbying is perhaps the most familiar tactic used by party leaders to build majorities and stifle dissent. It often consists of offering concrete benefits in exchange for support: favorable treatment for a bill or amendment, a choice committee assignment, appointment to a leadership position, special funding to a district or state, campaign assistance, or even a spot on an overseas trip (Sinclair 1995, 75; Smith 2007, 58–62; Ripley 1967, 73). Lobbying can also take the form of persuasion or "personal appeals to members for help" (Green 2013; Ripley 1967, 73). When Lyndon Johnson was Senate majority leader, his greatest strength lay not in demanding loyalty or punishing dissenters but in employing the so-called Johnson Treatment, which consisted of "supplication, accusation, cajolery, exuberance, scorn, tears, complaint, [and/or] the hint of threat" (Evans and Novak 1966, 104).

In 2003, when House Republicans passed a Medicare bill that garnered the votes of a handful of Democrats, then minority leader Nancy Pelosi gave one such Democrat "a ten-minute lecture on why he had to reverse his vote when the bill came back." "Was it a warm and fuzzy conversation?" recalled the lawmaker. "No. But that's what a good leader does" (Eilperin 2006, 63). Even Joe "Czar" Cannon, a Speaker from the early 1900s who had considerable procedural powers, was not averse to using persuasion. He once approached a group of potential freshmen defectors on a bill and "made no threats" but explained to them why dissent would endanger "a career of public life and party usefulness [that] lay before them" (*Washington Post* 1906). Persuasion can also include threats, though they must be used judiciously; as Speaker Jim Wright once argued, threats "don't work and they make enemies" (Barry 1989, 314; Ripley 1967, 73). In the mid-2000s, for instance, Minority Leader Pelosi threatened to deny Democrats access to services at the party's campaign headquarters if they failed to pay their dues (Eilperin 2006, 24).

Anecdotal and other evidence strongly suggests that lobbying—whether through persuasion, quid pro quos, or threats—does induce loyal behavior.

Research has found a relationship in Congress between the distribution of pork-barrel projects and support for major bills (Evans 2004).[19] On one occasion, a House Democrat who had recently received funding for her district later admitted to switching her vote on a defense spending bill after a subcommittee chairman "came right up to me and . . . said, 'You change that [vote] and change it right now or I'm taking that money out of there'" (Lochhead 2015).

There are many accounts of bills and procedural motions passing—even victory for the House majority party's nominee for Speaker—following last-minute lobbying by party leaders (Draper 2012, 64; Green 2010; Ripley 1967, 73–76; Sinclair 1995, 247–48, 251).[20] Studies of whip counts (the internal polling of how lawmakers plan to vote) have revealed what Tom DeLay called "growing the vote," in which some lawmakers are initially uncertain about or opposed to measures but are subsequently converted (Burden and Frisby 2004; Draper 2012, 81; Evans 2011; Evans and Grandy 2008). In 2014, efforts by Speaker Boehner and his allies to persuade colleagues to contribute to the party's campaign operations induced a number of them to pony up (Choma 2014; Isenstadt and Sherman 2014).

Collective Lobbying

In addition to lobbying individual party members, leaders may try to pressure or persuade many would-be dissidents at once. For instance, some votes are labeled "party votes" in advance, signaling that how legislators cast their ballots will be remembered the next time they ask for a favor (Barry 1989, 429; Sinclair 1995, 244). Speakers of the House sometimes deliver a speech on the House floor close to a vote to convince wavering lawmakers to support the party (Green 2010, ch. 2). Other tactics in this category include threatening to schedule votes over a weekend should a bill fail, summoning lawmakers to party meetings to share information or hear persuasive speeches, and declaring publicly that a measure will pass so that would-be opponents feel compelled to support the measure, lest their defections result in a defeat that embarrasses their leaders (Forgette 2004; Green 2015).

Inclusive Decision-Making

Known as the "politics of inclusion," this tactic involves consulting with likely opponents in advance, or granting them decision-making authority, so they have a shared stake in the outcome (Farrell 2001, 471; Sinclair 1995, 75–77). In the 1970s, for instance, Speaker Tip O'Neill (D-MA) strategically appointed key lawmakers to a special ad hoc committee he created to review and modify a complex energy bill (Farrell 2001, 465–68). Thirty years later, Speaker Nancy Pelosi held "meetings and after meetings with all the diverse Democratic groups" on health-care reform, following a strategy of "relentless inclusion that involved letting everyone have their say" in order to marshal a majority in favor of President Barack Obama's health-care legislation (Lochhead 2015). An anecdote about independent-minded Representative Buddy MacKay (D-FL) perhaps best sums up this technique's value. When told by Speaker Jim Wright, "I like team players," MacKay replied, "I like to play on a team as long as I'm in the huddle when the play is called" (Barry 1989, 259).

Offering Benefits for Higher Levels of Loyalty

Besides awarding scarce goods in exchange for future loyalty, leaders may opt to reward lawmakers *after* they demonstrate fealty to the party. The idea is not only to guarantee their continued fidelity but also to have them "serve as an example for other members" to entice them to be more loyal in the future (Pearson 2015, 169). Studies have found correlations between greater party loyalty on certain matters and getting better committee assignments, having one's legislative proposals considered on the floor, and securing party campaign funds (Cox and McCubbins 1993; Leighton and López 2002; Pearson 2015).

It should be noted that the frequency and effectiveness of these tactics depend to a great extent on the goals and skills of party leaders.[21] Discipline is more likely to be enforced when leaders prioritize policy enactment over winning or keeping control of Congress (Pearson 2015, 36–37). Additionally, some leaders are simply better at lobbying and counting votes than others (Draper 2012, 77, 270, 278; Sherman 2013). Party leaders who suffer high-profile losses may lose their aura of influence, making it harder for them to build majority coalitions later. In 2008, after House leaders failed to pass a bank bailout bill in the wake of the collapsing economy, a former whip observed, "When you lose a vote like that, your ability to have discipline dissipates" (Ota 2008).

Leaders are also more likely to succeed if they have credibility among, are trusted by, and have done favors for rank-and-file party members. Republican whip Tom DeLay was extremely skilled at counting votes, but he was also successful because he had built a reservoir of goodwill by doing small favors, like providing barbecue chicken when the House met late in the evening (Baker 2000, 45). Speaker Nancy Pelosi, whose prodigious fund-raising and work ethic engendered loyalty among her fellow Democrats, was often able to convince party liberals to compromise on core policy issues because her own leftward leanings were above reproach (Lochhead 2015). By contrast, Speaker

Boehner was distrusted by a number of Republican freshmen elected in 2010, and after tearful pleas to his party to pass a budget bill in January 2013 got him nowhere, one reporter at the time said, "He's been crippled" (Draper 2012, 132; Klein 2013; Strong 2013).

Creating a Culture of Loyalty

Most scholars of Congress concur that lawmakers' behavior stems from their careful calculation of how to best achieve individual electoral and policy goals (Mayhew 1974). Nonetheless, certain kinds of legislator behavior—such as voting loyally on procedural matters that are less transparent to voters and have little, if any, ideological content—do not seem as readily explainable by individual calculations of self-interest (Evans 2011, 11). Collective concerns that divisions will tarnish the party's image and thus hurt individual lawmakers' chances of reelection could be one reason why legislators are loyal even on these issues (Cox and McCubbins 1993; F. Lee 2009, 18). The contrasting philosophies of Congressmen Dent and Brat about party loyalty, however, suggest another explanation: norms of behavior and strength of party identity matter. For instance, a member of Congress noted that when the House votes for Speaker, "there's no law that mandates that you have to vote for your political nominee, but the *tradition* has been that you do" (Gehrke 2015; emphasis added). Similarly, scholars have noted, "The expectation of supporting your party on procedural votes is now very strong" (Evans 2011, 11; Sinclair 2006, 177; 2012, 33).

If norms and party identity are important, then a subtler and longer-term leadership strategy other than distributing rewards or sanctions is to establish an expectation of party loyalty among the rank and file and deepen their party identity. Leaders may then rely on those expectations and that deep-seated identity to maximize party unity—even on nonideological matters or when lawmakers and party leaders disagree on policy. For example, Democratic House minority whip Steny Hoyer (D-MD) has said that his goal as party leader is to develop a "psychology of consensus." "I [want] people to get up in the morning," he said, "and think, 'I want to be with the team'" (Dumain and Fuller 2013). Tom DeLay, for one, would appeal to party identification as a tactic of persuasion: some legislators, he once remarked, "just understand the dynamics of teamwork, sticking together, working with each other, *that you appeal to*" (quoted in F. Lee 2009, 47; emphasis added).[22]

There are several ways party leaders can develop and enhance party identity and norms of loyalty. One is to recruit candidates to run for Congress who are more likely to embrace party loyalty as an end in itself. Representatives and senators who have previously served in elected office or worked in state and local party organizations often have "a strong psychological identification with their parties" (Rieselbach 1973, 88; Smith 2007, 56). That in turn may translate into loyalty: House Republicans who formerly served as party leaders in state legislatures, for instance, have been less likely to defy their party's agenda-setting power (Green forthcoming).[23]

Candidates recruited and endorsed by party leaders may also feel some obligation to those leaders—obligation that can be converted into support for the party. Rewards, sanctions, party-centered traditions like regular lunch meetings, and team-building exercises may also help establish and enforce norms of behavior (Goodin 2013; Green 2015). Norms are important to develop among new members especially. Representative Joe Cannon once advised a group of potentially disobedient freshmen House Republicans to "give and take" as lawmakers, while Speaker Sam Rayburn (D-TX) famously reminded newly elected Democrats to "go along to get along" (*Washington Post* 1906; Champagne 1984, 161). By contrast, Majority Whip Kevin McCarthy (R-CA) reportedly liked the rebelliousness of many of the freshmen elected in 2010 and "wasn't going to quash their spirit, even if he had the power to do so" (Draper 2012, 130).

If party identification and norms of loyalty become well established, rank-and-file members may help enforce them (Smith 2007, 56). When moderate House Democrats provided the votes to pass Republican legislation in the 1980s, it was other Democrats, not party leaders, who were most intent on punishing them (Rohde 1991, 78–81). In the early 2000s, when some Democratic members of prized committees proved reluctant to donate money to the party's coffers, one legislator warned, "People are saying, 'Why should you serve on an exclusive committee if you aren't willing to participate?'" (Billings 2004). In 2003, after Representative David Wu (D-OR) voted at the last minute in favor of a major Republican Medicare bill that narrowly passed, fellow congressman Barney Frank (D-MA) warned Wu that his vote would haunt him for a while, for "he had underestimated how personally lawmakers take party defections on key votes" (Eilperin 2006, 65).

Leaders, then, can help inculcate party loyalty not just with deal making and case-by-case persuasion but by fostering a culture of loyalty and intense party identity. But norms are also less durable than procedures or electoral incentives, and failure to regularly enforce them, especially with new lawmakers, can cause their rapid deterioration (Rohde, Ornstein, and Peabody 1985). In early 2007, for instance, newly ascendant majority Democrats in the House allowed some in their ranks to vote for a Republican motion to recommit, rejecting the norm that such motions were measures of party loyalty. As a result, "they suddenly made the motion to recommit real" (in the words of one Republican aide), and the motion was soon used regularly, sometimes successfully, by Republicans to alter or defeat Democratic bills (Green 2015, 175; Sinclair 2012, 44).

Conclusion

As measured by voting behavior, today's Congress is at its highest level of polarization since the late nineteenth century. Representatives and senators seem less willing than ever to cross party lines, and the two major parties are frequently unwilling to pursue interparty compromise or cooperation. However, as recent events have shown, party loyalty is not an inherent feature of congressional life. Some Republicans in Congress (the House especially) have openly rebelled against their party's policymaking, procedural, organizational, and electoral authority, and even among Democrats there are signs of disunity, such as on the floor vote for Speaker.

These developments have underscored the critical task of party leaders in Congress to maintain their party's authority over vote outcomes, the legislative agenda, the selection of leaders, and electioneering activities. That authority cannot be presumed to exist but must be regularly monitored and protected, especially when new members of Congress arrive in Washington, DC. Evidence shows that offering rewards, not meting out punishments, is usually the best way to accomplish that task, and if party leaders can instill strong party identification and norms of compliance, they can further bolster party loyalty and, by extension, the authority of their party.

Perhaps the best recent illustration of what happens when leaders ignore this was John Boehner's challenging tenure as Speaker of the House. Many Republicans first elected to Congress in 2010 identified less with their party and were skeptical of its leaders, so their loyalty to Republican leaders was far from assured. But Boehner and other leaders made a series of moves that exacerbated intraparty tensions. Fulfilling a campaign promise, they banished "earmarks" (targeted benefits in bills), meaning they had fewer goods to trade in exchange for votes. Lawmakers were whipped less on votes than in the past, and early defections by GOP dissenters went unanswered (or met with little more than a "thwack on the back and a disapproving shake of [Boehner's] head"), encouraging future dissent (Draper 2012, 135; Kane and Fahrenthold 2013; Stanton 2012; Stanton and Palmer 2011). Boehner eventually began imposing punishments on rebellious colleagues, but they usually proved counterproductive and were held up by rebels as proof of their "true" conservatism. When a fight over President Obama's signature health-care law led to a partial shutdown of the federal government in October 2013, Boehner reportedly admitted to Obama that he had wanted to avoid a shutdown, but "I got overrun" (Bresnahan et al. 2013). Boehner eventually resigned from the Speakership midterm, only the second Speaker to do so in American history.[24]

The challenge facing congressional leaders today is how to maintain, if not rebuild, frayed norms of party loyalty. There are potent countervailing pressures both outside Congress (from interest groups, the blogosphere, activist constituents) and within (from maverick incumbents and organized factions like the House Freedom Caucus) that may continue to keep congressional parties divided. How those pressures will be overcome and whether party leaders will be skilled enough to overcome them remains to be seen.

Notes

1. Examples included a compromise budget bill to reopen the federal government in October 2013 (H.R. 2775, 113th Congress), an increase in the debt limit in February 2014 (S. 540, 113th Congress), and a Homeland Security spending bill in March 2015 (H.R. 240, 114th Congress).

2. Committee chairs often use the same techniques outlined here to impose discipline; see, e.g., Plungis (1999) and the Rostenkowski example below. Presidents may also impose sanctions or offer rewards to increase loyalty (Birnbaum and Rogers 1993).

3. In the House agenda control is usually exercised via special rules, while in the Senate it can be exercised via bills that may be subject to limitations on amendments (like reconciliation bills; see chapter 5), creative procedural mechanisms (like filling the amendment tree; see chapter 8), or agreements between leaders of both parties to limit amendments (Beth et al. 2009; King, Orlando, and Rohde 2012; Hanson 2014; Lynch and Oleszek 2014; Wallner 2013).

4. Smith (2007, 49–50) refers to the second and third causes of party discipline as "indirect" and "direct" forms of influence, respectively. However, perhaps a more precise analogy is with the three dimensions, or "faces," of power: having one's own preferences subtly shaped by others (the third dimension), being constrained in one's choice of action (the second dimension), and being subject to persuasion or threats (the first dimension) (Gaventa 1980, 5–13).

5. In 2014, for example, the least loyal Democrats in each chamber were Senator Joe Manchin III (from the Republican state of West Virginia) and Collin Peterson (from a swing district in Minnesota), and the least loyal Republicans were Senator Susan Collins (from Democratic Maine) and Representative Chris Gibson (from a Democratic-leaning district in New York) (Carney 2015).

6. In 2014, Jones had the second-lowest loyalty score among House Republicans, voting with a majority of his party just 70.8 percent of the time (Carney 2015).

7. Lawmakers who announce their intention to defect are less likely to face leaders' wrath than those who do not, because "vote-counters hate being surprised" (Pershing 2003). Since most party leaders are elected by party members, disciplining those

members risks undermining their support within the party. The desire to discipline lawmakers is also likely to vary by leader (see Pearson 2015 and Rohde 1991, 38, 172).

8. "Outcome" could mean a majority, but it could also mean unanimity, either within the party or on the final vote, for strategic or political reasons.

9. The tools themselves have changed in scope over time; generally speaking, since the 1970s party leaders (primarily in the House) have accrued more power over committee assignments, committee chairmanships, the legislative agenda, and how bills are referred to committees (Rohde 1991, 23–25).

10. This authority is significant enough in the U.S. House that Cox and McCubbins (2005) call the House majority party a "procedural cartel." They tend to emphasize this authority negatively (i.e., its use in blocking bills), though it can be used to enact legislative proposals too (Smith 2007, 53–54; Jones 1968).

11. Jenkins and Stewart (2013) call this an "organizational cartel."

12. This may also include supporting the party's nominee for president. Refusal to do so has occasionally been met with punishment (see table 3.1).

13. The origins of this extreme polarization have been researched in great depth (Masket 2011, Nivola and Brady 2006, Noel 2013, Rohde 1991, Sinclair 2006, and Theriault 2008).

14. Ballots cast "present" for speaker are not counted toward the total number of votes, thereby reducing the number of votes needed for a candidate to win, and may thus be seen differently by party leaders than, say, voting against the party's nominee (Beth and Heitshusen 2015).

15. The process by which Congress investigates and punishes violations of chamber rules or codes of conduct is more formalized than how party disloyalty is dealt with, and chamber rules permit a range of punishments, including reprimand, censure, and even expulsion (Maskell 2008, 2013).

16. Note that congressional leaders are not the only ones who can impose punishments for disloyalty. Representative Mark Meadows (R-NC), for instance, claimed that when he proposed ousting John Boehner as Speaker, his fund-raiser "fired him"; "He just said I can't raise any more money in this town for you because of what you just did" (Siegel 2015).

17. Punishments are probably more acceptable among the rank and file when meted out for ethical or legal violations, since such violations tarnish the reputation of the party as a whole (Smith 2007, 28).

18. It is also useful to leave the door open to defectors so they have an avenue to return to the party's good graces, rather than remaining outcasts. In 1981, House Democratic leaders let most partisans who defected on a major budget bill return to the fold. Said Jim Wright, "We welcome the sinners back" (Shribman 1981).

19. One drawback to this approach is that it may encourage lawmakers to behave as potential dissenters in order to trade their votes for scarce goods.

20. Sometimes last-minute votes are the result of "pocket votes" secured in advance (King and Zeckhauser 2003; Sinclair 1995, 247).

21. In addition, leaders with friends and allies may be able to rely on their support on politically difficult votes (Green forthcoming; Smith 2007, 57).

22. Evidence has also shown that lawmakers most loyal to the party in general are those most likely to be converted by party leaders on whipped votes (Burden and Frisby 2004).

23. It may be no coincidence that the more loyal Dent, prior to joining Congress, had served fourteen years in the state legislature, whereas Brat had never previously held elected office.

24. Ironically, Boehner himself had once recognized the folly of using punishment, warning committee chairs in 2011 that doing so would "just make martyrs out of" rebels (Draper 2012, 278).

References

Baker, Peter. 2000. *The Breach: Inside the Impeachment and Trial of William Jefferson Clinton.* New York: Scribner.

Barry, John M. 1989. *The Ambition and the Power.* New York: Viking Press.

Beth, Richard S., and Valerie Heitshusen. 2015. "Speakers of the House: Elections, 1913–2015." Congressional Research Service. Washington, DC: Library of Congress.

Beth, Richard S., Valerie Heitshusen, Bill Heniff, and Elizabeth Rybicki. 2009. "Leadership Tools for Managing the U.S. Senate." Paper presented at the American Political Science Association Annual Meeting, Toronto, Ontario, Canada, September 3–6.

Billings, Erin P. 2004. "Peterson, in Ag Bid, Pays Up." *Roll Call,* November 22.

Birnbaum, Jeffrey H., and David Rogers. 1993. "Clinton Pursues Strategy to Pass Stimulus Bill." *Wall Street Journal,* April 13.

Blake, Aaron. 2015. "John Boehner Just Endured the Biggest Revolt against a House Speaker in More Than 150 Years." *Washington Post,* January 6.

Bolton, Alexander. 2009. "Sen. DeMint Battling NRSC Chair Cornyn over Conservative Primary Candidates." *Hill,* December 21.

Bresnahan, John, Manu Raju, Jake Sherman, and Carrie Budoff Brown. 2013. "Anatomy of a Shutdown." *Politico,* October 18.

Burden, Barry C., and Tammy M. Frisby. 2004. "Preferences, Partisanship, and Whip Activity in the U.S. House of Representatives." *Legislative Studies Quarterly* 29: 569–90.

Carey, John M. 2007. "Competing Principals, Political Institutions, and Party Unity in Legislative Voting." *American Journal of Political Science* 51: 92–107.

Carlson, Peter. 1993. "Dan Rostenkowski Goes Down in History." *Washington Post Magazine,* October 17.

Carney, Eliza Newlin. 2015. "Standing Together against Any Action." *Congressional Quarterly Weekly Report,* March 16.

Champagne, Anthony. 1984. *Congressman Sam Rayburn.* New Brunswick, NJ: Rutgers University Press.

Choma, Russ. 2014. "Republican Dues Crackdown Pays Off." *Opensecrets,* August 22, https://www.opensecrets.org/news/2014/08/republican-dues-crackdown-pays-off (accessed October 30, 2015).

Cooper, Kenneth J. 1994. "Straying Lawmakers May Face Revived Party Discipline on Hill." *Washington Post*, December 17.

Cox, Gary W., and Mathew D. McCubbins. 1993. *Legislative Leviathan: Party Government in the House*. Berkeley: University of California Press.

———. 2005. *Setting the Agenda: Responsible Party Government in the U.S. House of Representatives*. New York: Cambridge University Press.

Deering, Christopher J., and Steven S. Smith. 1997. *Committees in Congress*, 3rd ed. Washington, DC: CQ Press.

Dent, Charlie. 2015. "Biography." Charlie Dent, http://dent.house.gov/index.cfm?p=Biography (accessed October 18, 2015).

Draper, Robert. 2012. *Do Not Ask What Good We Do: Inside the U.S. House of Representatives*. New York: Free Press.

Dumain, Emma, and Matt Fuller. 2013. "Hoyer Holds the Line." *Roll Call*, September 24.

Eilperin, Juliet. 2006. *Fight Club Politics: How Partisanship Is Poisoning the House of Representatives*. Lanham, MD: Rowman & Littlefield.

Evans, C. Lawrence. 2011. "Growing the Vote: Majority Party Whipping in the U.S. House, 1955–2002." Paper presented at the 10th Annual Congress and History Conference, Brown University, Providence, Rhode Island, June 9–10.

Evans, C. Lawrence, and Claire E. Grandy. 2008. "The Whip Systems of Congress." In *Congress Reconsidered*, edited by Lawrence C. Dodd and Bruce I. Oppenheimer, 189–216. 9th ed. Washington, DC: CQ Press.

Evans, Diana. 2004. *Greasing the Wheels: Using Pork Barrel Projects to Build Majority Coalitions in Congress*. New York: Cambridge University Press.

Evans, Rowland, and Robert Novak. 1966. *Lyndon B. Johnson: The Exercise of Power*. New York: New American Library.

Farrell, John A. 2001. *Tip O'Neill and the Democratic Century*. Boston: Little, Brown.

Fenno, Richard F., Jr. 1973. *Congressmen in Committees*. Boston: Little, Brown.

Foerstel, Karen. 2001. "Rep. Traficant Pleads Not Guilty, Challenges Federal Probers' Integrity." *Congressional Quarterly Weekly Report*, May 12.

Forgette, Richard. 2004. "Party Caucuses and Coordination: Assessing Caucus Activity and Party Effects." *Legislative Studies Quarterly* 29: 407–30.

French, Lauren, and Jake Sherman. 2015. "House Conservatives Lash Out at Boehner's 'Culture of Punishment.'" *Politico*, June 22.

Fuller, Matt. 2015. "Freedom Caucus to Oppose Any Spending Bill with Planned Parenthood Money." *Roll Call*, September 10.

Gaventa, John. 1980. *Power and Powerlessness: Quiescence and Rebellion in an Appalachian Valley*. Urbana: University of Illinois Press.

Gehrke, Joel. 2015. "McCarthy's Path to Speaker May Not Be as Clear as It Seems." *National Review*, October 2.

Goodin, Emily. 2013. "Weekly Lunches Give Senators a Chance to Air Their Differences." *Hill*, May 7.

Green, Matthew N. 2010. *The Speaker of the House: A Study of Leadership*. New Haven, CT: Yale University Press.

———. 2013. "Congressional Leadership and the Power of Persuasion." Paper presented at the American Political Science Association Annual Meeting, Chicago, Illinois, August 29–September 1.

———. 2015. *Underdog Politics: The Minority Party in the U.S. House of Representatives.* New Haven, CT: Yale University Press.

———. 2016. "The Multiple Roots of Party Loyalty: Explaining Republican Dissent in the U.S. House of Representatives." *Congress and the Presidency.*

Hanson, Peter. 2014. *Too Weak to Govern: Majority Party Power and Appropriations in the U.S. Senate.* New York: Cambridge University Press.

Heberlig, Eric S., and Bruce A. Larson. 2012. *Congressional Parties, Institutional Ambition, and the Financing of Majority Control.* Ann Arbor: University of Michigan Press.

Ho, Catherine, and Kelsey Snell. 2015. "Export-Import Bank Supporters Move to Force House Vote." *Washington Post*, October 9.

Hunter, Kathleen. 2011. "Cardoza-Pelosi Relationship Turns Chilly." *Roll Call*, February 15.

Isenstadt, Alex. 2013. "House Tea Partiers Not Anteing Up." *Politico*, October 20.

Isenstadt, Alex, and Jake Sherman. 2014. "House GOP Cracks Down on Dues." *Politico*, July 11.

Jenkins, Jeffrey A., and Charles Stewart III. 2013. *Fighting for the Speakership: The House and the Rise of Party Government.* Princeton, NJ: Princeton University Press.

Jones, Charles O. 1968. "Joseph G. Cannon and Howard W. Smith: An Essay on the Limits of Leadership in the House of Representatives." *Journal of Politics* 30: 617–46.

Kackley, Rod. 2015. "Freedom Caucus Members Decry 'Fear and Intimidation' of Boehner Era." *PJ Media*, October 12, http://pjmedia.com/blog/freedom-caucus-members-decry-fear-and-intimidation-of-boehner-era (accessed October 30, 2015).

Kane, Paul, and David A. Fahrenthold. 2013. "Boehner's Laid-Back Approach Seen as Boon, Bane for House Republicans." *Washington Post*, June 29.

Killian, Linda. 1998. *The Freshmen: What Happened to the Republican Revolution?* Boulder, CO: Westview Press.

King, Aaron S., Francis J. Orlando, and David W. Rohde. 2012. "Beyond Motions to Table: Exploring the Procedural Toolkit of the Majority Party in the United States Senate." In *Party and Procedure in the United States Congress*, edited by Jacob R. Straus, 173–94. Lanham, MD: Rowman & Littlefield.

King, David C., and Richard J. Zeckhauser. 2003. "Congressional Vote Options." *Legislative Studies Quarterly* 28: 387–411.

Klein, Ezra. 2013. "Why Boehner Doesn't Just Ditch the Far Right." *Wonkblog* (blog), *Washington Post*, October 1.

Krehbiel, Keith. 1993. "Where's the Party?" *British Journal of Political Science* 23: 255–66.

Leary, Alex. 2014. "Bilirakis Loses Leadership Post over Floor Vote." *Tampa Bay Times*, February 21.

Lee, Frances E. 2009. *Beyond Ideology: Politics, Principles, and Partisanship in the U.S. Senate.* Chicago: University of Chicago Press.

Lee, Timothy B. 2015. "The House Freedom Caucus, Explained." *Vox,* October 9.

Leighton, Wayne A., and Edward J. López. 2002. "Committee Assignments and the Cost of Party Loyalty." *Political Research Quarterly* 55: 59–90.

Lochhead, Carolyn. 2015. "Nancy Pelosi's Leadership Style Helps Her Avoid Crises like GOP's." *San Francisco Chronicle,* October 16.

Lynch, Megan S., and Mark J. Oleszek. 2014. "Recent Innovations in Special Rules in the House of Representatives." In *The Evolving Congress,* Congressional Research Service, 113th Cong., 2nd sess., S. Prt., 113–30, 245–58. Washington, DC: Government Printing Office.

Lyons, Richard L. 1969. "McCormack Beats Back House Revolt." *Washington Post,* January 3.

Mann, Thomas E., and Norman J. Ornstein. 2012. *It's Even Worse Than It Looks: How the American Constitutional System Collided with the New Politics of Extremism.* New York: Basic Books.

Marcus, Ruth. 2005. "The Woman Warrior." *Washington Post,* May 24.

Maskell, Jack. 2008. "Expulsion and Censure Actions Taken by the Full Senate against Members." Congressional Research Service. Washington, DC: Library of Congress.

———. 2013. "Expulsion, Censure, Reprimand, and Fine: Legislative Discipline in the House of Representatives." Congressional Research Service. Washington, DC: Library of Congress.

Masket, Seth E. 2011. *No Middle Ground: How Informal Party Organizations Control Nominations and Polarize Legislatures.* Ann Arbor: University of Michigan Press.

Mayhew, David R. 1974. *Congress: The Electoral Connection.* New Haven, CT: Yale University Press.

New York Times. 2015. "House Votes Violating the 'Hastert Rule.'" *Inside Congress,* http://politics.nytimes.com/congress/votes/house/hastert-rule (accessed December 4, 2015).

Newhauser, Daniel. 2015. "Three Booted from GOP Whip Team as Leaders Crack Down." *National Journal,* June 16.

Nivola, Pietro S., and David W. Brady, eds. 2006. *Red and Blue Nation? Characteristics and Causes of America's Polarized Politics,* vol. 1. Washington, DC: Brookings Institution Press.

Noel, Hans. 2013. *Political Ideologies and Political Parties in America.* New York: Cambridge University Press.

Ota, Alan K. 2005. "No Pat on the Back for GOP as Intraparty Issues Dominate." *Congressional Quarterly Weekly Report,* January 10.

———. 2008. "Leadership Battles Break Out in House." *Congressional Quarterly Weekly Report,* November 10.

Overby, Peter. 2010. "DeMint Increases Clout by Banking on Conservatives." NPR, November 12.

Pathé, Simone. 2015. "Walter Jones' Leadership Letter Solidifies Outsider Image ahead of Rematch." *Roll Call,* October 15.

Pearson, Kathryn. 2015. *Party Discipline in the U.S. House of Representatives.* Ann Arbor: University of Michigan Press.

Pershing, Ben. 2003. "Bass off Whip Roster Again." *Roll Call*, July 7.

Plungis, Jeff. 1999. "The Driving Force of Bud Shuster." *Congressional Quarterly Weekly Report*, August 7.

Rieselbach, Leroy N. 1973. *Congressional Politics*. New York: McGraw-Hill.

Ripley, Randall B. 1967. *Party Leaders in the House of Representatives*. Washington, DC: Brookings Institution Press.

Rogers, David. 2015. "How Boehner Might Rethink His Speakership." *Politico*, March 4.

Rohde, David W. 1991. *Parties and Leaders in the Postreform House*. Chicago: University of Chicago Press.

Rohde, David W., Norman J. Ornstein, and Robert L. Peabody. 1985. "Political Change and Legislative Norms in the U.S. Senate, 1957–1974." In *Studies of Congress*, edited by Glenn R. Parker, 147–88. Washington, DC: CQ Press.

Sherman, Jack. 2013. "A House in Chaos." *Politico*, May 1.

Sherman, Jack, and Anna Palmer. 2015. "Behind Boehner's Crackdown on Conservatives." *Politico*, June 24.

Shribman, David. 1981. "House Democrats Offering 'Amnesty' to Defectors." *New York Times*, September 17.

Siegel, Josh. 2015. "Home in North Carolina, Mark Meadows Reflects on Move to Oust John Boehner with 'No Regrets.'" *Daily Signal*, August 24.

Sinclair, Barbara. 1995. *Legislators, Leaders, and Lawmaking: The U.S. House of Representatives in the Postreform Era*. Baltimore: Johns Hopkins University Press.

———. 2006. *Party Wars: Polarization and the Politics of National Policy Making*. Norman: University of Oklahoma Press.

———. 2012. *Unorthodox Lawmaking: New Legislative Processes in the U.S. Congress*. 4th ed. Washington, DC: CQ Press.

Smith, Steven S. 2007. *Party Influence in Congress*. New York: Cambridge University Press.

Stanton, John. 2012. "Who's Afraid of John Boehner?" *Roll Call*, February 29.

Stanton, John, and Anna Palmer. 2011. "McCarthy: Whipping without a Hammer." *Roll Call*, March 21.

Strong, Jonathan. 2013. "Speak Softly or Carry a Big Stick." *Congressional Quarterly Weekly Report*, January 14.

Theriault, Sean M. 2008. *Party Polarization in Congress*. New York: Cambridge University Press.

Wallner, James I. 2013. *The Death of Deliberation: Partisanship and Polarization in the United States Senate*. Lanham, MD: Lexington Books.

Washington Post. 1906. "House Has Revolt: Strong Combine Goes Counter to President's Plans." *Washington Post*, January 9.

Weisman, Jonathan. 2013. "Texas Senator Goes on Attack and Raises Bipartisan Hackles." *New York Times*, February 15.

Wong, Scott, and Cristina Marcos. 2015. "The Dozen Rebels Targeted by GOP Leaders." *Hill*, June 27.

Woodward, Bob. 2012. *The Price of Politics*. New York: Simon & Schuster.

4

The Motion to Recommit in the U.S. House

Jennifer Hayes Clark

THE RULES OF THE GAME IN CONGRESS can often be as important as policy questions before the legislators. Conventional wisdom holds that, in the U.S. House of Representatives, the majority party dominates while the minority party possesses few powers that will allow its members to meaningfully participate in the policymaking process. Indeed, the Speaker of the House, who serves as the highest-ranking member and in the modern era is always a member of the majority party, has the ability to appoint and remove committee members, schedule legislation for the floor, and determine members of conference committees. Not only does the House minority party lack sufficient numbers to pass legislation on its own, but its members generally also lack the prerogatives, or rights, necessary to guarantee them a seat at the table during decision-making. Conversely, in the U.S. Senate, each senator has the right to take the floor to speak with generally no limits. This grants members who are opposed to bills the ability to filibuster and also gives members of the minority party a seat at the decision-making table, as sixty senators are required to invoke cloture, which ends a filibuster.

In the U.S. House, there are fewer rules that preserve minority rights. One rule is the discharge petition, which allows members who can garner signatures from a majority of House members to remove a bill from a congressional committee and bring it to the floor. This can be an important right for minority-party members as it allows members to circumvent committee chairs, who maintain power over whether a bill receives a hearing or markup.[1] While the discharge petition has the potential to allow the minority to move otherwise blocked legislation to the floor, its power is somewhat limited.

More often, the minority party uses a procedure after a bill has come to the floor—the motion to recommit (MTR). The motion to recommit, established by Rule XIX of the U.S. House of Representatives' standing rules, permits opponents of a measure to offer an alternative for consideration prior to offering the previous question. In this chapter, we explore the motion to recommit in the House. We examine how the rules have evolved with respect to the motion to recommit, its usage over time, and its success in conferring real policy gains to members of the minority party.

Rules and Procedures of the U.S. House

Article I, Section 5 of the Constitution states that each chamber shall determine its own rules of legislative proceedings. Shortly following the seating of each new Congress, members come together to determine the rules and procedures that govern the legislative process. The adoption of legislative rules at the beginning of the session, however, is anything but pro forma. According to former House Republican leader Bob Michel, "Procedure hasn't simply become more important than substance—it has, through some strange alchemy, become the substance of our deliberations. Who rules House procedures, rules the House—and to a great degree, rules the kind and scope of political debate in this country" (Oleszek 2007). Representative John Dingell stated more bluntly, "If you let me write procedure and I let you write substance, I'll screw you every time." The rules determine whose legislation receives consideration on the House floor, who can offer amendments, and who has veto authority. In theory, representative institutions might embrace equal participation among all members. In practice, institutional rules and norms confer unequal weight, empowering some at the expense of others, thereby determining who wields influence over legislative outcomes.

Partisan theorists argue that majorities structure the rules in ways to enhance their power and achieve their most preferred policy outcomes. In their book *Legislative Leviathan,* political scientists Gary Cox and Mathew McCubbins (1993) argue that the majority party acts as a cartel usurping power to craft rules that facilitate moving policy toward the majority party's ideal position (and away from the median voter in the chamber). Cox and McCubbins's partisan cartel theory holds that the majority party successfully advances its policy objectives not simply through cohesive majorities but also through the strategic structuring of legislative rules and procedures that provides the majority-party control over the legislative agenda.

The majority-party leadership has various mechanisms, including regular party caucus meetings, party whips, and representation of diverse actors in leadership positions, to communicate party interests to rank-and-file members and to extract information about legislative preferences, thereby reducing uncertainty about legislative outcomes. Leadership can then utilize this information to craft bills that will pass the full chamber (*positive agenda control*) or to block legislation that internally divides the party from consideration on the floor (*negative agenda control*).

Positive agenda control refers to the ability to secure adoption of bills that some group, typically the majority party, favors. Although the U.S. Congress has a reputation as an institution plagued by gridlock, the House majority can at times marshal cohesive majorities that successfully pass legislation. One means of assessing the power of the Speaker is to investigate instances in which he or she is able to forge a cohesive majority to pass a policy in spite of ideological rifts within the party ranks. In other words, the ability of leaders to exercise positive agenda control often necessitates that members be willing to support the party when it is perhaps unpopular to do so. Party leaders have a variety of tools at their disposal to promote discipline among members. These carrot-and-stick methods include the leaders' institutional prerogatives to determine the composition and makeup of congressional committees, to schedule legislation on the floor, and to steer distributive benefits to members' legislative districts (see, for example, Carroll and Kim 2010). Cox and McCubbins (2005, 47–48) argue that centrist members may be induced to support majority-party policies through distributive benefits (e.g., pork-barrel projects for their districts). Centrists may withstand policy losses if provided real distributive benefits by their party leaders.

Negative agenda control refers to the ability to prevent bills that are unfavorable to a group, often the majority party, from being considered on the floor. This often occurs through the use of special rules, which govern how major bills are considered on the floor (e.g., whether amendments are allowed), to structure the options available to members when a bill comes before the House. Scholars have cited an increasing number of *closed rules*, which call for a simple up or down vote and no amendments, being issued by the House Rules Committee. Walter Oleszek (2007) finds that in the 95th Congress (1977–1978), only 15 percent of special rules were restrictive (i.e., closed); yet in the 110th Congress (2007–2008), 85 percent of special rules were restrictive. This is cited as evidence that, over time, majority-party leaders increasingly attempt to exercise negative agenda control through these special rules.

A second theory, known as the conditional party government theory, was developed by political scientists John Aldrich and David Rohde (1998, 2001). The conditional party government theory argues that the costs and benefits accrued from rank-and-file members' delegation of authority to the leadership vary according to the ideological homogeneity within the party and differentiation/polarization between the parties. Delegating authority to leadership is less costly to members when their party is internally cohesive and polarized from the other party. This is an important distinction of the U.S. Congress, where party discipline—even in the current polarized era—is much lower than party discipline in other legislatures around the world, such as the United Kingdom's House of Commons (Spirling and McLean 2007). In the United States, legislators have strong incentives to cultivate a personal vote (given the electoral rules); therefore, in some instances, the costs of voting with the party outweigh the benefits, particularly when it conflicts with the preferences of the constituency on a highly salient issue. Thus, the costs and benefits of delegating authority to the party leadership are clearly affected by the ideological character of the membership of the party in Congress (Rohde 1991).

Critics of the partisan theory have contended that the decisions of legislators are primarily driven by their ideological preferences and that the inclusion of partisanship into the model does not contribute anything significant to the explanation (Krehbiel 1993, 1998). The informational theory of congressional organization contends that legislative institutions are created to facilitate the gathering of information to reduce the level of uncertainty faced by legislators when formulating policy. Since the U.S. House is a majoritarian institution and the rules are subject to change by a simple majority of the membership, stacking the deck to favor some interests over others may prove especially difficult. Keith Krehbiel (1993, 1998) contends that preferences of legislators alone are sufficient to explain legislative behavior, and the inclusion of party into the model does not significantly improve its predictive power. From Krehbiel's perspective, the median voter in the chamber ultimately controls policy; therefore, his model predicts centrist legislative outcomes.

Scholars have argued that partisan influence in legislative politics may take various forms, including the ability to block unfavorable legislative proposals and amendments, arm-twisting to ensure that members vote for the party's proposal, rewarding party discipline with the appointment of influential or beneficial committee assignments, and so forth. The partisan cartel theory focuses in large part on the negative agenda control powers of political parties (i.e., the ability of the majority party to keep proposals that it dislikes off the floor and to prevent its policy proposals from losing on the floor). It is in majority party's best interest to use its prefloor procedural powers to prevent legislation that would be less favorable than the status quo from coming to the floor, receiving a roll call, and possibly being passed.

The Motion to Recommit in the U.S. House

The motion to recommit is a parliamentary procedure used to refer a motion that is under consideration on the floor back to committee. The motion to recommit, as established by Rule XIX of the U.S. House of Representatives' standing rules, permits opponents of a measure to offer an alternative for consideration prior to offering the previous question. The motion to recommit may be offered in various forms. The first type of motion to recommit is commonly referred to as a "straight" motion to recommit. The straight motion to recommit is a motion offered without instructions and allows for no debate. If the motion is adopted by the chamber, the underlying bill is returned to committee. There is no promise that the bill will receive further consideration by the House, and therefore opponents of a measure may use the "straight" motion to recommit to effectively dispose of legislation by bottling it up in committee in hopes that it will not be returned to the floor for further consideration.

Opponents of a measure may also offer the motion to recommit with "forthwith" instructions. A motion to recommit forthwith contains amendatory language that is considered on the House floor without being referred back to committee. A successful motion to recommit with instructions to report back forthwith allows any amendatory language included in the motion to be adopted immediately without the measure leaving the House floor. Finally, the motion to recommit with "nonforthwith" instructions returns the measure back to committee with no real assurance that the committee will ever act on the bill. In some instances, the motion to recommit will instruct the committee to "promptly" act and report back to the House; however, this has no true effect in urging the committee to act. This last form of the motion to recommit may include amendatory language, can instruct further research or hearings on a matter, and can urge action on the part of the committee; however, these actions are simply advisory and do not in fact require the committee to take any action on the measure.

Beginning in the 111th Congress (2009–2010), the Democratic leadership made reforms to the motion to recommit. The rule change eliminated the opportunity for the minority (or the bill's opposition) to make a motion to recommit a bill to committee with instructions to report nonforthwith or promptly. The right of the opposition to the bill to instruct the committee to report forthwith remains. The former (MTR with amendments nonforthwith) removes the bill from the floor for committee consideration, where it may remain indefinitely. This ultimately can kill the bill. The motion to recommit with amendments forthwith keeps the bill on the floor, where the amended proposal is considered and voted on for final passage immediately.

The leaders urging this change argued that it was essential, since the motions to recommit promptly were killing legislation and causing considerable delays in the legislative process. Thus, members opposed to legislation are still granted a final opportunity to amend the legislation (or to offer some alternative to that being considered); yet their ability to obstruct through use of this procedure is now more limited. This remains the sole opportunity for members opposed to the bill to amend it; however, the motion to recommit offered must be germane (i.e., relevant) to the underlying measure.

The motion to recommit has been hailed as an important right of the House minority party, which lacks the institutional tools available to its counterpart in the U.S. Senate (Binder 1997; Wawro and Schickler 2006). Unlike the filibuster (see chapter 10) and other tools available for the minority to obstruct the majority party's policy agenda (see chapter 8), Keith Krehbiel and Adam Meirowitz (2002) argue that the motion to recommit affords members of the minority party the opportunity to positively shape the legislative agenda through offering policy alternatives to legislation currently under consideration. Before touting the motion to recommit as the great equalizer between the parties in the House, we must consider a few points concerning how the motion has worked in practice, the limitations placed upon the minority party's amendatory powers, and its place in the broader policymaking context.

Although this procedural right has existed since the 1st Congress (1789–1791) and may be traced back to the British parliament, the motion to recommit has operated differently over time. This institutional prerogative recently has been touted by members of the majority party as evidence of their commitment to procedural fairness. In rebuffing claims of abusive majority-party tactics at the beginning of the 108th Congress (2003–2004), Representative David Dreier (2003, 18), who served as chairman of the Rules Committee, stated, "If my colleagues look at the reforms that we have maintained we initiated once we became a majority and frankly built upon, they do, in fact, increase the accountability and the deliberative nature of this Congress. We have items that are included in this measure which guarantee the minority the right to offer a motion to recommit on legislation."

In an essay on the motion to recommit, Donald Wolfensberger (2003, 28) characterizes the motion to recommit as "a convenient last bastion of institutional fairness in an otherwise unfair process." A historical view casts doubt on the perspective of the motion to recommit as a legislative prerogative that affords the minority meaningful influence in the policymaking process. Although the procedural right has existed in the codified rules since the inception of Congress, in the earlier congresses the motion was frequently used to further majority-party interests, thereby limiting its use as a tool for the minority party. In the early years, the motion to recommit was frequently used by the bill's supporters to correct technical errors in the language of the bill. The relevant language concerning the motion to recommit did not make any explicit reference to the opposition or minority party.

Only during the 1909 rules changes did reformers include language that explicitly referenced the opposition or minority party. Consequently, the Speaker was given great discretion in determining who could offer the motion to recommit and frequently ruled that the motion to recommit was intended to provide an opportunity for supporters of a bill to clean up the language before the final adoption of the measure. On the matter concerning a motion to recommit a legislative, executive, and judicial appropriation bill during the 62nd Congress (1911–1913), House Speaker Joseph Cannon (1936, 393) clarified the intent of the motion stating, "The object of this provision was, as the Chair has always understood, that the motion should be made by one friendly to the bill, for the purpose of giving one more chance to perfect it, as perchance there might be some error that the House desired to correct."

Others have likewise interpreted the motion to recommit as a tool for the majority party to make small technical changes before legislation is adopted. In the 61st Congress (1909–1910), Representative John Dalzell (1909, 31) described the motion in the following way: "We all know that the motion to recommit, under existing practice, has been used not to secure recommittal, but to prevent recommittal. The custom has grown up to have a Member of the majority party move to recommit and then to have his colleagues vote the motion down."

Thus, early interpretations of the motion to recommit undermined the opposition's authority to participate meaningfully by advancing its own policy alternatives into the discussion. In fact, this interpretation of the motion to recommit also facilitated the majority party's efforts in controlling the legislative agenda. However, Wolfensberger (2003) points out that from 1880 to 1909, Speakers were much more inclined to recognize members of the minority party than members of their own party to offer the motion to recommit. Nonetheless, the lack of clear language concerning who should be recognized to offer the motion to recommit in the event of multiple authors of motions served to empower the Speaker. Consequently, between 1880 and 1909, the minority party's rights were far from guaranteed and rested upon the goodwill of the Speaker at that time.

The rules changes of 1909 clarified the intent of the motion to recommit as a tool of the opposition. Specifically, the House amended what is now Rule XIX, clause 2(a), to include language stating that the Speaker give preference to "a Member, Delegate, or Resident Commissioner who is opposed to the measure" to offer the motion to recommit. This rules change seemingly benefitted the minority party by taking the guesswork out of determining who should be recognized to offer the motion to recommit. By 1932, House precedents interpreted this rule as granting preferential recognition to a member of the minority party opposed to the underlying measure. The new recommit rule stated, "After the previous question shall have been ordered on the passage of a bill or joint resolution, one motion to recommit shall be in order, and the Speaker shall give preference in recognition to a Member who is opposed to the bill or joint resolution."[2]

Moreover, the rule prohibited the Rules Committee from reporting "any rule or order that would prevent the motion to recommit from being made as provided in paragraph 4 of Rule XVI." These changes in the language concerning the motion to recommit seemingly strengthen the prerogatives of the minority party to offer policy alternatives. However, there are still reasons to doubt that these changes have substantially increased involvement of the minority party in legislative decision-making.

Following the 1909 rules changes, one of the first major changes to minority-party rights occurred in 1934, when Speaker Henry Rainey (D-IL) determined that the Rules Committee had the ability to issue special rules that prohibit all amendments and limit (but do not completely prohibit) amendatory language offered by the motion to recommit. The justification in limiting motions to recommit with amendatory language was that the 1909 rule only pertained to the straight motion to recommit. Speaker Rainey argued that only a straight motion to recommit was guaranteed to the opposition. According to Wolfensberger (1991), this limitation set the stage for the majority party to begin issuing special rules to curb the ability of the minority to offer motions to recommit with instructions. The issuance of restrictive rules by the Rules Committee dates back to 1883 (Nelson 1994). However, restrictive rules did not become commonplace until the mid-1970s (Bach and Smith 1998; Sinclair 1994, 1997). The rise in closed and semiclosed rules, which place restrictions on amending by the Rules Committee, was accompanied by other tactics, including the "king of the hill," to restrict the ability of the minority party to offer a motion to recommit with instructions. These restrictions were in addition to those already in place, such as the requirement of germaneness and stipulations of the Senate Pay-as-You-Go Rule (Lynch 2008).

With the Republicans' takeover of the House during the 1994 midterm election, the new leadership pushed a broad package of reforms as part of the Contract with America, including changes in the rules and procedures of Congress. Included in their proposed changes was a section titled "Affirming the Minority's Right on Motions to Recommit." In short, the new Republican majority altered the standing rules of the House to ban special rules that prevented a motion to recommit. This came after several decades of being in the minority party and complaining of perceived abuses in legislative procedures.

Finally, Brian Webb (2012) argues that the motion to recommit has been used by the minority party as a strategy to cross-pressure members of the majority party. Members of the minority party may present particular amendments to bills under consideration on the floor that pit majority-party members' constituents and their party leadership against one another. If majority-party members vote in accordance with party leader wishes, they risk alienating their constituencies and vice versa. This presents an opportunity for the minority party to capitalize electorally through this cross-pressuring.

One important instance in which the minority party offered a motion to recommit that "split" the majority party and placed majority-party members in a tough position was on the issue of health-care reform in the 111th Congress (2009–2010). Specifically, one issue that threatened to derail President Barack Obama's (and congressional Democrats') chief policy accomplishment of comprehensive health reform was whether taxpayer funds could be used for abortion coverage. A leading pro-life Democrat in the House, Representative Bart Stupak of Michigan, offered an amendment with Republican Representative Joseph Pitts of Pennsylvania, that prohibited any taxpayer funds from covering abortions, and it passed in the House. It was, however, unable to pass the Senate. In order to get these pro-life Democrats to support the Senate bills, which was ultimately necessary to ensure the comprehensive health-care bill was passed, Stupak negotiated an agreement with the White House that President Obama would issue an executive order with language similar to that of the Stupak-Pitts amendment that had previously passed the House.[3]

After the executive order had been signed, and while the Patient Protection and Affordable Care Act was being considered on the House floor, House Republicans offered a motion to recommit with the exact language of the Stupak-Pitts amendment. If this motion to recommit had passed, then it would have prevented the legislation from being enacted since the Senate would not agree to such language. Thus, pro-life Democrats were faced with the challenge of voting for a motion to recommit that addressed their concerns with the health-care bill (yet the bill failing) or voting against the motion to recommit and passing the health-care bill and trusting that the executive order would address their concerns. Ultimately, the motion to recommit failed and the Patient Protection and Affordable Care Act was enacted along with an executive order concerning the public funding of abortions. This example illustrates how, although motions to recommit rarely pass in the House, minority-party members may seek to cross-pressure majority-party members with the hopes that this will result in electoral gains down the line.

Use of the Motion to Recommit in the U.S. House over Time

Since the 104th Congress (1995–1996), the minority party has frequently exercised its prerogative to offer the motion to recommit. Figure 4.1 shows contemporary trends in the motion to recommit (104th–114th Congresses). These data were compiled using the Library of Congress's THOMAS database. During the 110th Congress (2007–2008), 120 motions to recommit were offered, with 72 including forthwith instructions and 47 including nonforthwith instructions. Prior to the 111th Congress (2009–2010), members could offer three types of MTRs: straight, forthwith, and nonforthwith. Over the course of this period, few "straight" motions to recommit had been offered. However, since the rules change in the 111th Congress, only forthwith MTRs are in order. Thus, in comparing total MTRs with forthwith instructions to the total of MTRs overall, we find the largest gulf in the 110th Congress, and the reforms offered during the 111th Congress were in response to this steep increase in the nonforthwith MTRs being offered during the 110th Congress. We then see a drop in total MTRs in the 111th Congress (compared to the 110th Congress), yet an increase in the number of forthwith MTRs.

Of the various types of motions, the motion to recommit with forthwith instructions is the most common. From the 109th (2005–2006) to the 110th (2007–2008) Congresses, there was a sharp increase in members offering the MTR with forthwith instructions as well as in the passage of forthwith instructions. There was also a substantial increase in motions to recommit with nonforthwith instructions between the 109th and 110th (2007–2008) Congresses. However, none of these motions passed during this period. During the 110th Congress, the minority party offered motions to recommit that spanned the legislative agenda from the Lobbying Transparency Act to the DC Voting Rights Bill. Since the 111th Congress (2009–2010), members may no longer offer a motion to recommit with amendments nonforthwith (or promptly). Subsequently, there was an increase in the motions to recommit forthwith. During the 111th Congress, there were 84 MTRs, and this increased to 115 in the 112th Congress (2011–2012) and 120 in the 113th Congress (2013–2014). Few passed in the 111th and 112th Congresses (two in each), while thirteen motions to recommit passed in the 113th Congress. In the first session of the 114th Congress (2015–2016), there have already been fifty-two motions to recommit, with five passing.

In more recent cases, the majority party has charged that the minority party is simply using its institutional prerogative for political gain. In a recent essay, Norman Ornstein (2010) argued, "The motion to recommit with instructions has for more than a decade become a hollow vehicle and a farce. . . . [T]he minority has eschewed the chance to use the motion to recommit

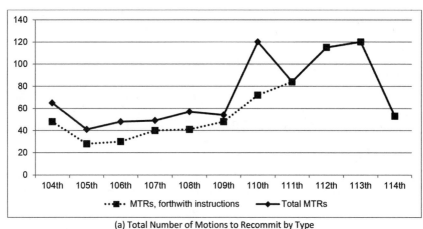

(a) Total Number of Motions to Recommit by Type

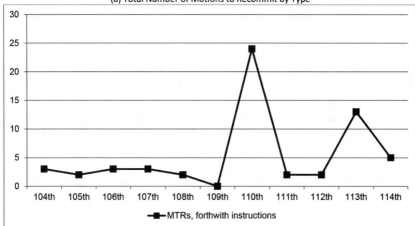

(b) Total Number of Motions to Recommit Adopted

FIGURE 4.1
Number of motions to recommit, 104th–114th Congresses.
Source: Data were compiled using the Library of Congress THOMAS database.

to offer constructive amendments to bills or to show a minority alternative vision, and instead has used the gotcha route." One recent example cited is the America COMPETES Act reauthorization, in which the bipartisan legislation focused on increasing our investment in science research and training. The motion to recommit offered by the minority required that any federal employee who had viewed or downloaded pornography be fired.

Although the motion to recommit is frequently used by members, it seldom is successful. This motivates us to consider why members would propose these motions and under what conditions the minority party (or opposition) might be successful in its MTR. Understanding the factors that shape voting outcomes on motions to recommit will enhance our knowledge about the role of parties in legislative decision-making and the institutions that enhance or diminish the ability of the minority party to participate in the policymaking process.

The Motion to Recommit and Partisan Theories of Legislative Politics

Does the motion to recommit undermine majority-party control over the legislative agenda and provide an opportunity for the minority party to exert influence over legislative outcomes? The party cartel theory developed by Cox and McCubbins (1993, 2005) predicts that the majority party should never suffer a loss from a motion to recommit. Indeed, they argue that the majority party should either defeat the motion through its superior numeric size (and voting cohesion among members) or keep unfavorable legislation off the House floor to begin with through tight control of the legislative agenda.

The conditional party government theory offered by Aldrich and Rohde (2001) predicts that party leaders are strongest and best able to promote the party agenda when the two parties are polarized from one another yet internally cohesive. Under these conditions, the costs for legislators to delegate power to their leadership are much less. Thus, the conditional party government theory suggests that the majority party will be most effective in staving off defeat via a motion to recommit when the majority party is more internally cohesive (high intraparty cohesion) and the two parties are more ideologically polarized (high interparty polarization). The nonpartisan theory espoused by Krehbiel and Meirowitz (2002) predicts that a large number of motions to recommit will be offered regularly and that these motions will pass.

To test these competing theories, I compiled a dataset of all motions to recommit offered between the 61st (1909–1910) and 114th (2015–2016) Congresses. Upon identifying whether a motion to recommit was offered, I then coded whether the motion had amendatory language and whether it contained a forthwith or nonforthwith instruction, whether the motion passed or failed, and whether the motion passed with a majority of the majority party in opposition to the motion (a majority-party "roll"). The nonpartisan theory suggests that motions to recommit will frequently (if not always) pass the House. The party cartel theory predicts a low passage rate of motions to recommit as they undermine majority-party policy priorities. Finally, the conditional party government theory suggests that the majority party will be more successful when it is internally homogeneous and ideologically distant from the minority party.

The average majority-party roll rate on motions to recommit is about 2 percent. The low rate of majority-party rolls on motions to recommit provides some limited support for the partisan theories. However, to provide a stronger test of the competing theories, I employed multivariate analysis of motion to recommit outcomes. Under what conditions do recommittal motions pass the House in the face of majority-party opposition?

I employed a number of independent variables that should influence majority-party roll rates on the motion to recommit. To assess the conditional party government theory, I constructed measures of the internal homogeneity of the majority party, which is simply the standard deviation of first-dimensional DW-NOMINATE scores for legislators (Poole and Rosenthal 1997). DW-NOMINATE scores were obtained using a scaling procedure on all competitive roll call votes (i.e., at least 5 percent voting in the minority) developed by Keith Poole and Howard Rosenthal. Roughly these scores provide us with a measure of legislators' ideological position relative to other members. Conditional party government theory suggests that majority-party rolls on the motion to recommit increase with majority-party ideological heterogeneity. Thus, as the majority party becomes more ideologically heterogeneous, the minority party may be better equipped to convince some members of the majority to join its recommittal efforts at the expense of their party.

The conditional party government theory predicts that as the two parties become more differentiated ideologically (i.e., greater polarization) the majority-party roll rate on motions to recommit should decline. Ideological polarization between the parties is measured as the absolute difference between the median party members' first-dimensional DW-NOMINATE scores. These measures have been employed frequently in the literature to measure ideology of individual members (Poole and Rosenthal 1997) as well as ideological dispersion within and between parties (Aldrich and Rohde 2001).

Drawing upon the earlier analysis of Jason M. Roberts (2005), the model includes a dummy variable controlling for recorded voting in the Committee of the Whole during the 92nd Congress (1971–1972). Roberts (2005) argues that the adoption of electronic voting technology produced an increase in the ability of the minority party to achieve a recorded vote on amendments. Likewise, the model also controls for the frequency of restrictions placed on amendatory instructions by House Democrats (Wolfensberger 1991). These restrictions are expected to have a negative impact on the number of rolls during a given Congress. Finally, I also include dummy variables for motions that concern social issues and appropriations issues.

The dependent variable for this analysis is a count (number of rolls per Congress); thus it is important that I control for the number of opportunities for the event to occur (King 1989). The number of rolls is potentially important theoretically, as Cox and McCubbins (2005) argue that one of the most important procedural powers of the majority party is to control the legislative agenda and to keep items that divide the party off the floor, thereby keeping the status quo intact. Majority-party roll rates have been used extensively in legislative research (Cox and McCubbins 2005; Gailmard and Jenkins 2007). However, Krehbiel (2007) notes a number of limitations of the measure and its ability to effectively measure "party influence." In cases where the majority party experiences deep divisions, it is unlikely that the majority leadership will place legislation on the calendar for consideration. Consequently, I include the natural log of the number of measures being voted upon to control for differential opportunities that the majority party will face a roll across different legislative sessions.

Table 4.1 presents the multivariate analysis of the number of majority-party rolls on recommittal motions per legislative session. The results of the analysis lend strong statistical support to the theory of conditional party government. Majority-party heterogeneity is positively associated with the majority-party rolls on recommittal motions. In instances where the majority party has greater ideological diversity, motions to recommit are much more likely to actually pass despite majority-party opposition to them. Interparty polarization is also statistically significant in the model and in the predicted negative direction. Thus, the majority party is much less likely to face a roll on a recommittal motion when its ideological distance is farther from the other

TABLE 4.1
Generalized Event Count Model of the Motion to Recommit

Predictor	Estimated Coefficient
Majority-party polarization (DW-NOM)	−1.95*
Majority-party cohesiveness (DW-NOM)	11.17*
Size of the majority party	−4.08*
Majority-party size × heterogeneity	1.33
ln(final passage votes)	0.06
Restrictions on instructions	0.19*
Social policy	3.44*
Appropriations issue	−1.76
Electronic voting	1.20
Constant	−1.59
Log-likelihood	−72.99

Note: *$p < 0.05$

party. This makes intuitive sense, as the minority party is less able to convince members of the majority party to join its coalition to pass the motion when the two parties are highly polarized.

The variable controlling for the size of the majority party is also statistically significant. Larger majorities are less likely to suffer rolls on motions to recommit. This again is intuitive, as a small minority would need to convince a greater number of members in the majority party to join them in passing the motion to recommit. The interactive variable (majority-party size × heterogeneity) did not reach the conventional levels of statistical significance. The results of the model also suggest that the majority party is more likely to face a roll on the motion to recommit on social issues. However, there is no statistically significant difference in the roll rates of appropriation bills. The baseline prediction of majority-party rolls is about 1.3, with all variables held constant. These results lend support to partisan theories and suggest a conditional relationship between party strength and recommittal rolls for the majority party. These results cast doubt upon the predictions of the Krehbiel and Meirowitz (2002) model. These empirical results further highlight the contingent nature of minority-party influence over legislative outcomes.

Conclusion

In 1809, Thomas Jefferson asserted that codified rules and procedures were vital in protecting the rights of the minority. Although institutional prerogatives granted to the minority may be a necessary condition for meaningful participation and influence in the legislative process, this research suggests that the rules alone are not sufficient for ensuring members of the minority party a seat at the decision-making table. The contingent nature of minority-party rights in legislative decision-making has been relatively unexplored in congressional scholarship, despite the fact that the American political system is founded upon the values of majority rule and minority rights.

The motion to recommit is one of the few institutional prerogatives afforded to the minority party in the U.S. House of Representatives. Although some have argued that this right firmly establishes a mechanism for the minority party to meaningfully participate in the policymaking process, norms and customs governing its practice demonstrate how the majority party may suppress minority-party influence in the legislative process even in the face of codified rules that seemingly empower the minority party.

The Republicans' outrage concerning the changes adopted by congressional Democrats at the beginning of the 111th Congress (2009–2010) suggests that they perceive the motion to recommit as a valuable right. Systematic

analysis of recommittal motions shows that the minority party is rarely successful in fundamentally shaping legislative outcomes. However, there may be
other ways, besides policy outcomes, that these motions provide benefits to
the minority. As Wolfensberger suggests, the value of the motion to recommit may come in the form of position taking (Mayhew 1974). Members of
the minority party may utilize their institutional prerogatives to put forth a
different vision, which they may draw upon come Election Day. On the flip
side, it may also be used as a means to force majority-party members to take
positions that may eventually be used against them in elections. Finally, the
mere suggestion of changing the rules may also be used by the minority to
cast the majority party as a tyrannical faction seeking a power grab to run
roughshod over the opposition.

Notes

1. A recent example of members circumventing the committee chair to bring a
bill to a vote on the floor occurred in October 2015 with a bill aimed at reforming the
Import-Export Bank of the United States. Specifically, the resolution (H. Res. 450)
that would allow for consideration of H.R. 597 was bottled up in the House Rules
Committee, and its sponsor, Representative Stephen Fincher (R-TN), initiated the
discharge petition, gathering the 218 signatures necessary to remove the bill from
committee to receive a vote on the House floor.
2. *Rules of the House of Representatives*, Rule XIX, clause 2(2)(a).
3. Executive Order 13535 was issued by President Obama on March 24, 2010. It
may be found at "Executive Order 13535—Ensuring Enforcement and Implementation of Abortion Restrictions in the Patient Protection and Affordable Care Act," U.S.
Government Printing Office, March 24, 2010, http://www.gpo.gov/fdsys/pkg/DCPD-
201000199/pdf/DCPD-201000199.pdf.

References

Aldrich, John H., and David W. Rohde. 1998. "Theories of Party in the Legislature
    and the Transition to Republican Rule in the House." *Political Science Quarterly*
    112: 112–35.
———. 2001. "The Logic of Conditional Party Government: Revisiting the Electoral
    Connection." In *Congress Reconsidered*, edited by Lawrence C. Dodd and Bruce I.
    Oppenheimer, 269–92. Washington, DC: CQ Press.
Bach, Stanley, and Steven S. Smith. 1998. *Managing Uncertainty in the House of Repre-
    sentatives: Adaptation and Innovation in Special Rules*. Washington, DC: Brookings
    Institution Press.

Binder, Sarah. 1997. *Minority Rights, Majority Rule.* New York: Cambridge University Press.

Cannon, Clarence. 1936. "The Motion to Refer as Related to the Previous Question." In *Cannon's Precedents*, vol. 8, sec. 2762, 393. Washington, DC: Government Printing Office.

Carroll, Royce, and Henry A. Kim. 2010. "Party Government and the 'Cohesive Power of Public Plunder.'" *American Journal of Political Science* 54: 34–44.

Cox, Gary W., and Mathew D. McCubbins. 1993. *Legislative Leviathan: Party Government in the House.* Berkeley: University of California Press.

———. 2005. *Setting the Agenda: Responsible Party Government in the U.S. House of Representatives.* New York: Cambridge University Press.

Dalzell, John. 1909. "Rules." *Congressional Record*, House of Representatives, 44, pt. 1 (March 15): 31.

Deschler, Lewis. 1994. *Deschler's Precedents.* Washington, DC: Government Printing Office, http://www.gpo.gov/fdsys/pkg/GPO-HPREC-DESCHLERS-V7/pdf/GPO-HPREC-DESCHLERS-V7-2-6-1.pdf.

Dreier, David. 2003. "Rules of the House." *Congressional Record*, House of Representatives, 149, pt. 1 (January 7): 18.

Gailmard, Sean, and Jeffery A. Jenkins. 2007. "Negative Agenda Control in the Senate and House: Fingerprints of Majority Party Power." *Journal of Politics* 69: 689–700.

King, Gary. 1989. "Variance Specification in Event Count Models: From Restrictive Assumptions to a Generalized Estimator." *American Journal of Political Science* 33: 762–84.

Krehbiel, Keith. 1993. "Where Is the Party?" *British Journal of Political Science* 23: 235–66.

———. 1998. *Pivotal Politics: A Theory of U.S. Lawmaking.* Chicago: University of Chicago Press.

———. 2007. "Partisan Roll Rates in a Nonpartisan Legislature." *Journal of Law, Economics, and Organization* 23: 1–23.

Krehbiel, Keith, and Adam Meirowitz. 2002. "Minority Rights and Majority Power: Theoretical Consequences of the Motion to Recommit." *Legislative Studies Quarterly* 27: 191–218.

Lynch, Megan S. 2008. "The Motion to Recommit in the House of Representatives: Effects, Recent Trends, and Options for Change." Congressional Research Service. Washington, DC: Library of Congress.

Mayhew, David. 1974. *Congress: The Electoral Connection.* New Haven, CT: Yale University Press.

Nelson, Garrison. 1994. *Committees in the U.S. Congress, 1947–1992.* Vol. 2: *Committee Histories and Member Assignments.* Washington, DC: CQ Press.

Oleszek, Walter J. 2007. *Congressional Procedures and the Policy Process.* Washington, DC: CQ Press.

Ornstein, Norman. 2010. "The Motion to Recommit, Hijacked by Politics." *Roll Call*, May 18.

Poole, Keith T., and Howard Rosenthal. 1997. *Congress: A Political-Economic History of Roll Call Voting.* New York: Oxford University Press.

Roberts, Jason M. 2005. "Minority Rights and Majority Power: Conditional Party Government and the Motion to Recommit in the House." *Legislative Studies Quarterly* 30: 219–34.

Rohde, David. 1991. *Parties and Leaders in the Postreform House*. Chicago: University of Chicago Press.

Sinclair, Barbara. 1994. "House Special Rules and the Institutional Design Controversy." *Legislative Studies Quarterly* 19: 477–94.

———. 1997. *Unorthodox Lawmaking: New Legislative Processes in the U.S. Congress*. Washington, DC: CQ Press, 1997.

Spirling, Arthur, and Iain McLean. 2007. "UK OC OK? Interpreting Optimal Classification Scores for the United Kingdom House of Commons." *Political Analysis* 15: 1–12.

Wawro, Gregory, and Eric Schickler. 2006. *Filibuster: Obstruction and Lawmaking in the U.S. Senate*. Princeton, NJ: Princeton University Press.

Webb, Brian. 2012. "Minority Party Strategies in the House of Representatives: Cross-pressuring and the Motion to Recommit." PhD diss., Georgia State University.

Wolfensberger, Donald. 1991. "Motion to Recommit in the House: The Rape of a Minority Right." U.S. Congress, House, Subcommittee on Rules of the House, *Roundtable Discussion on the Motion to Recommit*, 102nd Cong., 2nd Sess. Washington, DC: Government Printing Office.

———. 2003. "The Motion to Recommit in the House: The Creation, Evisceration, and Restoration of a Minority Right." Paper presented at the History of Congress Conference, University of California, San Diego, December 5–6.

5

Evolution of the Reconciliation Process, 1980–2015

James V. Saturno

IN RECENT DECADES, policy choices made by Congress and enacted into law have become increasingly entwined with the budget process. Congress has developed and adapted that process to fit its changing institutional needs. Reconciliation has been a major part of this, but scholars have largely neglected it as a specific object of study, and it remains an often misunderstood part of the budget process. This chapter discusses reconciliation both as a particular set of procedures and as part of an ever-changing political dynamic.

There are descriptions of the reconciliation process in most books about the contemporary Congress (Oleszek et al. 2015; Gold 2004), but many of these discuss reconciliation as a static, technical part of the budget process, following a single predictable path that uses it as a device for majoritarian decision-making in the Senate. While reconciliation procedures can be used to create a legislative opportunity in which a simple majority will be sufficient for Senate passage, emphasizing this feature in isolation misses the way that other features place significant limits on its use (Beth et al. 2009).

Discussion of reconciliation has also been integrated with case studies of recent major legislation enacted as reconciliation bills (Sinclair 2011). These studies, however, typically focus on those specific legislative actions rather than on the broader context of the reconciliation process itself. More recently, there have been efforts to examine the role of reconciliation within a broader policy context, but these generally underestimate the dynamic nature of the reconciliation process itself and how it has been molded to fit the needs of Congress. For example, Chris Den Hartog and Nathan W. Monroe (2011) include reconciliation in their study of the power of the majority party in the

Senate, but the finding that the majority is particularly successful in getting reconciliation measures to final passage does not enhance understanding of how the process works or when it is used. A more successful study by Molly E. Reynolds (2015) attempts to examine when and why certain policy questions have been addressed through the reconciliation process, particularly with respect to its utility as a way for the majority to identify itself with specific policies. All of these are useful for building an understanding of reconciliation, but what is necessary is also an understanding of the different ways in which the process can be deployed.

A limited view of reconciliation has also permeated general perception, especially in the press. For example, in the aftermath of the 2014 election that returned a Republican majority to the Senate, various press outlets began speculating about the possible use of reconciliation. One thing this speculation focused on was the idea that reconciliation was something that would allow the new majority to achieve its policy goals without the need to muster a supermajority of sixty senators to defeat a filibuster. Richard Arenberg (2014) wondered whether a new Republican majority might abuse this process to pass a "laundry list" of legislative initiatives. In January, when the new majority was sworn in, former chairman of the Senate Budget Committee, Judd Gregg (R-NH), described reconciliation as "one of those Beltway terms that causes normal Americans to bang their heads against the wall and ask 'are these Washington types for real,'" but he also stated that it was "a tool of considerable force if used well." He warned, however, that reconciliation was not a "magic bullet." Instead, reconciliation legislation designed to pass on a party-line vote would simply end up vetoed by the president, "a brave but doomed charge of the light brigade" (Gregg 2015). None of this, however, gave a very clear picture of how reconciliation actually works, and readers are left wondering exactly what reconciliation is and is not.

The Reconciliation Process Explained

Reconciliation is an optional, expedited legislative process that consists of several stages, beginning with congressional adoption of the budget resolution. As provided under the Congressional Budget Act of 1974 (P.L. 93-344, as amended), the purpose of reconciliation is to allow Congress the opportunity to make a certain measure (or measures) privileged for consideration and to use an expedited procedure when considering it. These expedited procedures are intended to allow Congress to more easily bring existing spending, revenue, and debt-limit laws into compliance (in a sense, to "reconcile" them) with current fiscal priorities established through a concurrent resolution on the budget. These procedures include compelling committees to draft legislative language to fit specific desired budgetary outcomes, packaging multiple initiatives into omnibus legislation, limiting amending opportunities, and limiting the duration of debate on the Senate floor.

If Congress intends to use the reconciliation process, reconciliation instructions to committees must first be included in the budget resolution. This feature alone places perhaps the most significant limitation on the use of reconciliation. Although a budget resolution can be adopted with a simple majority, because bicameral agreement on the budget resolution is a necessary first step, the House and Senate must collectively agree on the need for reconciliation and its broad contours. If such an agreement can be achieved, reconciliation instructions can then trigger the second stage of the process by requiring specific committees to develop and report legislation that would change laws within their respective jurisdictions related to spending, revenues, or the debt limit.

If a committee is instructed to submit legislation reducing spending (or the deficit) by a specific amount, that amount is considered a minimum, meaning that a committee may report greater net savings. If a committee is instructed to submit legislation increasing revenues by a specific amount, that amount would also be considered a minimum. If a committee is instructed to decrease revenue, however, that amount would be considered a maximum. Although there is no procedural mechanism to ensure that legislation developed by a committee in response to reconciliation instructions will be in compliance with the instructed levels, if a committee does not report legislation or such legislation is not fully in compliance with the instructions, procedures are available that would allow either chamber to move forward with reconciliation. For example, legislative language that falls within the jurisdiction of the noncompliant committee can be added to a reconciliation bill during floor consideration that will bring the bill into compliance. These methods vary by chamber.

In the House, if a committee is not in compliance with its instructions, the Budget Act provides that the Rules Committee should make in order amendments that would achieve the instructed results. In the Senate, it would be in order for any senator to make a motion to commit (or recommit) the reconciliation bill to the noncompliant committee with instructions that it report the measure back to the Senate forthwith with an amendment that would bring the committee into compliance. Such a motion would effectively allow any senator to craft legislative language within the directed committee's jurisdiction that would bring it into compliance.

In the development of legislation in response to reconciliation instructions, the policy choices remain the prerogative of the committee. In some instances, reconciliation instructions have been couched in terms of particular options or assumptions regarding how an instructed committee might be expected to achieve its reconciliation target, but such language has not been considered binding or enforceable.

Once a specified committee develops legislation, the reconciliation instruction may further direct the committee to report the legislation for consideration in its respective chamber or to submit the legislation to the Budget Committee to be included in an omnibus reconciliation measure. If it will be included in an omnibus measure, the Budget Act requires that the Budget Committee report such a measure "without any substantive revision."

Reported legislation is then eligible to be considered under expedited procedures in both the House and the Senate. As with all legislation, any differences in the reconciliation legislation passed by the two chambers must be resolved before the bill can be sent to the president for approval or veto.

Although reconciliation instructions may include target dates for committees to submit their legislative language, there is no requirement that the Budget Committee, in either chamber, must report a reconciliation bill by that date. On occasion, the House or Senate Budget Committee has delayed reporting an omnibus bill to accommodate an instructed committee or the scheduling needs of the leadership. As a consequence, the target date included in reconciliation instructions is not necessarily indicative of a timetable for consideration of reconciliation legislation.

In the House, consideration of reconciliation legislation has historically been governed by special rules reported from the House Rules Committee. These special rules have established the duration of a period of general debate as well as a limited number of amendments (if any) that may be considered before the House votes on final passage.

In the Senate, rules, precedents, and practices do not place general limits on the consideration of legislation, including the content of amendments or the duration of their consideration. For reconciliation, however, a distinguishing feature is that specific limits are placed on both. The Budget Act limits total debate time on the measure, including all amendments, motions, or appeals, to twenty hours, equally divided and controlled by the majority and minority. After debate time has expired, senators may continue to offer amendments and make other motions or appeals, but without further debate. This period is often referred to as a "vote-a-rama." Although no further debate time is available, the Senate has typically agreed by unanimous consent to accelerated voting procedures, allowing a nominal amount of time to identify and explain an amendment before voting. The Budget Act imposes no procedural limit on the duration of a vote-a-rama, so the Senate has sometimes needed to devote significant periods of floor time to the consideration of reconciliation measures (U.S. Congress 2009). Despite this, the limit on debate time has meant that, in practice, it has been unnecessary for the Senate to invoke cloture in order to reach a final vote on a reconciliation bill.

In addition to the limit on debate time, the Budget Act places limits on the subject matter and budgetary impact of the bill and any amendments. This may be enforced through senators raising points of order.[1] Although the presiding officer may rule on whether the point of order is well taken, in practice senators will typically make a motion to waive the application of the rule. In most cases, a motion to waive requires a vote of at least three-fifths of all senators (sixty votes if there are no vacancies) to be successful. If the motion fails, the presiding officer will then rule the provision or amendment out of order.

Perhaps the best-known limit on the content of reconciliation bills is the so-called Byrd Rule (Section 313 of the Budget Act). This rule prohibits including extraneous provisions in the measure or offering them as amendments, meaning it prohibits the inclusion of nonbudgetary provisions in reconciliation legislation or provisions that are otherwise contrary to fulfilling the intent of reconciliation (such as increasing the deficit in years beyond the period covered in a committee's instructions). If a Byrd Rule point of order is sustained against a provision in the bill as reported, the provision is stricken, but further consideration of the bill may continue. If the point of order is sustained against an amendment, the amendment's further consideration would not be in order.

Rules also place other limits on the content of reconciliation bill amendments. For example, all amendments must be germane to the bill, meaning that amendments generally cannot be used to expand a bill's scope beyond the provisions reported from an instructed committee (although a motion to commit or recommit that would bring a committee into compliance with its instructions would not be limited by this rule). Limits on amendments' budgetary impact also exist. Amendments, for example, may not increase the level of spending (or reduce the level of revenues) provided in the bill unless offset. Together, these rules have the effect of protecting the policy changes proposed by an instructed committee in ways that are not generally available under the Senate's regular procedures.

Early Origins

Reconciliation, like many congressional practices, has evolved and changed over its three decades of use. Because of the central role reconciliation has played in the enactment of significant legislation, understanding the process and its evolution is critical to understanding the modern Congress. More importantly, reconciliation provides a window to see how Congress has evolved broadly and how the House and Senate leaderships have applied procedural tools in new or innovative ways to accomplish certain goals.

Reconciliation first became a powerful tool because it could be used to supersede the normal prerogatives of committee chairs over committee agendas. Specifically, it was intended to induce greater committee participation in legislation to implement budgetary goals consistent with the budget resolution. The overall goal of deficit reduction was at odds with the committees' desires. Nevertheless, as demonstrated by its early usage, reconciliation was committee centered. Policy choices and formulation of legislative language, as well as subsequent conference negotiations, were dependent on the participation of committee members. Any authority over policy choices exercised by leadership was indirect.

Over time, however, reconciliation, like congressional policymaking generally, has become increasingly leadership centered, with party leaders responsible for directing or developing major policy initiatives. As a result, wide participation by rank-and-file membership has become more limited, especially for the minority party. This has been especially true since a series of late-1990s budget surpluses, which caused a breakdown of the previous consensus on deficit reduction. Since then, reconciliation's primary use has shifted from achieving a budgetary outcome to enabling a bicameral majority to pass signature legislation. Understanding this evolution and how reconciliation works involves understanding the impact of three contributing factors: committee prerogatives regarding the content of legislation, the ability of the minority to play a meaningful part in the legislative process, and the evolving role of leadership, especially in the Senate. This chapter uses case studies drawn from several reconciliation measures since the 1980s to trace the use of reconciliation in an effort to better understand how Congress evolves to meet new institutional challenges.

The Congressional Budget Act of 1974

The Congressional Budget Act of 1974 was the culmination of an extended period of budgetary conflict between Congress and the president. In particular, the Richard M. Nixon administration had raised the related issues of statutory spending limits and presidential discretion over spending to an unprecedented level (Schick 1980; Fisher 1975). One criticism Nixon leveled at Congress was that it took action on "the various spending programs as if they were unrelated and independent actions." What was needed to remedy this was "that an annual spending ceiling be set first, and that individual program allocations then be tailored to that ceiling" (U.S. President [Nixon] 1974).

Rather than refute the criticism, Congress took it to heart, even as tensions with the Nixon administration increased. Instead of ceding greater control over the budget to the president, however, Congress responded by creating a Joint Study Committee on Budget Control, which ultimately produced a recommendation that Congress create a legislative vehicle that would enable it to set fiscal policy and budgetary targets independently of presidential initiative. This new budget resolution garnered support from members of Congress for a variety of reasons. Some hoped that having such a tool would make it easier for Congress to use the budget to stimulate the economy; others hoped that it would allow them to strengthen overall congressional control over priorities; and still others expected that it would lead to spending restraint and reduced deficits (Fisher 1984, 171).

As originally enacted, the Congressional Budget Act provided for two budget resolutions each year: a first one to be adopted in the spring to set nonbinding targets and a second one in the fall to reaffirm or revise the first and establish binding and enforceable targets. Because budget resolutions are concurrent resolutions, they represent an agreement between the House and the Senate but do not become law. Consequently, although the fiscal policy and budgetary targets agreed to in a budget resolution might presuppose that policy changes would be necessary to achieve the desired budgetary outcomes, a budget resolution could not, by itself, achieve such changes. Instead, they would be implemented through one or more subsequent measures.

The Initial Conception of Reconciliation

To facilitate the ability of Congress to achieve its fiscal goals, the Budget Act also provided for a procedure called reconciliation that would allow the Budget Committees to include language in the second budget resolution instructing specific committees to produce changes to previously passed or enacted legislation in order to achieve the binding targets. In order to facilitate the consideration of such legislation, the Budget Act allowed the Budget Committees to package the proposed changes into an omnibus measure and provided for an expedited procedure to limit Senate floor debate time to twenty hours and require that all amendments be germane.

Reconciliation, then, was set up as a two-step process that required language (instructions) in a budget resolution as a trigger to allow expedited procedures to be used in the Senate. What defines reconciliation legislation as a unique and significant tool for implementing policy is that its relationship to the budget resolution means that it is intended to work within a budgetary context. Although, as detailed below, much has changed with respect to the use and operation of reconciliation since the Budget Act was enacted in 1974, this remains the basic relationship that defines today's structure and process. Without bicameral agreement on a budget resolution to open the door and establish its broad contours, there can be no reconciliation legislation.

As contemplated in the initial setup of the Budget Act, reconciliation was attempted exactly once. Although the second budget resolution for fiscal year 1976 (H. Con. Res. 466, 94th Congress [1975–1976]) made no direct reference to reconciliation, it did call for an economic stimulus by including language providing that "the House Committee on Ways and Means and Senate Committee on Finance shall submit to their respective Houses legislation to reduce revenues by approximately $6,400,000,000." On December 15, 1975, the Senate began consideration of H.R. 5559 (94th Congress), a tax measure that had previously passed the House. As passed by the House, it had not been specifically labeled a reconciliation bill, but in the Senate, Senator Russell Long (D-LA), Senate Finance Committee chairman, asserted that the bill, as reported by his committee with a substitute, was intended to carry out the provision in the budget resolution and should be considered under the terms for reconciliation legislation provided in the Budget Act (Riddick and Frumin 1992, 622–23).

The use of procedures that would limit amendments was not without controversy. After H.R. 5559 was vetoed by President Gerald Ford, later consideration of a different economic stimulus measure, H.R. 9968 (94th Congress), was done without the use of reconciliation procedures. It is important to recognize that this first attempt to use expedited reconciliation procedures aimed neither to supersede the Finance Committee's prerogatives to initiate legislation nor to avoid the need to invoke cloture. Rather, it was the committee's attempt to utilize an expedited procedure to advance its agenda and limit the potential for floor modification of its policy choices.

Over the next several years, Congress did not use reconciliation again in this manner. No committees attempted to use reconciliation procedures to limit floor action. Nor did leadership attempt to use reconciliation to dictate what policy questions should be addressed by committees. Instead, even though budget resolutions adopted between 1976 and 1979 included assumptions of future legislative savings as part of their overall budget targets, these savings were to be achieved through the regular legislative process. The budget resolution might include assumptions about the makeup of these savings, but these assumptions were not binding and did not require specific response.

Perhaps it is not surprising, therefore, that Congress had only limited success with achieving such legislative savings. The Senate Budget Committee did attempt to report reconciliation instructions in the second budget resolution in 1977 (S. Con. Res. 43, 95th Congress [1977–1978]), but these instructions did not survive conference negotiations with the House. The Senate

Budget Committee also included reconciliation instructions in the second budget resolution in 1979 (S. Con. Res. 36, 96th Congress [1979–1980]), but the House report stated that the House Budget Committee had not included reconciliation language, in part because "there may be practical difficulties inherent in the reconciliation process" (H. Rept. 96-435). Once again, reconciliation procedures ultimately were not used to expedite consideration of any proposed spending-reduction legislation.

First Use of Modern Reconciliation Procedures, 1980

When the House Budget Committee reported the first budget resolution in 1980, it acknowledged the lack of previous success in using the Budget Act's new procedures to achieve a balanced budget. The committee called for implementation of an "extraordinary" procedure in the form of reconciliation to achieve deficit reduction. Furthermore, it intended to tie this untried procedure to the first budget resolution, instead of the second, as contemplated in the Budget Act. The report accompanying the budget resolution (H. Con. Res. 307, 96th Congress [1979–1980]), stated, "Due to the necessity of acting quickly and effectively . . . and realizing that there may not be time to act on reconciliation instructions before the end of the Second Session of the 96th Congress, the Committee has included reconciliation instructions in the first budget resolution" (H. Rept. 96-857).

The move to include reconciliation instructions in the first budget resolution was not without controversy. During floor consideration, Representative Morris Udall (1980, 10153), chairman of the House Interior and Insular Affairs Committee, stated his concern that if the inclusion of reconciliation instructions in the first budget resolution was to become routine, the first resolution would effectively set spending ceilings, not just targets, and that "many weeks before relevant hearings could be held on which rational decisions could be based, irrevocable ceilings would be established with which all spending would have to conform."

When a conference report was agreed to on June 12, 1980, eight House and nine Senate committees were instructed to recommend savings. These recommendations were then packaged into an omnibus measure by each Budget Committee and considered on the floor in each chamber. In the Senate, two separate measures were considered: the Reconciliation Act (S. 2885) passed 89–0 on June 30, 1980, and the Revenue Reconciliation Act (S. 2939) passed by voice vote on July 23. In the House, the Omnibus Budget Reconciliation Act (H.R. 7765) was considered and passed 294–91 on September 4. The Senate then amended the House bill with the text of both Senate bills on September 17 and asked for a conference. The conference agreement was passed

334–45 by the House on December 3 and 83–4 by the Senate on the same day, before being signed into law on December 5 (P.L. 96-499).

The Omnibus Budget Reconciliation Act established a template for future action in a number of ways. First, it made reconciliation instructions a part of the first budget resolution rather than the second. This change altered the concept of reconciliation. If the original idea had been that reconciliation could be used to adjust pending legislation to conform to the enforceable levels in a second budget resolution, this change was a recognition that the reality had been that the second budget resolution had instead largely adjusted the priorities in the first budget resolution to accommodate the enactment of any budgetary legislation passed in the interim. Reconciliation might be a powerful expedited process, but it was unclear how it might be used.

The second budget resolution was adopted too late in the congressional session for reconciliation to be used to instruct committees to develop potentially complicated legislation. Attaching reconciliation instructions to the first budget resolution meant that committees would have the time necessary to develop legislation that could make changes in the base of existing mandatory spending programs in order to achieve a specific budgetary outcome. Instead of budgetary outcomes being a secondary effect resulting from policy preferences, under this new arrangement reconciliation could allow a desired budgetary outcome to be a driving force in the development of policy options.

Second, reconciliation instructions are directed at specific committees and involve specific amounts by which the budgetary impact of existing laws should be changed. In the development of legislation in response to reconciliation instructions, however, the policy choices made remain largely the prerogative of the instructed committee.

Third, the participation of instructed committees does not end with reporting legislation to the House or Senate Budget Committee. The Budget Act does not empower the Budget Committees to usurp the jurisdictions of other committees through the reconciliation process. Although both the House and Senate appoint members from the Budget Committees to oversee overall conference proceedings, members from instructed committees are appointed to negotiate substantive matters within their respective jurisdictions. In 1980—the first time this process was used—the House appointed six members from the Budget Committee as conferees for the whole bill and fifty-seven other members as limited-purpose conferees on one or more of ten subconferences organized to consider portions of the bill. In the Senate, five senators from the Budget Committee were appointed as conferees for the whole bill, and thirty-five others were appointed as limited-purpose conferees (Final House Calendars, 96th Congress, 67–70).

Each of these aspects illustrates the proposition that, while reconciliation was a new and powerful tool to direct committees to achieve particular budgetary outcomes, committees retained much of their autonomy. Although the budget resolution required committees to act, neither the Budget Committees nor the leadership was in a position to determine the specific policy changes that would be chosen. Not only would committees themselves initially develop the policy choices that would go into the legislation, but the Budget Committee was explicitly barred from changing it. Furthermore, because reconciliation rules limited the scope of amendments that could be offered during floor consideration and conference negotiations would be led by members from the House and Senate committees of jurisdiction rather than the Budget Committees, the policy choices made by instructed committees would largely be protected from change.

The success of this new, 1980 version of reconciliation resulted from two factors: (1) it required that committees participate in implementing a budgetary outcome decided outside each committee's own initiative, and (2) it provided an incentive for that participation by protecting the committee's choices more than the regular legislative process. At this point, reconciliation was not yet perceived as a procedure designed to create a partisan advantage for the majority, particularly in the Senate, as demonstrated by the large, bipartisan majorities in both chambers that voted in favor of the reconciliation bill.

It should also be noted that Representative Udall's concerns about the effect of attaching reconciliation instructions to the first budget resolution proved to be prescient, as doing so ultimately sounded the death knell for the idea of a two-budget resolution system. If reconciliation instructions could be used to require a committee to achieve a specific budgetary outcome, then the levels agreed to in the first budget resolution were an enforceable ceiling and not simply a target. Furthermore, if the levels in the first budget resolution could be enforced, what was the purpose of the second budget resolution? Over the next several years, Congress was to determine that the second budget resolution was no longer a useful exercise. In 1982, the first budget resolution included a provision stating that if Congress had not completed action on a second budget resolution by October 1, then the first budget resolution would be deemed to be the second resolution. Similar provisions were included in the first budget resolutions in 1983, 1984, and 1985, as well as before the Budget Act was amended to eliminate the need even for this.

Reconciliation and the Reagan Administration, 1981

If 1980 demonstrated that reconciliation had the potential to be a powerful tool, 1981 showed how broadly it might be applied and raised concerns about the need for limits. One change between 1980 and 1981 was an expansion in the number of instructed committees. Ultimately, the conference report on the first budget resolution instructed fifteen House committees and thirteen Senate committees, including the Senate Appropriations Committee, to achieve savings.

In addition to an increase in the number of committees involved, the contents of the instructions were also expanded. For the first time instructions were framed to cover multiple fiscal years to capture the future budgetary impact of any resulting program or policy changes. Savings achieved for the coming fiscal year would need to be sustained or increased in succeeding years in order to achieve the multiyear savings in the instructions. Instructions were applied not only to direct spending but also to authorizations of discretionary appropriations as well, so that committees were directed to achieve savings by reducing authorizations within their jurisdiction in order to require a reduction in appropriations. As adopted in the conference report on the budget resolution, about two-thirds of the directed savings were to be achieved through such cuts in authorizations, although the instructions allowed committees to substitute savings in direct spending programs for cuts in authorizations. The Senate Appropriations Committee was also instructed to achieve savings and subsequently achieved this through enactment of rescissions (that is, cancellation of previously enacted appropriations) in a supplemental appropriations bill (P.L. 97-12).

The extent of the instructions and the intent to use reconciliation to implement a significant part of the Ronald Reagan administration's agenda were a major part of the debate on the budget resolution. During House consideration of the budget resolution conference report, Representative Del Latta (R-OH), ranking Republican on the Budget Committee, responded to concerns that this expanded version of reconciliation would usurp the traditional authority of committees. He explained that despite the expanded nature of the instructions, committees would retain the latitude to make decisions about which programs to target and that so long as the amount of savings in direct spending and changes in authorizations met the level in reconciliation instructions, the Budget Committee would not seek to dictate the precise program cuts (Latta 1981, 10311).

Beginning with consideration of the budget resolution and continuing through consideration of reconciliation, amendments offered by Representative Latta allowed the Republican minority in the House, in coalition with conservative Democrats, to exploit the majoritarian nature of House rules generally to take control of the budget process. One aspect of this was that, because of its omnibus nature, the reported reconciliation bill was so broad and encompassed so many policy issues that it was not possible for the majority Democrats to use germaneness to limit the breadth of policies addressed in the substitute offered by the conservative coalition. This also meant that the conservative coalition could minimize the number of votes necessary to bring the House measure more closely into alignment with the policy choices made in the Senate.

Conference procedures on the 1981 reconciliation bill followed the pattern set the previous year. Conferees from the House and Senate Budget Committees would again shepherd the legislation through the process, but the substantive policy negotiations would be handled by subconferences involving members from the committees of jurisdiction. Ultimately, 192 members, including ten representatives from the House Budget Committee and sixty-nine senators, including seven from the Senate Budget Committee, participated in the conference (Final House Calendars, 97th Congress, 2-2-4). President Reagan signed the bill into law on August 13 (P.L. 97-35).

The success of reconciliation in 1981 involved a number of procedural decisions that were ultimately abandoned in later years. First, instructions directed at reducing authorizations of discretionary appropriations or requiring rescission of previously enacted discretionary appropriations did not become a permanent feature of reconciliation. Second, senators raised concerns about the possible use of reconciliation to require them to make decisions about dozens of issues, many with little or no budgetary impact, with only limited opportunities to debate or amend. In 1981, these concerns led the Senate majority leader to offer an amendment at the beginning of Senate consideration to strike a long list of extraneous provisions that had been included by the instructed committees (Senate Amendment 171, 97th Congress, *Congressional Record*, June 22, 1981, 13209–12), which ultimately led to the Senate's adopting a rule in 1985 prohibiting their inclusion.

A desire to use reconciliation so that the Senate would need only a simple majority to pass legislation, however, does not appear to have been a significant aspect of reconciliation in 1981. Reconciliation made it possible for the Reagan administration and congressional allies to quickly achieve a significant part of a legislative agenda that included wide-ranging spending reductions and tax cuts by using its expedited procedures to pass omnibus legislation. The success with reconciliation in 1981 made it possible for Congress to revamp such diverse programs as Food Stamps and the Strategic Petroleum Reserve, to merge various education, health, and social service programs into new block grant programs, and to achieve budgetary savings from dairy price supports, unemployment insurance, and student assistance programs, all in one bill, all in less than six months.

The Reconciliation Process, 1982–1989

Over the next several years, congressional consensus on the continuing need for deficit reduction produced a general acceptance of reconciliation as a regular part of the annual budget cycle. This consensus was bolstered by budgetary control mechanisms enacted beginning with the Balanced Budget and Emergency Deficit Control Act of 1985 (P.L. 99-177), also referred to as Gramm-Rudman-Hollings. By prescribing specific deficit targets to be enforced by presidential sequester orders if Congress did not meet these targets, this act (and its successors) kept deficit reduction a key part of fiscal policy debates. As a consequence, reconciliation legislation was considered in every year for the remainder of the decade except 1984 and 1988. In all but one case (the Tax Equity and Fiscal Responsibility Act of 1982), reconciliation measures were passed in the Senate by a majority greater than the three-fifths threshold that would have been necessary to invoke cloture if they had been considered under the regular rules for consideration. This, however, is not to suggest that there were no further procedural innovations or controversies and no significant policy disputes.

One of the reasons why reconciliation had been successful for the Reagan administration in 1981 had been the ability to take advantage of the omnibus nature of reconciliation to obviate concerns about the germaneness of floor amendments. As a consequence, in 1982 the House Democratic leadership ultimately chose to bring separate measures from four different committees to the floor rather than have them submit their recommendations to the Budget Committee. This was done despite inclusion in the budget resolution (S. Con. Res. 92, 97th Congress [1981–1982]) of reconciliation instructions for nine House committees to submit their recommendations to the House Budget Committee. The four separate bills were subsequently joined together into a single measure by unanimous consent in order to facilitate negotiations with the Senate over what became the Omnibus Reconciliation Act of 1982 (P.L. 97-253).

In addition, reconciliation in 1982 also saw the consideration of a separate measure providing for tax increases as a part of the reconciliation process, the Tax Equity and Fiscal Responsibility Act of 1982 (P.L. 97-248). By considering each committee's recommendations separately, this approach allowed germaneness to keep the potential scope of amendments limited. Although this answered a specific concern of the majority leadership about maintaining control over the legislative agenda, it raised the counterconcern that in providing separate consideration for each committee's recommendations separately, the focus would be on the policy issues rather than budgetary impact, making the job of deficit reduction more difficult. As a consequence,

Congress returned to the use of omnibus bills for reconciliation the following year, although separate reconciliation bills for spending and revenues were used again in 1997 and 2005.

Another significant action in the 1980s involving the consideration of reconciliation legislation was the adoption of a rule by the Senate prohibiting the inclusion of extraneous issues in reconciliation bills. This had been a significant concern starting in 1981 when Majority Leader Howard Baker (R-TN) offered an amendment to strike extraneous provisions. Baker stated that while some nonbudgetary matters might be necessary, the inclusion of extraneous provisions generally was harmful to the character of the Senate, because allowing such provisions to be considered as part of reconciliation meant that time and germaneness limits would impede the exercise of minority rights. It would also create "an unacceptable degree of tension between the Budget Act and the remainder of Senate procedures and practice" (Baker 1981, 13209). Democratic senator from West Virginia Robert Byrd (1981, 13210), the minority leader, echoed this concern and asked, "What controversial measure will not be viewed as a future candidate for inclusion in a reconciliation bill?"

This concern over the potential for committees to try to use reconciliation as a pathway to avoid regular Senate procedure continued over the next several years, ultimately prompting the Senate to adopt a rule to prohibit extraneous matters in reconciliation bills. Modified several times since its initial approval in 1985, what is now known as the Byrd Rule was considered as an amendment during Senate consideration of the Consolidated Omnibus Budget Reconciliation Act of 1985 (U.S. Congress 1993, 198–246). The amendment was a bipartisan effort by Senate leadership to retain the budgetary focus of reconciliation. The germaneness requirement could be used to prevent senators from expanding the scope of the measure through amendments offered during floor consideration. Nothing in the Budget Act, however, limited the content of legislation submitted by committees in response to their reconciliation instructions. Republican majority leader from Kansas Robert Dole (1985, 28973) stated that reconciliation was "never intended as the answer for every amendment." Senator Byrd (1985, 28968) was more explicit in stating, "Senate committees are creatures of the Senate, and, as such, should not be in the position of dictating to the Senate as is being done here. By including material not in their jurisdiction or matter which they choose not to report as separate legislation to avail themselves of the non-deliberative reconciliation process, Senate committees violate the compact which created both them and the reconciliation process. . . . The Senate must protect itself from this attack by its own committees." Although reconciliation would continue to evolve after this point, the decision to adopt the Byrd Rule was critical for keeping reconciliation at least nominally a budgetary tool, rather than allowing it to become simply a device to avoid the need for cloture.

In most other respects, the reconciliation process in the 1980s generally followed the path that had been outlined in 1980 and 1981, providing various procedural incentives to promote the participation of committees. Using the two-stage process of the budget resolution to establish budgetary parameters and trigger reconciliation meant that committees were empowered to make most of the policy decisions as long as they stayed within those parameters. Legislation developed by committees was then shepherded through a pro-tected lawmaking process by the Budget Committees, with a reduced likeli-hood of floor amendments and a virtually guaranteed response from the other chamber. It was also important that committees not only exercised authority at the beginning of the process to determine the policies submitted for initial inclusion in reconciliation but also had the last word on negotiating the final form of the policies that got enacted through participation in large conference committees, comprised primarily of limited-purpose conferees organized into numerous subconferences.

Budget Summitry and Reconciliation, 1990

Statutory deficit targets had ensured that deficit reduction was the driving force behind reconciliation since the Balanced Budget and Emergency Deficit Control Act of 1985 had become law. Each year the budget resolution focused on how the target could be achieved so that a presidential sequester order requiring across-the-board spending cuts could be avoided. In both recon-ciliation and other legislation, Congress took actions to reduce the deficit that were often criticized as a "smoke and mirrors" approach—that is, the projected budgetary impact of program adjustments consistently rested on economic or technical assumptions that didn't come to pass or administrative actions that had only illusory impact, such as pushing the timing of spending actions into future years. This approach meant that by 1990 there was a gap between the projected deficit for the following fiscal year and the statutory deficit target that was too great for Congress to address through actions that would simply push things into future years.

The deficit target for fiscal year 1991 was $64 billion, but the deficit pro-jected by the Office of Management and Budget was $147.3 billion, requir-ing outlay cuts for defense programs of $41.7 billion (34.7 percent) and for nondefense programs of $41.7 billion (31.6 percent). Faced with a looming sequester of this magnitude, in the fall of 1990, President George H. W. Bush and congressional leaders agreed to negotiations on spending reductions and tax increases sufficient to avoid this dire result. The result was a five-year, $500 billion deficit-reduction plan implemented principally through the Omnibus Budget Reconciliation Act of 1990 (P.L. 101-508). Another result was that direct negotiation between Congress and the president was seen as a useful path for developing the policies to be included in successful efforts to use reconciliation when Congress and the presidency were held by different parties; bipartisan Republican majorities and President Bill Clinton would use this tactic again in 1996 and 1997.

The process of getting to that point was indicative of a subtle shift that meant a greater centralization of decision-making about reconciliation in congressional leadership. Even in 1981, when the contours of policies included in reconciliation largely followed the Reagan administration's agenda, it had been left to committees to develop the actual content. In 1990, President Bush's previous pronouncements about not increasing taxes meant that any deficit-reduction package would need to be negotiated directly between Congress and the administration. The conference on the budget resolution (H. Con. Res. 310, 101st Congress [1989–1990]) had been delayed so that it could incorporate the result of the prolonged negotiations and allow them to come to the floor of the House and Senate for approval and trigger implementation through reconciliation. This effectively bypassed the regular process so that all that would be left to the committees would be to write the legislative language and fill in the details of the agreement. When the House rejected the conference because of dissenting votes from both conservative Republicans, led by Minority Whip Newt Gingrich (R-GA), and liberal Democrats, led by Representative David Obey (D-WI), further negotiations were required.

A revised conference report was able to gain the support of most of the Democratic members who had opposed the initial version of the summit agreement and was subsequently approved in the House and Senate, triggering the reconciliation process. As with previous reconciliation bills, a large group of House and Senate conferees was appointed. Because there was little room to rewrite the agreement between Congress and the president, however, conference action was completed quickly. Although it had taken months to negotiate a deficit-reduction package, congressional action was completed in a matter of weeks due to the expedited procedures available through the reconciliation process.

Single Party Reconciliation, 1993 and 1995

In the 1990s it became apparent that one of the chief advantages of reconciliation was the ability for a simple majority to pass the bill in the Senate. The

1990 reconciliation experience had demonstrated that party lines and partisan preferences were hardening. No longer was a general consensus on the need for deficit reduction guaranteed to be strong enough to overcome this partisanship.

In 1993, the realities of partisanship became clearly manifest when Congress was asked to use reconciliation to enact deficit-reduction legislation as part of President Clinton's economic program. The administration asked Congress to accomplish this through a combination of entitlement spending reductions and tax increases. As the budget resolution moved through the legislative process, it became apparent that the Republican minority, particularly in the House, was not willing to negotiate over a deficit-reduction package that included tax increases. As a consequence, the budget resolution (H. Con. Res. 64, 103rd Congress [1993–1994]) was passed by the House with no Republican votes, signaling that the minority's support for deficit reduction did not include a willingness to increase taxes. A similar sentiment played out during Senate consideration where the resolution was also adopted with no Republican votes.

As finally adopted, the budget resolution included reconciliation instructions to thirteen House and twelve Senate committees. As committees developed responses to their instructions, a number of conservative Democrats in both the House and Senate began to back away from their support for the tax increases in the deficit-reduction package. In particular, opposition to energy taxes in the recommendations of the House Ways and Means Committee cost support from some members from energy-producing states. The reconciliation bill (H.R. 2264) survived initial consideration in the House, still without any Republican support. In the Senate, initial passage required the vote of Vice President Al Gore to break a tie, 50–49 (Senate roll call vote 190, *Congressional Record*, June 24, 1993, 14172).

The precarious situation was not improved during conference negotiations so that the vice president's tie-breaking vote was again necessary to secure final passage, 51–50 (Senate roll call vote 247, *Congressional Record*, August 6, 1993, 19871). In both chambers it was necessary for the majority Democrats to pass the legislation without a single Republican vote and largely without Republican participation in the process.

After the election of 1994, with new Republican majorities elected in both the House and Senate, the circumstances were reversed. Under Newt Gingrich as the new Speaker of the House, Republicans made changes in party conference rules to centralize decision-making authority in the House, empowering the Speaker with a greater say in determining committee membership (and chairmanships) as well as giving him an expanded role in managing the legislative agenda. These changes meant that while committees were not under the direct control of the leadership, it would be less likely for their work to be at cross-purposes. For the new majority to carry out its agenda and deliver on a campaign pledge to make reductions in spending sufficient to produce a balanced budget within seven years, bringing the legislation to the House floor using the reconciliation process would be crucial. Reconciliation could facilitate its ability to move complex omnibus legislation through the legislative process, and to do so quickly. In the Senate, the new majority recognized that deficit reduction built around spending cuts would not easily gain bipartisan support but that using reconciliation would enable Republicans to avoid the need for Democratic votes to invoke cloture.

A significant aspect of House consideration of the reconciliation was that the leadership stepped in to supplant policy choices made by committees. A special rule reported by the House Rules Committee (H. Res. 245, 104th Congress [1995–1996]) to provide for consideration of the reconciliation bill (H.R. 2491) provided for an amendment in the nature of a substitute to be considered as adopted in the House in lieu of the text of the reconciliation bill as reported. This amendment brought the bill more closely into alignment with leadership preferences, particularly with regard to Medicare and farm policy. The Seven-Year Balanced Budget Reconciliation Act of 1995, as amended, was passed by the House with the vote divided largely along party lines. The Senate version of the reconciliation bill was similarly passed on a party-line vote.

Although the conference largely followed the previous pattern of having a large number of conferees negotiate the final version in smaller subconferences, the number of conferees was reduced compared to some earlier reconciliation conferences. In addition, among the House delegation of seventy-one were several party leaders who also served on the Budget Committee: Majority Leader Dick Armey (R-TX), Whip Tom DeLay (R-TX), and party conference chair John Boehner (R-OH). The Senate appointed a delegation of forty-three. Final action on the conference report in both the House and Senate remained divided along party lines before the bill was subsequently vetoed by President Clinton.

These two cases together demonstrate the changing political context in which reconciliation was considered in the 1990s. While the bipartisan consensus in favor of deficit reduction remained, the differing approaches of the two parties now made it difficult to bring them together. As a consequence, the ability to employ reconciliation as a tool for majoritarian decision-making in the Senate took on newfound importance. If the minority might choose not to participate in negotiations where they perceived little likelihood of an outcome that would improve their electoral prospects, as in 1993, or if the majority might choose not to accommodate policy preferences of members from the minority whose votes would not affect the outcome, as in 1995, the utility of reconciliation as a policymaking tool could be changing as well. In addition, the increasing importance of involvement of congressional leadership (1995) or direct negotiation with the president (1990, 1993) also meant that the committees could not be considered the primary source for policy choices embodied in the bill.

Reconciliation and Partisan Politics, 1999 and Beyond

By the late 1990s the budget and economic outlook had improved sufficiently that the federal budget had moved from deficit to surplus in fiscal year 1998 for the first time in three decades. In fact, the budget would be in surplus for four consecutive years. Without a need to use reconciliation for deficit reduction, the Republican majority employed the process four times in five years to promote tax cuts with little, if any, support from the minority in either chamber.

In both the first and second sessions of the 106th Congress (1999–2000), bicameral Republican majorities passed tax-cut measures, only to have them vetoed by President Clinton. Reconciliation instructions to reduce revenues had previously been included in budget resolutions, and in 1996 the Senate established by precedent that such instructions were allowable in a budget resolution as a general principle (*Congressional Record*, May 21, 1996, 11937–39; sustained on appeal, 53–47, Senate roll call vote 152, *Congressional Record*, May 23, 1996, 12355). Tax cuts, however, generally needed to be limited to the time frame provided in the budget resolution. Because of the Byrd Rule, tax cuts that reduced a surplus or caused a deficit outside that time frame would be considered extraneous.

This ruling would prove to be critical in 2001, after the election of President George W. Bush, when the 107th Congress (2001–2002) again included reconciliation instructions to reduce revenues in the budget resolution. In addition, to facilitate the enactment of longer-term changes in the tax code, the period covered by the budget resolution was extended to ten years. This extended period would allow tax cuts in reconciliation to be phased in and sunset over the next decade. In both 2001 and 2003, Republican majorities used this idea to structure tax cuts to fit within the limits imposed by the Byrd Rule and enact reconciliation bills without Democratic support. In failure and success, these reconciliation bills effectively moved the concept of reconciliation away from omnibus legislation intended to reduce the deficit or enact a major economic initiative, as under Presidents Reagan and Clinton, to instead promote a specific policy.

A change in both the House and Senate majority in the 2006 election, followed by the 2008 election of President Barack Obama, set the stage for a further step in the evolution of reconciliation. One of the first major policy initiatives from the Obama administration was reform of health care. The Byrd Rule was seen as a major obstacle to using reconciliation as a vehicle for reform. A significant part of the proposed reform would depend on provisions that would likely be considered nonbudgetary and therefore extraneous to the purpose of reconciliation. Leaving these things out of the legislation would leave it weakened and incomplete, but including them would require three-fifths of senators to vote to keep them in the bill or the use of regular Senate procedural rules to consider it, likely necessitating a three-fifths vote to invoke cloture.

Despite a nominal majority of sixty in the Senate, the Democratic leadership knew that keeping the entire party conference together through the entire process (or gaining any Republican votes) would be difficult, so it took a two-pronged approach. The budget resolution would include reconciliation instructions to those committees with significant health-care jurisdiction, but this approach would be a backup strategy to utilize reconciliation only if the regular process broke down. In addition, these instructions were structured to require only a *de minimus* positive budget impact to give the instructed committees maximum flexibility in developing legislation.

Although Senate Majority Leader Harry Reid (D-NV) had managed to steer a health-care reform measure through initial consideration in the Senate, the significant difficulty of negotiating the differences between the House and Senate approaches remained. On January 19, 2010, when Senator Scott Brown (R-MA) won a special election to succeed the late Senator Ted Kennedy (D-MA), the Democratic majority was reduced to fifty-nine seats, and the strategy of using the regular rules of the Senate came to an end. Rather than simply abandon the progress made thus far, the House and Senate leadership instead chose to take advantage of the majoritarian nature of House rules to have the House pass the Senate's bill, clearing it for the president without the need for any further Senate votes. Because a significant portion of House Democrats wanted the opportunity to make changes to the Senate-passed bill, however, reconciliation would be used as a way to initiate legislation to make further changes to reform health care, including changes to the bill that had just been enacted. This decision allowed reconciliation to be used to take advantage of its majoritarian decision-making mechanism, despite the policy limitations that went along with it. Ultimately, the two measures together fulfilled the Obama administration's health-care reform initiative.

Understanding the Limits of Reconciliation

Overall, the development and use of reconciliation in the 1980s does not provide much evidence of its being viewed as a tool to promote a partisan agenda or facilitate majoritarian decision-making in the Senate. The reason why could be as simple as the divided control of Congress for much of the decade. Democratic majorities in the House were paired with Republican majorities in the Senate between 1981 and 1987. Given this situation, it was an institutional arrangement that both reconciliation bills and the budget resolutions necessary to trigger them would, of necessity, be largely bipartisan decisions. The idea of reconciliation in this era as a bipartisan phenomenon is supported by the voting record. Of the ten reconciliation bills considered in the Senate between 1980 and 1989, only one of them was passed with fewer than sixty votes.[2]

Looking deeper, however, to examine the collective legislative histories of all reconciliation bills in this era yields a richer understanding of why reconciliation was so consistently supported by bipartisan supermajorities. Reconciliation was viewed during this era primarily in terms of its budgetary context rather than specific policy outcomes. There was consistent bipartisan support for the idea of deficit reduction, and the ability to use expedited consideration of omnibus legislation to achieve this meant that reconciliation was an important instrument for carrying this out. Using reconciliation instructions in the budget resolution to assign responsibility to specific committees for achieving these savings was ultimately the chief aim of reconciliation in the 1980s. Bipartisan majorities ensured that the collective goal of deficit reduction would prevail over the possible incentives of individual committees not to act so that the collective action failures experienced in the 1970s could be overcome.

The changing political circumstances in the 1990s meant that the previous congressional consensus that saw reconciliation primarily as a tool for deficit reduction began to fall apart. A desire to produce a particular budgetary outcome was not the only factor driving the process. Whereas committees had previously had wide latitude to find savings through policy changes within their jurisdictions without significant policy preferences imposed by the leadership, by the 1990s there was a reversal of this relationship. Budgetary impact was not forgotten or ignored as a factor, but the policies embodied in reconciliation legislation became increasingly an exercise in defining partisan policy preferences (Reynolds 2015). Reconciliation could still be used as a vehicle to enact broad fiscal and budgetary legislation, especially when negotiated directly between Congress and the president (1990, 1996, 1997, 2005), but a change that occurred in the 1990s was that leadership came to view reconciliation increasingly as an opportunity for a bicameral congressional majority to express its policy preferences without the need for a supermajority vote in the Senate. In 1993, this meant reconciliation could be used to implement the agenda of a new Democratic president supported by a bicameral Democratic majority. In 1995, 1999, and 2000, it meant that reconciliation could be used to define the policy preferences of a bicameral Republican majority in opposition to the views of a Democratic president, even though all three attempts were ultimately vetoed. By 2001, then, it seemed that the budgetary impact of reconciliation had become not merely of secondary importance but often beside the point.

The majoritarian aspects of the reconciliation process were integral to enacting the revenue-reduction policies favored by both a new Republican president and bicameral Republican majorities in 2001 and 2003. Bicameral Democratic majorities in 2007 and 2009 and a bicameral Republican majority in 2015 took another step away from the 1980s implementation of reconciliation by not framing reconciliation instructions primarily in terms of budgetary impact. In these cases, reconciliation instructions required committees to submit legislation reducing the deficit by a *de minimus* amount ($750 million in 2007 and $1 billion in 2009 and 2015) over the period covered by the budget resolution. These *de minimus* instructions effectively meant that while the provisions in reconciliation legislation still needed to have a positive net budgetary effect, this was clearly secondary to utilizing the majoritarian features of the process to enact policy preferences.

Another way in which the relationships and priorities established in the 1980s have been reversed is that whereas in the 1980s reconciliation was seen as a way to implement the fiscal policies in the budget resolution, in the 2010s one of the primary uses of the budget resolution has been to trigger the reconciliation process. The idea of this reversal is supported not just by the decline in the frequency with which budget resolutions have been adopted but by the virtual disappearance of budget resolutions without reconciliation instructions.

If one accepts the idea that Congress should make an annual decision about the size of the budget, the failure of Congress to adopt a budget resolution in 1998, 2002, 2004, 2006, 2010, 2011, 2012, 2013, and 2014 might be a cause for concern. This, however, misses the broader context in which the budget resolution exists. The failure to adopt a budget resolution does not necessarily mean that no decision has been made about the size of the budget. Prior decisions about the level of discretionary spending in the form of spending caps in statutory budget control measures were undoubtedly a major part of the reason why there was less need to adopt a budget resolution in certain years.

In 2002, 2004, 2006, and 2010, there were no such statutory caps in effect, so the answer is likely more complicated and nuanced. Interestingly, with the exception of 2011 and 2013, each of the years without a budget resolution is the second year of a congress. The likely importance of this factor is bolstered by the fact that the group includes the second year of each congress other than the 106th (1999–2000) and 110th (2007–2008) Congresses.

Partisan differences between the chambers appear to be an important contributing factor. No budget resolution was adopted in the five years after 2000 in which the House and Senate were controlled by different parties (2002, 2011, 2012, 2013, and 2014). The pattern, however, is consistent enough over the entire period that partisan differences between the chambers do not appear likely to be the only cause.

If the answer is indeed tied to the second year of a congress, the next question is why. One possible answer is that congressional leadership, especially in the Senate, seems to act as if consideration of a budget resolution is not always a very good use of the limited amount of time available, particularly when the decision about the level of discretionary spending has already been made through some other means. In general, it appears that the pattern shown in table 5.1 supports the idea that there is greater interest in making an effort to adopt a budget resolution in the first year of a congress (or administration), when there is likely a greater desire to make fiscal or policy decisions involving changes in direct spending or revenues and to use the budget resolution to trigger access to reconciliation in order to facilitate the enactment of policies to implement them. In the second year of a congress, major changes are less likely to be part of the legislative agenda. Reconciliation legislation has been passed in the second session of a congress only once in recent years (2000). Conversely, there has been only one year (2008) in which a budget resolution was adopted when no reconciliation bill was passed.

This pattern illustrates that while reconciliation may have evolved into a tool through which policy goals can be achieved in the Senate with a simple majority vote, there are significant limitations. The first is the need to adopt a budget resolution with reconciliation instructions that will allow committees to develop legislative language to implement those policies. Although the process for adopting a budget resolution is characteristically majoritarian, the need to appropriately tailor the language of the budget resolution and reach bicameral agreement limits its availability. The Senate, therefore, cannot unilaterally choose to use reconciliation. It must first come to an agreement with the House, so it is no surprise that there have been no reconciliation bills considered in recent years in which the House and Senate have been under different partisan control.

Second, since 2001 the Senate has operated on advice from the Office of the Parliamentarian interpreting the language in Section 310 of the Budget Act as permitting only one reconciliation bill for any of the three purposes enumer-

TABLE 5.1
Reconciliation Legislation, 106th–113th Congresses

Congress	Year	Reconciliation Act
106	1999	Taxpayer Refund and Relief Act of 1999 (H.R. 248, vetoed)
	2000	Marriage Tax Relief Reconciliation Act of 2000 (H.R. 4810, vetoed)
107	2001	Economic Growth and Tax Relief Reconciliation Act of 2001 (P.L. 107-16)
	2002	—
108	2003	Jobs and Growth Tax Relief Reconciliation Act of 2003 (P.L. 108-27)
	2004	—
109	2005	Deficit Reduction Act of 2005 (P.L. 109-171); Tax Increase Prevention and Reconciliation Act of 2005 (P.L. 109-222)
	2006	—
110	2007	College Cost Reduction and Access Act of 2007 (P.L. 110-84)
	2008	—
111	2009	Health Care and Education Reconciliation Act of 2010 (P.L. 111-152)
	2010	—
112	2011	—
	2012	—
113	2013	—
	2014	—

Source: Final Calendars of the House of Representatives for each respective congress.
Note: Shading indicates fiscal years for which no budget resolution was agreed to.

ated in the act (that is, spending, revenues, and debt limit).[3] This approach allows omnibus legislation but prevents the use of reconciliation procedures to allow multiple bills to be considered under expedited, majoritarian procedures so that it is not possible to use reconciliation as a means for establishing more general majoritarian decision-making in the Senate.

Third, the rules applied by the Senate to limit the contents and budgetary impact of reconciliation legislation (primarily Sections 310 and 313 of the Budget Act) limit the ability to apply the advantages of limited debate time and passage by simple majority to general, nonbudgetary policies, even in the context of reconciliation legislation.

Taken together, these factors demonstrate that while reconciliation can provide a Senate majority with the ability to overcome some procedural obstacles in some circumstances, these circumstances are extremely limited. Most successful policy legislation continues to depend on the Senate's operating under its regular rules.

When there is a bicameral majority, however, reconciliation can be a powerful tool to promote policies that highlight that majority's preferences. In this sense, the value of the current approach to reconciliation is that it serves not simply as a procedural device to avoid the need for cloture but also as a way to promote the party. Since the 1990s this has proven to be true in most instances in which reconciliation has been used, regardless of whether the majority is the same party as the president.

A wide range of interests can drive institutional change within Congress, and more than one interest can be significant in bringing about any change. Furthermore, different interests can be more or less important at different times (Schickler 2001). In 1980, reconciliation was used to provide the necessary incentives to induce committees to produce omnibus legislation to achieve a desired budgetary outcome. Congressional experience with reconciliation since that initial use, however, shows it to be a more complex and multifaceted process that can be employed for a variety of purposes. Furthermore, none of the innovations described in this chapter make earlier usage obsolete. Using reconciliation to highlight congressional policy preferences even in the face of a presidential veto does not prevent it from being used as a tool for deficit reduction; focusing reconciliation on a single policy area in one year does not prevent it from being used as a vehicle for omnibus legislation in another. In short, reconciliation is not simply one thing; it has evolved and developed and been molded by Congress to fit that body's procedural needs.

Notes

* This chapter reflects the views of the author and does not necessarily reflect the view of the Congressional Research Service or the Library of Congress.

1. Raising a point of order is an action taken by a senator on the floor to suggest that legislation (or an amendment) violates a specific rule at the time it is being considered. If a point of order is sustained by the presiding officer of the Senate, it is generally not in order for the Senate to continue consideration of the matter in question. Points of order, however, are not self-enforcing limits. That is, the presiding officer generally does not make a ruling unless the question has been raised by a senator from the floor.

2. There were two reconciliation bills voted on in the Senate in 1980 that were later combined with a single House bill. The Tax Equity and Fiscal Responsibility Act of 1982 passed in the Senate 50–47.

3. See, for example, discussion of the number of reconciliation bills in relation to the number of tax bills that might be considered in the 107th Congress that appears in "Big Breaks for Married Couples Offered in Latest House Tax Bill."

References

Arenberg, Richard A. 2014. "Would a New Senate Majority Abuse the Budget Reconciliation Process?" *Constitution Daily*, November 3.

Baker, Howard. 1981. "Omnibus Reconciliation Act of 1981." *Congressional Record*, Senate, vol. 127, part 10, June 22.

Beth, Richard S., Valerie Heitshusen, Bill Heniff Jr., and Elizabeth Rybicki. 2009. "Leadership Tools for Managing the U.S. Senate." Paper presented at the Annual Meeting of the American Political Science Association, Toronto, Ontario, Canada, September 3–6.

"Big Breaks for Married Couples Offered in Latest House Tax Bill." *CQ Weekly Report*, March 24, 2001, 653–54.

Byrd, Robert. 1981. "Omnibus Reconciliation Act of 1981." *Congressional Record*, Senate, vol. 127, part 10, June 22.

———. 1985. "The Consolidated Omnibus Budget Reconciliation Act of 1985." *Congressional Record*, Senate, vol. 131, part 21, October 24.

Den Hartog, Chris, and Nathan W. Monroe. 2011. *Agenda Setting in the U.S. Senate: Costly Consideration and Majority Party Advantage.* New York: Cambridge University Press.

Dole, Robert. 1985. "The Consolidated Omnibus Budget Reconciliation Act of 1985." *Congressional Record*, Senate, vol. 131, part 21, October 24.

Fisher, Louis. 1975. *Presidential Spending Power.* Princeton, NJ: Princeton University Press.

———. 1984. "The Budget Act of 1974: A Further Loss of Spending Control." In *Congressional Budgeting: Politics, Process, and Power*, edited by W. Thomas Wander, F. Ted Hebert, and Gary W. Copeland. Baltimore: Johns Hopkins University Press.

Gold, Martin. 2004. *Senate Procedure and Practice.* 2nd ed. Lanham, MD: Rowman & Littlefield.

Gregg, Judd. 2015. "There Are No Magic Republican Bullets." *Wall Street Journal*, January 5.

Latta, Delbert. 1981. "Conference Report on House Concurrent Resolution 115, First Concurrent Resolution on the Budget—Fiscal Year 1982." *Congressional Record*, House, vol. 127, part 8, May 20.

Oleszek, Walter J., Mark J. Oleszek, Elizabeth Rybicki, and Bill Heniff Jr. 2015. *Congressional Procedures and the Policy Process*, 10th ed. Washington, DC: CQ Press.

Reynolds, Molly E. 2015. *Exceptions to the Rule: Majoritarian Procedures and Majority Party Power in the U.S. Senate.* PhD diss., University of Michigan.

Riddick, Floyd, and Alan S. Frumin. 1992. *Riddick's Senate Procedure: Precedents and Practices.* 102nd Cong., 2nd sess., S.Doc. 101–28. Washington, DC: Government Printing Office.

Schick, Allen. 1980. *Congress and Money.* Washington, DC: Urban Institute.

Schickler, Eric. 2001. *Disjointed Pluralism: Institutional Innovation and the Development of the U.S. Congress.* Princeton, NJ: Princeton University Press.

Sinclair, Barbara. 2011. *Unorthodox Lawmaking: New Legislative Processes in the U.S. Congress*, 4th ed. Washington, DC: CQ Press.

U.S. Congress, Senate Committee on the Budget. 1993. *Budget Process Law Annotated—1993 Edition*, by William G. Dauster, 103rd Cong., 1st sess., S. Prt. 103–49, October. Washington, DC: Government Printing Office.

———. 2009. *Senate Procedures for Consideration of the Budget Resolution/Reconciliation*. Hearing of February 12, 111th Cong. 1st sess., S. Hrg. 111-106. Washington, DC: Government Printing Office.

U.S. President (Richard M. Nixon). 1974. "Special Message to the Congress on Federal Government Spending." In *Public Papers of the President of the United States 1972*, no. 238, 741–44. Washington, DC: Government Printing Office.

Udall, Morris. 1980. "First Concurrent Resolution on the Budget—Fiscal Year 1981." *Congressional Record*, House, vol. 127, part 7, May 7.

6

Post-Committee Adjustment in the Contemporary House

The Use of Rules Committee Prints

Mark J. Oleszek

"TALK TO LEADERSHIP, it's their strategy," Chairman Bill Shuster (R-PA) suggested to the reporter asking about changes made to a surface transportation bill (H.R. 3763, 114th Congress [2015–2016]), known as the "Highway Bill," after it left his committee but before it was brought to the House floor for debate (Mejdrich 2015a). The Transportation and Infrastructure Committee had completed its work on a six-year plan for the construction and maintenance of highway, rail, and mass-transit projects, but before being called up for chamber consideration the bill was adjusted in ways the chairman did not seem especially thrilled with. The modified version reduced by $9 billion the amount of money available for new construction projects, and it included funding mechanisms contained in the Senate's version of the bill (H.R. 22) that some members thought would not add up (Curry 2015).[1] "I'm deeply discouraged by the phony pay-fors," lamented Representative Reid Ribble (R-WI), a member of the House Transportation Committee (Mejdrich 2015b).[2] In addition, while the committee bill would have enabled the Federal Transit Administration to oversee public transit systems that fail to meet minimum safety standards specified by law, those provisions were not included in the version put before the House.[3]

The strategy Chairman Shuster was alluding to involved a plan by the House majority leadership to bring the revenue provisions of the House committee version of the bill more in line with the Senate's version, while preserving the policy language of the committee's bill in anticipation of conference committee negotiations with the Senate.[4] So, after it was reported from committee, the bill was modified, and a new version was presented on the House floor in the form of Rules Committee Print 114-32.[5] Box 6.1[6] provides an illustration of a Rules print.

Most provisions of Rules Print 114-32 included the exact language recommended by the Transportation Committee, but in what has become common practice, House majority leadership, in concert with the Rules Committee, made "post-committee adjustments" to the bill by way of a "special rule" recommended by Rules and adopted by the whole House. Rather than setting the committee-reported version of H.R. 3763 as the legislative text for House floor consideration, the special rule made the Rules print version of the bill in order instead. Moreover, using "self-executing" language, the rule did not

---

Box 6.1. A Rules Print

October 27, 2015

RULES COMMITTEE PRINT 114-32

[Showing the text of H.R. 3763, the Surface Transportation Reauthorization and Reform Act of 2015, as ordered reported by the Committee on Transportation and Infrastructure with modifications.]

In the matter proposed to be inserted by the amendment of the Senate to the text of the bill, strike section 1 and all that follows through division B and insert the following:

DIVISION A—SURFACE
TRANSPORTATION
SECTION 1. SHORT TITLE; TABLE OF CONTENTS.
(a) Short Title. —This Act may be cited as the
"Surface Infrastructure Reauthorization and Reform Act
of 2015."
(b) Table of Contents.—The table of contents for
this Act is as follows:
DIVISION A—SURFACE INFRASTRUCTURE
Sec. 1. Short title; table of contents.
Sec. 2. Definitions.
Sec. 3. Effective date.
Sec. 4. References.

allow a separate vote to take place on whether the post-committee adjustments should remain a part of the text. Adoption of the special rule meant that those adjustments were made automatically.

The use of "self-executing" special rules by the Rules Committee is not a new practice, but it can arouse the ire of committees and members on occasion, especially to the degree that leadership is perceived to be trespassing on policy ground occupied by committees. Democratic Representative Jared Polis (2014, H7403) of Colorado, a member of the Rules Committee, described these rules this way: "They [the Rules Committee majority] use a self-executed amendment in the rule. That means that by passing this rule there is a special amendment that actually becomes part of the bill. We don't even have the opportunity to debate the merits of that amendment, whatever they are, but any other ideas from Democrats or Republicans are closed down."

What is new is the method by which post-committee adjustments are being made: by establishing a Rules Committee print—drafted by the Rules Committee in consultation with the House majority leadership—as the baseline text for consideration on the floor in lieu of the committee-reported version. According to Donald Wolfensberger (2015, 11), a former staff director of the Rules Committee and a close congressional observer, this approach can obscure detailed changes to the text and make it difficult to ascertain how, if at all, the Rules print differs from the version recommended by committee(s): "More recently, the Rules Committee has simply substituted the language of a 'Rules Committee Print' for committee-reported language, as the new base bill for amendment purposes. In so doing, it is sometimes inserting new leadership-blessed language without having to use the self-executing language or even to explain the changes." In the view of a former House parliamentarian, "This [post-committee adjustment] technique has taken hold more frequently in contemporary Congresses as measures emerging from committees are sometimes extensively rewritten, often with additional and non-germane matter, merely by a vote on the special order of business resolution and not by the traditional presentation and vote on separate amendments following the standing committee stage" (McKay and Johnson 2010, 428).

Historically, the House has initiated floor debate on the basis of committee-reported legislation. Congressional hearings, oversight activities, and relatively stable memberships allow committees to develop policy expertise on issues within their jurisdiction. Recently, it has become common for the House to begin floor proceedings with the text of a Rules print. In many cases the language of the print is the same as the committee-reported bill(s), but in some instances the text is adjusted before it reaches the floor. This chapter examines the development in the use of Rules prints as a way of executing post-committee adjustments and is organized into four sections. The first section provides an overview of how legislation gets considered on the House floor and the important role of the Rules Committee in organizing the chamber's business. The second section describes how special rules from the Rules Committee have evolved in how they make post-committee adjustments to legislation. The third section provides an empirical assessment of the degree to which post-committee adjustments have been made in the form of Rules Committee prints. The fourth section offers concluding observations.

Business on the House Floor: The Role of the Rules Committee and "Special Rules"

Floor time for legislation is a precious commodity in the workload-packed and deadline-driven environment of Capitol Hill. Thousands of legislative proposals are introduced each congress, many of which are considered at length by one or more congressional committees, but only a relative few are brought to the House floor for consideration by the entire body. Congress simply lacks the time necessary to consider every measure its members introduce or its committees report. Choices must therefore be made regarding what proposals the House will consider, when it will do so, and under what (if any) procedural limitations on floor debate and amendment. It makes little sense for the House to consider bills in the order in which its committees report them, for such an automatic procedure would disregard differences in the importance and urgency of various bills and make it impossible for the House to meet deadlines, such as the enactment into law of the twelve annual appropriations bills by the beginning of a new fiscal year.[7]

In addition to constraints imposed by time, House Rule XIV prescribes a daily order of business to occur on the chamber floor unless the House decides otherwise (as it often does). While Rule XIV specifies a daily order of business, it does not bind the House to a fixed routine. For action to occur in contravention of Rule XIV, privilege must be conferred to the measure the House wishes to consider. Privilege, in this context, refers to the special legislative status accorded to a limited class of measures that can be called up for floor consideration at any time, so long as another piece of legislation is not already pending before the chamber. Other House rules confer privilege to certain subjects so as to allow the daily order of business to be interrupted or supplanted entirely.

There are three main ways bills become privileged and eligible for floor consideration. First, various House rules confer privilege to certain kinds of measures reported by specific committees. Privileged measures include appropriations bills reported by the Appropriations Committee, budget resolutions and reconciliation bills produced by the Budget Committee (see chapter 5), resolutions reported by the Ethics Committee that sanction members for bad behavior, measures recommended by the House Administration Committee that address matters such as contested elections and internal expenditures of the House and its committees, and proposals from the Rules Committee either to amend the standing rules of the House or to affect the order of business on the House floor.[8] The House rulebook grants these measures privileged access to the floor due to their special importance to the House's ability to meet its constitutional responsibilities.

Second, House Rule XV makes in order certain kinds of legislative business on designated days of each week or month. On those particular days, Rule XV allows specific categories of legislation to become privileged for floor consideration. The most common of these special procedures is suspension of the rules. On Monday, Tuesday, and Wednesday of each week, motions are in order to suspend House rules and pass individual bills or take other legislative actions (House Rule XV, clause 1). The second and fourth Mondays of each month are reserved for floor action both on motions to discharge committees from further consideration of bills and bills concerning the District of Columbia (House Rule XV, clauses 2 and 4). Bills listed on the Private Calendar become privileged during the first and third Tuesdays of each month (House Rule XV, clause 5), while a rarely used procedure called Calendar Wednesday sets aside each Wednesday for committees to call up bills they have reported but that are not otherwise privileged for consideration under the chamber's standing rules. However, the rule states in part that the call of committees on Wednesdays occurs only if the committee chair "or other member authorized by the committee, has announced to the House a request for such call on the preceding legislative day" (House Rule XV, clause 6). Few such requests have been made in recent years.

These various procedures facilitate floor action on the measures they apply to, but they do not enable the House to take up many of the most important pieces of legislation on which members wish to act, including tax bills, program authorizations, and other proposals that cannot surmount the two-thirds vote threshold required of suspension motions. So these measures become privileged in a third way—by the House voting on a resolution, recommended by the Rules Committee, to make in order one or more bills for floor consideration. These "order of business" resolutions—more commonly called "rules" or "special rules"—are themselves privileged for consideration if offered at the direction of the Rules Committee.[9] These rules reported by the Rules Committee are considered "special" in the sense that they create floor procedures that are tailored to the unique set of circumstances that accompany the piece(s) of legislation to which they apply. If a special rule is adopted by a majority vote of the House, then the legislation specified in the rule becomes privileged for consideration, with floor debate and amendment opportunities (if any) proceeding on the basis of the procedures specified in the special rule.

By conferring privileged access to the floor to measures that lack this status, special rules provide flexibility to the House over how it conducts its business.[10] Special rules often set additional terms of consideration as well, such as the amount of floor time available for debate, the specific amendments that can be offered, and whether points of order can be raised against its consideration.[11] In crafting a special rule, the Rules Committee can devise whatever procedures it considers most suitable for floor action on a particular bill. With few exceptions, special rules can address, create, or avoid almost any parliamentary situation. The latitude the committee has in setting the terms of debate and amendment means that the committee's actions and inactions can be as controversial as they are important.

The Rules Committee, of course, does not act unilaterally. Each resolution it recommends must achieve a majority vote on the House floor to become binding, which occurs after a period of debate (customarily one hour) and a roll call vote that usually divides the House along party lines. Almost always, the House votes in support of the special rule because its provisions work as an effective ally of the House's majority-party leadership. Some call the Rules Committee the "Speaker's Committee" for this reason.[12]

As has been the case since the mid-1970s, a close connection exists today between the House's majority leadership and the Rules Committee. This connection is maintained in two important ways. First, the Speaker and the minority leader nominate their respective party members to the committee, subject to a vote of approval from their entire party caucus or conference. Second, while the party ratio on most other standing committees approximates the overall partisan composition of the chamber, on the Rules Committee the majority party enjoys a membership advantage of nine to four. This deliberate partisan imbalance reflects the vital role the committee plays in controlling the House's floor agenda and defining the policy choices that come before the chamber.

As a bridge between the House's committee system and the chamber floor, the Rules Committee is instrumental in helping the House majority leadership manage floor time. This responsibility is established in House Rule X, which provides the committee with legislative jurisdiction over measures affecting "the order of business of the House." If the Rules Committee does not grant a special rule for a bill reported from committee, that bill is unlikely to reach the floor and so cannot become law. In current practice, when writing a special rule, the Rules Committee not only determines what particular bills will reach the House floor but also for how long they may be debated and to what extent they can be amended.

The kinds of provisions contained in special rules have shifted over the years, largely in response to the composition and needs of House majorities at various times.[13] One key point that emerges from this line of research is that special rules regulate floor activity to a far greater extent than they once did. Over time, they have become more detailed, more complex, and more restrictive on amending activity, a trend that is independent of what political party happens to constitute a chamber majority at a particular time. Procedural innovations of the majority party in their construction of special rules are often adopted by the minority party upon assuming majority status.

Almost all special rules, regardless of their length or complexity, set parameters for the debate and amendment of legislation identified in the rule.[14] Some do even more than that—for instance, by adjusting the language of a committee-reported bill prior to its consideration on the floor. These "post-committee adjustments" are not new to the House, but the frequency with which such adjustments are made has increased noticeably in recent congresses, especially in the context of a Rules Committee print.

There are three main ways in which the text of committee-reported legislation can be modified by a special rule prior to House floor consideration: by incorporating certain provisions into the bill through language contained in the special rule resolution; by modifying the bill through an amendment printed in the Rules Committee report that accompanies the special rule resolution; and by setting a Rules Committee print containing new language as the basis for floor consideration. To be sure, the use of Rules prints is properly understood as a logical extension of past procedural innovations of the Rules Committee and should not be viewed as constituting a significant departure in the way the House conducts its business. The next section describes the procedural development in the use of Rules prints as a method of adjusting legislation after it leaves committee.

Setting the Baseline for House Floor Consideration

When the Rules Committee wants to confer privilege to legislation by way of a special rule, it often uses a bill reported from committee(s) as the baseline for debate and amendment on the House floor. As repositories of expertise on issues within their jurisdiction, congressional committees represent a division of labor within the House that facilitates the consideration of thousands of introduced measures across a wide range of subjects. By reporting a measure favorably, a committee is signaling to the House that the proposal has been sufficiently vetted and deserves consideration by all members.

Legislative changes recommended at the committee level often serve as the basis for floor debate and amendment. Usually, committee-endorsed changes are packaged together as an all-encompassing "amendment in the nature of a substitute" that seeks to replace introduced text in its entirety with language adopted during committee markup proceedings. While committee-endorsed amendments often benefit from procedural protections contained in a special rule, leadership deference to the work of committees is not absolute. If the views expressed by a committee diverge from the policy preferences of the majority party as understood by the Speaker, then recommended changes to a bill might instead come in the form of a leadership-crafted amendment printed in a Rules Committee report that accompanies a special rule resolution.

Displayed in Box 6.2 is a portion of text from H. Res. 23, a special rule adopted during the 113th Congress (2013–2014) that enabled the House to expediently consider legislation providing relief to the victims of Hurricane Sandy in New York and New Jersey. As the rule states in part, "It shall be in order to consider as an original bill for the purpose of amendment under the five-minute rule the amendment in the nature of a substitute printed in Part A of the report of the Committee on Rules accompanying this resolution." This language specifies that when the House takes up H.R. 152, a supplemental spending bill reported by the Appropriations Committee, the text of that bill will be replaced in its entirety with language printed in Part A of the Rules Committee report (H. Rept. 113-1) on H. Res. 23. Following the replacement of text, the Part A amendment effectively becomes the baseline for floor consideration with debate and amendment proceeding on the basis of subsequent provisions of H. Res. 23.

Alternatively, rather than make in order an amendment printed in its committee report, the Rules Committee may draft a Rules Committee print and make that proposal, through a special rule, the basis for floor consideration. Typical language used to this effect is displayed in Box 6.3, which contains the text of H. Res. 107, a "print" rule adopted during the 113th Congress (2013–2014). As H. Res. 107 states, in part, "An amendment in the nature of a substitute consisting of the text of Rules Committee Print 113-3 shall be considered as adopted." As before, the effect of this sentence is to replace the text of the reported bill, H.R. 890, with the language of Rules Committee Print 113-3.

Table 6.1 illustrates the number and percentage of "print" rules—defined here as special rules that set a Rules Committee print as the baseline for floor consideration—in relation to the total number of special rules granted by the

---

Box 6.2. Prelude to a Print Rule

H. RES. 23

Resolved, That at any time after the adoption of this resolution the Speaker may, pursuant to clause 2(b) of rule XVIII, declare the House resolved into the Committee of the Whole House on the state of the Union for consideration of the bill (H.R. 152) making supplemental appropriations for the fiscal year ending September 30, 2013, and for other purposes. The first reading of the bill shall be dispensed with. All points of order against consideration of the bill are waived. General debate shall be confined to the bill and shall not exceed one hour equally divided and controlled by the chair and ranking minority member of the Committee on Appropriations. After general debate the bill shall be considered for amendment under the five-minute rule. It shall be in order to consider as an original bill for the purpose of amendment under the five-minute rule the amendment in the nature of a substitute printed in part A of the report of the Committee on Rules accompanying this resolution. That amendment in the nature of a substitute shall be considered as read. All points of order against that amendment in the nature of a substitute are waived. No amendment to that amendment in the nature of a substitute shall be in order except those printed in part B of the report of the Committee on Rules. After disposition of such amendments, the Chair shall put the question on the amendment in the nature of a substitute.

Source: "Providing for Consideration of H.R. 152, Disaster Relief Appropriations Act, 2013." 2013. *Congressional Record* 159 (January 15): H99.

Rules Committee since the beginning of the 106th Congress (1999–2000). Both in number and as a percentage of all special rules, the use of print rules has increased dramatically in recent years.

In most cases a Rules Committee print contains language that is identical (or very similar) to the committee-reported version. Rules Print 113-12, for instance, mirrors the text of H.R. 1911, which was reported by the Committee on Education and the Workforce on May 9, 2013. Although the language of both measures is equivalent, selecting a Rules print as the basis for debate and

Box 6.3. A Print Rule

H. RES. 107

Resolved, That upon the adoption of this resolution it shall be in order to consider in the House the bill (H.R. 890) to prohibit waivers relating to compliance with the work requirements for the program of block grants to States for temporary assistance for needy families, and for other purposes. All points of order against consideration of the bill are waived. An amendment in the nature of a substitute consisting of the text of Rules Committee Print 113-3 shall be considered as adopted. The bill, as amended, shall be considered as read. All points of order against provisions in the bill, as amended, are waived. The previous question shall be considered as ordered on the bill, as amended, and on any amendment thereto to final passage without intervening motion except: (1) one hour of debate equally divided and controlled by the chair and ranking minority member of the Committee on Ways and Means; and (2) one motion to recommit with or without instructions.

Source: "Providing for Consideration of H.R. 890, Preserving the Welfare Work Requirement and TANF Extension Act of 2013." 2013. *Congressional Record* 159 (March 13): H1365.

TABLE 6.1
Number and Percentage of Print Rules, 106th–113th Congresses (1999–2014)

Congress (Years)	Number of Special Rules	Number of Print Rules	Percentage of Print Rules
106th (1999–2000)	267	1	0
107th (2001–2002)	191	0	0
108th (2003–2004)	192	1	<1
109th (2005–2006)	193	3	2
110th (2007–2008)	220	0	0
111th (2009–2010)	165	0	0
112th (2011–2012)	129	27	21
113th (2013–2014)	105	47	45

Source: Data are drawn from http://www.congress.gov, an online database of congressional activity, by searching the text of House resolutions for the phrase "Rules Committee Print." Figures on the number of special rules are drawn from Rules Committee activity reports for each congress.

amendment offers several advantages to the majority leadership and members generally. First, Rules prints made in order under the terms of a special rule can be easily located and retrieved in portable document format (PDF) from the Rules Committee website for inspection by all members, as well as the general public. Transparency in lawmaking can be enhanced when the Rules Committee acts as a legislative clearinghouse in this way. Second, Rules Committee staff can quickly post the text of a measure online in the form of a Rules print. This can be especially beneficial to members who intend to offer amendments because page and line numbers in a Rules print are fixed at the outset, whereas additional time is occasionally needed for the Government Printing Office to publish and distribute bills that have been reported from committee.[15]

While many Rules prints contain the same language found in a committee-reported bill, others may depart from the reported version in slight or significant ways. Some Rules prints contain additional material in comparison to the reported version; others subtract one or more sections or titles, and some do both.[16] These changes may reflect post-committee adjustments of a minor or technical nature, or they may codify more substantive agreements based on negotiations that occur after committees complete their work. Negotiations of this sort often involve the relevant committee(s) of jurisdiction, especially the chair(s) and majority-party leader(s).

Like all special rules, print rules involve majority-party leadership input and review. After a committee has reported a measure, it may become evident that there are issues—a lack of votes for chamber enactment, for instance, or jurisdictional disputes involving two or more committees—that require corrective action by the leadership and the Rules Committee. Print rules can serve this purpose by enhancing the ability of the majority party to build a winning coalition in support of its policy proposals.

Decisions by the Rules Committee to establish a Rules print as the legislative baseline for floor action—rather than an amendment in the nature of a substitute printed in a Rules Committee report (as was the case earlier with H. Res. 23)—reflect a change in practice whose importance should not be overstated. Both techniques can be used to adjust legislative text after it has left committee and before it is placed on the House floor for debate and amendment (assuming the rule allows amendments to be offered). The frequency with which post-committee adjustments are being made by way of a Rules Committee print, however, has increased. The next section offers an empirical assessment of post-committee adjustments made in the context of a Rules print.

Post-committee Adjustments in Rules Committee Prints

On the first page of each Rules print, just below its legislative title, is a sentence that identifies the textual sources a Rules print is derived from (see Box 6.1).[17] A typical sentence reads as follows: "Showing the text of H.R. 803 as ordered reported by the Committee on Education and the Workforce."[18] In this particular case, as the quoted sentence clearly implies, the Rules print contained language that was identical to the committee-reported version of H.R. 803. Of the eighty-eight Rules prints considered by the House from 1999 to 2014, exactly half of them contained the same language that was reported from committee.

In other instances, a Rules print contained different language than was reported from committee. When this occurs, the sentence atop a Rules print will be written in such a way as to alert members and staff that the language of the print is not the same as that in the committee-reported version of the bill. If the language adjustment is considered minor or of a technical nature, the sentence might read as follows: "Showing the text of H.R. 624 as ordered reported by the Permanent Select Committee on Intelligence with a modification."[19] Changes that are considered minor also might be identified as "technical changes" or "modifications."

The Rules Committee uses different language to convey changes of greater significance. For instance, Rules Print 113-2 included much of the same text as S. 47, a Senate bill to reauthorize the Violence against Women Act, but added new language in Title VIII on immigration while also dropping three other titles from S. 47. In this case, the sentence used to indicate these changes read as follows: "Showing a new text for S. 47." Alternatively, more significant changes might be summarized with sentences that read, "Showing the text as ordered reported with changes recommended by the committee chair(s)" or "Showing text based on H.R. _____."

Generally speaking, the summary sentence atop a Rules print conveys the magnitude and significance of any post-committee adjustments contained in the print. Most prints included no such changes, but those that did tended to use a typology of identically worded sentences to describe the nature of the changes that were made. This typology is displayed below, with sentences rank-ordered according to the significance of textual changes they are meant to convey, from no change to a major revision:

1. Showing the text as ordered reported
2. Showing the text as ordered reported with a technical change (or technical changes)

3. Showing the text as ordered reported with a modification (or modifications)
4. Showing the text as ordered reported with changes recommended by the committee chair(s)
5. Showing text based on H.R._____
6. Showing new text

Beyond the language of the summary sentence itself, post-committee adjustment can be assessed by comparing the number of sections in a Rules print to the number of sections in the corresponding reported bill(s).[20] Differences in these numbers provide a useful measure of the degree to which a bill has been modified after it leaves committee.[21] Of course, sections of legislation are not all of equal importance. New sections might entail only minor changes of limited policy significance, while others could address entire new policy areas, including ones that fall outside the purview of the reporting committee(s). Section counts do not distinguish between important sections and less important sections. This method also does not account for language changes that occur within a same-named section of a bill and print, but it is usually the case that the language of both sections is equivalent when the summary sentence of a Rules print identifies an unmodified committee-reported bill as its textual source. If the number and wording of sections are the same in both the print and the reported bill and the summary sentence suggests some modification was made, then examination of both texts is required to ascertain any differences in wording.

An important feature of Rules prints is that they allow the Rules Committee to combine two or more bills that are awaiting floor action into a single bill for House consideration.[22] Of the eighty-eight Rules prints created during the 1999–2014 period, sixteen (18 percent) combined multiple bills in a single print. All sixteen of these cases occurred in recent congresses: seven in the 112th Congress (2011–2012) and nine in the 113th Congress (2013–2014).[23] When multiple bills are joined in a print, the sections of all incorporated bills are compared to the sections of the print.[24]

Section counts of Rules prints and committee-reported bills are presented in two ways in table 6.2: as the number of sections across all prints and associated bills during a congress and as the number of print sections added or subtracted from reported bills.[25] The first measure provides a rough estimate of the amount of legislation presented to the House in the form of a print, and the second measure captures the degree to which legislation has been modified after being reported from committee. The last column of table 6.2 displays the percentage of print sections that did not correspond with sections in reported bills during a given Congress.

TABLE 6.2
Comparison of Sections Included in Rules Prints and Reported Bills

Congress (Years)	Rules Prints	Reported Bills	Print Sections	Bill Sections	Sections Added to Print	Sections Subtracted from Print	Section Difference	Percentage Change
106th (1999–2000)	1	1	131	118	13	0	13	11
107th (2001–2002)	0	0	0	0	0	0	0	0
108th (2003–2004)	1	1	242	225	17	0	17	8
109th (2005–2006)	3	3	120	139	0	19	19	14
110th (2007–2008)	0	0	0	0	0	0	0	0
111th (2009–2010)	0	0	0	0	0	0	0	0
112th (2011–2012)	28	64	1,476	1,421	189	134	323	23
113th (2013–2014)	49	84	1,977	1,963	29	49	78	4

Source: Data displayed in table 6.2 were collected by the author based on an examination of sections contained in Rules prints and associated reported bills.
Notes: Six Rules prints of the 113th Congress were excluded from analysis for lack of a committee-reported bill as a basis for comparison. In some cases, the text of an introduced bill or a bill that had already passed the House was included in the print alongside one or more reported bills. Of the sixty-four bills subject to a Rules print in the 112th Congress, nine were something other than the reported version; two were in introduced form, and seven had already passed the House. The eighty-four bills presented as Rules prints during the 113th Congress included eight introduced bills and one that had previously passed. The inclusion of language from an introduced bill in a Rules print tends to occur in the beginning months of a new congress, a time when many committees have yet to complete their review of bills referred to them, and as Congress nears adjournment.

As these data suggest, the Rules Committee has made increasing use of Rules prints as the textual basis for floor debate and amendment, especially since 2011. The 112th Congress (2011–2012) saw the most pronounced use of post-committee adjustment in the form of a Rules print as evidenced by a section difference of 323 between prints and reported bills during those two years. By comparison, the 113th Congress (2013–2014) considered forty-nine Rules prints, twenty-one more than during the 112th Congress, but the overall difference between print and bill sections during that time totaled seventy-eight, a roughly 75 percent drop from the prior two years.

The first identified use of a Rules print in lieu of a committee-reported bill occurred on July 1, 1999, but the practice did not become routine until the 112th Congress (2011–2012). During the initial phase of this now institutionalized practice, each Rules print was devoted to a single reported bill. Only recently have prints containing multiple bills become common. Early prints (including the very first one) appear to have modified bills to about the same degree as in recent congresses, at least on the basis of section counts, but a sharp drop in post-committee adjustment during the 113th Congress (2013–2014) suggests a continued evolution in the use of Rules prints for this purpose.[26] Whether Speaker Paul Ryan (R-WI) and the Rules Committee will continue to employ Rules prints in the ways they have in the past remains to be seen, especially in light of pressure on the new Speaker from some majority Republicans to enhance the role of committees in the legislative process.[27] Part of this enhancement might be to minimize significant changes to committee-reported bills through Rules prints.

Concluding Observations

A theme introduced at the outset is worth returning to here: the constant press of time, especially floor time, in today's Congress fosters creativity in how the House processes its workload. With more to do and less time to do it, the House majority leadership faces difficult choices regarding what measures to schedule for floor consideration and under what conditions to do so. At least to some degree, innovations like the use of Rules prints can be understood as a solution to time limitations and other demands inherent in modern lawmaking. Joining separately reported bills, for instance, expands the scope of subject matter that members may debate on the floor. In several instances, the texts of previously adopted House bills were added to committee-reported bills in the context of a Rules print, perhaps to help the majority leadership build a winning coalition in support of the overall legislative package. Prints may also embody the product of negotiations between and among committees when jurisdictional disputes arise, or they may be adjusted by the leadership to achieve particular goals. They can also be quickly posted online for all to see, thereby allowing members additional time to study the proposal and contemplate amendments to it.

In an era of intense partisan polarization, the strategic demands of what scholars call "message politics" can also shape the work of the Rules Committee (Evans 2001). Leadership deference to the work of committees tends to vary by issue, with "message" issues—subjects that voters most closely associate with one or another political party—being the most likely to receive active leadership involvement at all stages of the legislative process (Petrocik 1996).[28] As the two political parties move further apart ideologically, their leaders tend to draw sharper policy distinctions in an effort to attract undecided voters and to energize supporters ahead of upcoming elections. They do this in a number of ways—for instance, through media and legislative strategy that reinforces the central themes a party stands for—with the goal of creating a favorable political message the party can run on. To this end, new special rule provisions can be understood as procedural tools that help to manage uncertainty on the House floor and enhance majority leadership control over the substance of policy the House considers.

As the political world around it changes, so too does the Rules Committee. Nevertheless, in designing its special rules, the Rules Committee is able to adjust to changing circumstances in service to the needs of the majority party. In the view of legendary Speaker Thomas Bracket Reed (R-ME), this is how it ought to be. As he famously remarked in 1888, "If the majority do not govern, the minority will and if the tyranny of the majority is hard, the tyranny of the minority is simply unendurable. The rules, then, ought to be so arranged as to facilitate the action of the majority" (quoted in Robinson 1930, 182).

Provisions of special rules have evolved significantly over the past century, and there is little question that they will continue to do so. New provisions will come into favor, while others will be discarded.[29] Still others might find their way into the standing rules of the House.[30] History demonstrates that the agenda-setting responsibilities of the Rules Committee will continue to adjust and adapt to changing political and legislative circumstances, as manifested through the creation and design of innovative special rules.

Notes

* This chapter reflects the views of the author and does not necessarily reflect the view of the Congressional Research Service or the Library of Congress.

1. Memorandum to Rules Chairman Pete Sessions, "Cost Estimate for Rules Committee Print 114-32," *Congressional Budget Office*, October 20, 2015.

2. Federal transportation projects are funded primarily by the Highway Trust Fund (and the gasoline taxes that go into it), but additional money was needed beyond what the trust fund could provide to keep H.R. 3763 deficit neutral. There were concerns, however, about the viability of particular budget offsets in the Senate version intended to close the gap between the estimated $305 billion in spending authorized by H.R. 3763 over a six-year period and the $208 billion in revenue expected to flow into the trust fund during that time.

3. On account of a questionable safety record and a series of high-profile accidents in recent years, many commuters in the Washington, DC, area expected the FTA to impose a measure of discipline on the subway system (Metro) that connects Maryland, Virginia, and the District. It should be noted that the author is an occasional Metro rider whose views of the system have been tainted by experience.

4. Strategically, by narrowing the range of differences between House- and Senate-passed versions of a bill, House leaders can structure opportunities for compromise that might arise in conference. (A conference committee is a temporary joint committee created for the sole purpose of reconciling differences between House and Senate versions of a bill.) House Rule XXII and Senate Rule XXVIII require conference reports—which embody the product of compromises reached during conference negotiations—to stay within the "scope of differences" between the House and Senate versions. For instance, if the House bill provides $1 million for a certain purpose and the Senate bill allocates $2 million, then the conference report is required to provide no less than $1 million and no more than $2 million for that purpose (or any amount in between). Furthermore, if both versions of a bill contain the same legislative text on a particular subject, then the conference report must also include that same text. In the end, the conference version of the highway bill combined House policy language with Senate funding mechanisms and was signed into law (P.L. 114-94) by President Barack Obama on December 4, 2015.

5. "Committee print" is a generic term used to describe a document or publication produced by a congressional committee. Committee prints are often numbered based on the Congress during which they were published and the order in which a committee produced them. For instance, Rules Print 114-32 was the thirty-second print drafted by the Rules Committee during the 114th Congress. Prints of all committees are available online at "Congressional Committee Prints," Government Printing Office, http://www.gpo.gov/fdsys/browse/collection.action?collectionCode=CPRT.

6. "Rules Committee Print 114-32," U.S. House of Representatives Document Repository, October 27, 2015, http://docs.house.gov/billsthisweek/20151102/CPRT-114-HPRT-RU00-AIHighways.pdf.

7. With a relatively light workload compared to today, early congresses did in fact consider measures in the order in which they were reported from committee and placed on the legislative calendar. This method of setting the chamber's agenda endured into the 1880s, at which point crowded calendars made it difficult for the House to reach legislation it wished to consider. Expressing widespread frustration among members with the use of legislative calendars, Representative Francis Cush-

man (R-WA) had this to say in 1902: "The Calendar! What a misnomer. It ought to be called a cemetery. For therein lie the whitening bones of legislative hopes." Cushman's remarks originally appeared in the *Congressional Record* (35, pt. 5 [April 17, 1902], 4320) and are reproduced in *A History of the Committee on Rules* (Washington, DC: Government Printing Office, 1983), 81.

8. Although appropriations bills, budget resolutions, reconciliation legislation, and conference reports are privileged for consideration under the standing rules of the House, in modern practice those measures usually come to the floor by way of a special rule from the Rules Committee.

9. Special rules are privileged for consideration on the basis of House Rule XIII, clause 5(a)(4).

10. Early on, special rules were called "special orders" because they proposed an order of business that did not adhere to the "regular order" prescribed in House Rule XIV. For an analysis of how special rules evolved from special orders, see Bach (1990).

11. House rules are not self-enforcing. Compliance requires members to raise points of order (parliamentary objections) on the floor at the time an alleged rule violation is taking place. The presiding officer (the Speaker or a designee) judges the merit of a timely made point of order based on current House rules and precedents, and that ruling may be subject to appeal by a vote of all members. It is quite rare for the House to overturn a ruling on appeal, but a successful appeal will create a new precedent that the House will follow when similar circumstances arise in the future. Precedents are the application of House rules to specific parliamentary situations.

12. Prior to the start of the 94th Congress (1975–1976), the rules of the Democratic Caucus—the House majority at that time—were amended in order to strengthen the linkage between the Speaker of the House and majority members on the Rules Committee. The caucus adopted a resolution drafted by Representative Richard Bolling (D-MO) to give the Speaker direct authority to nominate (or renominate) all Democratic members of the Rules Committee, subject to caucus approval. The Republican Conference follows the same appointment procedure.

13. Special rules can be described any number of ways based on their provisions. "Open" rules, for instance, allow any floor amendments to be offered that otherwise comply with House rules, while "closed" rules prevent amending activity altogether. "Structured" rules, also called "modified-closed" rules, allow only certain members to offer amendments, while "compound" rules make two or more measures privileged for consideration though adoption of a single special rule. "MIRV" rules combine two or more separately passed measures into a single bill at the engrossment phase of proceedings, similar to how MIRV missiles contain multiple warheads that can be independently targeted so as to maximize first-strike capabilities. As described here, "print" rules set a Rules Committee print as the baseline for floor debate and amendment. See Bach and Smith (1988) for an authoritative account of the history and development of special rules and the kinds of provisions they contain.

14. Special rules sometimes are used for very specific purposes, such as designating a Thursday or a Friday as a suspension day or waiving certain layover requirements that normally apply to committee-reported legislation, including special rule resolutions themselves. The vast majority of special rules design procedures for considering specific pieces of legislation.

15. Bills, resolutions, committee reports, and other materials that require printing are delivered each evening in electronic format to the GPO from the offices of the House Bill Clerk and Tally Clerk. Printing and distribution then proceed along two tracks. Material placed on a "priority list" is usually ready to be delivered to congressional offices by 7:30 a.m. the following morning, while material that lacks a priority designation can take longer to distribute. In printing bills, priority is determined by the nature of the bill itself, the current stage it has reached in the legislative process, and the chamber from which it originated. Appropriations bills are considered the highest priority for printing purposes, followed by conference reports. Enrolled bills, which represent the final version of legislation that both chambers have agreed to, are prioritized next, followed by engrossed bills (the official copy of a measure as enacted by one chamber). At the low end of the priority scale are reported bills and introduced bills. Finally, all else being equal, Senate bills are usually printed before House bills.

16. In some cases a Rules print will combine the text of two or more measures into a single document at the outset of floor proceedings. For instance, Rules Print 112-17, the Jumpstart Our Business Startups Act, included text from H.R. 1070, H.R. 2167, H.R. 2930, H.R. 2940, H.R. 3606, and H.R. 4088. When multiple measures are merged into a Rules print, it is often (but not always) the case that the subjects of the various proposals have a direct connection to one another. In this case, for instance, the six measures that were combined in Rules Print 112-17 all dealt in some way with the ability of small businesses to access private capital. The multiple measures assembled in a Rules print may also be at different stages of the legislative process. For instance, in Rules Print 112-17, three of the bills (H.R. 1070, H.R. 2930, and H.R. 2940) had already passed the House as stand-alone measures, two (H.R. 2167 and H.R. 3606) had been marked up in committee and ordered reported (but had yet to see any floor action), and one (H.R. 4088) remained in its introduced form.

17. Seven Rules prints did not include this summary sentence. Most of these instances occurred prior to the 112th Congress, when the use of Rules prints was less institutionalized than it is today.

18. This sentence is drawn from Rules Print 113-4, reflecting the reported version of H.R. 803, the SKILLS Act.

19. This sentence comes from Rules Print 113-7, a version of H.R. 624 that includes modifications to the "sunset" provision of section 3. Sunset provisions allow legislation to expire after a given period—five years following enactment in this case—unless Congress takes positive action to keep the legislation on the books. It should be noted that House leadership protocols of the 114th Congress, which represent the Speaker's commitment to what might be called "best legislative practices," require most pieces of legislation to include a sunset provision of seven years or less before floor consideration may occur. Additional leadership protocols currently in effect include limitations on how commemorative legislation is considered, guidance on the drafting of constitutional authority statements for inclusion in a bill as required by House Rule XII, and budgetary requirements that apply to the authorization of new programs.

20. Bills can be organized by divisions, titles, and sections, with sections representing the smallest unit. Bills of less than fifty pages tend to contain only sections. Titles are included in longer bills that address a wide range of subjects or address a single

subject in considerable depth. Legislation of significant length, such as an omnibus appropriations bill, may also contain divisions. In this case, divisions would correspond to the particular appropriations bills included in the omnibus package.

21. In most cases a committee-reported version of the legislation had been produced prior to the assembly of a Rules print, thereby allowing a direct comparison to be made between the reported text and the text of the associated Rules print. In five instances, a Rules print included legislative text that did not emerge from a House committee. Those five prints are excluded from analysis because the texts of those prints are not directly comparable to committee-reported legislation.

22. Joining bills in this way can facilitate legislative efficiency and save the House time. In assessments of the work of Congress, the number of bills that pass during a given two-year period is often used as a basis for judgment. Prevalent use of multiple-bill prints, however, would depress the number of bill passages even as the substance of policy that is considered in committee and on the floor remains the same. For more on the difficulty of assessing congressional performance, see Straus (2014).

23. Multiple-bill prints usually contain several titles, where each title contains a separately reported bill.

24. The first section of a bill (or print) usually states the bill's legislative title, such as the Smarter Solutions for Students Act, a bill (H.R. 1911) reported from the Committee on Education and the Workforce and considered by the House during the 113th Congress in the form of Rules Print 113-12. To facilitate the comparability of section counts between bills and prints, only one section that expresses a legislative title is counted when multiple bills are combined in a print. Otherwise, prints containing multiple bills would appear to have fewer sections since each of the separate bills would include a section devoted to its title.

25. The number and wording of print sections were used as a baseline for comparison with sections that might have been added or subtracted from reported bills.

26. During the 114th Congress, for instance, the special rule (H. Res. 125) governing consideration of Rules Print 114-8 for H.R. 5, the Student Success Act, provided for a modification of the print in the form of an amendment printed in the Rules Committee report accompanying the rule. This approach combines the two methods of adjustment discussed in section 2 and gives the Rules Committee greater flexibility in designing procedures for the consideration of legislation. Instances in which one special rule makes two or more Rules prints eligible for floor consideration have also become more common recently.

27. As the first session of the 114th Congress winds down, twenty-seven Rules prints have been presented for debate on the House floor, a rate that slightly outpaces the consideration of Rules prints during the 113th Congress. Twenty-six of these instances, however, occurred prior to the election of Representative Paul Ryan as Speaker on October 29, 2015.

28. The Republican Party, for instance, tends to be associated with tax reduction, school choice, military readiness, crime suppression, and more traditional family values. Subjects often identified with the Democratic Party include health care, public education, Social Security, and environmental protection.

29. For instance, so-called queen-of-the-hill rules—special rules that make in order a series of amendments to the same text—were once quite common, but those provisions have fallen out of use in recent years. For more on queen-of-the-hill rules and their king-of-the-hill counterparts, see Saturno (2012).

30. For example, the ability of the majority party to postpone and cluster recorded votes until later in the day was integrated into House Rule XVIII, clause 6(g) at the outset of the 107th Congress (2001–2002). Prior to that, the power to do so could be granted only by way of language contained in a special rule.

References

Bach, Stanley. 1990. "From Special Orders to Special Rules: Pictures of House Procedure in Transition." Paper presented at the annual meeting of the American Political Science Association, San Francisco, California, August 30–September 2, http://stanistan.org/docs/1/4.pdf.

Bach, Stanley, and Steven S. Smith. 1988. *Managing Uncertainty in the House of Representatives: Adaptation and Innovation in Special Rules.* Washington, DC: Brookings Institution Press.

Curry, Tom. 2015. "House Panel Approves Six-Year Highway Bill; Funds in Question." *CQ News*, October 22.

Evans, C. Lawrence. 2001. "Committees, Leaders, and Message Politics." In *Congress Reconsidered*, edited by Lawrence C. Dodd and Bruce I. Oppenheimer, 217–43. 7th ed. Washington, DC: CQ Press.

McKay, William, and Charles W. Johnson. 2010. *Parliament and Congress: Representation and Scrutiny in the Twenty-First Century.* New York: Oxford University Press.

Mejdrich, Kellie. 2015a. "House Highway Bill Strategy Opens Window for Ex-Im Bank Renewal." *CQ Weekly*, October 28.

———. 2015b. "Senate Clears Five-Year Highway Bill; Ex-Im Renewal." *CQ Weekly*, December 3.

Oppenheimer, Bruce I., et al. 1983. *A History of the Committee on Rules.* Washington, DC: Government Printing Office.

Petrocik, John R. 1996. "Issue Ownership in Presidential Elections, with a 1980 Case Study." *American Journal of Political Science* 40: 825–50.

Polis, Jared. 2014. "Providing for Consideration of H.R. 3522, Employee Health Care Protection Act of 2014." *Congressional Record*, House, daily edition, 160 (September 10).

Robinson, William A. 1930. *Thomas B. Reed: Parliamentarian.* New York: Dodd Mead.

Saturno, James V. 2012. "Toppling the King of the Hill: Understanding Innovation in House Practice." In *Party and Procedure in the United States Congress*, edited by Jacob R. Straus, 35–60. Lanham, MD: Rowman & Littlefield.

Straus, Jacob R. 2014. "Comparing Modern Congresses: Can Productivity Be Measured?" In *The Evolving Congress*, Congressional Research Service, 113th Cong., 2nd sess., S. Prt. 113–30, 217–41. Washington, DC: Government Printing Office.

U.S. Congress. 2015. *Constitution, Jefferson's Manual, and Rules of the House of Representatives*. H.Doc. 113-181, 113th Congress, 2nd sess. Washington, DC: Government Printing Office.

Wolfensberger, Donald R. 2015. "Changing House Rules: From Fair Game to Partisan Tilt." Paper presented at the Conference on Congress, the Constitution, and Contemporary Politics, Washington, DC, American Enterprise Institute, October 16.

7

Longitudinal Analysis of One-Minute Speeches in the House of Representatives

Colleen J. Shogan and Matthew E. Glassman

CONSIDERABLE ATTENTION ABOUT ideological polarization in Congress, both in the media and within the discipline of political science, has generated intellectual interest in political parties and the role they play in the legislative process. Nonetheless, the House of Representatives is not simply comprised of two separate teams competing for press coverage and desired policy outcomes. Anyone who has worked on Capitol Hill or devoted considerable time to observing Congress knows that there are 435 voting members in the House, each trying to create his or her own political identity. Members achieve these personalized goals by choosing their staff carefully, determining how to spend their limited time, crafting relationships with party leaders, sponsoring specific pieces of legislation, and communicating their cautiously crafted political personas to House colleagues, press outlets, and constituents.

The latter activity has changed recently with the development of the Internet and social media. Every House member has a website on which the congressional office can portray the elected representative, within certain guidelines, as it deems politically beneficial. Press releases do not necessarily need to find their way into the printed stories of reporters covering Congress or the district. Instead, they are now independent vehicles for information, directly available for public consumption via Twitter or an enterprising blogger.

Even more dynamic is the presentation of members of Congress on social media. In 140 characters or less, members take policy positions, advocate, talk about their districts, describe official actions, or commemorate important occasions (Glassman, Straus, and Shogan 2013). Social media use by elected representatives continues to evolve and may change models of representation in important ways. Right now, congressional scholars are still trying to make sense of the data presented to them through social media, given that initial member adoption occurred largely in the 111th (2009–2010) and 112th (2011–2012) Congresses (Straus et al. 2013).

For a longitudinal examination of how members of Congress have changed portrayals of their political and representative personas, a consistent data source is needed. One-minute speeches in the House can serve that purpose. Despite the proliferation of communication outlets available today—from websites to social media—members still come to the House floor in the (relatively) early morning hours, line up, and wait for their opportunity to give a sixty-second speech on any topic of their choosing. Given that members of Congress guard their time as a precious resource, it is almost a marvel that such a practice continues. This analysis of one-minute speeches attempts to explicate the rationale for the tradition's continued existence.

Even more importantly, how has the content and tone of these one-minute speeches evolved over time? If one-minute speeches have changed in composition or tenor, then their development might be a revealing indicator of larger institutional, political, and representational changes in Congress. The scholarly literature on polarization has examined legislative productivity but not congressional deliberation or debate (Quirk and Bendix 2011). Studying House floor rhetoric may increase knowledge about the effects of polarization and its complicated interaction with the institutional operations of Congress.

We are particularly interested in possible changes to the behaviors of incumbent legislators identified by David R. Mayhew (1974) in *Congress: The Electoral Connection*. In his classic book, Mayhew identifies three observable behaviors exhibited by virtually all members of Congress: position taking, credit claiming, and advertising. *Position taking* refers to judgmental statements about politics, policies, or governmental actors. *Credit claiming* is proffering a belief that a member of Congress is personally responsible for causing the government or another entity to do something desirable. *Advertising* is any effort to disseminate a member's name to create a favorable image without mentioning specific issues or policy content (Mayhew 1974, 49–61).

Our examination of one-minute speeches can help answer a number of questions about Congress and its evolution. More than forty years after the publication of *Congress: The Electoral Connection*, are members still engaging in these activities? Has increased ideological polarization affected how members of Congress portray themselves to their colleagues, constituents, and the media? Furthermore, in today's nationalized media climate, have elected members moved from a "person-intensive" district-based approach to a "policy-intensive" national representational style (Fenno 2000)?

One-Minute Speeches

House floor speeches are an understudied source of information about member behavior and preferences (Pearson and Dancey 2011). One-minute speeches occur with regularity, and the Speaker of the House determines the number of speeches on a given day. There may not be a large number of members on the House floor during one-minute speeches; yet every House office is tuned in to C-SPAN to watch morning proceedings in the chamber. Regardless of physical location, members and staff watch one-minute speeches—or at least monitor the subjects being discussed—with considerable interest in what is being said on the floor.

Both parties in the House have organized communication entities to promote partisan messages—namely, the Democratic Message Board and the Republican Theme Team. Although the parties can present an organized message on the House floor during one-minutes if they so choose, the majority party has the power to limit the number of one-minute speeches on a given day. Members do not need to reserve time with their party leadership to give one-minute speeches. Consequently, one-minute speeches reflect a mixture of party messaging, member policy priorities, and district concerns.

Protocol concerning one-minute speeches has been consistent since August 8, 1984, with one-minutes alternating between the majority and the minority, and with the Speaker of the House reserving the right to limit or reschedule such speeches (Schneider 2015). The Speaker, or the presiding officer, recognizes members for one-minutes according to the order in which they are seated on each side of the aisle.

Previous research analyzing the use of one-minutes has examined the role of party messaging (Morris 2001; Harris 2005), the characteristics of House members who speak on the floor during unconstrained time (Maltzman and Sigelman 1996; Morris 2001), the partisan content of recent one-minute speeches (Green 2013), the prevalence of backbenchers giving floor speeches (Maltzman and Sigelman 1996; Rocca 2007), and the role gender plays in the frequency of one-minute speeches (Pearson and Dancey 2011). Several scholars (Green 2013; Morris 2001; Harris 2005) have analyzed one-minute speeches for content, usually coding for broad categories such as the purpose of the speech or the relationship of the speech's topic to the party's daily message. Even though the Speaker's orders concerning one-minutes have been consistent since 1984, there has been little longitudinal work on the content or partisan tone of one-minute speeches. Morris (2001, 114) calls for further examination of one-minutes that focuses on a "look across time for specific changes in speaking behavior."

Our research examines a random sample of one-minute speeches from three points: 1989, 1999, and 2009. These three years correspond, respectively, to the first sessions of the 101st, 106th, and 111th Congresses. Each speech has been analyzed using a robust coding structure to measure content and tone. Mayhew's three behaviors of incumbent legislators (position taking, credit claiming, and advertising) serve as the anchor of the substantive content category. In this respect, we build on previous research, which claimed that activities such as position taking were common in one-minute speeches but did not measure this specific behavior (Rocca 2007).

Hypotheses

We hypothesize that House members will exhibit all three incumbent behaviors over time. Due to increased polarization of congressional parties, we further hypothesize that the tone of the speeches will grow more negative over time, with higher frequencies of critical mentions focused on the opposing party and the president. Lastly, as a by-product of larger macropolitical trends that encourage the nationalization of politics and public policy, we hypothesize that recent one-minute speeches will be more "wonky" in nature (i.e., using statistical information to bolster or frame arguments) and will focus more on national and international, rather than local, issues of interest.

Concerning the individual characteristics of the speakers, we predict that members in the ideological extreme of their party will give one-minute speeches more frequently than moderates. Furthermore, we hypothesize that critical mentions of the opposing party will be higher with ideological speakers. This would corroborate the findings of Douglas B. Harris (2005). Furthermore, we anticipate that the relationship between a member's ideology and the critical tone of one-minute speeches will intensify over time, a likely by-product of increased polarization in Congress.

Calls for bipartisanship will be relatively uncommon in one-minute speeches, given that their format of alternating between parties contributes to partisan posturing on the House floor. We also anticipate that ideologically extreme members will engage in "position taking" more frequently, choosing to use one-minutes to make a partisan or policy argument rather than to bring attention to their district in a nonpolitical way through "advertising."

Methodology/Coding

For our analysis of one-minute speeches, we collected a random 10 percent sample of one-minute speeches given in 1989, 1999, and 2009. The year

1989 is the first in which the *Congressional Record* is available electronically through the Legislative Information System (LIS), a legislative database available to members of Congress and their staffs. Similar congressional information is available to the public on the Congress.gov website. The other two years (1999 and 2009) were chosen in ten-year increments after 1989. All one-minute speeches given in a particular year were exported from LIS and placed into a spreadsheet. Each speech was assigned a unique identification number. A random number generator chose 10 percent of the identification numbers for each year, which were then assigned randomly to each author for coding. Each author then matched up his or her assigned identification numbers with the speeches in the spreadsheet, located the speeches in the *Congressional Record*, and coded those speeches. In total, 706 speeches were coded after eliminating speeches from nonvoting delegates and repeated speeches in the sample. Coding was equally distributed among the authors.

Devising a robust and stable coding plan proved more challenging than anticipated. Three trial rounds of coding speeches refined the definitions of the coded variables and the overall scope of the coding. Over 90 percent of the time, the authors gave a speech the same code, providing the study with high intercoder reliability.

The three behaviors of incumbent members identified by Mayhew (1974) were augmented by one additional behavior ("calls to action") that was identified in an early coding trial. A call to action is a particular type of position taking, but the frequency of this behavior warranted its own category. A call to action is a specific request or demand that a particular action should be taken by a political actor, the American people, or those listening to the speech. These four behavioral categories were not exclusive; for example, one speech could contain both credit-claiming and position-taking rhetoric.

Coding also included the scope of the issue being discussed (local, national, or international). This category also was not exclusive. For example, a speech might emphasize a local problem (affecting the congressional district) but also include an argument about a broader national issue. Furthermore, we coded mentions of other institutions: the House, the Senate, the president or presidency, the member's party, and the opposing party. Other content coding included a "policy wonk" variable that measured whether the speaker used at least two pieces of statistical information to substantiate his or her argument. Finally, all explicit bipartisan appeals were coded.

Several measures captured the tone of the speech. Each mention of an institution (House, Senate, president/presidency, the speaker's party, and the opposing party) was coded as favorable, critical, or neutral. An explanation of our coding rules is available in the appendix at the end of this chapter.

Overview of Data

LIS provides an accurate count of the number of one-minute speeches given since 1989. Figure 7.1 shows the frequency of one-minute speeches from the 101st (1989–1990) through the 114th (2015–2016) Congresses. One-minutes decreased in frequency in the late 1990s and then resurged in the mid-2000s. The highest frequency occurred in 1995, the first year of a House GOP majority after several decades of Democratic control.

In general, first sessions yield more one-minutes than second sessions, most likely due to the congressional schedule limiting time in session during campaigns that occur in the second year of a congress.

Analysis

Analysis of the data is concentrated on three lines of inquiry: the demographics of members of Congress who give one-minute speeches in comparison to the chamber as a whole, the behaviors measured in the speeches over time, and the relationship between ideological extremeness and speech composition.

Table 7.1 compares the demographics of members in our sample who gave one-minute speeches in comparison to the chamber's population. The data indicate that Democrats gave one-minute speeches at a less frequent rate than their chamber membership might predict. This occurred in all three congresses examined. Republicans outperformed their Democratic colleagues in terms of frequency of one-minute speeches.

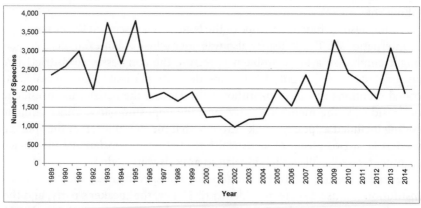

FIGURE 7.1
One-minute speeches, 1989–2014.

TABLE 7.1

Demographics of One-Minute Speakers in Sample

	101st Congress		106th Congress		111th Congress	
	Sample (%)	Chamber (%)	Sample (%)	Chamber (%)	Sample (%)	Chamber (%)
Democrats	53.0	57.7	44.9	48.8	46.3	58.8
Republicans	47.0	42.3	55.1	51.2	53.7	41.2
Men	93.9	93.4	88.7	87.2	80.2	84.4
Women	6.1	6.6	11.3	12.8	19.8	16.6
Freshmen	14.1	9.7	8.9	9.7	13.7	14.9
Nonfreshmen	85.9	90.3	91.1	90.3	86.3	85.1
Liberals*	25.2	29.8	25.6	24.3	31.3	29.2
Conservatives*	30.2	20.2	38.9	25.7	25.0	20.7
Extreme liberals**	11.5	11.9	7.7	9.7	13.1	11.8
Extreme conservatives**	14.4	8.1	17.8	10.2	9.4	8.2

*Liberals/conservatives are defined as DW-NOMINATE ideology scores in extreme half of party.
**Extreme liberals/conservatives are defined as DW-NOMINATE ideology scores in extreme 20 percent of party.

In the 111th Congress (2009–2010), female members' frequency of one-minute speeches exceeded their chamber membership, which is in keeping with findings by Kathryn Pearson and Logan Dancey (2011). In 1990, freshmen members might have viewed one-minutes as a helpful tool to promote their names; yet freshmen in later congresses (106th and 111th) did not give one-minutes speeches at a disproportionate frequency.

"Conservative" members routinely give one-minute speeches frequently, while "liberal" members are much closer to the proportion of the chamber. "Extreme conservatives" also issued one-minutes at a high level, although the difference between the rates of frequency in the 111th Congress (2009–2010) largely disappeared. This could be attributed to the advent of social media and its high rate of early adoption among the most conservative members of Congress (Straus et al. 2013). Once social media provided a cheap, easily accessible, and largely unlimited forum to express viewpoints, take positions, and claim credit, the chamber's most conservative members may have decided that one-minute speeches had lost some of their political luster. Lastly, the data suggest that historically, Democrats may not have fully utilized one-minute speeches as a messaging tool. With respect to one-minutes, the "liberal" voice within the House Democratic caucus was not as strong as the "conservative" voice within the GOP. This data partially supports the findings of Jonathan S. Morris (2001) but indicates that ideological conservatives give one-minutes at a proportionately higher rate than ideological liberals.

The next line of inquiry is the substantive content of the speeches. Figure 7.2 shows the percentage of speeches across time for each of Mayhew's three categories of incumbent behavior, with the addition of the fourth "calls to action" category. Across all congresses, the most common type of one-minute speech was one in which the member took a position. Approximately 70 percent of one-minute speeches included position taking.

Advertising increased over time (11.9 to 21.6 to 28.1 percent). This is an interesting finding, since advertising is generally the opposite of position taking. When members advertise, they create a "favorable image" utilizing "messages with little or no issue content" (Mayhew 1974, 49). In the 111th Congress (2009–2010), members often combined advertising (usually concerning district issues) with position taking, perhaps in an attempt to merge local concerns with broader national issues.

In the following example, Representative Kathy Castor (2009, 17052) advertises a local investment of money while also taking a position on healthcare legislation:

> Ms. CASTOR of Florida. Mr. Speaker, I rise today to inform the House that the economic recovery plan is working in my district. Yesterday, I was at the Johnny Ruth Clark Community Health Center in South St. Petersburg, Florida, *where*

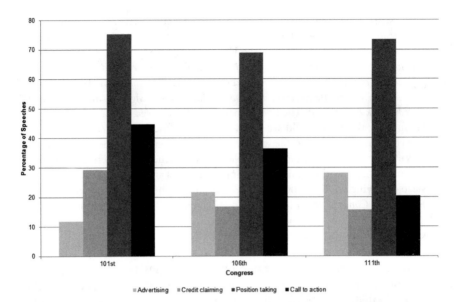

FIGURE 7.2
Congressional behavior in speeches.

we made the announcement that $1 million will go to expand that community health center. That community health center is the lifeline for that community, for the neighbors and businesses in that community. It's going to allow them to build new patient exam rooms. This $1 million grant comes on the heels of a half million dollar grant that will allow them to hire new doctors, nurses, and medical professionals, very important because our community health centers are the places where folks receive quality, affordable health care. *Fortunately, in our health care reform bill, we are going to make an additional investment in our community health centers.* They are the lifelines to our communities. This is one of the only ways we're going to make quality health care affordable and convenient for families and small businesses throughout our neighborhoods. (Emphasis added.)

Two incumbent activities in one-minute speeches decreased over time. Credit claiming steadily declined (29.2 to 16.7 to 15.7 percent). Members may have found more efficient outlets, such as their official websites, in which to claim credit. The following one-minute speech includes a credit claim:

Mr. CHABOT. Mr. Speaker, President Clinton ran an ad in his first presidential campaign back in 1992 in which he said he wanted to end welfare as we know it. Then what happened? Well, he had a Democrat-controlled Congress for the first 2 years of his term, and what did they do on welfare reform? Nothing. The American people decided it was time for a change in 1994, just 2 years later, and elected a Republican majority in the House for the first time in 40 years. *The Republican Congress passed welfare reform; the President vetoed it. And then we passed it again, and then he vetoed it a second time. We finally passed it a third time shortly before the election, and the President finally signed it into law, and then he took credit for it.* The liberals had ranted and raved that welfare reform, because it passed, we would see people starving in the streets. Well, just about everybody now agrees that the welfare reform has been one of the greatest success stories in years. Millions of people who were stuck, who were trapped on welfare are now working and supporting themselves and their own children instead of relying on their fellow taxpayers to support them. *Mr. Speaker, it took a Republican Congress to get the job done.* (Chabot 1999, 14720; emphasis added.)

Calls to action also declined over time (44.7 to 36.5 to 20.4 percent). While the data cannot tell us why this behavior occurred less frequently, it might be that members have come to see one-minute speeches as venues for position taking or commemorating local achievements but as an ineffective mechanism for "rallying the troops" to support a particular political action. In the following speech, Representative Charles G. Douglas (1989, 18541–42) asks for a specific action to solve a policy problem:

Mr. DOUGLAS. Mr. Speaker, for 28 days, the gentleman from Mississippi [Mr. Smith] has been rising and will rise to point out that this House has not yet entered the drug war. In fact, we are not even fighting a good skirmish yet. We have 28 standing committees and 46 subcommittees spread over this so-called drug war. I just wanted to praise the gentleman from Mississippi for pointing out that by the time we get back here in September and Mr. Bennett gives us his action plan for that drug war, it is going to be fanned out over so many committees nothing is going to be done. If World War II had been fought that way, one committee would deal with helmets, one committee would do tanks, one would do jeeps, another would do uniforms, and we would probably still be fighting World War II. I think it is obvious that we need one committee, as the gentleman from Mississippi has pointed out. *He is one of the few Members who has actually had to fight the drug war when he served as sheriff, and I think we ought to listen to him, and we ought to act, and we ought to make this House streamlined so that we can enter the drug war rather than pretend we are fighting the drug war.* (Emphasis added.)

Figure 7.3 shows the content scope of coded speeches. In each congress, between 75 and 80 percent of one-minute speeches in the sample addressed a domestic national policy issue (e.g., the budget deficit, tax policy, Medicare). There was a notable increase from the 106th (1999–2000) to 111th Congress

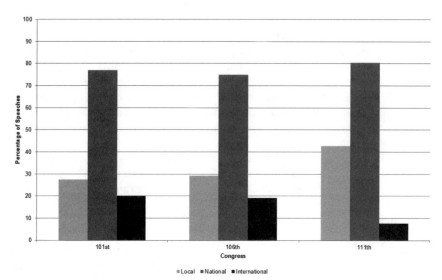

FIGURE 7.3
Coded speeches, by scope.

(2009–2010) in the percentage of speeches addressing local issues (such as unemployment in the member's district or commemoration of a local sports team).

International issues were never popular for one-minute speeches but decreased in frequency over time (from 19.9 to 19.2 to 7.7 percent). These findings do not confirm or invalidate Richard Fenno's description of an emerging "policy-intensive" national representative style. Members certainly focus on national issues in one-minute speeches. The modest rise of local issues in one-minute speeches over time, however, indicates that House members have not forgotten their districts. Indeed, members in the most recently coded Congress in the sample (111th) continued to talk about national concerns but frequently related those concerns back to their districts, often using an anecdote about recent town hall meetings to substantiate their arguments. All politics is still local but perhaps viewed through the prism of national policymaking, as evidenced in the following one-minute speech:

> Mr. LAMPSON. Mr. Speaker, I rise this morning to tell all of my colleagues about a brave 6-1/2-year-old girl named Keeley Woodruff from Beaumont, Texas. Yesterday, Keeley braved Vagus Nerve Stimulator implant surgery to stop the more than 50 epileptic seizures that she has suffered daily since she

was 1 1/2 years old. Well, this stimulator has proved to be a safe and effective therapy for patients with severe epilepsy, but it has not been approved by the State of Texas for patients under 12 years old. *The bottom line is that costs associated with this life-changing procedure often are not covered.* Mr. Speaker, thanks to the fast action and cooperation among a University of Texas medical branch physician; the manufacturer, Cyberonics; and Medicaid this procedure was allowed for Keeley. And thankfully her parents, Rob and Christi, informed me that she has only suffered two seizures since the surgery. While Keeley's story has a happy ending, there are many other children who face the same situation, and very soon I will be in contact with Texas and Medicaid officials to see what can be done to approve this device for all children under 12 years old. Mr. Speaker, we as Members of Congress must do all we can to make sure that medical policy keeps pace with medical technology. (Lampson 1999, 18609–10; emphasis added.)

A one-minute speech was coded as "policy wonk" if it contained two or more policy-related statistics. One-minute speeches used statistics slightly more frequently over time. Generally, between 15 and 20 percent of one-minute speeches in both parties contained "policy wonk" arguments. The exception was during the 111th Congress (2009–2010), when 30.4 percent of Republican one-minute speeches invoked two or more policy-related statistics. This was largely due to the consideration of health-care reform during that session of Congress; GOP members frequently offered statistics to rebut Democratic arguments about reform. As hypothesized, members do not use one-minute speeches to make bipartisan appeals. Over time, only 1 to 3 percent of one-minute speeches included a bipartisan appeal.

Figure 7.4 displays the percentages of speeches in which the president of the United States was mentioned and in which the opposing party was mentioned. During each of the three congresses in our sample, a greater percentage of one-minute speeches by members belonging to the opposite party as the president mentioned the president than did speeches by members belonging to the president's party. Specifically, during the 101st Congress (1989–1990; George H. W. Bush), 39.3 percent of Democratic one-minute speeches mentioned the president versus 23.1 percent of Republican speeches. During the 106th Congress (1999–2000; William J. Clinton), 30.4 percent of Republican one-minute speeches mentioned him. Democrats only mentioned Clinton in 10.7 percent of their speeches in 1999, most likely avoiding mentions of Clinton after his 1998 impeachment. During the 111th Congress (2009–2010; Barack H. Obama), 31.5 percent of Republican one-minute speeches mentioned the president versus only 17.2 percent of Democratic one-minutes.

In each of the congresses in our sample, a greater percentage of the one-minute speeches of members belonging to the minority party in the House explicitly mentioned the opposing party in comparison to one-minute

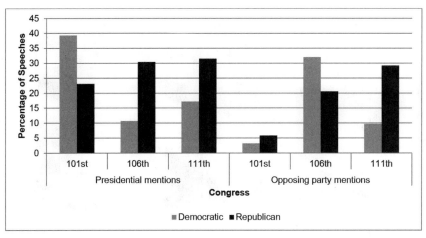

FIGURE 7.4
Presidential and opposing party mentions.

speeches given by members in the majority party. This difference grew more pronounced over time. In 1989, the Republicans mentioned the Democrats in 5.8 percent of their speeches, and the Democrats mentioned Republicans in 3.2 percent. Although the Republicans as the minority party engaged in opposing party mentions at a higher rate, it is worth noting that the overall frequency was quite low. By 1999, it was much more common to mention the opposite party, and it was now the minority-party Democrats (32.0 percent) who did so more frequently than the Republicans (20.6 percent). In 2009, the Republicans mentioned the Democrats in 29.2 percent of their speeches, in comparison to 9.7 percent of Democratic speeches mentioning Republicans.

Have one-minute speeches grown more critical? Figure 7.5 shows the percentage of one-minute speeches that were coded as "critical" when the opposite party or the president of the United States was mentioned. For the POTUS mentions, only members of the party opposite the president (Democrats in the 101st, Republicans in 106th and 111th) were included. What was the tone of speeches when members talked about the opposite party or the opposing party president? First, the percentage of one-minute speeches mentioning the other party in a negative context increased consistently over time (78.0 to 90.4 to 96.4 percent). In general, the prevalence of mentioning the other party in a critical context likely reflects the finding that a greater percentage of one-minute speeches of members belonging to the minority party in the House mention the other party. Since the minority party does not set the agenda in the House, one-minute speeches provide the minority a consistent opportunity to register objections on the floor. Mentioning

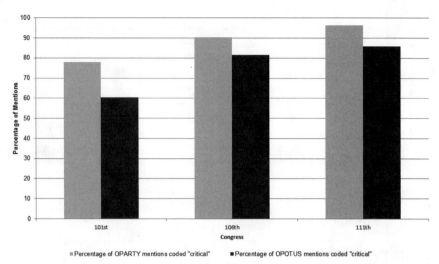

FIGURE7.5
Critical mentions of opposing party and president.

the other party has always involved a critical tone, but in the 101st Congress (1989–1990), such mentions were quite rare. In the 106th (1999–2000) and 111th (2009–2010) Congresses, "shots across the aisle" became more frequent and more critical. Finally, the most recent Congress in our sample yields an impressive statistic worth emphasizing. In 2009, when a House member in our sample mentioned the opposing party in a one-minute speech, 96.4 percent of the time it was a critical comment or argument.

When a member of the opposite party mentioned the president, how critical or negative was the remark? The percentage of critical mentions increased over time (60.4 to 81.4 to 85.7 percent). Figure 7.5 shows that a greater percentage of one-minute speeches by members belonging to the opposite party as the president mention the president than do speeches from members of the president's own party. When the results in Figures 7.4 and 7.5 are considered together, the data shed light on why presidents often remain on their end of Pennsylvania Avenue and are reluctant to venture to Capitol Hill. When presidents are talked about on the House floor during one-minutes, it is largely by members of the opposite party, and increasingly over time, those comments have been critical of the president. Members belonging to the president's party speak favorably of him, but since, in comparison, they don't speak of him very often in one-minute speeches, members of the opposing party dominate the rhetorical discourse about the president on the floor.

Figure 7.6 shows the relationship over time between the ideology of a one-minute speaker and the overall tone of one-minute speeches. The balance

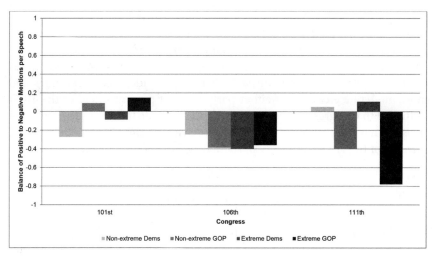

FIGURE7.6
Balance of favorable and critical mentions of the president and opposing party, by party and ideology.

indicating the tone of speeches on the *y*-axis was calculated by subtracting the number of critical mentions of both the president and the opposing party from the total number of positive mentions of both the president and the opposing party. That difference was then divided by the total number of one-minute speeches analyzed in that subpopulation to provide a "tone ratio" that can be compared across time and across ideological groupings of members. If the overall tone of the speeches is favorable, the balance is positive on the *y*-axis. If the overall tone of the speeches is critical, then the value on the *y*-axis is negative.

In 1989, Democrats were negative in tone, most likely due to criticisms of President George H. W. Bush in one-minute speeches. Republicans were positive for the converse reason. Interestingly enough, in 1999, all subgroups of members were critical in their mentions of the opposing party and the president. Democrats were critical of the Republicans, who controlled the House chamber, and that negative tone was not offset by positive affirmations about President Clinton. As mentioned, after impeachment, Clinton did not receive many positive affirmations on the House floor, even from fellow Democrats. In 2009, the ideological extreme of the House GOP grew quite negative due to the fact that the Democrats controlled the White House and the House chamber. In the 111th Congress, the GOP extremists represented a significant jump in the balance of critical versus favorable mentions in one-minute speeches. Figure 7.5 demonstrates an increase in the critical tone of one-minute speeches over time, and figure 7.6 shows that ideological extremists grew much more critical in comparison to their more ideologically moderate copartisans. This difference in tone occurred in the most recent Congress in our sample; such a large disparity between the ideological extremes and more moderate elements of either party was not present in either the 101st or the 106th Congress. It seems plausible to conclude that House one-minute speeches have grown more critical or negative over time, and the ideological extreme of the House minority party may be largely responsible for the shift.

Concluding Thoughts

Several conclusions can be drawn from the analysis of the data. Based upon the sample, there may be a relationship between the frequency of one-minute speeches and political party. That relationship is likely affected by a member's ideology. Over time, ideologically conservative members have made strategic use of the floor time provided by one-minutes. However, 2009 results indicate that such behavior may be waning as social media and technology provide communication outlets with less restriction and a lower investment of time.

Mayhew's 1974 categories of incumbent member behavior still ring true. The observations in *Congress: The Electoral Connection* remain valid four decades later. House members utilized one-minute speeches to engage in these behaviors and have done so throughout the years represented in the sample. Members have consistently used one-minutes for position taking. However, in perhaps a slightly surprising result, advertising has increased modestly. This finding is substantiated by the increase in "local" issue mentions, since "advertising" often includes a district component. Members may increasingly view their representational activities through a national policy lens, but they have not forgotten to tout local concerns or important district activities and accomplishments.

Lastly, increased polarization in Congress is not without substantial consequences. The negative tone of one-minute speeches has increased over time. Opposing party mentions of the president were always critical, but the proportion of such discourse has increased over time. It is important to note that in 1989, it was relatively rare for a member to talk about the opposing party. Such mentions had become more frequent by 1999. Combining the growth in frequency and the change in tone, the data strongly substantiates the claim that one-minute speeches have grown more negative over time. Furthermore, by examining the ideology of members who engage in one-minute speeches, we have shown that recent conservative House minority Republicans were much more negative than the more moderate wing of their party.

The question of how changing congressional rhetoric affects the operations of the institution is a good one. Increasingly negative one-minute speeches probably do not promote bipartisanship. Negotiation and compromise in politics often require trust and reciprocity, and trading barbs daily on the House floor likely mitigates such deeply held beliefs. However, as Mayhew observed, members of Congress do not operate in a vacuum. They are motivated primarily by the desire for reelection, engaging in behaviors to increase the likelihood of that outcome. In other words, negative rhetoric has increased in the House not because members necessarily prefer such discourse. Instead, members likely believe that such speech enhances their future electoral prospects. The rationale for such a calculated decision rests upon the larger complicated, competitive, and antagonistic reality of contemporary American national politics.

Note

* The views expressed herein are those of the authors and are not presented as those of the Congressional Research Service or the Library of Congress. The authors thank Greg Gelzinis for his editorial and research assistance.

References

Castor, Kathy. 2009. "Community Health Centers." *Congressional Record*, House of Representatives, 155, pt. 13 (July 8): 17052.

Chabot, Steve. 1999. "It Takes a Republican Congress to Get the Job Done." *Congressional Record*, House of Representatives, 145, pt. 10 (June 30): 14720.

Douglas, Charles G. 1989. "Congress Must Truly Fight the Drug War." *Congressional Record*, House of Representatives, 135, pt. 13 (August 3): 18541–42.

Fenno, Richard. 2000. *Congress at the Grassroots: Representational Change in the South, 1970–1998.* Chapel Hill: University of North Carolina Press.

Glassman, Matthew Eric, Jacob R. Straus, and Colleen J. Shogan. 2013. "Social Networking and Constituent Communications: Members' Use of Twitter and Facebook during a Two-Month Period during the 112th Congress." Congressional Research Service. Washington, DC: Library of Congress.

Green, Matthew N. 2013. *Underdog Politics: The Minority Party in the U.S. House of Representatives.* New Haven, CT: Yale University Press.

Harris, Douglas B. 2005. "Orchestrating Party Talk: A Party-Based View of One-Minute Speeches in the House of Representatives." *Legislative Studies Quarterly* 30: 127–41.

Lampson, Nicholas V. 1999. "Keeping Pace with Medical Technology." *Congressional Record*, House of Representatives, 145, pt. 13, July 29: 18609–10.

Maltzman, Forrest, and Lee Sigelman. 1996. "The Politics of Talk: Unconstrained Floor Time in the U.S. House of Representatives." *Journal of Politics* 58: 819–30.

Mayhew, David R. 1974. *Congress: The Electoral Connection*. New Haven, CT: Yale University Press.

Morris, Jonathan S. 2001. "Reexamining the Politics of Talk: Partisan Rhetoric in the 104th House." *Legislative Studies Quarterly* 26: 101–21.

Pearson, Kathryn, and Logan Dancey. 2011. "Elevating Women's Voices in Congress: Speech Participation in the House of Representatives." *Political Research Quarterly* 64: 910–23.

Quick, Paul, and William Bendix. 2011. "Deliberation in Congress." In *The Oxford Handbook of the American Congress*, edited by Eric Schickler, Frances Lee, and George Edwards, 550–74. New York: Oxford University Press.

Rocca, Michael S. 2007. "Nonlegislative Debate in the U.S. House of Representatives." *American Politics Research* 35: 489–505.

Schneider, Judy. 2015. "One-Minute Speeches: Current House Practices." Congressional Research Service. Washington, DC: Library of Congress.

Straus, Jacob, Matthew Eric Glassman, Colleen J. Shogan, and Susan Navarro Smelcer. 2013. "Communicating in 140 Characters or Less: Congressional Adoption of Twitter in the 111th Congress." *PS: Political Science & Politics* 46: 60–66.

Appendix

(A) Coding categories:

Advertising: Creating a favorable image of oneself but in messages with little or no issue content. These are nonpolitical messages. This is undertaken to emphasize personal qualities, such as experience, knowledge, concern, or sincerity. This is a member attempting to associate himself with positive entities, organizations, or occurrences that are nonpolitical in nature.

Credit claiming: Generating a belief that the member is personally responsible for causing the government to do something desirable. This could be for particularized benefits or general benefits.

Position taking: Public enunciation of a judgmental statement on anything likely to be of interest to political actors.

Call to action: A specific request or demand that a particular action should be taken by Congress, another government agency or entity, or the president. General calls, such as "The president must create jobs now," are included. Calls for the president or Congress to "consider" or "think" about an issue (non-action-oriented) are not included.

Please note the following caveats for the coding categories:

- These categories are not exclusive.
- All "calls to action" are inherently also "position taking." But "position taking" does not have to be marked in the positive coding of "calls to action."

(B) Geographical scope

Is the issue being discussed local, national, or international in scope? Local is coded if the district or state is mentioned, even to substantiate an argument about a national issue. Local can be regional or geographic, such as the Great Lakes region.

(C) Mentions

Was the House, the Senate, the president, Congress, the speaker's own party, or the other party mentioned in the speech? For the president, this includes references to the presidency, the White House, a specific president, or the administration. It does not include specific departments or agencies.

(D) Wonk variable

Did the speaker use statistical or empirical information to substantiate his argument? At least two statistical pieces of information need to be present.

(E) Bipartisanship

Did the speaker call for bipartisan action, or for the parties to "work together" or "come together" to achieve a purpose? The speech includes an explicit bipartisan appeal, or an explicit call for both parties to work together.

(F) Tone thermometer

When the president, the speaker's own party, the other party, the House, the Senate, or Congress (as a whole) is mentioned, is the tone either

F = favorable or positive or praising

C = critical or negative

N = neutral (only mentioned in passing)

III
SENATE

8

A Good Leader Never Blames His Tools

The Evolving Majority-Party Toolkit in the U.S. Senate

Aaron S. King, Frank J. Orlando, and David W. Rohde

"It is easy to conjure up visions of the sort of zero-sum politics parties could import into a representative assembly. . . . It should be obvious that if they wanted to, American congressmen could immediately and permanently array themselves in disciplined legions for the purpose of programmatic combat. They do not."

—Mayhew 1974, 97–98.

"The magic number in the Senate is not 60, and it's not 51—a majority. The most important number in the Senate is one. One senator. That's how it was set up. That's how our founders designed it. Every senator has the power to introduce legislation and until recently, offer amendments. . . . No single senator should be able to decide what the rights of another senator should be. That's tyranny."

—Coburn 2014, S6591.

THESE EPIGRAPHS ILLUSTRATE THE great differences between the Senate in the early 1970s and the Senate today. Over forty years ago, an expert on congressional politics had difficulty imagining a world where parties would wage war against each other. Two generations later, a senator gave his farewell speech and bemoaned the majority leader's trampling the rights of individual members. While party control has shifted back and forth a handful of times since David Mayhew's seminal work, politicians, pundits, and academics alike have watched as partisan brinksmanship and dysfunction have stymied the legislative productivity of the chamber once known as the world's most deliberative body.

Given this change, we expect members of a polarized chamber will cast roll call votes in a more partisan manner. When parties are more cohesive internally and farther apart from each other, we expect votes will frequently pit one party against the other (Rohde 1991). Yet, following ideological concerns is not what Senator Tom Coburn and experts had in mind when they complained about the institutional struggles of the upper chamber. Obstruction by the minority party has led to a massive increase in filibuster threats that hold up nominations and hamper key pieces of legislation. The majority party frequently bypasses the committee process in order to place bills on the floor with minimal alteration. Then, once bills reach the floor, the majority limits opportunities to amend legislation using a number of procedural tools. In this chapter, we focus on attempts to curtail amending activity in an effort to achieve partisan goals.

While the House developed majoritarian techniques to limit amendments, senators have historically treated the ability to offer amendments to a bill as a birthright. Using a detailed longitudinal dataset, we show that senators are losing the ability to offer and receive roll call votes on amendments, particularly those that could threaten the majority party. As a result, the majority party benefits from restricting amending activity, both in terms of passing preferred policies and in improving its members' collective and individual electoral goals. We argue that procedural tools, which senators treat differently from the substantive votes that the public can more easily comprehend, allow the majority party to block unpalatable amendments. We examine the evolution of four chief instruments of the majority-party toolkit, which changes over time in response to the institutional and political context. We conclude with an analysis of the procedural implications of the latest change in party control of the Senate.

Past Research

Though the Constitution grants the upper chamber half of the legislative responsibilities of Congress, the extant literature pays less attention to the Senate. In particular, the focus on party effects in the Senate has, until recently, been sparse. Sarah A. Binder and Steven S. Smith (1998) found that partisan and political considerations, as opposed to concern for protecting the institutional role of the chamber, drive decisions in the Senate. Andrea Campbell, Gary W. Cox, and Mathew D. McCubbins (2002) found that throughout the Senate's history, roll rates (how often a party loses a vote that succeeds) for the minority party are much higher than for the majority party. Interbranch relations exacerbate the partisan nature of the chamber, and the divide between parties grows in discussion of legislation on the president's agenda (Lee 2008). There is little doubt that the Senate parties are more ideologically diverse than parties in the House, but researchers have identified several tactics majority-party leaders use to rein in the individual freedoms that senators enjoy (Evans and Lipinski 2005).

Other research provides a longitudinal account of the transformation from an individualistic chamber to a more partisan institution (Sinclair 2005). Evidence shows the Senate parties have been infiltrated by a number of ideological "Gingrich senators," or former members of the House who were elected into the Senate, which fundamentally changed how business gets done (Theriault 2013). In the modern Senate, conflict goes above and beyond ideological disagreement as partisan teams compete for power (Lee 2009). Commentators and scholars are not the only observers taking note of increased partisanship in the Senate; stock prices of energy firms fluctuated after the Jim Jeffords switch in 2001, as the changing majority status had significant implications for a pending energy bill (Monroe and Den Hartog 2005). While the Senate still prides itself on the leverage that individual members can exert, a majority of scholars now acknowledge the growth of partisanship and the important role of political parties in the upper chamber.

The edited volume *Why Not Parties?* deals specifically with party effects in the Senate (Monroe, Roberts, and Rohde 2008). One of the more noted weapons the majority can use is the motion to table (MTT), specifically the motion to table amendments (Gold 2008; Oleszek 2014). Bryan W. Marshall, Brandon C. Prins, and David W. Rohde (1997, 1999) showed that motions to table were a favorite way to stop members of the minority from altering bills on the floor. Chris Den Hartog and Nathan W. Monroe (2008) argued that MTTs were a cost-effective way for the majority party to manipulate the agenda. While receiving less attention until recently, cloture votes have become increasingly partisan; this tool not only stops debate but also limits the ability to amend legislation (Butler and Sempolinski 2012). The tactic of "filling the amendment tree" has also gained importance in recent years (Smith 2014; Gailmard and Jenkins 2007). Richard S. Beth et al. (2009) undertake an in-depth look at the diverse tactics that the majority leadership has at its disposal and conclude that the Senate does not lack for tools, but the tools used depend on a variety of factors.

Theoretical Perspective

It is well established that parties matter in the House. Here, we join the chorus of scholars who argue that parties also matter in the Senate. Members of both chambers face many of the same incentives, and while the institutional frame-work of the Senate makes it more difficult for members of the majority party to bend outcomes in their direction than in the House, they have developed a series of tools that help to accomplish their goals. Majority-party members of both chambers prefer to protect themselves from damage the minority party wishes to inflict. The majority would like to prevent the minority from altering legislation that the majority has crafted or from passing legislation that the majority party does not prefer. The majority would also like to limit its exposure to taking stands on issues where the party and its constituents disagree.

While these incentives are more straightforward for House members who serve electorally homogenous districts, senators serving diverse electorates create a unique context. Senators represent more moderate general election constituencies than their House counterparts, and so the tension between their desire to win in November and in the primary is much greater. There-fore, party leaders must work hard to set the agenda and realize preferred policy outcomes while being attentive to the diverse electoral needs of their caucus. Party leaders can incentivize behavior by offering rewards for mem-bers who stick with the party in the face of a disappointed constituency, such as campaign funds, favored committee positions, and opportunities to climb the leadership ladder of the chamber.

The party also offers disincentives for failing to support its agenda by threatening to take away prized chairmanships, encouraging primary chal-lengers, and condemning senators with leadership aspirations to the back bench. Still, it is suboptimal for leadership to encourage senators to put reelection in jeopardy. Casting controversial votes and compiling an overly partisan voting record in a moderate state may lead to lower probabilities of reelection (Canes-Wrone, Brady, and Cogan 2002). In order to ensure pas-sage of an agenda and protect members electorally, the majority party must find a way to control the legislative agenda to avoid putting its caucus in dif-ficult situations.

In order to further their goals, majority members must move to block dangerous minority-party amendments. For example, restricting floor ac-tivity helps to keep off the agenda killer amendments that can make a bill so unsatisfactory that it will not pass, leading to an embarrassing legislative defeat (Jenkins and Munger 2003). Here it is important to reemphasize why majority-party members prefer to restrict amendments from emerging rather than simply voting them down. First, debate on the subject can consume a great deal of time that could be valuable for other legislative purposes. More importantly, however, voting on the substantive content of the amendment could leave a paper trail of a senator acting in opposition to either party or constituency preferences that could prove fatal in a future election. Voting against the party may jeopardize the party agenda and disappoint fellow partisans, while voting against the perceived wishes of one's constituents may lead to the immediate threat of removal from office after the next election. While party leaders want their agendas passed (and therefore need some level of cohesiveness), they also prefer to keep their party's members out of electoral peril. After all, loyal party members have limited use if they are ushered out of office at the end of their terms.

The ways in which managers in the party friendly House achieve this agenda control is well documented (Rohde 1991; Cox and McCubbins 1993; Aldrich 1994). Gatekeeping committee chairs and a strong Rules Committee keep damaging amendments off the floor. The public is not knowledgeable enough to understand the institutional intricacies that bar popular amendments from consideration (Fenno 1978; Farquharson 1969). Therefore, the majority party can control the flow of amendments with impunity. The Senate is quite different. Senators are much more likely to be cross-pressured than their House counterparts, as they represent far less homogenous districts. This complicates the majority's job when trying to tilt outcomes in its favor. Beyond the electoral differences between the chambers, the Senate never developed a procedure to quickly cut off debate and limit amending activity, as the House did. The possibilities for the minority to put certain majority members in tight spots are endless. In the parlance of cartel theory, majority-party senators have less negative agenda power relative to their counterparts in the House (Cox and McCubbins 1993, 2005).

While a cartel model applies directly to the House, we believe that a costly consideration model fits better with the Senate (Den Hartog and Monroe 2008). There are scarce resources available to the majority party to achieve its goals. The majority leadership must utilize its own set of skills to lower agenda-setting costs and pass legislation in as efficient a manner as possible. While these tools pale in comparison to the strength of those in the House, the Senate majority does have some strategies at its disposal to restrict amending activity, influence outcomes, and protect members of its caucus.

Procedural Tools in the U.S. Senate

We argue that the value of different tools varies based on circumstances. Cohesion, relevance, majority size, and leadership style are all relevant factors that can explain why we see different tools being used at different times. The majority party in the Senate lacks a procedural silver bullet; instead, the majority party relies on several imperfect tools to assist it in reaching its goals.

In the remainder of this chapter, we analyze the ever-changing nature of the majority-party toolkit and address four tools: motions to table amendments, budgetary points of order, cloture, and filling the amendment tree.

Motions to Table Amendments

As we have shown previously (King, Orlando, and Rohde 2012), a simple way for the majority to restrict amendments is by tabling them. A motion to table has the effect of killing the amendment. According to Senate procedure, a motion to table is privileged and must be voted on without debate. Furthermore, MTTs are not susceptible to filibuster. This means that once the MTT has been raised, there is no way for a senator to protect his or her amendment except by defeating the tabling motion. Another attractive feature of the tabling motion is that it only needs a simple majority to pass. Motions to table allow the majority to restrict amendments in an efficient manner. As with the other tools that we will discuss below, the procedural context of the MTT obfuscates the true meaning of the vote and serves to shield senators from casting unpopular votes.

Budgetary Points of Order

The motion to table is only one way the majority can restrict amending activity. A senator can raise a point of order at any time if a bill, conference report, or amendment violates a provision of several budgetary rules that govern debate on budget and appropriation matters (Saturno 2011). The common pattern involves a senator offering an amendment, followed by a member of the opposite party raising a point of order against the amendment on the grounds that it violates one of several rules, including a provision of the Congressional Budget Act of 1974, requirements of the Balanced Budget and Emergency Deficit Control Act of 1985 (Gramm-Rudman-Hollings) or the Senate Pay-as-You-Go Rule (PAYGO), or the rules laid out in the budget act for that year. Senators may raise points of order for several reasons, such as violations of the germaneness requirement, exceeding of the budget authority, failure to offset expenses properly, or creation of long-term budget deficits. If the presiding officer upholds the point of order, the amendment falls unless the provision cited in the point of order is waived. More often than not, the sponsor of the original amendment who attempts to waive the point of order is a member of the minority party.

As with the motion to table, raising a point of order is an efficient way for the majority to restrict the ability of the minority to amend bills. Consider the example of a Republican majority invoking the germaneness requirement against tacking amendments that deal with immigration onto budget or reconciliation bills as a way to keep the underlying bill on track. While raising a point of order achieves the same goal as an MTT, it may be a more attractive tool when it applies. Members can explain that they are simply supporting the integrity of the budget process when upholding a point of order. The most important advantage of the budgetary point of order is the fact that it requires a supermajority, or sixty votes, for the minority to overcome it and to proceed to consideration of the amendment (since 1985). This difference from the MTT creates two benefits for the majority party. First, it is much easier for the majority to control the agenda with forty-one votes as opposed to a majority. Second, the fact that the majority only needs forty-one votes to keep an amendment off the floor means that some of its members have more freedom to vote in line with the preferences of their constituencies on the budget-waiving vote. Where it applies, the budget waiver is an even more efficient tool than the MTT.

Cloture

While the first two tools discussed involve stopping amendments when they hit the floor, cloture is an option to stop amendments before they materialize. While cloture is best known for its ability to cut off debate, it can also be used as a part of the majority-party toolkit to restrict amendments (Beth et al. 2009). In addition to prohibiting a filibuster, cloture also saves floor time, decreases the overall number of amendments offered, and requires that those amendments be germane. Once cloture is invoked, only amendments already filed are in order. Outside a unanimous consent agreement, this is the closest parallel the Senate has to the restrictive rules of the House. Cloture restricts senators (often in the minority) from proposing amendments to derail bills and cause difficult decisions. While cloture is an extremely powerful tool, it is relatively costly, as invoking cloture requires a three-fifths supermajority.

Filling the Amendment Tree

Finally, a tactic that has been growing in popularity is referred to as "filling the amendment tree." Depending on the type of bill and degree of amendments offered, a certain number of slots are available to amend the bill. Once all of the spots are taken, the Senate must take action on the amendments already pending on the bill before allowing other amendments to be offered. It is important to note that this tactic only temporarily delays dangerous amendments from receiving consideration. There are, however, two main ways to permanently protect a bill in the case of filling the amendment tree.

First, one of the amendments filling the tree can be offered in the nature of a substitute for the entire bill. Often times, these are friendly amendments that only change the underlying bill in superficial ways. If that amendment passes, then the entire bill has been altered and can no longer be amended. This allows the bill to reach a final vote intact and protects members of the majority from having to make the difficult decisions outlined above.

The second tactic used to make the filling of the amendment tree permanent happens in concert with the cloture strategy. If cloture is filed after the tree has already been filled, no further amendments will be in order as long as the tree stays filled until the expiration of the time limit that flows from a successful cloture vote. Even if those amendments fail, no new amendments are in order to alter those parts of the bill that remain unchanged. While this tactic can sometimes prohibit members of the majority party from offering their own amendments, this tool is valuable because the amount of negative agenda control action required of rank-and-file members is minimal. In sum, each of these tools has strengths and weaknesses, depending on the political and institutional context.

Analysis

In order to undertake the longitudinal analysis necessary to study the use of partisan procedural tools in the Senate, we utilize data from the newly expanded Political Institutions and Public Choice Senate Database (Rohde 2015). The dataset includes roll calls coded by issues and vote types, which enables us to make important comparisons over time. These data covers the Senate from 1969 to 2014, or from the 91st to the 113th Congresses. In addition, our analysis includes a preliminary look at the first session of the 114th Congress (2015–2016), through December 1, 2015, to see how procedural strategies changed under the new Republican majority leader Mitch McConnell.

We have combined our data on vote types with certain vote-level characteristics, including the level of partisanship present on each vote, which signals how the leadership uses different strategies. Of course, we acknowledge that not all of the activity in the Senate takes place on the roll call record. For example, it is rather difficult to examine the practice of filling the amendment tree in our data. Throughout the analysis, we seek to mesh our large data with expert accounts of activity that takes place off the Senate floor. Still, with over eighteen thousand roll call votes, the magnitude of this dataset allows us to observe the evolution of Senate procedure over the past forty-five years. As shown in figure 8.1, the usage of these procedural tools, as a proportion of all roll call votes, varies greatly over time.[1]

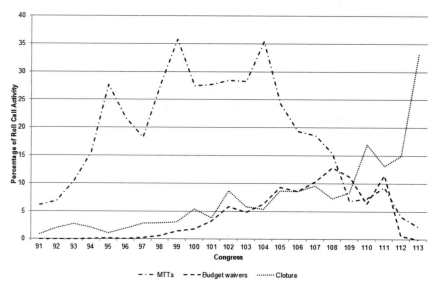

FIGURE 8.1
Usage of procedural tools in the U.S. Senate, 91st–113th Congresses.

We have made the case that the majority party uses four procedural tools (MTTs, budget waivers, cloture, and filling the amendment tree) to limit amending activity and help the party reach its collective and individual goals. Therefore, the first question we must examine is whether these votes are indeed partisan in nature. We achieve this by comparing procedural votes with votes that are substantive in character. We employ two different standards to determine how hotly contested a vote is between the parties. First, we identify party-unity votes where at least half of one party opposes at least half of the other party. Second, we utilize a higher standard of party unity, where 90 percent of one party must oppose 90 percent of the opposing party. We find that the types of votes based on party tactics are, in fact, more partisan than other votes in the Senate. In figure 8.2, we present the proportion of roll calls for each vote type that are party-unity (50–50) votes.

All types of votes are becoming more partisan over time; however, procedural votes are more partisan than final-passage votes. In fact, the last three congresses have been the most partisan in our entire dataset. This lends credence to the belief that ideological sorting has taken place over time, meaning liberal and conservative senators are more likely to belong to the Democratic and Republican parties, respectively. Yet, when one looks deeper into the data, it is clear to see that member behavior varies depending on the type of vote in question. On substantive votes that the public can easily

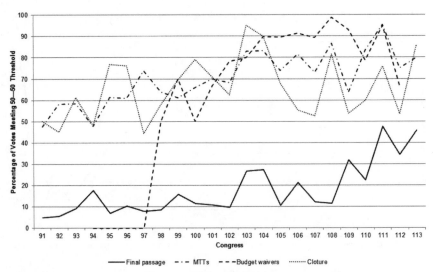

FIGURE 8.2
Partisanship on procedural votes in the U.S. Senate, 91st–113th Senates.

comprehend, there is less division between the parties. For example, on votes that determine final passage of a bill, the most partisan Congress (111th, 2009–2010) had 47 percent of roll calls meeting the 50–50 party-unity standard. Furthermore, in eleven of the twenty-three congresses we study, none of the final-passage votes met the 90–90 party-unity standard. This is not surprising according to our theory; final-passage votes leave little flexibility for cross-pressured senators. When facing a decision that will leave either one's party or one's voters disappointed, final-passage votes do not afford the sort of institutional confusion that officeholders can exploit when explaining activity to their constituents.

Is voting behavior on amendments different from that on final passage? Amendments are often less visible to constituents than the act of sending a piece of legislation to the president's desk. The data bear this out. Amending activity is clearly more partisan than final-passage activity. In the 113th Congress (2013–2014), 74 percent of amendments that received a recorded roll call met the 50–50 standard of party unity, while just over a third managed to reach the 90–90 standard. Partisanship plays a much larger role on these often contentious amendments than on the much more visible terminal vote on legislation. Still, these votes are often straightforward enough for constituents to comprehend and for opponents to exploit.

We predict that procedural votes should be even more partisan than amendment votes, and we find that the high level of partisanship on amendments is surpassed by that of procedural votes that are specifically designed to kill amendments already on the floor. In all but one of the congresses we examine (the 109th, 2005–2006), MTTs met the 50–50 party-unity standard at a higher rate than a purely policy-driven amendment vote. For the more restrictive party standard, the gap is becoming even larger. Over the last three congresses, amendments reached this threshold about one-quarter of the time. In comparison, motions to table amendments met the 90–90 party-unity standard two-thirds of the time. We observe an even stronger pattern of partisanship on budget-waiving votes. Since the 104th Congress (1995–1996), roll calls waiving budgetary points were partisan (50–50) over 90 percent of the time. In the same period, those votes have been hyperpartisan (90–90) over half of the time. The richness of our data allows us to demonstrate that these procedural tools are much more partisan than the amendments they intend to kill.

In order to show that the majority party uses tabling motions and budget waivers to achieve party goals, we must also show the majority using these tools to kill amendments it deems toxic to its agenda. We find ample evidence to support this claim. If the MTT is a tool the majority uses to protect the underlying bill and minimize the electoral risk that its members face in advancing their agendas, we should see that members of the majority party move to table amendments more often than do their counterparts in the minority. Turning to the data, this holds true in each congress we analyze. From the 102nd (1991–1992) to the 112th (2011–2012) Congresses, majority motions to table outnumbered minority motions 4:1. In the 111th Congress (2009–2010), all but one of the sixty-five MTTs originated with the majority party. Besides identifying the origin of motions to table, it is equally important to examine the targets of this procedural tool; if used for partisan gain, MTTs should disproportionately target amendments from the minority party, and our data confirm this. During the much less partisan early era of our analysis, MTTs targeted majority and minority amendments at a similar rate. Since the 96th Congress (1979–1980), however, MTTs have targeted minority amendments at an ever-increasing rate, with three attempts to kill minority amendments for every one attempt to kill a majority amendment.

Tabling motions are important procedural tools; yet this tactic is just one part of the majority-party toolkit (King, Orlando, and Rohde 2012). Next, we analyze the use of budgetary points of order. As outlined above, a senator can raise a point of order against an amendment if it violates one of several rules, such as a provision of the Congressional Budget Act of 1974, Gramm-Rudman or PAYGO requirements, or the rules laid out in a the budget act of that year. Oftentimes, the senator who offered the original amendment then moves to waive the relevant portion of the budgetary rules referenced in that point of order. The senator who offered the original amendment then moves to waive the relevant portions of the budget act holding up a vote. The chamber must agree to the motion prior to voting on the underlying amendment. Because of this pattern, we expect to see members of the minority party offering a disproportionate share of budget-waiving votes. If the budgetary point of order truly is a partisan tool, then members of the majority should use it to stop dangerous minority amendments (as a result, a minority senator would then move to waive the relevant budget rules referenced in the point of order). We see this borne out in the data. From the 102nd Congress (1991–1992), when budget-waiving activity began to increase, to the 111th Congress (2009–2010), the last to feature widespread usage of budget waivers, the dominant pattern involved a member of the minority attempting to waive a point of order raised by a member of the majority. In the 108th Congress (2003–2004), for example, seventy-nine of the eighty-five budget-waiving votes pitted a member of the minority attempting to save his or her amendment against a majority member's point of order.

It is important to remember that there is nothing stopping the minority from raising points of order or attempting to table majority amendments, but the fact that this happens less often is evidence of two important points. First, the majority is less dissatisfied with the bills that reach the floor and has less incentive to amend legislation. Second, the minority is less inclined to try to stop amendments because the majority rarely uses plenary time to force members of the minority to take stands on difficult issues. Of course, these data also reflect the fact that the majority has more votes, and so its efforts to suppress amendments via these tools are more likely to succeed.

While both of these amendment-killing strategies are part of the majority-party toolkit, each device is more useful in certain circumstances. We see that their usage varies over time, which corresponds to key institutional differences. First, the tabling motion has been around for far longer than the budgetary point of order, which was not a viable option until the mid-1980s. In addition, the budgetary point of order only applies where a senator can convince the presiding officer that a motion violates either the Congressional Budget Act or the Gramm-Rudman requirements. MTTs are in order for any amendment, including those that do not affect the budget. Although budgetary points of order are less flexible than MTTs, they have one major advantage: they require sixty votes to waive a point of order. In other words, a coalition of only forty-one senators can sustain a point of order. Majority-party members raise points of order far more often than do their counterparts in the minority. Because of the leeway that it affords to certain members while still offering a high likelihood of success, the point of order is a more efficient tool where it applies.

The data illustrate the changing usage of these tools over time. As the chamber became more partisan, the use of the motion to table grew in regularity. The earliest congresses in our dataset feature a high proportion of amending activity. When party strength in Congress was at its lowest ebb, votes on amendments made up over half of the votes per legislative session. Save for a brief resurgence in the first decade of the twenty-first century, votes on amendments fell from comprising almost three-fifths of the votes in a congress to about a third. As straightforward votes on amendments declined, tabling motions increased. In fact, an enlarged number of MTTs almost perfectly compensates for the vanishing proportion of amendments. In short, the number of amendments was consistent between the 1970s and the next two decades, but in the polarizing context of the 1980s and 1990s, a large proportion of those amendments were tabled before they could reach an up or down vote. As we have shown, minority amendments were the most likely to fall upon the table. By the 104th Congress (1995–1996), over 35 percent of recorded votes were motions to table amendments. From that point on, however, there has been a gradual decline in MTT usage.

Although budgetary points of order were a viable tool to restrict amendments from the mid-1980s, it was not until the Republican Party gained control of the Senate in 1995 that this particular instrument became a staple in the majority party's arsenal. The use of points of order against amendments accounted for around 2 percent of all roll calls in the five congresses preceding the change in majority control to over 10 percent in the five congresses after. Under the leadership of Trent Lott, Republicans felt comfortable using the efficiency of the budgetary point of order to their advantage. Predictably, when the use of one tool increases, the use of another declines. Instances of motions to table declined for important reasons. First, the amount of focus spent on issues related to the budget increased in the 1990s, which led to an increase in the opportunity to raise budgetary points of order. Second, party leaders replaced the tabling motions that they once used to kill budget-related votes with a superior tool.

Through the 109th Congress (2005–2006), motions to table and budgetary points of order were the main instruments used to keep amendments from reaching an up or down vote, but when Democrats took control of the Senate away from Republicans in January 2007, new tools surfaced. Just as a change in majority status led to the rise of the budgetary point of order in 1995, the leadership style of Harry Reid and the institutional context of the final days of the George W. Bush administration led to new tactics. While the previous tools we discussed seek to kill amendments that have already been offered, Senate Democrats sought the assistance of new tools that keep harmful amendments off the floor altogether.

Let us first turn our attention to cloture. The increased usage of this tactic is a direct result of the emergence of a more intransigent minority. While the minority party had been comfortable attempting to change policies through the amending process, polarization and the changing character of the membership of the Senate led to a minority party that became less interested in altering legislation and more interested in gumming up the works. Threatening (and actually attempting) to filibuster legislation became more and more common. As the Republicans in the minority shifted their strategy to slowing down business on the floor, Democrats countered with their own new strategy. In fact, there were nearly five hundred roll call votes on cloture between the 110th (2007–2008) and 113th (2013–2014) Congresses, which is nearly equal to the sum of cloture votes during the twelve previous congresses. Recall that cloture votes serve more than one purpose. Their primary role is to cut off debate on a topic and thus save time on the floor, but they also serve to limit the number and scope of amendments allowed on the underlying bill. Once the chamber agrees to a cloture motion, only those amendments previously filed are in order. In addition, these amendments must be germane, or relevant, to the content of the bill. The fact that cloture can restrict amendments led to several situations in which the Democratic leadership sought cloture even in the absence of an immediate filibuster threat.

When we analyze cloture votes for their partisan nature, we find that these roll calls are hotly contested and becoming more so over time. In the last Senate under Harry Reid's leadership, over half of the 218 cloture votes met the hyperpartisan 90–90 standard of party unity. With votes on cloture greatly decreasing the number of amendments offered to bills, the need to table amendments or raise budgetary points of order against them greatly diminished. In the 113th Congress (2013–2014), senators raised a paltry fifteen motions to table against amendments. Even more strikingly, there was not a single budget-waiver vote.

Once again, the increase in prominence of a new partisan tactic to restrict hostile amending activity has rendered tried-and-true tools almost obsolete. Still, cloture is far from a perfect partisan tool. After all, for the cloture motion to be successful, it requires support from three-fifths of the Senate. With a few notable exceptions, the majority party rarely reaches a filibuster-proof threshold, as it needs the help of some senators in the minority party to shut off debate and stop the flow of future amendments. It is costly and time-consuming for the majority party to invoke cloture, especially on contentious issues. While there are benefits, this strategy often proves too costly for the majority party to employ.

The last tool we analyze, filling the amendment tree, is also the most difficult to study because of the lack of roll call records associated with it. This tactic is possible because only a certain number of amendments are in order on a bill at a given time. If the tree is full, the chamber cannot consider any additional amendments to a bill. There are relatively few drawbacks to this method, save for its curtailing members of one's own party from offering their amendments in the future. The majority party also uses this tool in concert with cloture, often filling the tree prior to invoking cloture. Once the cloture motion passes, only those amendments filling the tree are in order.

Data from the Congressional Research Service (2015) indicate that the number of times that the majority party has employed this tool has increased greatly since 2006. Majority Leader Reid filled the amendment tree ninety-five times over a period of eight years. By comparison, from 1985 to 2006, the tree was filled just forty times. Still, no matter how many amendments the Democrats tried to keep off the floor, nothing could keep them from handing the gavel over to a new leader, Mitch McConnell, after the 2014 elections. Once again, a new party and leader in control have led to a reexamination of the majority-party toolkit.

Partisanship and Procedure in the 114th Senate

From 2007 through 2015, with the Senate under Democratic control, the Republican leader, Mitch McConnell of Kentucky, complained frequently about Democratic leader Harry Reid's use of procedural tools to block the Republicans from getting votes on their proposals and amendments. In particular, McConnell objected to Reid's frequent resort to filling the amendment tree. When the GOP succeeded in regaining control of the Senate in the 2014 elections, McConnell promised to restore the "regular order" in the Senate, contending, "The Senate needs to be fixed" (Weyl 2014, 5).

Among McConnell's promised revisions were relying more on committee deliberations for producing legislation for the floor and providing greatly expanded opportunities for members to offer amendments. "McConnell has made breaking what he calls the 'logjam' in Washington his No. 1 priority" (Bolton 2015, 1). In the early weeks of the new Congress, his actions reflected his promises. The first major bill, to approve the Keystone XL oil pipeline, was freely open to amendments. Indeed, an analysis by PolitiFact (a journalistic fact-checking site) indicated that the Senate had voted on more amendments in January 2015 (thirty-three) than it had in all of 2014 (fifteen) (Sanders 2015).

The pattern of the Congress's first month was not a prelude to the return to regular order that McConnell had promised. For example, in late January Senator McConnell engineered a series of votes to table Democratic amendments and refused to permit their sponsors a minute each to explain them (Lesniewski 2015). Then, as the year passed, McConnell began to resort more often to filling the amendment tree to prevent the consideration of Democratic amendments. Bills affected by this tactic included a Homeland Security appropriations bill in March, National Security Agency reform and legislation on trade promotion authority in June, and a transportation bill in July.

A McConnell spokesman indicated that the senator's objections to Reid's employing the tactic were because the frequency increased in the later years of his leadership. But, in fact, an analysis conducted by the Congressional Research Service (2015) on the number of times the Senate majority leader or his designee had resorted to filling the tree from 1985 through late September 2015 showed that the evidence did not provide clear support for this contention. Through September 2015, McConnell had filled the tree eleven times. This was more than Reid had done in any full odd-numbered year in the four congresses in which he had been majority leader. The frequency in those years was between seven and nine. On the other hand, in the four even-numbered years (when the legislative workload tends to be heavier), Reid had filled the tree between twelve and seventeen times. Whether McConnell will surpass the numbers for even-numbered years, of course, remains to be seen.

What this early account of the new Republican Senate seems to indicate is that even for leaders who profess to desire a more open and less structured process in the Senate, the demands of trying to produce legislation will create circumstances in which they feel compelled to resort to procedural devices to mitigate the ability of opponents to delay or block action.

Concluding Remarks

Through analysis of the roll call record and journalistic accounts, we have demonstrated that the majority party uses a variety of tools to restrict the minority from offering amendments that could be damaging to its policy and electoral objectives. The usage rates of these tools have changed over time based on a variety of factors. At first, strategies killed amendments already on the floor, but then new strategies emerged that enabled the majority party to preclude minority amendments from reaching the floor at all. Changes in majority-party status often lead to changes in procedural strategies; yet the tactic of using procedural tools to reach goals remains consistent. This reinforces the notion that the "tyranny" mentioned by outgoing Senator Coburn is not a Republican or Democratic issue but a majority-party issue. The tools may change, but the intent to produce outcomes desired by the majority party while protecting its electoral fortunes remains strong.

If the tools that we discussed are so valuable, why do we ever see amendments offered by the minority making it to the floor at all? In the House, after all, procedural tactics have all but eliminated dangerous amendments. First, although the tools in the Senate have many desirable characteristics for agenda control, they are not nearly as efficient or costless as those used in the House. Restrictive rules in the House that determine what amendments are in order are still the gold standard for curtailing amending activity. These special rules allow majority-friendly amendments to receive consideration, while barring others from even reaching the floor. This is not possible in the Senate. Furthermore, these special rules in the House are extremely difficult to explain to the public. While potential opponents could conceivably explain to constituents that a tabling vote in the Senate had substantive implications, it is far more difficult to do this when discussing a vote that governs debate on a bill.

Perhaps more importantly, the appetite for hard-edged procedural warfare remains greater in the House than in the Senate. Despite the evidence we present that supports the notion that the Senate is a partisan institution, we do not argue that the Senate is as partisan as the House. Although both the Republican and Democratic caucuses in the Senate have become more cohesive over the years, they are not as unified as their counterparts in the House. Senators serve more ideologically diverse districts than their House counterparts, and this tends to produce members who are more ideologically moderate. As a result, majority members in the Senate may be leery of delegating too much power to the leadership to invoke cloture or fill the amendment tree. After all, these blunt tools do not discriminate in the types of amendments that they restrict. Senators who desire to offer amendments either to alter policy or take a position will be hesitant to empower the majority leader to exercise too much control on the floor, and the majority leader has no choice but to respond to the will of his party members.

Although procedural tool usage in the Senate still pales in comparison to its usage in the House, such methods are playing an ever-expanding role in the makeup of the chamber. If the Senate continues to polarize, it will be impossible to explain behavior on the floor without understanding the tactics used by the majority party to limit the influence of the minority. As majority control shifts between parties, old instruments will continue to fade away, and new instruments will take their place. Perhaps if a tool is overused, it will become sufficiently politicized that it can no longer provide electoral cover. Perhaps a party will become cohesive and large enough to fundamentally change the rules and stack the institutional deck in its favor. No matter what the future holds, the procedural toolkit will be very valuable to the majority party in the Senate.

Note

1. It is difficult to represent the act of filling the amendment tree in relation to other tools. Because the tactic can take place outside the roll call process, we cannot include it as a proportion of recorded roll call votes. Similarly, because filling the amendment tree involves multiple procedures that may not be recorded, it is difficult to compare their degree of partisan use relative to the other tools.

References

Aldrich, John H. 1994. "A Model of a Legislature with Two Parties and a Committee System." *Legislative Studies Quarterly* 19: 313–39.

Beth, Richard S., Valerie Heitshusen, Bill Heniff, and Elizabeth Rybicki. 2009. "Leadership Tools for Managing the U.S. Senate." Paper presented at the annual meeting of the American Political Science Association, Toronto, Ontario, Canada, September 3–6.

Binder, Sarah A., and Steven S. Smith. 1998. "Political Goals and Procedural Choice in the Senate." *Journal of Politics* 60: 398–416.

Bolton, Alexander. 2015. "McConnell Grabs the Wheel in the Senate." *Hill*, January 6.

Butler, Daniel M., and Joseph Sempolinski. 2012. "Non-policy Determinants of Legislators' Procedural Votes: Evidence from Vote Switching between Cloture and the Underlying Motion." Unpublished manuscript, Yale University.

Campbell, Andrea, Gary W. Cox, and Mathew D. McCubbins. 2002. "Agenda Power in the U.S. Senate, 1877 to 1986." In *Party, Process and Political Change in Congress: New Perspectives on the History of Congress*, edited by David W. Brady and Mathew D. McCubbins, 146–65. Palo Alto, CA: Stanford University Press.

Canes-Wrone, Brandice, David W. Brady, and John F. Cogan. 2002. "Out of Step, Out of Office: Electoral Accountability and House Members' Voting." *American Political Science Review* 96: 127–40.

Coburn, Tom. 2014. "Farewell to the Senate." *Congressional Record*, Senate (daily edition), 159 (December 11): S6590–92.

Congressional Research Service. 2015. "Annual Breakdown of Instances in Which Opportunities for Floor Amendment Were Limited by the Senate Majority Leader or His Designee Filling or Partially Filling the Amendment Tree, 1985–2015." September 28.

Cox, Gary W., and Mathew D. McCubbins. 1993. *Legislative Leviathan: Party Government in the House*. Berkeley: University of California Press.

———. 2005. *Setting the Agenda: Responsible Party Government in the U.S. House of Representatives*. New York: Cambridge University Press.

Den Hartog, Chris, and Nathan W. Monroe. 2008. "Agenda Influence and Tabling Motions in the U.S. Senate." In *Why Not Parties?*, edited by Nathan W. Monroe, Jason M. Roberts, and David W. Rohde, 142–58. Chicago: University of Chicago Press.

Evans, C. Lawrence, and Dan Lipinski. 2005. "Obstruction and Leadership in the US Senate." In *Congress Reconsidered*, edited by Lawrence C. Dodd and Bruce I. Oppenheimer, 227–48. 8th ed. Washington, DC: CQ Press.

Farquharson, Robin. 1969. *Theory of Voting*. New Haven, CT: Yale University Press.

Fenno, Richard F. 1978. *Home Style: House Members in Their Districts*. Boston: Little, Brown.

Gailmard, Sean, and Jeffrey A. Jenkins. 2007. "Negative Agenda Control in the Senate and House: Fingerprints of Majority Party Power." *Journal of Politics* 69: 689–700.

Gold, Martin B. 2008. *Senate Procedure and Practice*, 2nd ed. Lanham, MD: Rowman & Littlefield.

Jenkins, Jeffrey A., and Michael C. Munger. 2003. "Investigating the Incidence of Killer Amendments in Congress." *Journal of Politics* 65: 498–517.

King, Aaron S., Frank J. Orlando, and David W. Rohde. 2012. "Beyond Motions to Table: Exploring the Majority Party Toolkit in the United States Senate." In *Party and Procedure in the United States Congress*, edited by Jacob R. Straus, 173–94. Lanham, MD: Rowman & Littlefield.

Lee, Frances. 2008. "Dividers, Not Uniters: Presidential Leadership and Senate Partisanship, 1981–2004." *Journal of Politics* 70: 914–28.

———. 2009. *Beyond Ideology: Politics, Principles, and Partisanship in the U.S. Senate.* Chicago: University of Chicago Press.

Lesniewski, Niels. 2015. "McConnell Shows He's the Boss of Openness." *Roll Call*, January 25.

Marshall, Bryan W., Brandon C. Prins, and David W. Rohde. 1997. "Theories of Legislative Organization: An Empirical Study of Committee Outliers in the Senate." Paper presented at the annual meeting of the Midwest Political Science Association, Chicago, Illinois, April 10–12.

———. 1999. "Fighting Fire with Water: Partisan Procedural Strategies and the Senate Appropriations Committee." *Congress & the Presidency* 26: 113–32.

Monroe, Nathan W., and Chris Den Hartog. 2005. "The Value of Majority Status: The Effect of Jeffords's Switch on Asset Prices of Republican and Democratic Firms." *Legislative Studies Quarterly* 33: 62–84.

Monroe, Nathan W., Jason M. Roberts, and David W. Rohde, eds. 2008. *Why Not Parties?* Chicago: University of Chicago Press.

O'Keefe, Ed. 2014. "Coburn Gives Tearful, Remorseful Farewell to the Senate." *Washington Post*, December 11.

Oleszek, Walter J. 2014. *Congressional Procedures and the Policy Process*. 9th ed. Washington, DC: CQ Press.

Rohde, David W. 1991. *Parties and Leaders in the Postreform House*. Chicago: University of Chicago Press.

———. 2015. *Political Institutions and Public Choice Senate Roll-Call Database*. Durham, NC: Duke University Press.

Sanders, Katie. 2015. "Senate Voted on More Amendments in January Than It Did in All of 2014." Politifact.com, February 2, http://www.politifact.com/punditfact/statements/2015/feb/02/phil-kerpen/claim-mitch-mcconnell-has-already-allowed-more-ame.

Saturno, James V. 2011. "Points of Order in the Congressional Budget Process." Congressional Research Service. Washington, DC: Library of Congress.

Sinclair, Barbara. 2005. "The New World of U.S. Senators." In *Congress Reconsidered*, edited by Lawrence C. Dodd and Bruce I. Oppenheimer, 1–22. 8th ed. Washington, DC: CQ Press.

Smith, Steven S. 2014. *The Senate Syndrome: The Evolution of Procedural Warfare in the Modern U.S. Senate*. Norman: University of Oklahoma Press.

Theriault, Sean M. 2013. *The Gingrich Senators: The Roots of Partisan Warfare in Congress*. New York: Oxford University Press.

Weyl, Ben. 2014. "The Tables Have Turned." *CQ Weekly*, November 6: 5–8.

9

The Electoral Politics of Procedural Votes in the U.S. Senate

Joel Sievert

IN THE FINAL WEEKS OF THE 111th Congress (2009–2010), Senate Majority Leader Harry Reid (D-NV) filed a cloture petition on the DREAM Act, an immigration reform proposal. Majority Leader Reid and his fellow Senate Democrats did not, however, expect to win this procedural battle. Earlier in the session, the Senate had failed to move forward with a similar proposal, and there was no indication that this proposal would have the votes needed to invoke cloture. Senate Democrats' primary objective was not to overcome a threatened filibuster or even to change policy; rather the cloture vote was an opportunity to "draw a clear and very public distinction between themselves and Republicans on the topic of immigration reform" (Lillis 2010). As expected, the cloture motion fell short of the sixty votes needed to invoke cloture, but it gave senators from both parties one last opportunity to affirm their position on immigration reform.

Despite the failure of the cloture motion, Senate Republicans were nonetheless displeased with Majority Leader Reid's decision to file a cloture petition in order to obtain an additional vote on immigration reform. Senator Lisa Murkowski (R-AK), who voted for the cloture motion, issued a statement criticizing the Senate majority leadership for bringing a bill to the floor that it knew would fail (Herszenhorn 2010). Republican senator from Alabama Jeff Sessions (2010, 22917) argued that it was emblematic of the Democratic leadership's behavior throughout the 111th Congress (2009–2010): "For 2 years, Democratic leaders have ignored the public. They have rammed through a lot of unpopular legislation. . . . So we are at it again, in these last hours, attempting to force through legislation that is not acceptable to the people." In his closing floor speech during debate over the cloture motion, Senator Reid (2010, 22934) fired back at Senator Sessions and the rest of the Senate Republicans with his own denunciation: "Some Republicans are trying to demonize these young men and women, who love this country and want to contribute to it and fight for it. The real faces of the DREAM Act are the dreamers." In the end, the decision to force another cloture vote on the DREAM Act largely achieved the Democratic leadership's goal of drawing a contrast between the two parties on the issue of immigration reform.

Although position taking is known to be important for members of Congress (Mayhew 1974), the decision to use a cloture vote for the express purpose of differentiating one party from another on a particular issue is surprising, given conventional accounts of procedural votes in the Senate. Prior research focuses largely on the policy consequences of the Senate's various procedural hurdles (Binder and Smith 1997; Madonna 2011; Wawro and Schickler 2007), rather than on the use of procedure for electoral politicking. The oversight can be explained, at least in part, by the fact that procedural votes are thought to be less salient than votes on amendments and final passage of legislation (Arnold 1990; Cox and McCubbins 2005; Froman and Ripley 1965). Recently, however, congressional scholars have given more attention to how, or if, the Senate majority can use procedural tactics to avoid electorally difficult votes (Carson, Madonna, and Owens forthcoming; Den Hartog and Monroe 2011; King, Orlando, and Rohde 2012; Smith, Ostrander, and Pope 2013).

Although recent studies disagree about the extent to which senators can use procedural tools to provide political cover, there is growing evidence that such cover is far from guaranteed (Smith 2014; Smith, Ostrander, and Pope 2013). Changes in the Senate's procedural environment over the last few decades, however, have led Senate leaders to adapt their strategies to find innovative ways to boost their electoral fortunes (Smith 2014). Indeed, the manner in which political opponents and the news media discuss procedural votes can have important implications for the electoral significance of these roll calls (Carson, Crespin, and Madonna 2014; Smith 2014; Smith, Ostrander, and Pope 2013). Furthermore, the Democratic leadership's action on the DREAM Act indicates that congressional leaders are willing to rely on procedural tools explicitly for the purpose of position taking.

The remainder of this chapter proceeds as follows. In the next section, I review previous research on procedural votes in Congress. From there, I outline the importance of roll call votes for electoral politics and discuss why procedural votes may have greater electoral importance than previously acknowledged. Next, I utilize several sources in order to highlight the role of procedural votes in modern Senate electoral politics. First, I discuss a series of case studies that highlight how senators, their opponents, and outside groups have used procedural votes for campaign advertisements. Second, I outline how one prominent interest group, Americans for Democratic Action (ADA), has incorporated procedural votes into its legislative scorecards over the last several decades. The primary objective is to demonstrate that votes of all types are open to interpretation and strategic misrepresentation come election season. Lastly, I conclude with general discussion about the implications of my findings.

Procedural Votes in Congress

The question of why legislators vote the way they do is of considerable interest to congressional scholars. John W. Kingdon (1989) posits that a legislator's decision is influenced by a number of factors that he or she may consider when deciding how to vote: constituent preferences, saliency, policy, and the position of party leaders both in and out of Congress. Although there will be cases in which one factor may dominate the decision-making process, legislators may have to balance multiple goals when deciding how to vote. Furthermore, changes in the context of each vote ultimately determine which considerations are brought to bear on a legislator's decision-making process. It can therefore be important to account for differences in the types of legislative proposals on which legislators are asked to vote to determine why they vote the way they do.

One important consideration is whether legislators are voting on a substantive or procedural question. Lewis A. Froman and Randall B. Ripley (1965) were among the first to systematically examine differences between legislators' votes on procedural motions and substantive votes (e.g., amendments or final-passage votes). They found that the House majority party was considerably more cohesive on procedural votes than on final-passage votes. Subsequent research on the House finds similarly high levels of party unity for votes on special rules (Monroe and Robinson 2008) and previous-question motions (Finocchiaro and Rohde 2008). These differences have led some scholars to posit that the House majority party's ability to influence policy depends on its ability to operate as a "procedural cartel" (Cox and McCubbins 2005).

The partisan nature of procedural votes is not, however, a House-specific phenomenon. Sarah A. Binder and Steven S. Smith (1997) provide evidence of a near monotonic increase in the level of partisanship on cloture votes from the 90th (1967–1968) through the 104th (1995–1996) Congresses. Frances E. Lee (2009) finds that Senate procedural votes in general, and not just cloture votes, are, on average, more partisan than votes on substantive questions. Furthermore, these differences are not the result of procedural votes being used exclusively for contentious policy issues. Lee compares procedural and substantive votes on the same policy issues and finds that procedural votes are still more partisan, even after controlling for the issue area.

What accounts for the stark differences between votes on procedural motions and substantive votes? One explanation points to the role of congressional parties. In the House, the majority-party leadership can use special rules and other procedural tools to exert influence over the legislative agenda that will benefit most members of the majority party (Cox and McCubbins 2005). It is argued that majority-party legislators will vote the party line on the procedural question even if they do not support the party's position on the substantive vote. For example, a special rule that limits amendments can serve both the electoral and policy interests of the majority party. By limiting amendments, a restrictive rule can secure policy outcomes that are not attractive to or electorally viable for all majority-party members (Jenkins and Monroe 2012; Monroe and Robinson 2008). The same rule, however, can also ensure that more moderate members are not forced to vote on amendments that might have undesirable electoral ramifications (Bach and Smith 1988).

In contrast, the Senate majority party is not able to exercise the same type of agenda control as its counterpart in the House (Smith, Ostrander, and Pope 2013).[1] Despite the Senate majority party's weaker agenda-setting power, senators' policy preferences alone do not account for the high levels of partisanship on procedural matters (Binder and Smith 1997; Lee 2009). Rather than party pressure, however, procedural partisanship in the Senate is argued to result from cooperation in order to further the party's collective interests (Crespin et al. 2015; Lee 2009) or to promote more efficiency in the legislative process (Carson, Madonna, and Owens forthcoming; Smith, Ostrander, and Pope 2013).

A second, and arguably related, explanation focuses on the saliency of procedural votes.[2] Prior studies posit that votes on procedural motions are less salient because it can be more difficult for constituents to identify the policy consequences of these votes (Arnold 1990; Cox and McCubbins 2005; Froman and Ripley 1965; Monroe and Robinson 2008). R. Douglas Arnold's (1990) concept of "traceability" is instructive for understanding the logic behind this argument. According to Arnold, an effect is not traceable unless citizens can identify an individual legislator's contribution to the observed policy effect.[3] Legislative procedure can be a particularly useful tool for leaders who want to help cover the contribution of individual legislators. Because procedural votes occur before the vote on an amendment or final passage, legislators can vote with their party on the procedural vote and then vote their electoral interests on the substantive question (Cox and McCubbins 2005; Jenkins and Monroe 2012; Monroe and Robinson 2008). Although the procedural vote was a crucial factor in making the substantive vote possible, the procedural vote adds complexity to the causal chain by introducing additional steps in the policy process. In doing so, it is argued to be more difficult for voters to identify an individual legislator's contribution to the policy outcome.

Arnold and several other studies that build on his basic framework contend that the added complexity has important electoral consequences. Specifically, these studies contend that legislators are less likely to be held electorally accountable for procedural votes than they are for substantive votes, even when a procedural vote effectively determines the final outcome (Arnold 1990; Carson, Crespin, and Madonna 2014; Monroe and Robinson 2008). In an institution where electoral pressures exert a strong influence over members' behavior, it is assumed that legislators will support their party on a procedural motion but vote against their party on passage whenever it is politically expedient (Den Hartog and Monroe 2011; Monroe and Robinson 2008).

These arguments, however, were developed to explain the procedural politics in the House, and it is not clear that the same logic can be applied to the Senate, at least not without some modifications (Smith, Ostrander, and Pope 2013). In particular, many Senate procedural votes will effectively prevent additional consideration of the bill or amendment. We can see this most clearly in the case of two commonly studied procedural tools: cloture and the motion to table. While failing to secure the sixty votes needed to invoke cloture does not, in and of itself, prevent further consideration of an amendment or bill, the most common outcome in this scenario is the defeat of the proposal.[4] In the case of the motion to table, there is no chance for additional legislative action once a proposal has been tabled, since the motion, which is not debatable, is equivalent to defeating the proposed amendment.

One effect of procedural tools that have the consequence of preventing further consideration of a proposal is that a procedural vote may be the only roll call on a given bill or subject. While senators may prefer a vote on the actual amendment or bill itself, procedural votes may become a tool for position taking, either by senators or outside groups, because they are the best option available under the existing political circumstances. Put differently, Senate procedural votes may be the only available option for both position taking and electoral branding. Indeed, the Democratic leadership scheduled an additional cloture vote on the DREAM Act precisely because it could not get a vote on passage.

Roll Call Votes and Electoral Politics

Interest in the electoral consequences of a legislator's voting behavior is understandable since roll calls are one of the most visible indications of where a legislator stands on salient issues. In this respect, roll call votes provide valuable information about how well a legislator represents constituents' interests and the types of policies he or she will pursue if reelected. Legislators and their potential opponents are therefore attentive to the reputation roll call votes project and attempt to use them to further their own electoral goals (Arnold 1990; Kingdon 1989; Mayhew 1974). Since roll call votes will ultimately be used to both promote and undermine an incumbent's electoral prospects, it should not be surprising that a legislator's voting record can have both positive and negative electoral effects.

In terms of positive benefits, roll call votes are an invaluable tool for legislators who wish to engage in position taking (Mayhew 1974). As a position-taking device, roll call votes allow legislators to claim support for issues that are popular with the public. It is important to note that the value of the position does not depend upon passing legislation. What matters is simply the opportunity to voice support for or opposition to an issue. David Mayhew (1974, 62) posits that the electoral requirement for a member of Congress is "not that he make pleasing things happen but that he make pleasing judgmental statements. The position itself is the political commodity." The important implication of this argument is that legislators have an incentive to cast multiple votes on an electorally beneficial issue, even if they know it will not change policy.

For example, since reclaiming majority control in 2011, House Republicans have held numerous votes on repealing the Affordable Care Act (ACA). The first round of votes occurred when the Democrats were still in the majority in the Senate, which means the House Republicans had no reasonable expectation that the repeal legislation would become law. Despite Republicans gaining a majority in the Senate, the House Republicans' most recent vote was still a symbolic act intended to reaffirm their opposition to the ACA, since President Barack Obama would veto the legislation if it did pass the Senate. The Senate Democrats' decision to schedule a cloture vote on the DREAM Act in the final month of the 111th Congress (2009–2010) is another example of structuring the legislative agenda purely for position-taking purposes. The important difference between these two examples, however, is that the latter involved a procedural vote, whereas the former entailed passing legislation. As noted above, the contrast between these two cases speaks to the fact that a procedural vote may be the only option available to senators who wish to take a position on a salient or electorally valuable issue.

A legislator's voting history can also harm his or her electoral fortunes (Canes-Wrone, Brady, and Cogan 2002; Carson et al. 2010). Members of Congress are concerned about and attempt to avoid being on the wrong side of a roll call vote (Arnold 1990; Mayhew 1974; Kingdon 1989). There are a number of different ways in which legislators can end up taking the incorrect position. Legislators who develop a voting record that is either too ideological (Canes-Wrone, Brady, and Cogan 2002) or too partisan (Carson et al. 2010) for their districts may be punished by voters on Election Day. Conversely, legislators from districts that are more lopsidedly partisan may be hurt electorally if they vote in support of bipartisan legislative proposals (Harbridge and Malhotra 2011) or if they are perceived as not being ideologically extreme enough.[5]

When legislators do end up on the wrong side of a roll call vote, they can expect to face difficult questions during their next electoral campaign. For example, legislators may have to address accusations that their support for party leaders, especially for the president, is out of step with their constituents' preferences. During the 2014 Senate elections, a number of vulnerable Democratic incumbents were targeted for voting with President Obama on 96 percent or more of votes on which he took a position (Lesniewski 2014). These high presidential-support scores were due in large part to the Senate majority leadership's decision to restrict amendment votes. In this case, the procedural strategy not only failed to provide coverage for vulnerable majority-party members but led them to accumulate a voting history that became an electoral liability. Not surprisingly, these incumbent senators faced a number of tough questions during their reelection campaigns and were portrayed by both their opponents and the National Republican Senatorial Committee as being in lockstep with the president (Lesniewski 2014). The strategy was successful as five of the eight incumbent Democrats that *Roll Call* identified as vulnerable failed to win reelection (Bowman 2014).

In sum, the electoral implications of a legislator's voting record are determined by one of two considerations. First, did he or she take an incorrect position on salient issues? Second, did the legislator cultivate a voting record that was not in agreement with constituents' preferences? If neither of these questions can be answered in the affirmative, a legislator may have little cause for concern. When the answer is less favorable, the chance that a legislator will be punished on Election Day can increase considerably. There is no requirement, however, that campaign communications from incumbents or challengers only use votes on substantive questions like amendments or the passage of legislation. In practice, the only requirement is that there be a vote that could plausibly support the claim one wants to make (Sellers 1998). Given that electoral campaigns are often fought in thirty- to sixty-second sound bites or in dueling press releases, it could be difficult for an incumbent to explain why a procedural vote does or does not substantiate the claim made in the campaign message.

An Electoral Side to Procedural Votes?

The argument that procedural votes are less visible and therefore not electorally costly rests on the assumption that certain types of roll call votes are treated differently in the electoral arena. It is not clear, however, that this distinction is in fact made in real-world politics (Carson, Crespin, and Madonna 2014; Smith, Ostrander, and Pope 2013). In order to demonstrate this point, it can be instructive to examine the different ways in which procedural votes are used to further electoral goals. Below, I consider two such examples.

First, electoral campaigns for the U.S. Senate are replete with messages about senators' legislative records and performances. Given the value of being able to point to specific votes or legislative actions (Arnold 1990; Grose, Malhotra, and Van Houweling 2015; Mayhew 1974; Sellers 1998), some opponents and perhaps even some senators will reference procedural votes as evidence of where the senator stands on key issues.[6] In support of this point, I document a series of cases where procedural votes appeared in candidates' and outside groups' campaign advertisements and press releases. Second, political candidates are not the only interested parties that might selectively use procedural votes to build a narrative about a senator's issue positions. Steven S. Smith, Ian Ostrander, and Christopher M. Pope (2013) found that interest groups were just as likely to include votes on the motion to table in their yearly scorecards as they were to include votes on amendments. I build on Smith, Ostrander, and Pope's analysis by examining how often interest groups included all types of procedural votes in their legislative scorecards. Interest group scorecards are particularly ideal for examining these questions because they capture the issues and votes an interest group believes were key during the previous legislative session.

Procedural Votes in U.S. Senate Campaigns

Roll call votes leave a paper trail that both supporters and opponents can use to portray an incumbent as either in or out of step with constituents. Senator's votes can be particularly important in electoral campaigns because they provide a concrete example to explain where a senator stands on an issue (Grose, Malhotra, and Van Houweling 2015; Sellers 1998). Indeed, Patrick J. Sellers (1998, 160) contends that a campaign message will be more effective when it can be tied to a candidate's legislative record and notes that these "background-supported messages" highlight the candidate's record and "indicate a history of commitment to a particular issue and position." Furthermore, the content of these messages can also be important in Senate elections because it influences what voters learn about their elected representatives (Krasno 1997).

Although many votes will not be salient enough to capture public attention when they are cast, it would be inaccurate to assume that these votes will be electorally irrelevant. If a particular vote is no longer part of the conversation about a senator's record, an opponent or an interested third party can bring it back to the public's attention prior to the election (Arnold 1990). More importantly, the meaning of a particular vote is often subject to interpretation and even manipulation come campaign season. The dubious interpretation of a vote is in fact the primary manner in which procedural votes are used to tie a candidate to a particular issue (Carson, Crespin, and Madonna 2014; Smith, Ostrander, and Pope 2013). In order to demonstrate this point more clearly, it can be helpful to look at examples from high-profile Senate elections in 2010, 2012, and 2014.

2010

In the closing month of the 2010 election, Majority Leader Reid and Republican nominee Sharron Angle were in a near statistical dead heat in the polls, with Angle enjoying a slight advantage.[7] During the last month of the campaign, Angle released a campaign advertisement with a devastating accusation that she hoped would pull her comfortably ahead of Senator Reid. The advertisement claimed that Senator Reid voted in favor of using taxpayer dollars to provide Viagra for child molesters and sex offenders.[8]

Although Angle's charge against Senator Reid was certainly attention grabbing, her claim rested on a relatively shaky reading of the roll call record. The vote in question was the result of an amendment offered by Senator Tom Coburn (R-OK) during consideration of the Affordable Care Act. Senator Coburn's amendment would have prohibited coverage of Viagra for sex offenders, but the amendment never received a direct vote. Instead, the Senate voted on a motion to table Senator Coburn's amendment, and the motion passed with fifty-seven votes in favor and forty-two votes against. Senator Reid did not in fact vote to provide taxpayer-subsidized Viagra to sex offenders; rather he voted to forgo considering an amendment on the subject. There is a clear substantive difference between what Senator Reid's vote actually did and what Angle claimed, but explaining this to voters in a concise manner could no doubt prove to be difficult.

Angle was not alone in using procedural votes to make claims about Senator Reid's legislative record. Clean Energy Works, a pro-environment group, ran a television advertisement that thanked Senator Reid for voting against a "big oil bailout worth $47 million" (Kiely 2010). The legislative action in question, however, was a vote on a cloture petition on the motion to proceed to consideration of Senator Lisa Murkowski's (R-AK) bill to block Environmental Protection Agency regulations. According to the Annenberg Center, the claim that the bill was in any way a bailout was based on suspect assumptions about the policy consequences of the bill (Kiely 2010). More importantly, Senator Reid never voted on the regulations or any purported bailout. Instead, he voted against ending debate on a motion that would allow for consideration of the legislation.

2012

In the 2010 election, the Senate Democrats lost six seats but retained their majority by a single seat. The Democrats' electoral woes were the consequence of pursuing an ambitious legislative agenda, which led to some incumbents' opting for strategic retirements or losing their reelection bids (Carson 2005). The 2010 West Virginia Senate race, however, revolved around different dynamics, as then Democratic governor Joe Manchin and the Republican nominee, John Raese, competed to fill the vacancy caused by Democratic Senator Robert Byrd's death. Although preelection public opinion polls suggested a close race, Manchin ultimately won by ten points.

The 2012 West Virginia Senate race was a rematch between Senator Manchin and Raese. Although Senator Manchin was not in office when the more controversial votes were cast in 2009 and 2010, Raese still tried to link Senator Manchin to President Obama and some of the more unpopular policies of his administration. Raese's decision made sense given West Virginians' political mood. According to the 2012 Cooperative Congressional Election Survey (CCES), only 41.41 percent of West Virginians approved of President Obama's job performance, and only 45.73 percent said they would have voted in favor of the ACA when it was passed in 2010 (Ansolabehere and Schaffner 2012).

Senator Manchin's more limited voting record and the fact that he did not vote on the ACA should have, in theory, represented a considerable challenge for the Raese campaign. In order to get around this potential setback, Raese relied upon Senator Manchin's votes on procedural motions. In the "Issues" section of his campaign website, Raese accused Senator Manchin of breaking his campaign promise to vote to repeal the ACA.[9] In this case, the vote in question was on whether to waive the Budget Act for Senate Minority Leader Mitch McConnell's (R-KY) amendment to an authorization bill for the Federal Aviation Administration. While Senator McConnell's amendment sought to repeal portions of the ACA, Senator Manchin voted not on the repeal but on whether or not Senator McConnell's amendment was germane. Similarly, one of Raese's press releases noted that Senator Manchin voted for the "liberal position" 85 percent of the time during his first two years in office.[10] The figure mentioned in the press release was based on votes compiled by the American Conservative Union. Of the seventeen votes listed in the press release, seven, or just over 40 percent, were votes on procedural motions.

What is surprising about this particular example is not that the Raese campaign relied on Senator Manchin's procedural votes for its messages but rather the extent to which it did so. It does, however, reaffirm the earlier observation that being able to point to some kind of legislative behavior is crucial for electoral campaigns. More importantly, it demonstrates that in real-world politics, the type of vote often matters little so long as it supports the broader narrative a campaign wishes to push. Indeed, this problem will only be exacerbated when a legislator has a more limited voting record.

2014

The 2010 and 2014 Senate elections share a number of similarities. For one, both elections saw the Democrats lose a sizable number of seats, with the latter leading to the first Republican majority in eight years. In both election years, a member of the Senate leadership faced a high-profile challenge. As discussed above, Senator Reid fended off a challenge from Sharron Angle during the 2010 election. In 2014, it was then Senate Minority Leader McConnell's turn to face a challenge from a well-funded opponent, Kentucky secretary of state Allison Lundergan Grimes.

Like Senator Reid before him, Senator McConnell was attacked for his vote on a procedural motion. In a July campaign advertisement, Grimes claimed that Senator McConnell had voted to increase senior citizens' Medicare costs by $6,000.[11] The accusation against Senator McConnell stemmed from his vote on the motion to proceed to consideration of a budget resolution authored by Representative Paul Ryan (R-WI). While Grimes later clarified that the $6,000 figure was based on several studies of the Ryan budget (Contorno 2014), Senator McConnell never had an opportunity to vote on the actual budget since the motion to proceed was not approved.

Senator McConnell was not the only incumbent senator up for reelection in 2014 to be attacked for a vote on a motion to proceed. In the North Carolina Senate race, the conservative political group Americans for Prosperity ran an advertisement accusing Democratic Senator Kay Hagan of taking an inconsistent position on health-care reform.[12] Americans for Prosperity's attack was based on Senator Hagan's vote against the motion to proceed to consideration of a resolution introduced by Senator Michael Enzi (R-WY).

Senator Enzi's proposal sought congressional disapproval of a rule on grand-fathered health-care plans under the ACA. While Senator Hagan's vote against the motion to proceed may indicate how she would vote on the bill, she never actually voted against the proposed change. The distinction is important since time considerations or general legislative efficiency, rather than policy considerations, can determine how senators vote on these types of procedural motions (Oppenheimer 1985; Smith, Ostrander, and Pope 2013).

Procedural Votes and Interest Group Ratings

Interest groups' legislative scorecards are intended to help identify which members of Congress are "friends" and which are "foes" of a particular organized interest (Fowler 1982). Since these groups focus on a limited set of votes relative to the full roll call record, it should not be surprising that interest groups will at times use procedural votes to characterize a senator's position on important issues (Smith, Ostrander, and Pope 2013). The primary contribution of this analysis is that it examines how often an interest group incorporates procedural votes into its legislative scorecards without taking into account the relationship between a specific procedural vote and its substantive counterpart. Such an examination makes it possible not only to assess the generalizability of Smith, Ostrander, and Pope's findings but also to examine the strategic choices interest groups make when constructing legislative scorecards.

In order to explore this question, I examined two sets of voting scores from the 97th (1981–1982) to the 113th (2013–2014) Congresses. The first set of votes comes from Americans for Democratic Action, a liberal organization whose scores attempt to quantify a legislator's overall liberalism.[13] The second set of votes are *Congressional Quarterly's* (CQ) key votes, which are votes CQ identifies as being the most influential votes in a given congress.[14] I include CQ's key votes for comparative purposes and to provide an approximate baseline for the overall saliency of procedural votes in a given congress. After identifying the votes that each group considered to be the most important in a given congress, I calculated the proportion of votes that were procedural in nature.[15] Figure 9.1 shows the proportion of each group that were procedural votes.

Overall, the ADA frequently uses votes on procedural motions to construct its legislative scorecards. During the more than three decades examined here, approximately 44 percent of the roll calls identified by the ADA were procedural in nature. Furthermore, there were four congresses in which procedural votes accounted for at least half of the ADA's key votes. Although there is

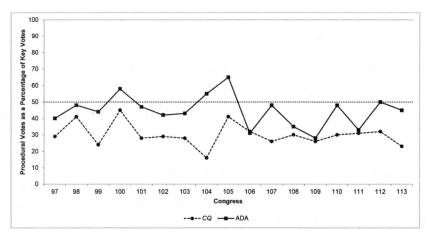

FIGURE 9.1
Procedural votes as percentage of key votes.

variability in how often the ADA utilizes procedural votes, the proportion is never less than 25 percent in any of the congresses examined here.

It is also instructive to compare the ADA scorecard with the *CQ*'s key votes. There is only one congress, the 106th (1999–2000), in which the ADA's scores include a lower proportion of procedural votes than the *CQ*'s key votes. The difference is quite small—only 1.2 percent—and is not substantively meaningful. Furthermore, the mean difference between the proportion of ADA and *CQ* key votes that are procedural is just over 14 percent across these seventeen congresses. In short, interest groups rely on procedural votes to identify "key votes" more than would be expected relative to a nonpartisan measure of the importance of procedural votes.

The calculations reported in figure 9.1 also mask some additional differences between the ADA scores and the *CQ* key votes. For example, votes on the motion to table and the motion to waive budgetary points of order were found more frequently in the ADA legislative scorecards than in the *CQ* key votes. A vote on the motion to table accounted for approximately 20.3 percent of the ADA's votes but just 12.8 percent of the votes identified by the *CQ*.[16] Similarly, a vote on budgetary points of order constituted 5.6 percent of the votes cataloged by the ADA, which was more than double the rate, 2.4 percent, at which the *CQ* included these votes in its key votes.

In sum, these differences suggest that interest groups may rely on procedural votes to sort out "friends" from "enemies" more than would be expected based on the saliency of procedural votes alone. Interest groups rely on procedural votes to identify "key votes" more than would be expected relative to a nonpartisan measure of the importance of procedural votes. In short, these time series provide additional evidence that senators cannot count on legislative procedure to insulate them from manipulation and subjective interpretations of what counts as a liberal (or conservative) position or a vote in favor of a specific issue.

Conclusion

Although congressional scholars frequently assume that legislative procedure can provide political cover for members of Congress, each of the examples discussed above runs counter to prior arguments about how this coverage should work in practice (Arnold 1990; Den Hartog and Monroe 2011). Indeed, these cases demonstrate that the additional complexity of procedure is hardly sufficient to insulate senators from electoral consequences. If anything, the complexity of legislative procedure may in fact make it easier for opponents and other interested parties to define a senator's voting history. For example, the accusation that a senator voted with party leaders over 90 percent of the time is easy to make in a campaign advertisement, press release, or speech. It can be a more difficult task, however, to come up with a concise explanation that many of these votes were procedural and might not carry the same policy repercussions as other votes. Rather than attempt to explain away their votes, senators may instead point to other legislative actions that demonstrate their stance on the issue.

Overall, the evidence presented here raises important questions about the idea that senators gain political coverage using the various procedural tools at their disposal. First, the Senate's rules themselves might make some procedural votes a viable and attractive option for position taking or for tying an incumbent to an unpopular issue. Since a number of the Senate's procedural motions effectively prevent additional consideration of a legislative proposal, the procedural vote will often be the only roll call on a given issue. Second, both Senate candidates and interest groups use procedural votes to build a narrative about a legislator's voting history and issue positions. These examples demonstrate that the connection between a roll call and the policy position it is said to represent may be tenuous at best and that all parties recognize the importance of finding *a vote* to corroborate their claims. Furthermore, it can be difficult for a candidate to explain the intricacies of and provide the proper context for a procedural vote. As such, there is little reason to expect Senate candidates to stop using these votes in campaign communications.

While the case studies about the use of procedural votes in electoral campaigns examined recent elections, the analysis of interest group scores indicates that the electoral side of procedural votes is not a recent development. Indeed, groups like the ADA have relied on procedural votes over the last three decades to identify their friends and enemies more than would be expected based solely on the importance and saliency of procedural votes alone. Furthermore, there is little reason to expect that these patterns will not be evident in earlier periods with regard to the divisive issues of the day. For example, during the 1960s, the ADA routinely included any cloture votes on civil rights legislation in its yearly scores. These votes fit squarely with the expectation that legislators and interest groups will be more likely to rely on Senate procedural votes for position-taking purposes because these will be the only votes on given issues.

These findings have several implications for broader issues related to the relationship between members of Congress and the public. If procedural votes are used to explain a senator's legislative positions, then we may have reason to be concerned about the quality of information constituents receive. Although some of these votes will likely reflect a senator's actual position on an issue, they can also distort a senator's legislative record. For example, the use of procedural votes to calculate how often an incumbent voted with party leaders will likely provide a biased measure of certain incumbents' issue positions. More importantly, these results suggest that these inaccuracies can have real consequences for incumbents come election time.

Notes

1. But see King, Orlando, and Rohde (2012) and chapter 8 for a discussion about how the Senate majority party may be able to use different procedural tools to exercise some level of agenda control.

2. The two explanations are related in that members of Congress are more likely to defer to party leaders precisely because procedural votes are less salient (Arnold 1990; Carson, Crespin, and Madonna 2014; Cox and McCubbins 2005; Froman and Ripley 1965).

3. A visible contribution by a legislator is one of three conditions Arnold (1990, 47–49) identifies as necessary for traceability. The other two conditions include a perceptible policy effect and an identifiable government action. All three conditions must be met in order for traceable effects to be present.

4. In the 112th Congress (2011–2012), there were thirty-two instances in which the Senate failed to invoke cloture and only three cases, out of five attempts, where the cloture motion was successful on reconsideration. During the 113th Congress (2013–2014), there were thirty-one cloture petitions that failed and only six successful attempts to invoke cloture upon reconsideration. In these two congresses, a failed cloture motion was the last legislative action for the proposal in question over 80 percent of the time.

5. The House and Senate incumbents, including then House majority leader Eric Cantor (R-VA), who recently faced primary challenges for not being "conservative enough" are illustrative on this point.

6. Grose, Malhotra, and Van Houweling (2015) found that when contacted about immigration reform, a number of senators highlighted their votes on a cloture motion to offer support for their stated position on the issue.

7. According to Real Clear Politics, in the polls over roughly the last month of the election, from October 1, 2010, onward, the average for Senator Reid and Angle were 45.64 and 47.64, respectively. "Nevada Senate—Angle vs. Reid," Real Clear Politics.

8. Angle, "Big Clue."

9. Raese for Senate. "West Virginia Senate Issues."

10. Raese for Senate. "West Virginia Senate Campaign News."

11. Grimes. "Question from Don—Retired Coal Miner."

12. Americans for Prosperity, "Tell Kay Hagan ObamaCare Hurts North Carolina."

13. Although it might be preferable to include more groups, particularly more issue-specific scores (e.g., the National Rifle Association), obtaining these votes over the full time span was not possible. Several groups either do not have publicly available archives of their scorecards or will only release their scorecards to dues paying members.

14. CQ has only compiled key votes through the first session of the 113th Congress. As such, the calculations reported in figure 9.1 are only for votes cast during the first half of the 113th Congress.

15. The following types of votes were coded as procedural votes: cloture, motion to table, motion to proceed, motion to recommit, motion to reconsider, germaneness, point of order, motion to waive the Budget Act, ruling of the chair, motion to instruct, and motion to suspend the rules. The following types of votes were coded as substantive votes: amendment, conference report, passage, veto override, nomination, treaty, and resolution.

16. In their analysis, Smith, Ostrander, and Pope (2013) compare the proportion of votes on amendments against the proportion of votes on the motion to table and conclude that interest groups use both types of votes at comparable rates. While this conclusion is not fully replicated in this analysis, the ratio of amendment to motion to table votes is much lower for the ADA than for CQ. Over 33 percent of the ADA's key votes were on amendments, which is 1.5 times more than the proportion of votes on the motion to table. In contrast, almost 27 percent of the votes CQ identified were amendments, which is more than twice the proportion of votes on the motion to table. As such, these data still support the general observation that interest groups focus more on motions to table votes than would be expected based on the saliency and importance of these votes alone.

References

Americans for Prosperity. "Tell Kay Hagan ObamaCare Hurts North Carolina." YouTube. https://www.youtube.com/watch?v=jODEmS_J_ho (accessed March 5, 2015).

Angle, Sharron. "Big Clue." YouTube. http://youtu.be/B5pK3TNsx8g (accessed March 5, 2015).

Ansolabehere, Stephen, and Brian Schaffner. 2012. "Cooperative Congressional Election Survey, Common Content 2012." Handle.net, http://hdl.handle.net/1902.1/21447.

Arnold, R. Douglas. 1990. *The Logic of Congressional Action*. New Haven, CT: Yale University Press.

Bach, Stanley J., and Steven S. Smith. 1988. *Managing Uncertainty in the House of Representatives: Adaptation and Innovation in Special Rules*. Washington, DC: Brookings Institution Press.

Binder, Sarah A., and Steven S. Smith. 1997. *Politics or Principle? Filibustering in the United States Senate*. Washington, DC: Brookings Institution Press.

Bowman, Bridget. 2014. "What Happened to 2014's Most Vulnerable Senators?" *Roll Call*, November 5.

Canes-Wrone, Brandice, David W. Brady, and John E. Cogan. 2002. "Out of Step, Out of Office: Electoral Accountability and House Members' Voting." *American Political Science Review* 96: 127–40.

Carson, Jamie L. 2005. "Strategy, Selection, and Candidate Competition in U.S. House and Senate Elections." *Journal of Politics* 67: 1–28.

Carson, Jamie L., Michael H. Crespin, and Anthony J. Madonna. 2014. "Procedural Signaling, Party Loyalty, and Traceability in the U.S. House of Representatives." *Political Research Quarterly* 67: 729–42.

Carson, Jamie L., Gregory Koger, Matthew J. Lebo, and Everett Young. 2010. "The Electoral Costs of Party Loyalty in Congress." *American Journal of Political Science* 54: 598–616.

Carson, Jamie L., Anthony J. Madonna, and Mark E. Owens. Forthcoming. "Regulating the Floor: Tabling Motions in the U.S. Senate, 1865–1946." *American Politics Research*.

Contorno, Steve. 2014. "Did Mitch McConnell Vote to Raise a Senior's Medicare Costs by $6,000?" Politifact.com, July 10.

Cox, Gary W., and Mathew D. McCubbins. 2005. *Setting the Agenda: Responsible Party Government in the U.S. House of Representatives*. New York: Cambridge University Press.

Crespin, Michael H., Anthony Madonna, Joel Sievert, and Nathaniel Ament-Stone. 2015. "The Establishment of Party Policy Committees in the U.S. Senate: Coordination, not Coercion." *Social Science Quarterly* 96: 34–48.

Den Hartog, Chris, and Nathan W. Monroe. 2011. *Agenda Setting in the U.S. Senate: Costly Consideration and Majority Party Advantage*. New York: Cambridge University Press.

Finocchiaro, Charles J., and David W. Rohde. 2008. "War for the Floor: Partisan Theory and Agenda Control in the U.S. House of Representatives." *Legislative Studies Quarterly* 33: 35–61.

Fowler, Linda L. 1982. "How Interest Groups Select Issues for Rating Voting Records of Members of the U.S. Congress." *Legislative Studies Quarterly* 7: 401–13.

Froman, Lewis A., and Randall B. Ripley. 1965. "Conditions for Party Leadership: The Case of the House Democrats." *American Political Science Review* 59: 52–63.

Grimes, Allison Lundegran. "Question from Don—Retired Coal Miner." YouTube. http://youtu.be/HnG72T6t3-s (accessed March 5, 2015).

Grose, Christian R., Neil Malhotra, and Robert Parks Van Houweling. 2015. "Explaining Explanations: How Legislators Explain Their Policy Positions and How Citizens React." *American Journal of Political Science* 59: 724–43.

Harbridge, Laurel, and Neil Malhotra. 2011. "Electoral Incentives and Partisan Conflict in Congress: Evidence from Survey Experiments." *American Journal of Political Science* 55: 494–510.

Herszenhorn, David. 2010. "Senate Blocks Bill for Young Illegal Immigrants." *New York Times*, December 18.

Jenkins, Jeffery A., and Nathan W. Monroe. 2012. "Buying Negative Agenda Control in the U.S. House." *American Journal of Political Science* 56, no. 4: 897–912.

Kiely, Eugene. 2010. "'Bailout' Baloney." FactCheck.org, July 2, http://www.factcheck.org/2010/07/bailout-baloney (accessed December 1, 2015).

King, Aaron S., Francis J. Orlando, and David W. Rohde. 2012. "Exploring the Procedural Toolkit of the Majority Party in the United States Senate." In *Party and Procedure in the United States Congress*, edited by Jacob R. Straus, 173–94. Lanham, MD: Rowman & Littlefield.

Kingdon, John W. 1989. *Congressmen's Voting Decisions*. Ann Arbor: University of Michigan Press.

Krasno, Jonathan S. 1997. *Challengers, Competition, and Reelection: Comparing Senate and House Elections*. New Haven, CT: Yale University Press.

Lee, Frances E. 2009. *Beyond Ideology: Politics, Principles, and Partisanship in the U.S. Senate*. Chicago: University of Chicago Press.

Lesniewski, Niels. 2014. "Vulnerable Senate Democrats Almost Always Voted with Obama." *Roll Call*, October 27.

Lillis, Mike. 2010. "Reid Files Cloture as House Poised to Vote on DREAM Act." *Hill*, December 7.

Madonna, Anthony J. 2011. "Winning Coalition Formation in the U.S. Senate: The Effects of Legislative Decision Rules and Agenda Change." *American Journal of Political Science* 55: 276–88.

Mayhew, David. 1974. *Congress: The Electoral Connection*. New Haven, CT: Yale University Press.

Monroe, Nathan W., and Gregory Robinson. 2008. "Do Restrictive Rules Produce Nonmedian Outcomes? A Theory with Evidence from the 101st–108th Congresses." *Journal of Politics* 70: 217–31.

"Nevada Senate—Angle vs. Reid." Real Clear Politics. http://www.realclearpolitics.com/epolls/2010/senate/nv/nevada_senate_angle_vs_reid-1517.html (accessed March 5, 2015).

Oppenheimer, Bruce I. 1985. "Changing Time Constraints on Congress: Historical Perspectives on the Use of Cloture." In *Congress Reconsidered*, edited by Lawrence C. Dodd and Bruce I. Oppenheimer, 393–413. 3rd ed. Washington, DC: CQ Press.

Raese for Senate. "West Virginia Senate Campaign News." http://www.raeseforsenate.org/index.php/category/west-virginia-senate-campaign-news (accessed March 5, 2015).

———. "West Virginia Senate Issues." http://www.raeseforsenate.org/index.php/category/west-virginia-senate-issues (accessed March 5, 2015).

Reid, Harry. 2010. "Recognition of the Republican Leader." *Congressional Record*, Senate, 156, pt. 15 (December 18): 22933–34.

Sellers, Patrick J. 1998. "Strategy and Background in Congressional Campaigns." *American Political Science Review* 92: 159–71.

Sessions, Jeff. 2010. "The Dream Act." *Congressional Record*, Senate, 156, pt. 15 (December 18): 22916–17.

Smith, Steven S. 2014. *The Senate Syndrome*. Norman: University of Oklahoma Press.

Smith, Steven S., Ian Ostrander, and Christopher M. Pope. 2013. "Majority Party Power and Procedural Motions in the U.S. Senate." *Legislative Studies Quarterly* 38: 205–36.

Wawro, Gregory J., and Eric Schickler. 2007. *Filibuster: Obstruction and Lawmaking in the U.S. Senate*. Princeton, NJ: Princeton University Press.

10

Partisanship, Filibustering, and Reform in the Senate

Gregory Koger

ONLY THE U.S. SENATE CAN make the outbreak of nuclear war seem ordinary. On November 21, 2013, the majority leader of the Senate, Harry Reid (D-NV), brought up the nomination for Patricia Ann Millett to the District of Columbia Court of Appeals, which had previously been blocked by a Republican filibuster. After a brief debate, Reid (2013, S8417) raised a point of order that "the vote on cloture under rule XXII for all nominations other than for the Supreme Court of the United States is by majority vote." Within minutes, senators affirmed Reid's argument by a 52–48 vote and cleared the path for simple majority cloture on nominations. Boom! The Democrats had just exercised the "nuclear option" to make a major change in the way the Senate works.

In order to appreciate the significance of this event, we must first understand the Senate filibuster, competition over the Senate agenda, and the contest over executive and judicial nominations in a partisan environment. In context, the events of November 21, 2013, mark a significant development in the history of the Senate. This chapter begins with a discussion of agenda setting: the goals and strategies of the majority party and the available responses of the minority party. Next, I apply this framework to the Senate and explain how the majority and minority parties in the Senate compete for partisan advantage, while they cooperate to run the chamber. In recent years, this has motivated an argument over the right of senators to filibuster, culminating in the "nuclear option" of November 21, 2013.

Partisan Agenda Setting: Goals and Strategies

Congressional parties strive to steer the agenda of the U.S. House and Senate to issues and proposals that provide them with political advantage. The leaders of the majority party have three agenda-setting strategies. First, they try to help party members develop *individual portfolios* of issue positions and personal accomplishments to help their personal bids for reelection. Second, leaders seek to maintain and expand the *coalition* of organized groups and demographic subsets that support their party; toward this end they schedule proposals to show support for these groups' policies, even if the legislation is not enacted into law. Third, leaders seek to maximize the *reputation*, or "name brand," of their party so that voters develop long-term loyalties or short-term biases toward their party (Cox and McCubbins 1993; Egan 2013; Pope and Woon 2008, 2009), at least on specific issues (Petrocik 1996).

One implication of the first goal is that party leaders may be very selective about which issues come up for a vote at all. A vote against a popular proposal or a powerful interest group can be used against party members in the next election cycle, so the best way to win the battle is to avoid it altogether. Second, the majority party may try to maximize its relative brand advantage over the opposing party by scheduling proposals that are popular, supported by the majority party's coalition, and opposed by some portion of the minority party's base coalition. These "wedge" issues force minority-party members to either cast an unpopular vote or disappoint some of their core supporters—perhaps leading to a challenge in their next party primary.[1] For example, Democratic majorities might schedule a bill to raise the minimum wage, which is typically very popular among Democratic and independent voters and often supported by many Republican voters as well. In one instance the Republican majority in the House scheduled dozens of votes to repeal or restrict the 2010 Affordable Care Act (or ObamaCare) in the belief that Republican and independent voters were highly opposed to the law while Democrats were only mildly supportive.

Finally, party leaders have an interest in addressing major national problems (e.g., the financial crisis of 2008) and meeting basic obligations like appropriating funds for government operations and raising the debt limit to avoid default; failure to do so could damage the majority party's reputation severely. For example, as discussed by Walter Oleszek in chapter 15, a disagreement over government funding in September and October 2013 led to a major shift in party reputation. At the beginning of this dispute, the two parties were essentially tied on the generic ballot polling question "Would you rather vote for the Republican or the Democrat in the next Congressional election?" The Democrats gained an advantage of about eight percentage points after three weeks of a government "shutdown," which occurs when the federal government's fiscal year begins on October 1 and there are no funds to pay for the continued function of an agency.[2] The shutdown—and accompanying media attention and competition between the parties to explain their perspectives on the breakdown in governance—provides a clear illustration of how a failure to govern effectively can affect a party's reputation.

Filibustering and Party Agenda Setting

While the majority party's goals are similar in the U.S. House and Senate, its power to set the agenda varies tremendously. In the House, the majority-party leaders enjoy a set of procedural advantages that enable them to dictate which issues come up, when they will be debated, and which amendments will be allowed. This can lead to much greater efficiency than in the Senate but also means that major legislation—such as the landmark health-care reform law of 2009–2010—often passes after a few hours of debate and just a single opportunity to amend the bill.

The majority party of the Senate, on the other hand, has limited power to set the chamber agenda. The Senate majority controls the committee system, which is an important incubator of policy proposals. For complex legislation such as the annual defense policy authorization bill, committees have real influence because they provide a forum for drafting the proposal for the Senate floor.

However, once a bill is ready for the Senate floor, the majority party has very limited power to determine if, when, and how that bill is debated. By tradition, the majority leader of the Senate enjoys the "right of first recognition" from the Senate's presiding officer.[3] This means that if the majority leader and any other senator stand up at the same time to make a motion, the presiding officer calls on the majority leader first. On its face, this gives the majority party agenda-setting powers similar to those of its House counterpart: its party leaders can propose bills for consideration, and a simple majority is required to approve these agenda-setting motions (Den Hartog and Monroe 2011). Unlike in the House, however, a motion to consider a bill is debatable. "Debatable" means that the motion is vulnerable to an organized effort by a senator or team of senators to debate it indefinitely, or threaten to do so. This is known as a filibuster.[4]

Filibustering in the Senate

Filibustering or obstructing is strongly associated with the U.S. Senate.[5] It is a staple of Senate lore that the practice of filibustering has been tolerated since its earliest days. Yet the filibuster of today is a far cry from the obstruction of the nineteenth century and the first half of the twentieth century (Koger 2010). Today's filibuster requires much less effort. Senators do not consume the time of the chamber with endless speeches or repeated votes on procedural questions; they simply threaten to do so and force the other legislators to overcome a filibuster that never actually happens. The rest of the Senate usually responds by attempting to use the Senate's "cloture" rule to impose a limit on debate.

Because it has gotten easier to filibuster over the last fifty years, obstruction has become so commonplace that it is built into the standard operating procedure of the Senate. Over the same period, senators have been increasingly likely to vote with their parties and against members of the opposing party (Koger and Lebo, forthcoming; Theriault 2008). While obstruction is not inherently partisan—filibusters have been waged by single legislators, a fraction of one party, or a bipartisan group based on common views—the ability of the minority party to filibuster has led to mixed incentives for senators. The Senate has a set of rules that forces senators to cooperate across party lines if they wish to accomplish anything; yet it is more and more difficult for senators to cooperate, if doing so means that the other party gains a public relations "win."

Senators, including the minority party working as a team, filibuster for four basic reasons. First, they simply object to the bill or nomination the majority party has proposed and wish to keep it from becoming law or to block it. This explanation is all too obvious because it is our default explanation for why senators filibuster and blinds us to the other uses of this power. The second reason is that senators hope the majority party will revise its bill to make it more acceptable to the members of the minority party. A team of senators might, for example, filibuster a farm program reauthorization bill they generally like in order to get better treatment of a sector they represent, such as wheat farms or dairy producers.

A third reason senators might filibuster a bill is to ensure adequate deliberation. In the contemporary Senate, this often happens when senators want a chance to offer amendments relevant to a bill, which they will block unless they get this opportunity. For senators, amendments are a tool both of policy (from the perspective of senators offering amendments, they "improve" the bill) and of politics. An amendment is a tangible sign of a senator's interest in an issue and his or her active participation in the legislative process. It is also a mechanism to force every other senator to publicly support or propose a specific policy.

Our fourth and final reason is similar: senators—particularly from the minority party—often filibuster to force a different issue onto the Senate's agenda. For example, a Republican majority might propose a reduction in business taxes, and the Democratic minority might counter by filibustering until the Republicans agree to also hold a vote on raising the minimum wage. This is more likely to occur when the minority party perceives that the majority party is proposing a bill that is purely political—intended to enhance the majority party' s reputation at the minority party's expense—and thus counters with its own "message" bill (Evans and Oleszek 2001). Or a subgroup of senators may filibuster to force action on a bill that the majority party is blocking because the majority party is internally divided on the proposal. For example, in June 2015 the Senate debated a bill to delegate "trade promotion authority"—a guarantee that any trade deals negotiated by the president would be approved or disapproved by a simple majority vote in both chambers of Congress without amendment. A subset of senators joined a filibuster even though they supported the bill. They bargained with Majority Leader Mitch McConnell (R-KY) to get a bill reauthorizing the Export-Import Bank onto the Senate agenda, and McConnell acquiesced.

Majority-Party Responses to Filibustering

In order to overcome these threats to waste time, majority leaders have four basic options: attrition, cloture, bargaining, and reform. For most of congressional history, legislators preferred to respond to time-wasting behavior by waiting it out: let the obstructionists talk until they are exhausted and give up, then win. This strategy of attrition, depicted in the 1939 movie *Mr. Smith Goes to Washington*, was effective as long as the majority had time to waste and remained near the Capitol in case there was a vote or quorum call. It was doubly effective because senators were often deterred from filibustering because they knew it was politically risky and physically difficult to do. However, by the mid-twentieth century the Senate (as an organization) and individual senators no longer had the spare time to outlast filibusters, even on crucial issues like civil rights (Koger 2010). In exasperation, they began to respond to filibusters with a procedural option that had lingered in the Senate rule book since 1917: cloture.

Cloture, a second option to respond to obstruction, is a process for limiting debate on a motion, bill, treaty, or nomination as provided in Senate Rule XXII. In order to invoke cloture, the majority party must (1) submit a petition to the Senate clerk with the signatures of sixteen senators who desire the limit on debate; (2) vote on the petition at noon on the second day after the petition is filed (so a petition filed on Tuesday receives a vote on Thursday); and (3) persuade sixty senators to vote for cloture unless, as discussed below, it is a cloture vote on a nomination for any position except the U.S. Supreme

Court.[6] If the majority party wins its cloture vote, then the debate on the motion or measure is limited in three ways: (1) all amendments must be "germane," or pertinent, to the measure on the floor; (2) each senator is limited to one hour of floor time; and (3) total floor debate is limited to thirty hours.

When discussing the Senate's cloture rule, most senators, scholars, and media focus on its supermajority threshold, noting that if any one senator threatens to filibuster, three-fifths of the Senate must agree to limit debate, or progress is stalled. But this overlooks the delay inherent in the rule. A measure can be filibustered multiple times—on the motion to bring it to the floor, on any key amendments, on passage, on motions to hold a conference committee with the House or to agree to the House's revisions to the measure, and on final approval of a conference report. At each step, it is possible that the Senate will have to go through the ritual of petition, wait, vote, and then "debate" for thirty hours. Thus the rule not only allows a minority of forty-one senators to filibuster indefinitely but allows a single senator to impose an exorbitant cost in Senate floor time to adopt a single measure. For most of the Senate's history, this power to extend debate within the Senate rules was rarely used to its maximum extent, but senators have reportedly been more likely to do so since 2008.

As figure 10.1 shows, roll call votes on cloture increased significantly from 2007 to 2013 and then skyrocketed in 2014. The number of cloture votes in

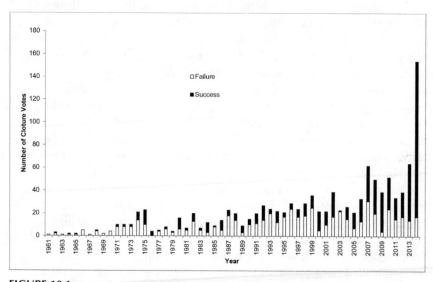

FIGURE 10.1
Annual cloture votes by outcome, 1961–2014.
Source: http://www.senate.gov/pagelayout/reference/cloture_motions/clotureCounts.htm

a year is not necessarily indicative of the level of obstruction; there may be filibusters that are resolved in some other way, or the Senate may vote on cloture even without a filibuster threat. More precisely, figure 10.1 illustrates the extent to which a majority responds to perceived threats by attempting to invoke cloture instead of bargaining or reforming.

The third possible majority response to obstruction is bargaining. Indeed, this is the primary reason that senators have preserved the right to filibuster: it forces them to bargain with each other. Historically, this has meant that senators can bargain for a more open floor debate, including votes on a wide range of amendments, and for changes in the substance of legislative proposals to make them acceptable to a broader coalition of senators (Koger 2010).

In recent years, it has become increasingly difficult for senators to arrive at legislative compromises. The underlying reason is probably that the partisan differences between states represented by each Senate party have grown. That is, there are fewer Democrats representing states that support a Republican candidate for president (and vice versa) than in previous years. It also means that the difference has increased in the Republican presidential vote shares of states represented by a typical Senate Democrat and a typical Senate Republican. This pattern is exhibited in figure 10.2, which shows the difference between the mean Republican presidential vote share in states represented by

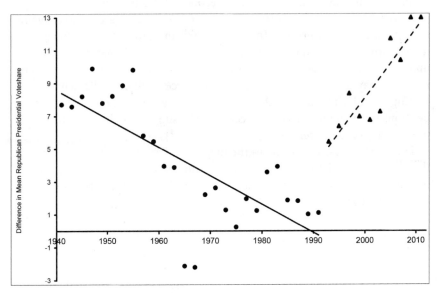

FIGURE 10.2.
Constituency polarization in the U.S. Senate.

Senate Democrats and Senate Republicans. Notably, this difference narrows for more than five decades from 1940 to 1992 (shown as dots with a solid trend line), then increases sharply from 1992 to 2010 (triangles with a dotted trend line).

This increasing difference in the constituencies of the Senate parties makes it more difficult for senators to reach compromise. In policy terms, it may be impossible for the majority party to craft legislation that satisfies the prefer-ences of its most ideologically pure members and the "moderate" members of the minority party. In political terms, the members of the minority party may find that they pay a political price for "collaborating with the enemy" by agreeing to a compromise, when in the past such bargaining was considered an act of reasonable statesmanship. Some combination of these factors made it impossible for Senate Democrats to entice a single Republican to support the Affordable Care Act when it passed the Senate in 2009 and 2010, despite con-siderable effort by Senate Finance Committee chairman Max Baucus (D-MT).

The increasing difficulty of bargaining also applies to the agenda-setting process. Since motions to proceed are "debatable," any individual senator can threaten to filibuster a bill unless she is allowed to offer her amendment(s) for a roll call vote. Collectively, the minority party can threaten to completely block a bill unless its members have ample opportunity to offer amendments. These demands are potentially costly to the majority party in two ways: First, the floor votes take up the time of the Senate and force senators to actually spend time in the Senate chambers. Second, majority-party members may wish to avoid voting on a proposal if the roll call vote can be used against them in the next campaign. In recent years, these negotiations have often moved slowly or stalled completely, so a single major bill may require several unanimous consent agreements to come to the Senate floor, or the major-ity party may attempt to invoke cloture to force a bill onto the Senate floor. During the 113th Congress (2013–2014), for example, 32 of the 220 cloture petitions were on motions to proceed to a bill, suggesting that this frustration was a common occurrence.

The fourth option available to the majority party is to reduce or eliminate the ability of legislators to filibuster. The next section discusses the conflict over Senate filibuster reform in depth, so here I will simply make some gen-eral observations.

Ultimately the majority of the Senate determines its rules. Article I of the Constitution states, "Each House may determine the rules of its proceedings." In the Senate, the conventional method for altering the rules is the Senate resolution, a type of legislation that is internal to the Senate. These resolu-tions can be filibustered, and the cloture threshold for a rules change is a little higher than the bar for all other items: two-thirds of all senators voting.[7]

However, these rules are subject to interpretation, and there are some questions that are outside the rules. For both reasons, senators are able to raise parliamentary points of order during the Senate's daily proceedings. The Senate's presiding officer announces a ruling on these questions, and then these rulings are subject to a simple majority vote to sustain or overturn the ruling. In fact, the House eliminated its filibuster in the early 1890s, beginning with a revolutionary precedent that nullified the primary methods of filibustering in January 1890 (Koger 2010). Such an action, should it ever occur, would serve to limit or eliminate obstruction by simple majority vote (Koger and Campos 2014).

Obviously, the fact that a simple majority of the Senate can end filibustering does not mean that the Senate should end filibustering or that it wants to. The case for majoritarianism is obvious: if a minority is blocking a majority from passing its proposals, the frustrated majority will presumably want to limit the right to filibuster so that its proposals will pass. But this rarely happens, and thus far no Senate majority has ended filibustering altogether. There are multiple reasons:[8]

1. For most of the Senate's history, filibustering was fairly rare, and majorities could usually overcome opposition and pass their legislation (Wawro and Schickler 2004; Koger 2010). Thus the incentive to restrict filibustering was low.
2. Filibusters during the era of attrition-based "talking" filibusters were a mechanism for intense minorities to have extra influence in the legislative process.
3. Even today, senators appreciate the ability to have special influence as individuals on their personal priorities.
4. Filibustering prevents the majority party from enacting extreme or highly partisan measures. This increases policy stability (the country does not lurch from right to left and back again as party fortunes vary) and protects members of the majority party for the demands of their party base.
5. Filibustering prevents the majority party from constraining floor debate for political purposes. In the U.S. House, the majority party has the procedural power to limit floor discussion and amendments to ensure that its priority legislation passes with a minimum of criticism and its members can avoid politically difficult votes, while the minority party often has little opportunity to bring up and articulate its own agenda. When senators say they do not want their chamber "to become like the House," this is one of the patterns they seek to avoid.
6. Even when they are in the majority, senators express reluctance to take away the benefits they enjoy while in the minority.

These defenses of the filibuster do not convince every senator. Some senators and outside observers have consistently supported reforms in Senate rules to abolish or limit the right to filibuster. For organized groups, support for cloture reform seems to increase as their policy agenda is blocked in the Senate. For senators, interest in cloture reform seems to wax and wane as their party's fortunes change. They even joke that they should print out a single set of talking points for each side and just swap them when there is a switch in majority status.

Filibuster Reform in the Senate, 2003–2015

From 2003 to 2015, senators engaged in a long-running debate over filibuster reform, with an escalating interest in ending obstruction in the Senate. During this period, the Senate majority party was the same as the president's party, except during the 110th Congress (2007–2008), with periods of unified government from 2003 to 2006 and 2009 to 2010. Filibusters against major legislation during these periods of unified government slowed the majority party's pace and forced the majority party to moderate its proposals (e.g., the Democrats reducing the size of their 2009 stimulus proposal), but both Republican and Democratic majorities were able to pass major agenda items when the majority party was internally united.

However, Senate consideration of presidential nominations has been much more conflictual. The U.S. Constitution states that the president shall nominate individuals for posts in executive agencies and for federal judicial positions, and the Senate shall "advise and consent" to these nominations. In other words, the president proposes names for the Senate to reject or accept. There is a critical distinction between judicial and executive nominations: once approved, judges retain their positions until they die, retire, or are impeached and removed by Congress, while most executive nominations expire when the nominating president leaves office.[9]

There are several reasons nominations have rarely faced filibusters in the past. Traditionally, presidents have consulted with senators before making nominations. For decades, senators have had a norm of supporting each other's objections if the president ignores a senator's views (Binder 2007). Once made, however, a nomination is not subject to "amendment," so filibustering is rarely needed to secure adequate floor deliberation. Furthermore, it seems that only a few nominations are filibustered because senators think the nominee is unqualified or will otherwise do a poor job.

Recently, however, nominations have become a common target for obstruction for several reasons. First, it has become easy. Beginning in the 1950s, the Senate developed a routinized system for senators to "hold" legislation and nominations from the floor for a few days while they studied committee reports, prepared floor amendments, or returned to the capital (Koger 2010, 173–76). In effect, a hold expressed opposition to a unanimous consent agreement on a measure. Senators have used holds for many purposes, as Walter Oleszek (2008, 1–2) explains: "There are so-called *informational* holds, where Senators wish to be informed or consulted before a measure or nomination is brought to the floor; *revolving* or *rotating* holds, where one Senator, and then another and so on, will place holds; *Mae West* holds, which suggest that the Senator(s) who employed the hold wants to bargain with the proponents of the legislation or nomination; *retaliatory*, or *tit-for-tat*, holds; and *choke* holds, where the objective is to kill the affected bill or nomination."

From 2003 to 2014, senators were highly likely to place revolving or choke holds on executive nominations. In placing holds, senators may wish to impede the work of agencies whose missions they oppose (e.g., Republicans seeking to delay actions by the Environmental Protection Agency during Democratic presidencies [Ostrander 2015]). Nominations have also served as a form of hostage taking using "Mae West" holds. Senators of the opposition party have been especially likely to place holds on executive nominations to bargain for information, agency decisions, or commitments from nominees about their future actions. For example, in 2005 and 2006 Senators Patty Murray (D-WA) and Hillary Clinton (D-NY) blocked two nominations for director of the Food and Drug Administration to force the agency to make a decision on whether "Plan B" birth control would be available without a prescription (Koger 2010, 191–92).

The use of holds to monitor and oversee agencies has probably been especially valuable to senators because the Senate's use of another classic monitoring device, the annual appropriations process, has increasingly been abandoned in favor of omnibus spending bills negotiated off the Senate floor (Hanson 2014). However, the cumulative effect of these holds has been very damaging to the nominees themselves, who sometimes wait months for the Senate to act for reasons that have nothing to do with their own qualifications. This has led to a "tragedy of the commons," in which the rational decisions of individual senators prove destructive to the agencies the Senate is trying to monitor and to the pool of qualified candidates for public service.

Judicial nominations have also been a frequent target for holds and floor filibusters. Senators have obstructed judicial nominees to influence the ideological balance of the federal bench in a specific district or an appellate circuit court region.[10] This obstruction is of special political significance because the federal judiciary has become a battleground for ideological and issue-oriented interest groups (Scherer 2005), particularly since the defeat of Robert Bork's

Supreme Court nomination in 1987 (Basinger and Mak 2012). These groups seek to advance their political agendas through the courts or to block other groups' legal strategies. Like the audience at a grade school fistfight, they egg on their respective champions and criticize weakness, moderation, and compromise.

The contest over judgeships reached a crisis point between 2003 and 2005. From 1995 to 2002, much of the contest over judicial nominations was focused on the Senate Judiciary Committee, which has jurisdiction over the nominations. During this period the majority party could slow down the process by acting slowly—or not at all—on judicial nominations. In 2003, however, the opposition party had to filibuster on the floor if it wanted to block nominations. The Democrats blocked ten appellate nominations (out of a total of thirty-four) despite repeated cloture votes on these nominees. This outraged the Republicans, who considered this obstruction a break with recent practice.[11]

The Republican majority in the 109th Congress (2005–2006), bolstered by a gain of four seats in the 2004 election, signaled that it would no longer accept obstruction of judicial nominations. Specifically, it expressed willingness to vote for a parliamentary ruling to end filibusters, which Republicans called the "constitutional option" because it ensured the Senate would fulfill its institutional obligation to consider nominations, while Democrats called this approach the "nuclear option" because this tactic would "blow up" the Senate in acrimony and retaliation (Koger 2008, 169). After some negotiations, Senate Majority Leader Bill Frist (R-TN) scheduled a critical vote on a judicial nomination on May 13, 2005: either the Democrats must give in, or the Republicans would eliminate the right to filibuster judicial nominations. In the end, a group of senators dubbed the "Gang of 14" arrived at a deal to avert the critical vote: three of five blocked judges would come to a final vote and pass, two would be blocked, and future nominees would only be filibustered in "extraordinary circumstances" (Koger 2008, 171). This agreement paved the way for the approval of two new Supreme Court justices in the summer of 2005: Chief Justice John Roberts and Samuel Alito.

Hold Reform

The "Gang of 14" agreement calmed the ferment for major reform for a while but did not address the underlying tragedy of the commons: senators were still free to hold nominations off the Senate floor anonymously for reasons other than concerns about the nominee's qualifications. At the time, Senator Trent Lott (R-MS), the majority leader, described senators' use of holds as "the most corrosive thing going on in the Senate right now" (Taylor

2006). This led to a series of actions to reduce the use of holds by making them public, with the hope that this would limit senators to holds they could publicly explain and defend.

In 2007 and 2011, the Senate adopted reforms to end the use of secret holds. First, in 2007 a provision of a broader ethics and lobbying reform bill required a senator to publicly declare his or her hold if (1) a party leader had blocked a measure on his or her behalf, and (2) six days had passed since the objection was made (W. Oleszek 2010). In other words, a hold would remain secret if the majority leader did not act on another senator's behalf or the senator who placed the hold did so for less than six days. Senators could evade this requirement by trading the hold on a bill or nomination with an allied senator. In 2011, the Senate adopted a standing order requiring senators to submit a statement to the *Congressional Record* for every hold request transmitted to a party leader, regardless of the duration of the hold or whether it would lead to delay on the Senate floor (M. Oleszek 2015).

Nominations and Cloture Reform

The Democratic success in the 2008 elections led to a period of unified government with large majorities—from 57 to 60 percent—in the House and Senate during the 111th Congress (2009–2010). Democrats and their supporters had high expectations for their legislative agenda; in modern politics, this was a rare window of opportunity to shift government policy. The Republicans, however, settled upon a strategy of strong opposition to the Democratic agenda, including obstruction of virtually every piece of major legislation. Two pieces of landmark legislation—the 2009 stimulus and the Dodd-Frank financial reform bill—passed with the support of a minimal number of Republicans, while the Affordable Care Act passed the Senate without Republican votes during a short period when the Democrats had a majority of sixty senators. Other Democratic agenda items, like additional stimulus measures, modest campaign finance reform, and possibly climate change legislation, were stifled in the Senate for lack of sixty votes for cloture.

Senate Democrats complained that the Republican obstruction was novel in two ways. First, some of this obstruction seemed to be purely strategic, based on politics rather than policy. Legislators pay a political price for co-operating as a party but benefit from legislative success (Carson et al. 2010; Koger and Lebo 2012; Lebo, McGlynn, and Koger 2007), so Republicans would come out ahead if they forced the Democrats to stick together as a party while minimizing their legislative accomplishments. An especially note-worthy example was the failure of a proposed deficit-reduction commission in January 2010, in which the critical votes against the proposal came from

Republican senators who had previously expressed their support by cosponsoring the measure (Rogers 2010).

Second, the Republicans seemed to be dragging out debates on issues as long as possible with the goal of consuming the overall supply of floor time on as few measures as possible. For example, the Republicans sometimes insisted on using up their entire allotment of fifteen hours of debate time after cloture had been invoked, even if there was no actual senator interested in speaking or offering amendments. Instead, the Senate would remain in session for hours, idly counting for a quorum. Or the Republicans extended the amending phase of a bill both by demanding a large number of amendments and also by agreeing to a limited number of amendments on any given day. The debate on the Dodd-Frank financial reform bill, for example, was extended for weeks by slow bargaining over floor debate agreements (Koger 2012). As for nominations, the Senate voted twelve times on whether to invoke cloture on nominations, with only one nomination defeated after a failed cloture vote: that of Craig Becker, nominated to the National Labor Relations Board (NLRB).[12]

The 112th Congress (2011–2012)

These complaints led to calls for reform (U.S. Congress 2010) at the start of the 112th Congress (2011–2012). Reforms included making holds public, reducing the number of nominations requiring Senate approval by about one-third, and eliminating the requirement that amendments be read aloud if they have been made publicly available (Koger 2011). Informally, Reid and McConnell agreed to refrain from filibusters against motions to proceed to measures, from Reid's "filling the amendment tree" to prevent other senators from offering amendments, and from altering the Senate rules by "nuclear option."

The 2010 elections brought two major changes to the Senate: a Republican majority in the U.S. House and the election to the U.S. Senate of a few Tea Party Republicans who were determined to resist President Barack Obama's agenda but also to remain independent of the Republican party leadership. The change in the House majority party meant that the Senate Republicans were no longer the greatest impediment to the Democratic agenda; the House majority party enjoys nearly total control over the chamber agenda. Divided party control of Congress led to a sharp reduction in legislative productivity, with major legislation often passing only after crisis bargaining over debt-limit increases, annual spending bills, or extension of the 2001/2003 Bush tax cuts.

Nominations remained a flash point for the Senate. There were only eleven votes on cloture for nominations, but cloture was rejected on six of these votes, and four nominations were defeated: those of three judges and the proposed director of the Consumer Financial Protection Bureau (CFPB). Out of frustration, President Obama used his recess appointment power to install the defeated CFPB director, Richard Cordray, and to fill three empty seats (out of five) on the NLRB during a short break in congressional activity (Cooper and Steinhauer 2012).[13]

The 113th Congress (2013–2014)

The Democrats retained the majority in the Senate after the 2012 election and returned to Congress with growing interest in reducing the effects of obstruction. Like Bill Frist in 2005, Harry Reid expressed the sentiments of many of his party members by threatening to "go nuclear" unless the Republicans agreed to make changes in the way the Senate operates (Raju 2013). This led to negotiations with Mitch McConnell, which yielded a package of incremental reforms (Koger 2013):

- Reducing postcloture debate time on executive nominations from thirty hours to eight, except for the most important positions[1]*
- Reducing postcloture debate on district court judges to two hours*
- Streamlining the process for holding a conference committee with the House on a bill, so it requires a single cloture vote (not three), two hours between filing and voting (not two days), and zero postcloture debate
- Two alternative agenda-setting methods: (1) a filibuster-proof, simple majority motion to proceed to a bill, provided the minority party has the unconstrained ability to offer two amendments,* and (2) a shortened cloture process on a motion to proceed if the cloture petition is signed by the minority-party leader and seven minority-party members

Notably, several of these reforms are focused on the time lags built into Rule XXII instead of on changing the cloture threshold. For low-level executive and judicial nominations, the critical question is not whether there are enough votes to overcome a filibuster but whether it is worth the Senate's time to do so. These reforms altered the equation for nominations and conference committees.

The reforms did not end partisan tension in the Senate. In February, Charles Hagel's nomination as secretary of defense failed one cloture vote only to survive another twelve days later. In March, Caitlin Halligan's nomination to the DC Circuit Court was blocked 51–41 and withdrawn by the

---

* Expired at the end of the 113th Congress (2013–2014).

White House. At about the same time, Rand Paul (R-KY), "filibustered" John Brennan's nomination as director of the Central Intelligence Agency by taking to the floor to speak against the nomination (with help) for over twelve hours (Ewing 2013).

In July 2013, Democratic frustration once again led to threats to use the "nuclear option" unless there were real changes in the nomination process. McConnell agreed to a tactical retreat, allowing votes on nominations for Cordray as director of the CFPB, for two new NLRB board members, and for the secretary of labor and director of the Environmental Protection Agency (Sanchez and Lesniewski 2013). This truce, however, was purchased with the tears of Republican moderates, who had to vote for cloture on controversial nominations in order to stave off Democratic reform. These votes were unpopular with conservative activists, and because multiple incumbent Republicans had been defeated in primaries since 2010, displeasing party activists could be career ending.

By late October 2013, the nominations process was stalled again. Cloture votes on four nominations failed: that for Mel Watts as director of the Federal Housing Finance Agency and three nominations for the DC Circuit Court. The revival of Republican obstruction triggered a nuclear option by the Democratic majority. On November 21, 2013, Reid moved to return to the nomination of one of the stalled DC judges, Patricia Ann Millett, then made a point of order that a simple majority was required to invoke cloture on all nominations other than those for the Supreme Court. The presiding officer, following the rules and precedents of the Senate, rejected this claim, but the presiding officer's ruling was subject to a simple majority vote. In a pair of 52–48 votes, the Senate supported Reid's "interpretation" of Rule XXII's three-fifths cloture threshold. Every Republican and three Democrats opposed Reid's interpretation, but the majority succeeded in changing the way the Senate works.

Nuclear Fallout

The immediate effects of the reform were clear: the Senate cleared a backlog of controversial nominations, starting with Millett and holding seventeen more cloture votes on nominations in the next eight weeks, with each nomination gaining cloture with fewer than sixty votes.

Did the Republicans retaliate? Remember that it is called the "nuclear option" because the minority party will retaliate with its remaining weaponry, leading to mutually assured destruction. The Republicans played their part in this narrative. While they could no longer block a nomination by mustering forty-one votes against it, they could require the majority party to invoke cloture on any and every nomination passing through the Senate, including many that would have previously gained approval without a roll call vote. Before 2013, the highest number of cloture votes on nominations in a year was the seventeen votes held in 2003. Then nineteen votes before the Senate "went nuclear" on November 21, 2013. From that day to the end of the 114th Congress (2015–2016), there were 131 cloture votes on nominations—more than the 112 votes total in the previous ninety-six years. Including votes on approval of nominations, 254 of the 366 Senate roll call votes in 2014 pertained to nominations. That is, just 30.7 percent of all 2014 votes were related to the other responsibilities of the Senate.[14]

What is the future of the Senate filibuster? The 2013 nuclear option transformed the debate over the filibuster in two ways. First, it took the critical topic of nominations off the table. This was an especially contentious issue with intense interest group lobbying for and against the right to obstruct nominations. Filibustering is still possible against Supreme Court nominations and most legislative proposals. These issues also arouse intense interest by outside groups, but senators tend to recognize the value of allowing obstruction on these issues due to the higher stakes—especially for Supreme Court nominations—and the role of obstruction in limiting the magnitude of policy changes and ensuring some degree of deliberation.

Second, the 2013 change laid bare the fragility of the Senate filibuster: it illustrated that a simple majority of senators can restrict filibustering whenever they choose. They do not need the previous-question motion used in the U.S. House, they do not have to wait until the first day of a new Congress, and they do not need the blessing of the Senate parliamentarian. They just need a simple majority of votes to establish a new precedent in the Senate. While I have long argued that this is the case (Koger 2002; Koger and Campos 2014), it was not universally acknowledged until the Senate's 2013 action.

As a consequence, the remainder of the Senate filibuster will be quickly criticized whenever a minority impedes a measure that is popular or supported by influential interest groups. At present, conservative Republican actors outside Congress have been calling for further limits on obstruction, and they have been joined by a few members of the U.S. House (Drucker 2015), even though changing Senate rules during the 114th Congress (2015–2016) will probably have zero effect on policy outcomes as long as the president is able to veto legislation. If the 2016 election results in another period of unified government, however, it is likely that the majority party in the Senate will be pressured by the rest of its party to do whatever it takes to ensure the passage of the party's agenda.

Conclusion

We live in very exciting times if you are interested in Senate parties and procedure. The current Senate is the flashpoint for two powerful forces: partisanship and tradition. The two major parties in the Senate have increasingly similar constituencies and cooperate to advance their policy agendas and electoral interests. As in the House, this makes control of the chamber's agenda—that is, deciding which issues come to the floor—a matter of intense interest and competition.

Unlike in the House, however, the minority party in the Senate retains the ability to block majority-party legislation, while individual senators have the power to waste a great deal of the chamber's time. This power stems from senators' ability to filibuster measures—to waste time, perhaps indefinitely. Senators use this power not only to block measures but to bargain for modifications to bills, to ensure their ability to offer amendments, and to bring new issues onto the Senate's agenda.

The Senate filibuster has been under attack for over a decade, particularly in the area of nominations. This is inevitable, as the two political parties find it harder to achieve compromises on legislation and nominations. This has led to a series of "Halt or I'll shoot" exchanges in which the majority party threatens to unilaterally limit the ability to filibuster unless the minority-party members refrain from obstruction and agree to some procedural reforms. On November 21, 2013, the Senate Democrats imposed the right to limit debate on almost all nominations except those for the Supreme Court. This leaves open the possibility of future reforms to restrict or eliminate the Senate filibuster.

Notes

1. However, in the interest of coalition maintenance, a majority party may advance controversial legislation that is demanded by a core constituency as a condition of its support in the next election. During the 111th Congress, this dynamic played out as Latino and business leaders sought comprehensive immigration reform and labor union leaders insisted that passage of the Employee Free Choice Act was the reward for their support during the 2008 election.

2. Polling data is available at "2014 Generic Congressional Vote," Real Clear Politics, http://www.realclearpolitics.com/epolls/other/generic_congressional_vote-2170.html.

3. The "presiding officer" is the person who monitors the floor discussion, calls on senators to speak, keeps track of debate time and the daily schedule, and makes decisions about parliamentary disputes, although these disputes are subject to ap-

peal. The U.S. Constitution designates the vice president of the United States as the Senate's presiding officer but allows the Senate to select a "president pro tempore" for those times when the vice president is not in the Senate. In modern practice, the vice president almost never presides over the Senate, only showing up for high-profile debates or to break a tie vote. The president pro tempore is customarily the most senior member of the majority party (Orrin Hatch, R-UT, in the 114th Congress) and usually delegates the tedious task of sitting through Senate sessions to a more junior senator.

4. More broadly, filibustering is the strategic use of delay in a legislative chamber. While the Senate filibuster is commonly associated with prolonged speaking because that was the most common tactic of the mid-twentieth century, my book on the subject describes and measures filibustering accomplished by repeatedly forcing votes on procedural motions or amendments or by refusing en masse to vote to deprive the chamber of a quorum (see Koger 2010).

5. Yet during the nineteenth century filibustering was prevalent in the U.S. House and has occurred in dozens of state and foreign legislatures.

6. The Senate can revise these requirements by unanimous consent. As noted below, the threshold for cloture on a rules change is two-thirds of those voting.

7. This threshold was set in 1959 for all legislation. When the threshold for ordinary legislation was reduced to three-fifths of the entire Senate in 1975, senators retained the higher bar for rules changes, presumably to discourage future reform efforts. In theory, two-thirds of those voting could be as few as two-thirds of a quorum of the Senate (one-half), so thirty-four senators. In modern practice, attendance is rarely so low that two-thirds voting is less than three-fifths of the Senate.

8. For a longer discussion of the arguments for and against the Senate filibuster, see Koger (2010, 189–200) and Senate Committee on Rules 2014.

9. Other executive positions, such as memberships on the Federal Reserve Board, are for fixed terms.

10. In a few cases, the party opposed to the president may block appellate nominees who are prospective Supreme Court nominees. Republicans claimed this was the case with Miguel A. Estrada.

11. But not completely unprecedented. The 1968 nomination of Abe Fortas for chief justice was defeated by a bipartisan filibuster (Koger 2010, 108).

12. For comparison to other new presidents, there were zero cloture votes in 1989–1990 (G. H. W. Bush), twelve in 1993–1994 (Bill Clinton), and four in 2001–2002 (G. W. Bush).

13. The Supreme Court later invalidated the appointments, stating that Congress was not in a long-term "recess." (*National Labor Relations Board v. Noel Canning et al.*, 573 U.S. ___, 2014).

14. The focus on nominations also reflects the electoral strategy of the Senate Democrats, who sought to insulate their incumbents from a poor national environment (midterm election, low presidential approval ratings) by "localizing" the 2014 elections. Part of that strategy was avoiding controversial policy debates on the Senate floor.

References

Basinger, Scott J., and Maxwell Mak. 2012. "The Changing Politics of Supreme Court Confirmations." *American Politics Research* 40: 737–63.

Binder, Sarah A. 2007. "Where Do Institutions Come From? Exploring the Origins of the Senate Blue Slip." *Studies in American Political Development* 21: 1–15.

Carson, Jamie, Gregory Koger, Matthew Lebo, and Everett Young. 2010. "The Electoral Consequences of Party Loyalty in Congress." *American Journal of Political Science* 54: 598–616.

Cooper, Helene, and Jennifer Steinhauer. 2012. "Bucking Senate, Obama Appoints Consumer Chief." *New York Times*, January 4, A1.

Cox, Gary W., and Mathew D. McCubbins. 1993. *Legislative Leviathan: Party Government in the House.* Berkeley: University of California Press.

Den Hartog, Chris, and Nathan W. Monroe. 2011. *Agenda Setting in the U.S. Senate: Costly Consideration and Majority Party Advantage.* New York: Cambridge University Press.

Drucker, David M. 2015. "Republican Fluster over Filibuster." *Washington Examiner*, September 23.

Egan, Patrick J. 2013. *Partisan Priorities: How Issue Ownership Drives and Distorts American Politics.* New York: Cambridge University Press.

Evans, C. Lawrence, and Walter Oleszek. 2001. "The Procedural Context of Senate Deliberation." In *The Contentious Senate: Partisanship, Ideology, and the Myth of Cool Judgement*, edited by Colton C. Campbell and Nicol C. Rae, 107–27. New York: Rowman & Littlefield.

Ewing, Philip. 2013. "Rand Paul Pulls Plug on Nearly 13-Hour Filibuster." *Politico*, March 6.

Hanson, Peter. 2014. *Too Weak to Govern: Majority Party Power and Appropriations in the U.S. Senate.* New York: Cambridge University Press.

Koger, Gregory. 2002. "Obstruction in the U.S. House and Senate: A Bicameral Analysis of Institutional Choice." PhD diss., University of California, Los Angeles.

———. 2008. "Filibustering and Majority Rule in the Senate: The Contest over Judicial Nominations, 2003–2005." In *Why Not Parties?*, edited by Nathan Monroe, David Rohde, and Jason Roberts, 159–77. Chicago: University of Chicago Press.

———. 2010. *Filibustering: A Political History of Obstruction in the House and Senate.* Chicago: University of Chicago Press.

———. 2011. "Senate Reform? Still Possible." *Monkey Cage*, February 2, http://the-monkeycage.org/2011/02/senate_reform_still_possible.

———. 2012. "The Filibuster Then and Now: Civil Rights in the 1960s and Health Care, 2009–10." In *The U.S. Senate: From Delay to Dysfunction*, edited by Burdette A. Loomis, 159–77. Washington, DC: CQ Press.

———. 2013. "Proposed Senate Reforms: Recap and Discussion." *Mischiefs of Faction*, January 24, http://www.mischiefsoffaction.com/2013/01/proposed-senate-reforms-recap-and.html.

Koger, Gregory, and Sergio Campos. 2014. "The Conventional Option." *Washington University Law Review* 91: 867–909.

Koger, Gregory, and Matthew Lebo. 2012. "Strategic Party Government and the 2010 Elections." *American Politics Research* 40: 927–45.

———. Forthcoming. *Strategic Party Government: Why Winning Trumps Ideology.* Chicago: University of Chicago Press.

Lebo, Matthew, Adam McGlynn, and Gregory Koger. 2007. "Strategic Party Government: Party Influence in Congress, 1789–2000." *American Journal of Political Science* 51: 464–81.

Oleszek, Mark J. 2015. "'Holds' in the Senate." Congressional Research Service. Washington, DC: Library of Congress.

Oleszek, Walter J. 2008. "'Holds' in the Senate." Congressional Research Service. Washington, DC: Library of Congress.

———. 2010. *Congressional Procedures and the Policy Process.* 3rd ed. Washington, DC: CQ Press.

Ostrander, Ian. 2015. "The Logic of Collective Inaction: Senatorial Delay in Executive Nominations." *American Journal of Political Science* 59: 1–10.

Petrocik, John R. 1996. "Issue Ownership in Presidential Elections, with a 1980 Case Study." *American Journal of Political Science* 40: 825–50.

Pope, Jeremy C., and Jonathan Woon. 2008. "Made in Congress? Testing the Electoral Implications of Party Ideological Brand Names." *Journal of Politics* 70: 823–36.

———. 2009. "Investigating the Dynamics of Party Reputations, 1939–2004." *Political Research Quarterly* 62: 653–61.

Raju, Manu. 2013. "Reid Threatens to Nuke Filibuster." *Politico*, January 22, http://www.politico.com/story/2013/01/reid-mcconnell-meet-on-filibuster-086551.

Reid, Harry. 2013. "Appealing Ruling of the Chair." *Congressional Record*, Senate (daily edition), 159 (November 21): S8417–18.

Rogers, David. 2010. "Senate Rejects Deficit Commission." *Politico*, January 26, http://www.politico.com/story/2010/01/senate-rejects-deficit-commission-032017.

Sanchez, Humberto, and Niels Lesniewski. 2013. "Deal Defuses 'Nuclear Option' in Senate (Updated)." *WGDB* (blog), *Roll Call*, July 16, http://blogs.rollcall.com/wgdb/nuclear-option-may-be-averted-in-the-senate.

Scherer, Nancy. 2005. *Scoring Points: Politicians, Activists, and the Lower Federal Court Appointment Process.* Stanford, CA: Stanford University Press.

Taylor, Andrew. 2006. "Lawmakers 'Hold' Up Senate." *Southeast Missourian*, September 18, http://www.semissourian.com/story/1168691.html.

Theriault, Sean M. 2008. *Party Polarization in Congress.* New York: Cambridge University Press.

U.S. Congress, Senate, Committee on Rules and Administration. 2010. *Examining the Filibuster: Hearings before the Committee on Rules and Administration.* S. Hrg. 111–706. 111th Cong., 2nd sess., April 22, May 19, June 23, July 28, September 22, and September 29. Washington, DC: Government Printing Office.

U.S. Congress, Senate. N.d. "Senate Action on Cloture Motions." http://www.senate.gov/pagelayout/reference/cloture_motions/clotureCounts.htm.

Wawro, Gregory, and Eric Schickler. 2004. "Where's the Pivot? Obstruction and Law-Making in the Pre-cloture Senate." *American Journal of Political Science* 48: 758–74.

11

Irregular Order

Examining the Changing
Congressional Amending Process

Michael S. Lynch, Anthony J. Madonna,
and Rachel Surminsky

I N THE 2008 PRESIDENTIAL CAMPAIGN, the burgeoning Great Recession
became a key platform issue between Senators Barack Obama (D-IL) and
John McCain (R-AZ). Senator Obama championed an aggressive increase
in federal spending as his campaign solution to mitigate the financial crisis.
Once he was sworn into office in January 2009, President Obama's top legislative priority was stimulating the economy. Shortly thereafter, an Obama-
supported multi-billion-dollar bill was drafted to slow the recession by providing a massive package of federal spending projects, targeted tax cuts, and
aid to states (Grunwald 2012).[1]

On January 15, 2009, House Democratic leaders introduced an $825 bil-
lion stimulus package in the form of H.R. 1: the American Recovery and
Reinvestment Act ("Stimulus Enacted" 2010). Given the amount of spending
and exorbitant tax cuts in the bill, House members were interested in voicing
their opinions about how much would be spent and on what. These opinions
manifested in a torrent of amendments; Democrats and Republicans proposed 206 unique amendments to the original bill.

In the House of Representatives, the majority party has a great deal of control over which amendments can be brought to the floor for consideration.
The House Rules Committee, dominated by the Democratic majority party,
issued rules for the bill's consideration that allowed for only eleven of the over
two hundred proposed amendments to be debated and receive votes on the
House floor.[2] Only eight of these eleven amendments passed, generating few
changes to H.R. 1's text. The tight controls Democratic leaders maintained on
amending prevented the bill from deviating from its original form. Adopted

amendments only increased the bill's spending by $3.7 billion—largely due to a successful amendment by Representative Jerrold Nadler (D-NY) that increased public transit spending. Democrats gave minority-party Republicans very few chances to amend the bill. Of the five Republican-proposed amendments that were allowed consideration, only two passed on the House floor—neither of which had much effect on the amount or type of spending included in the bill.[3] Party leaders' control over the amending process allowed the House to bring the bill to a final-passage vote a mere thirteen days after the bill's initial introduction. On January 28, H.R. 1 passed 244–188, with 244 Democrats voting for the package and all Republicans and 11 Democrats voting against it.[4]

On February 2, Senate Majority Leader Harry Reid (D-NV) introduced the Senate's version of the bill.[5] The Senate's initial version was even more comprehensive than the House's, with a total price tag of $940 billion ("Stimulus Enacted" 2010). Unlike their House counterparts, Reid and Senate Democrats did not have the ability to control the consideration of amendments to the bill. The rules of the Senate empower individual senators with a greater ability to propose amendments and alter the policy content of bills. Senators proposed a whopping 416 amendments to the Senate's version of the stimulus plan: Democrats proposed 224 amendments and Republicans 192.

The Senate began a marathon eight-day session of debating and voting on the amendments proposed to H.R. 1.[6] The key change to the bill came in the form of a substitute amendment cosponsored by Susan Collins (R-ME) and Ben Nelson (D-NE). This substitute amendment, negotiated by a group of moderate Democrats and Republicans, proposed a new version of the bill that replaced Reid's initial $940 billion version with a $780 billion package. The amendment slashed federal spending while increasing the dollar amount devoted to tax cuts.

The bipartisan coalition's substitute amendment highlights another key feature of the U.S. Senate: the filibuster. In the upper chamber of Congress, senators have the right to unlimited debate. The most effective way to stop such endless debate is to pass a cloture motion requiring sixty votes. If cloture is invoked the filibuster is broken and a vote on the bill can occur. Without cloture, passing controversial legislation can be extremely difficult (see chapter 10). As current Senate majority leader Mitch McConnell (R-KY) has argued, "I think we can stipulate once again for the umpteenth time that matters that have any level of controversy about it in the Senate will require 60 votes" (Herszenhorn 2007).

Following McConnell's logic, Obama could rely on all of the Senate's fifty-eight Democrats to support the stimulus package; Reid needed to gain the support of at least two Republican senators to acquire the critical sixtieth vote, blocking the threat of a Republican filibuster.[7] The Collins-Nelson amendment had the support of three key Republican senators: Collins, Olympia Snowe (R-ME), and Arlen Specter (R-PA). A compromise was struck. If the three senators' desired changes were incorporated into the bill, they would join Democrats to invoke cloture. On February 9, the Collins-Nelson amendment received a 61–36 vote on cloture, paving the way for the amended bill to pass the Senate.[8] Collins, Snowe, and Specter remained key figures during the House-Senate conference committee, working out the differences between the two chambers' bills.

The final $787 billion version of the bill was clearly influenced by the moderate Republicans' ability to use the amendment process to modify the content of the bill. While the final version of the American Recovery and Reinvestment Act did provide an aggressive stimulus package for the economy, the spending was not as bold as Obama and his allies had wanted. The amending process of the U.S. Congress, specifically of the Senate, markedly tempered the content of the stimulus package. Leveraging their votes for cloture allowed senators to alter the content of policy proposals, bringing the bill's substance closer to their preferences and the moderate final version of the bill.

Not all amendment activity in the Senate has such a clear impact on policy. For example, in March 2010, the Senate was considering the Health Care and Education Reconciliation Act. This bill sought to make a number of revenue and financing changes to the Affordable Care Act (ACA). Republican senators, who strongly opposed the initial ACA, were similarly opposed to the new proposed changes. Senator Tom Coburn (R-OK) proposed an amendment that barred the Affordable Care Act from providing insurance coverage of Viagra for child molesters and rapists. The sponsors of the bill argued that if any amendments to the bill were allowed to pass, it would extend the amount of time it would take to pass the bill and might ultimately lead to the bill's defeat. Democratic leaders, therefore, urged their members to vote no on the amendment for procedural reasons. Senator Max Baucus (D-MT) argued, "This is a serious bill. This is a serious debate. The amendment offered by the Senator from Oklahoma makes a mockery of the Senate, the debate, and the American people. . . . It is a crass political stunt aimed at making 30-second commercials, not public policy" (Holan 2010). While the amendment failed, it still put Democrats in the awkward position of voting against an amendment that could be construed as supporting insurance coverage of Viagra for sex offenders. Baucus's claim that the vote was "aimed at making 30-second commercials" turned out to be true: several Republican congressional candidates featured the vote in 2010 midterm election ads (see chapter 9 for a discussion of procedural votes).[9]

While amendments allow senators to influence the policy content of bills, as seen in the American Recovery and Reinvestment Act, amendments also have less noble uses. Senators can use amendments to delay the consideration of bills. At other times, senators, like Coburn, use amendments to force their ideological opponents to vote on politically controversial issues that frequently have nothing to do with the substantive content of bills. There is an inherent tension between senators' use of amendments as a positive policy tool to craft compromise legislation and senators' use of amendments as a political tool to attack opponents, reducing the efficiency of the Senate.

In recent years, this tension over amending has become the centerpiece of many debates over the functionality of Congress. House Speaker John Boehner's (R-OH) resignation in September 2015 and the subsequent withdrawal of his heir apparent, Majority Leader Kevin McCarthy (R-CA), were seen by many to be a response to frequent criticism from conservative members of the Republican caucus of Boehner's leadership style (Steinhauer 2015; Steinhauer and Herszenhorn 2015; Dumain and Fuller 2015).[10] A chief target of these critiques—which often called for a return to "regular order"—was Boehner's usage of restrictive rules to restrict floor amendments (Drutman 2015).[11] Similarly, Republicans made Senate Majority Leader Harry Reid's (D-NV) blocking of floor amendments in that chamber through filling the amendment tree a central focus of the 2014 midterm elections.[12] The new Senate majority leader, Mitch McConnell (R-KY), has since come under fire from members of both parties for restricting amending opportunities in the same way.[13] In this chapter, we shed some light on this debate by outlining the basics of the amending process and discussing the legislative and political consequences of amending in today's Congress.

The Amending Process

Amendments in the House and Senate can be differentiated using three general categorizations: (1) degree—whether the amendment changed the text of the measure or a pending amendment; (2) form—what the amendment did to the measure or amendment's text; and (3) effect—what influence the amendment had on the overall outcome of the measure or amendment.

Degree

In the House and Senate only certain amendments can be proposed or, in the language of Congress, are "in order." *First-degree* amendments modify the text of the bill being amended. *Second-degree* amendments change the text of a first-degree amendment that has been proposed but not dispensed with.[14]

Form

Amendments can modify the text of a bill in three different ways. An *amendment to insert* adds new text to a bill or pending amendment without removing any of the existing text. An amendment to remove text from a measure or pending amendment without adding new text is a *motion to strike*. An *amendment to strike and insert* strikes language and then adds new language to a measure.

- Insert: "The bureau will be allocated $15,000 and fifteen staff members [next year]."
- Strike: "The bureau will be allocated $15,000 and fifteen staff members next year."
- Strike and insert: "The bureau will be allocated $15,000 [$16,000] next year."

Effect

How an amendment changes the substance of a bill determines its third criterion for classification (Davis 2015a, 3–5). A *perfecting amendment* will change some language of a bill or amendment to, presumably, improve it. A perfecting amendment can be a first- or second-degree amendment to insert, strike, or strike and insert.

An amendment that is crafted to change a larger portion of the language of a bill or pending amendment is a *substitute amendment*. A substitute amendment replaces a large portion of a bill's language, while the goal of a perfecting amendment is to modify the existing language (Davis 2015b, 5). When a first-degree amendment changes an entire paragraph, section, or title or the entire text of a bill, it is designated an *amendment in the nature of the substitute* or a *substitute amendment*. If a second-degree amendment moves to change the entire language of a first-degree amendment, it is also referred to as a substitute amendment. Substitute-type amendments are restricted to the strike and insert form because they move to remove and replace text.

The designation of amendments as perfecting or substitute is a nuanced distinction. An amendment's structure, language, and presentation on the floor are factors that largely determine how the amendment will be categorized in the *Congressional Record*. The importance of a perfecting or substitute amendment largely depends on its substance. A substitute amendment may replace an entire section of the bill, only modifying spelling and grammatical errors. A perfecting amendment may change only a few words, altering millions of dollars of appropriations in a budgetary measure.

How Are Amendments Dispensed With?

All proposed amendments must be dispensed with by either the House or Senate according to each chamber's rules and procedures. Amendments are considered in a specific order when voting occurs in the House and Senate; this order is dependent on the precedence of priority.[15] Amendments will be voted on in the reverse order that they were proposed; this allows for all second-degree modifications to an amendment to be considered before the first-degree base amendment is voted on.

Points of Order

Before debate begins on a proposed first- or second-degree amendment, a member may make a *point of order* against the proposed amendment to challenge whether that amendment is in order.[16] Amendments can be challenged for a variety of reasons. For example, an amendment may be out of order in the House if it is not *germane*—meaning it is not strictly related to the content of a bill.[17] It is not the role of the presiding officer of the House or Senate— also referred to as the chair—to question whether an amendment is in order; it is up to members to enforce the rules of the floor. The amount of debate allotted to consider a point of order is generally at the discretion of the chair.[18]

At the conclusion of debate, with the consultation of the chamber's parliamentarian, the presiding officer will make a ruling on the point of order. If the chair upholds the point of order, the amendment is struck down and not considered. If the chair rejects the point of order, regular debate on the amendment ensues. In certain situations, any member may appeal the chair's decision.[19]

Withdrawal and Modification

Even after an amendment has been proposed and debated, the amendment's sponsor may withdraw the amendment, as long as there has been no action taken on that amendment. In the House and Senate, "action" is defined as (1) a vote taken on the amendment; (2) a motion to the previous question or a calling of the yeas and nays for voting; or (3) the adoption of a second-degree amendment to the first-degree amendment. Another member who did not author the amendment can move to withdraw an amendment if no action has been taken on the amendment and the motion is approved by unanimous consent. For certain reasons, such as satisfying a point of order, the amendment's original author may modify the amendment. Unless action has been taken on an amendment, as defined above, its author can modify the amendment at any time.

Motions to Table

Before a vote is called for on the question of agreeing to an amendment, a motion can be made at any time to table that amendment. This motion reflects that the chamber no longer wants to consider the amendment further. If the motion to table is rejected, debate proceeds. If the motion to table is adopted, it will kill the amendment without a formal vote being taken. A motion to table an amendment can be made even if there is an unresolved second-degree amendment attached to a first-degree amendment being tabled. Tabling amendments is especially common in the Senate. Since the Senate's tabling motion is nondebatable, meaning it is not subject to filibusters, a simple majority can defeat an amendment—this is the motion that Senate Democrats used to defeat Coburn's amendment barring insurance coverage for Viagra for sexual predators.

Voting

A vote can be taken on an amendment in three different forms: voice vote, division, and roll call (Oleszek et al. 2015, 296). The *voice vote* is the de facto form of voting in both the House and the Senate. When the question on the motion to pass the amendment is raised, the members call out yea or nay to voice their stance on the amendment. The presiding officer decides the outcome of the vote.[20]

After a voice vote on an amendment, a member may request a roll call vote on the amendment.[21] A *roll call* vote is a formal record of both totals of yeas and nays and individual member positions, with senators calling out their positions and House members recording their positions on electronic voting stations. Once a roll call vote is taken, members cannot request another vote type.[22]

Amending in the House and Senate

The differences in amending between the House and Senate, as demonstrated in our introduction, are fundamentally rooted in the two chambers' different procedural rules. One of the defining factors of the House of Representatives is the Committee on Rules.[23] The Rules Committee decides if, when, and in what order legislation is put on the House Calendar to be considered by the chamber. A *special rule* is used to give a bill privilege—moving it to the top of the House Calendar to be given immediate consideration.[24] The Rules Committee is instrumental in controlling how much amendment activity will occur on the floor through special rules. The Rules Committee can propose three types of special rules: *open*, *closed*, and *structured*.

- Open rules: In general, any amendment can be proposed to a bill under open rule without restriction. The House rules still apply to amendments under open rule. For example, if a nongermane amendment is proposed it may be struck down if a point of order is raised against it.[25]
- Closed rules: No amendments may be offered to the bill unless the committee from which the bill was reported offers them.
- Structured rules: Only specific amendments may be offered; these restrictions are specified in the special rule or in the Rules Committee report. Usually the Rules Committee will announce to members that a structured rule will be in place for an upcoming bill. Members will submit proposed amendments, and the Rules Committee will decide which amendments will be allowed under the rule.

The procedures and rules of the Senate are significantly different than those of the House, precipitating a less structured amending process that also strengthens minority-party rights. In the Senate there is no agenda-setting body comparable to the Rules Committee to regulate legislation and establish special rules for consideration. Once a standing committee has taken up and amended a bill, it reports the legislation back to the floor, where it is placed on the Calendar of Business. While there are formal rules that dictate the scheduling of legislation, these formal rules are rarely used, and a system of informal agreements usually determines how legislation is scheduled.[26]

In the House, the Speaker controls the floor, choosing who is recognized and in what order. The Senate requires that any member who seeks the floor be given recognition in the order that it was sought. The majority leader has the right of first recognition, which means the majority leader will always be recognized first if multiple senators are seeking recognition. Because of this the majority leader has an advantage in scheduling legislation, offering amendments, and proposing motions. This tool helps the majority leader control the agenda of the Senate and influence the Senate's amending process.

Debate on the floor of the Senate is not restricted by the time-limiting rules found in the House. Senators do not have to abide by House rules that restrict the amount of time each member can speak. Instead, Paragraph 1(a) of Rule XIX states that a senator is limited to two speeches per question per legislative day but imposes no other limits on debate. The Senate also lacks the House's previous-question motion, which allows a simple majority to end debate and conduct a final-passage vote on a bill. Once recognized, a senator can speak for as long as he or she desires, which can result in a filibuster. A *filibuster*, broadly defined, is any dilatory or obstructionist tactic that blocks a measure by preventing a vote from being taken (Beth and Heitshusen 2014, 4). Perhaps the most famous filibuster in American history was Strom Thurmond's (D-SC) of the Civil Rights Act of 1957, which lasted twenty-four hours and eighteen minutes. While lengthy speeches like Thurmond's are rare in the modern Senate, the threat of filibuster is often enough to influence how majority leaders choose to schedule legislation. A filibuster can be ended if three-fifths of all senators, normally sixty, vote to invoke cloture. *Cloture* effectively means closing the debate on the pending question (see chapter 10).

To both prevent potential filibusters and improve the efficiency of the Senate, *unanimous consent agreements* may be proposed before a bill is brought to the floor.[27] Unanimous consent agreements specify terms and conditions under which the bill will be considered. The Senate majority leader, often in consultation with the minority leader, will negotiate the terms of these agreements with members. These agreements can mimic special rules in the House, specifying what amendments can be offered, creating time agreements for debate, or indicating when consideration will begin and end. Because the agreements require the consent of all senators, unanimous consent agreements usually provide for a much more open amending process than exists under House special rules.

An amendment under consideration in the Senate does not have to adhere to the germaneness requirement, which limits the contents of amendments in the House. There are few rules for germaneness in the Senate; therefore any amendment can be offered, regardless of its relation to the content of the underlying bill. [28]

The Politics of Senate Amendments

Senate rules allow individual senators more access to the amending process, especially as compared to the House, where the majority party keeps a tight lid on amendments. While untrammeled access to the floor gives individual senators the opportunity to improve the policy content of bills via amendments, it can also be adulterated, acting as a mechanism to score political points by forcing tough votes on opponents. The American Recovery and

Reinvestment Act shows how amendments can engender compromise and deliberation. Coburn's "no insured Viagra for sexual predators" amendment shows how amendments can increase partisan politics, slowing the Senate's productivity. This crux naturally extends the question: are amendments used primarily for lawmaking or for partisan politics in the modern Senate? Recent patterns of amending and topical political controversies seem to point to the latter, galvanizing a more partisan and less efficient U.S. Senate.

Patterns of Amending

Using data from the University of Georgia Amendments Project, we observe several patterns.[29] First, amending is far more prevalent in the Senate than it is in the House. Anthony J. Madonna and Kevin R. Kosar (2015) examine four congresses between 1995 and 2009 and find that almost 80 percent of all congressional amendments are debated and voted on in the Senate, with the remaining 20 percent being considered in the House.[30] This is not surprising, given that the open process in the Senate contrasts heavily with the more draconian, majority-party-controlled process in the House.

Second, the amount of amending activity has trended upward in recent years. The number of amendments proposed in the Senate per Congress has increased. In the 102nd Congress (1991–1992), senators offered about 2,650 amendments to landmark bills; in the most recent Congress, the 113th (2013–2014), senators offered over 4,100 amendments to landmark bills (Kosar and Madonna 2015). This increase in Congress-level amending is matched at the bill level. Figure 11.1 reports the average number of amendments proposed for each landmark bill. In the 111th Congress (2009–2010), landmark bills were subjected to an average of 116 amendments per bill (Madonna and Kosar 2015).

Third, amendments are more frequently being dispensed with via recorded voting. From 1877 to 2010, only about 14 percent of amendments received a recorded vote in the Senate. Since 1995, the average number of recorded votes has risen to around 35 percent (Madonna and Kosar 2015). This is an especially interesting statistic in considering whether amendments are primarily tools of lawmaking or weapons of partisanship. If a senator is using an amendment vote for political purposes, it is necessary to have a record of members' positions so that it can be reported back to constituents and injure ideological opponents. This stark increase in requests for roll call amendment voting seems to imply that members are increasingly interested in creating a durable record of voting on amendments.

Fourth, more amendments are being proposed, and a greater proportion of them are being rejected.[31] From 1877 to 2010, an average of 46 percent of

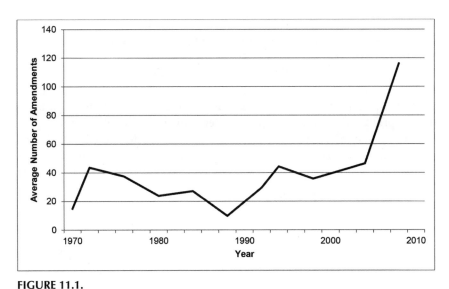

FIGURE 11.1.
Average number of Senate amendments offered to each landmark bill.
Source: This figure originally appeared in Kosar and Madonna (2015). The data were provided by the University of Georgia Amendments Project.

proposed amendments failed. Since 1995, the failure rate has risen to over 80 percent.[32] The increased number of failing amendments implies that senators are not invested in the passage of their amendments and are instead using them to achieve electorally political ends rather than policymaking results.

Politicized Amending

The Senate's recent consideration of the Keystone XL Pipeline Approval Act shows how these trends have come to epitomize lawmaking in the modern Senate. As Senate Majority Leader Mitch McConnell (R-KY) tried to move the contentious bill through the Senate, he was confronted by 247 amendment proposals. Roll call votes were taken on forty-two of these amendments. Despite the deluge of legislative activity, only seven amendments successfully altered the content of the bill.

During the bill's consideration, minority-party Democrats were especially ineffective in their efforts to influence policy via the amendment process. Democrats proposed 108 amendments, of which only one secured passage. Senator Sheldon Whitehouse's (D-RI) two amendments requiring campaign finance disclosures from "certain persons benefitting from the tar sands development" are archetypical examples of partisan-driven proposals. Both amendments, if voted down by Republicans, would allow Democrats to attack conservatives in upcoming elections for not supporting campaign finance reform. Whitehouse's first amendment was defeated via a party-line tabling motion. His second amendment failed 52–44, with all Republicans and a single Democrat voting no.

Even the Democrats' sole successful amendment to the Keystone XL Pipeline Approval Act is hardly a story of legislative success. Whitehouse proposed an amendment "to express the sense of the Senate that climate change is real and not a hoax." This amendment, which had no substantive impact on the final bill, passed with ninety-nine yea votes and only Senator Roger Wicker (R-MS) voting nay (Wolfensberger 2015).

Vote-a-ramas

Another example of the Senate working hard yet having minimal impact on policy is the "vote-a-rama" on budget resolutions. A vote-a-rama is an extended number of back-to-back Senate votes that begin after debate time for the resolution has expired but before the budget resolution receives a final-passage vote. A budget resolution acts as a framework for congressional appropriations rather than a binding set of instructions; therefore budget resolutions and their amendments do not have the power of law. The resulting legislation can be thought of as more a suggestion than substantive policy.

A key feature of the vote-a-rama is rapid-fire voting with essentially no debate between votes. Typically, each amendment's sponsor and a designated amendment opponent are given thirty seconds each to debate that amendment, followed by a roll call vote lasting ten minutes.[33] Extremely limited debate precipitates votes that occur in a very short time. During the Senate's 2015 budget resolution vote-a-rama, forty-three amendments were "debated" and given roll call votes in under sixteen hours.

Given this blistering pace and the general lack of substantive importance, it is not surprising that vote-a-rama amendments tend to be of a highly political nature. During the 2015 vote-a-rama, presidential candidates Senator Rand Paul (R-KY) and Senator Marco Rubio (R-FL) both proposed failing amendments that highlighted their support for the military (Sullivan 2015). Senator Brian Schatz (D-HI) offered an amendment supporting same-sex spouses' ability to access Social Security and veterans' benefits; the amendment drew the support of eleven Republicans. It is clear that all voting does not lead to lawmaking. Senator Chris Murphy (D-CT) summed it up nicely when he said, "There's a lot of smoke and not a lot of fire. So much of this is for show" (quoted in Sullivan 2015).

Filling the Amendment Tree

Senate leaders have long sought to find ways to successfully pass legislation in the face of minority-party obstruction. One of the few tools that majority-party leaders have at their disposal is the right of first recognition. Because Senate traditions allow the majority leader to be recognized before all other members, majority leaders can use this power to set the Senate's agenda and limit amendment activity. The process by which leaders accomplish this is called *filling the amendment tree* (see chapter 8). This has been a controversial but effective method of limiting minority-party amending activity in recent congresses.

Filling the amendment tree relies on Senate procedural practices that only allow a limited number of amendments to be offered at any one time. Some of these amendments have to be disposed of before other amendments can be offered. If the majority leader seeks recognition and proposes enough space-holder amendments to fill all the allowable spots, then there are no spots remaining for other senators to propose amendments. Majority leaders place all of their filler amendments to "fill the amendment tree" and effectively block other senators from offering new amendments.[34]

As discussed earlier, this controversial practice has been used with increasing frequency in recent congresses.[35] In the 113th Congress (2013–2014), minority-party Republicans repeatedly complained about Reid's use of this tactic. During the 2014 congressional elections, Minority Leader McConnell promised that if voters granted Republicans a majority in the Senate and made McConnell the majority leader, he would adopt a more open amending process. By allowing all senators access to the amending process, McConnell argued, "the Senate can be returned to the place of great debates, contentious debates, but where you can still get outcomes on things where you have at least 60 senators" (Hulse 2014).

In 2014, Republicans won a majority in the Senate, and McConnell was elected the new majority leader—his opportunity to open up the process had arrived. After only a few weeks on the job, Senator McConnell had allowed more amendment votes than Senator Reid had in all of 2014 (Sanders 2015). But this open process came at a cost. As highlighted in our discussion of the Keystone XL Pipeline Approval Act, Democratic senators capitalized on the more open process to propose countless amendments, many of which spawned votes that were politically damaging to Republicans. Republican senators also made use of the open process to propose more amendments. To control amendments, McConnell began to rely on filling the amendment tree to increase efficiency in the chamber. Filling the tree helped McConnell pass the USA Freedom Act, a funding bill for the Homeland Security Department, and the recent Bipartisan Budget Act. McConnell had idealistic expectations for an open process; senators were happy to take full political advantage of this opportunity. Majority leaders' decision to fill the tree will continue to be met with criticism in the future, but in a highly polarized Senate, it remains one of the few tools the majority leader can use to improve the efficiency of the chamber.

Conclusions

While the rules and procedures of the Senate allow all senators to engage in careful debate and deliberation over important bills, senators are instead debasing the Senate's open amending process to score political points, leading to slower legislative productivity in the chamber. The end result seems to be an increase in gridlock and a general reduction in lawmaking.

Unfortunately, there is not an easy way for the public to fix this problem. The Senate's current partisan use of amendments can only be reformed through Senate action. Much like McConnell's promise to quit filling the amendment tree, promises for reform often run headlong into partisan realities. Each party wants to generate a record of accomplishment for itself and a record of failure for its opponents to help achieve electoral success. Moreover, any potential reforms of the amending process will likely necessitate supermajority support, given the Senate's lack of a simple-majoritarian means for ending debate. In the current polarized political environment, there does not seem to be a clear path for bipartisan reform of the amending process. Minority-party obstruction, amendments of limited substantive importance, filling the amendment tree, and other forms of "irregular order" are likely to remain the norm in the Senate's near future.

Notes

* The authors would like to thank Kevin Kosar for comments and Keith T. Poole, Joshua Clinton, John Lapinski, and Jason Roberts for making data available. Finally, the authors would like to thank Nathaniel Ament-Stone, Rain Ammons, Whitney Arp, Matthew Baker, Ethan Boldt, Jason Byers, Lauren Corbett Bryant, Ananda Costa, Shellea Crochet, Michael Evans, Jason Fern, James Floyd, Matthew Fowler, Vinita Gandhi, David Gelman, Sophie Giberga, Hannah Greenberg, Casey Grippando, Cody Hall, Leyall Harb, Sharne Haywood, Daniel Helmick, Kyle Hollimon, Eric Howell, Nick Howard, Dory Ille, Taylor Johnston, Da Hae Kim, Cody Knapp, Megan Mayfield, Annabel McSpadden, Kayce Mobley, Amber Morgan, Erin Munger, Wes Nichols, Mark Owens, Justin Pinkerton, Elaina Polson, Scott Riley, Matthew Roberts, Melissa Siegel, Joel Sievert, Veselin Simonov, Laine Shay, Melissa Strickland,

Kelsey Thomas, Javier Trejo, Adam Veale, Michael Watson, and Andrew Wills for their research assistance.

1. Approximately 45 percent of the final bill's cost was allocated to federal spending projects, 37 percent was directed to targeted tax cuts, and 18 percent was given as aid to assist states with budget issues stemming from the financial crisis. For a detailed breakdown of the bill's spending provisions, see Letter from Douglas W. Elmendorf to Nancy Pelosi, CBO, February 13, 2009, https://www.cbo.gov/sites/default/files/111th-congress-2009-2010/costestimate/hr1conference0.pdf.

2. The House Rules Committee issued a structured rule for H.R. 1. Under a structured rule, members are asked to submit amendments to the Rules Committee. The Rules Committee considers all proposed amendments and decides which should be given consideration on the House floor. For a detailed discussion of structured rules and their use, see Lynch, Madonna, and Roberts (forthcoming).

3. While Republicans proposed 101 amendments to H.R. 1, only two were ultimately successful. Bill Shuster's (R-PA) amendment instructed states that stimulus funds for highway maintenance were not to be used to replace existing state funding. Todd Platts's (R-PA) amendment, a bipartisan measure that was also sponsored by Chris Van Hollen (D-MD), inserted the entire text of the Whistleblower Protection Enhancement Act into H.R. 1.

4. For a complete summary of all legislative activity on the American Recovery and Reinvestment Act, see "Bill Summary and Status, 111th Congress (2009–2010), H.R.1, All Congressional Actions with Amendments," Library of Congress, http://thomas. loc.gov/cgi-bin/bdquery/z?d111:HR00001:@@@S. A lone Republican, Ginny Brown-Waite (R-FL), did not vote on the measure.

5. Technically, Reid introduced Senate Amendment 98, which was a substitute amendment to the completed House bill. This is a frequent tactic that the Senate uses to work on its own version of a completed House bill.

6. These data come from the University of Georgia Amendments Project (http:// spia.uga.edu/faculty_pages/mlynch/amendment.php). Many of these amendments were to Reid's Amendment 98. When this version of the bill was withdrawn from the Senate floor and replaced with Collins and Nelson's Senate Amendment 570, many of the underlying amendments were no longer in order and were not ultimately considered on the Senate floor.

7. Al Franken (D-MN) was eventually declared the winner in his 2008 Senate election against Norm Coleman (R-MN), but because he won by fewer than one thousand votes, a recount and ensuing legal battles meant that he was not seated in the U.S. Senate until July 2009—almost a half year after his term should have started. While Joe Lieberman (I-CT) and Bernie Sanders (I-VT) were both technically independents, they caucused with Senate Democrats and are generally viewed as members of the Democratic Party.

8. After this key cloture vote, the final amended version of the bill passed the Senate by a vote of 61 to 37.

9. An example of such an ad can be viewed at Angie Drobnic Holan, "Ed Perlmutter Voted for Viagra for Sex Offenders, Paid for by Health Care Bill? Nope," PolitiFact,

October 26, http://www.politifact.com/truth-o-meter/statements/2010/oct/26/ameri-can-action-network/viagra-sex-offenders-paid-health-care-bill-nope.

10. For example, Representative Justin Amash (R-MI), a member of the conserva-tive House Freedom Caucus, asserted that he objected to Boehner not because he "isn't conservative enough" but rather because he "doesn't follow the process" (Sher-man 2014).

11. The concept of "regular order" is fairly ambiguous, or in the words of Walter Oleszek (2014), it is a "flexible construct." Perhaps more cynically, Senator Mike Lee (R-UT) argued that calls to return to regular order are made only "when it serves [members] interests" (Lee 2015).

12. Republicans featured Reid's handling of the chamber in attack ads in competi-tive Senate races in North Carolina, Alaska, Kansas, Kentucky, Louisiana, and Geor-gia (Kosar and Madonna 2015). The ads led vulnerable Democrats like Mark Begich (D-AK) to denounce Reid's tactics in formal statements (Everett 2014).

13. For example, during debate over H.R. 2, the Medicare Access and CHIP Reau-thorization Act of 2015, Senator Jeff Sessions (R-AL) lambasted McConnell for only allowing votes on six amendments (Haberkorn 2015). See also Binder (2015) and Kosar and Madonna (2015).

14. Third-degree amendments, amendments that alter a second-degree amend-ment, are not considered in order except by unanimous consent.

15. For a more complete discussion of the principle of procedure in terms of amendment voting order, see Oleszek et al. (2015, 288–90).

16. Certain special rules may have provisions to waive points of order against spe-cific amendments. Further, when the House is operating under a motion to suspend the rules, all points of order are waived. For a more complete discussion, see Davis (2015a, 38–39).

17. For a complete discussion of the germaneness rule, see U.S. Congress, House, Committee on Rules (2012).

18. See Lynch, Madonna, and Owens (n.d.) for a discussion of chair rulings in the Senate and Lawrence (2013) for more on chair rulings in the House.

19. For a complete discussion, see Brown (1996).

20. A division vote is also possible but is rarely used in the modern Congress. In a division vote, members stand up to show they are either in favor of or against an amendment. The presiding officer conducts a headcount to determine the outcome. A division, or *standing*, vote records totals on both sides but not the individual posi-tions of members.

21. The Constitution requires that votes be recorded at the "desire of one-fifth of those present," meaning that one-fifth of the chamber must support a member's request for a recorded vote.

22. A member on the prevailing side may offer a motion to reconsider the adopted amendment, which will allow the amendment to be rescinded or amended further. A member must second the motion to reconsider for a vote on the motion to occur. Most often, the motion to reconsider will be offered along with a motion to lay the motion to reconsider on the table to prevent the motion from being utilized.

23. The Rules Committee, also referred to as the Speaker's Committee, is a thirteen-person standing committee generally consisting of nine majority and four minority members. This supersized majority-party advantage highlights the importance of the Rules Committee in controlling policy outcomes (Cox and McCubbins 2005, 2007). Additionally, committee members are expected to be loyal partisans. In a move that generated criticism from many conservatives, Speaker Boehner used his influence to deny seats on the Rules Committee to two Republicans who opposed his election as Speaker (Sherman and Breshnahan 2015; Sherman and Palmer 2015; Dumain 2015).

24. The Rules Committee has established its procedure for reporting a special rule using a combination of House rules, committee rules, and long-established practices. See Lynch, Madonna, and Roberts (forthcoming) for more on amending under special rules.

25. A similar type of rule is a modified open rule. A modified open rule puts some restrictions on amending through requirements that place time constraints on debate and preprinting requirements for amendments.

26. A senator may bypass the committee referral process and place a bill directly on the calendar of business. For a full discussion, see Heitshusen (2014, 6).

27. See Smith and Flathman (1989) and Ainsworth and Flathman (1995) for more on the politics of unanimous consent agreements.

28. Amendments must be germane to general appropriations bills and budget measures, bills under cloture, and certain unanimous consent agreements; for further discussion, see Davis (2015b, 23).

29. Madonna and Kosar (2015) provide a detailed discussion of the collection of this data and an initial analysis of it.

30. Madonna and Kosar (2015) examine the 104th, 106th, 109th, and 111th Congresses. The data used do not consider amendments proposed in the House—only amendments allowed consideration by the House Rules Committee are assessed.

31. Many proposed amendments never received consideration on the floor.

32. It is interesting to note that this increase in failing amendments is occurring alongside an increase in minority-sponsored amendments. While minority-party senators sponsored around 40 percent of amendments from the 1950s to the 1980s, that proportion has increased recently, rising to a high of over 60 percent of all amendments by 2010.

33. See Hennessey (2010).

34. See Oleszek et al. (2015, 291–94) for a detailed description of filling the amendment tree.

35. Former Senate Majority Leader Robert Byrd (D-WV) is frequently credited with first using this tactic (Madonna and Kosar 2015).

References

Ainsworth, Scott, and Marcus Flathman. 1995. "Unanimous Consent Agreements as Leadership Tools." *Legislative Studies Quarterly* 20: 177–95.

Beth, Richard S., and Valerie Heitshusen. 2014. "Filibusters and Cloture in the Senate." Congressional Research Service. Washington, DC: Library of Congress.

Binder, Sarah. 2015. "Why Can't Mitch McConnell Keep His Promises?" *Monkey Cage* (blog), *Washington Post*, May 26, https://www.washingtonpost.com/blogs/monkey-cage/wp/2015/05/26/why-cant-mitch-mcconnell-keep-his-promises.

Brown, William Holmes. 1996. "Points of Order; Parliamentary Inquiries." *House Practice: A Guide to the Rules, Precedents, and Procedures of the House*, 12–13. Washington, DC: Government Printing Office.

Cox, Gary W., and Mathew D. McCubbins. 2005. *Setting the Agenda: Responsible Party Government in the U.S. House of Representatives*. New York: Cambridge University Press.

———. 2007. *Legislative Leviathan: Party Government in the House*. 2nd ed. New York: Cambridge University Press.

Davis, Christopher M. 2015a. "The Amending Process in the House of Representatives." Congressional Research Service. Washington, DC: Library of Congress.

———. 2015b. "The Amending Process in the Senate." Congressional Research Service. Washington, DC: Library of Congress.

Drutman, Lee. 2015. "The House Freedom Caucus Has Some Good Ideas on How the US House Should Operate." *Vox*, October 20.

Dumain, Emma. 2015. "Boehner Adds 2 Rules Republicans—Not the Ones He Booted." *Roll Call*, April 14.

Dumain, Emma, and Matt Fuller. 2015. "McCarthy Shocks Conference by Dropping Speaker Bid." *Roll Call*, October 8.

Everett, Burgess. 2014. "Mark Begich Blasts Harry Reid on Amendments." *Politico*, June 30.

Grunwald, Michael. 2012. *The New, New Deal: The Hidden Story of Change in the Obama Era*. New York: Simon and Schuster.

Haberkorn, Jennifer. 2015. "Bipartisan Senate Ends Flawed Medicare Payment Formula." *Politico*, April 14.

Heitshusen, Valerie. 2014. "The Legislative Process on the Senate Floor: An Introduction." Congressional Research Service. Washington, DC: Library of Congress.

Hennessey, Keith. 2010. "What Is a Vote-a-rama?" Keithhennessey.com, http://keithhennessey.com/2010/03/25/vote-a-rama.

Herszenhorn, David. 2007. "How the Filibuster Became the Rule." *New York Times*, December 2.

Holan, Angie Drobnic. 2010. "Ed Perlmutter Voted for Viagra for Sex Offenders, Paid for by Health Care Bill? Nope." Politifact.com, October 26.

Hulse, Carl. 2014. "McConnell Vows a Senate in Working Order, if He Is Given Control." *New York Times*, March 3.

Kosar, Kevin R., and Anthony J. Madonna. 2015. "Gridlock Governing: Toxic Amendments and Partisan Calculating May Land Senate Republicans in the Minority Once Again." *USA Today*, October 16.

Lawrence, Eric D. 2013. "The 1899 Publication of Hinds' Precedents and the Institutionalization of the House of Representatives." *Legislative Studies Quarterly* 38: 31–58.

Lee, Mike. 2015. "Congress Needs Uber-Level Innovation." *Federalist*, October 15.

Lynch, Michael, Anthony Madonna, and Mark E. Owens. n.d. "Procedural Uncertainty, the Parliamentarian, and Questions of Order in the United States Senate." Working paper.

Lynch, Michael S., Anthony J. Madonna, and Jason M. Roberts. Forthcoming. "The Cost of Majority Party Bias: Amending Activity under Structured Rules." *Legislative Studies Quarterly*.

Madonna, Anthony J., and Kevin R. Kosar. 2015. "An Open Amending Process in the Modern U.S. Senate: An Appraisal." R Street Policy Study No. 42, October, http://www.rstreet.org/wp-content/uploads/2015/10/RSTREET42.pdf.

Oleszek, Walter J. 2014. "The Evolving Congress: Overview and Analysis of the Modern Era." In *The Evolving Congress*, prepared by the Congressional Research Service, 3–60. 113th Cong., 2nd sess., S. Prt. 113–30. Washington, DC: Government Printing Office.

Oleszek, Walter J., Mark J. Oleszek, Elizabeth Rybicki, and Bill Heniff Jr. 2015. *Congressional Procedures and the Policy Process*, 10th ed. Washington, DC: CQ Press.

Sanders, Katie. 2015. "Senate Voted on More Amendments in January Than It Did in All of 2014." Politifact.com, February 2, http://www.politifact.com/punditfact/statements/2015/feb/02/phil-kerpen/claim-mitch-mcconnell-has-already-allowed-more-ame.

Sherman, Jake. 2014. "The Obsession of the House Freedom Caucus." *Politico*, October 15.

Sherman, Jake, and John Bresnahan. 2015. "Boehner Takes Revenge." *Politico*, January 6.

Sherman, Jake, and Anna Palmer. 2015. "Behind Boehner's Crackdown on Conservatives." *Politico*, June 24.

Smith, Steven S., and Marcus Flathman. 1989. "Managing the Senate Floor: Complex Unanimous Consent Agreements since the 1950s." *Legislative Studies Quarterly* 14: 349–74.

Steinhauer, Jennifer. 2015. "John Boehner, House Speaker, Will Resign from Congress." *New York Times*, September 25.

Steinhauer, Jennifer, and David M. Herszenhorn. 2015. "Kevin McCarthy Withdraws from Speaker's Race, Putting House in Chaos." *New York Times*, October 8.

"Stimulus Enacted to Pump Economy with $575.3 Billion in New Spending." 2010. In *CQ Almanac 2009*, edited by Jan Austin, 7-3-7-7. 65th ed. Washington, DC: CQ-Roll Call Group. http://library.cqpress.com/cqalmanac/cqal09-1183-59538-2251295.

Sullivan, Sean. 2015. "Senate Passes Budget after Lengthy, Politically Charged 'Vote-a-rama,'" *Washington Post*, March 27.

U.S. Congress, House, Committee on Rules. 2012. "The Germaneness Rule." In *Basic Training: Parliamentary Process, Facts, and Strategies*. House of Representatives, Committee on Rules, https://rules.house.gov/sites/republicans.rules.house.gov/files/112-BT-Germaneness-20120207.pdf (accessed October 29, 2015).

———. 2015. "About the Committee on Rules—History and Processes." House of Representatives, Committee on Rules, https://rules.house.gov/about.

U.S. Congress, Senate. 2015. "Unanimous Consent Agreements." United States Senate, http://www.senate.gov/reference/glossary_term/unanimous_consent_agreement.htm.

Wolfensberger, Don. 2015. "Keystone Process Tells Tale of Two Houses." *Roll Call*, February 24.

12

From Base Closings to the Budget

Exceptions to the Filibuster in the U.S. Senate

Molly E. Reynolds

F OLLOWING THE 2014 MIDTERM ELECTIONS, Congress returned to Washington in January 2015 with both houses controlled by Republicans for the
first time in eight years. Standing in the way of Republicans' major legislative
initiatives, however, was the threat of a filibuster from Senate Democrats
and a potential veto by President Barack Obama. In the opening weeks of
the 114th Congress (2015–2016) alone, major press coverage highlighted the
need for sixty votes in the Senate to pass a wide range of policies, including
an authorization of the Keystone XL Pipeline (Sullivan 2015), a revision of
President Obama's executive action on immigration (O'Keefe 2015), a repeal
of the Affordable Care Act (Weisman 2015b), and changes to the Dodd-
Frank financial reform law (Weisman 2015c). The embrace of the Senate as
a supermajoritarian body—in which more than a simple majority of votes is
needed for most legislative actions—extends, moreover, beyond the media to
the members of the chamber itself. In 2005, for example, Democratic Senator
Charles Schumer (2005, 8988) of New York went as far as to declare, on the
Senate floor, "The Senate is not a majoritarian body."

Many scholars (Koger 2010) have embraced this notion of the Senate as
supermajoritarian. Others, including Keith Krehbiel (1991) and Gregory J.
Wawro and Eric Schickler (2006), have countered this perception by arguing
that the Senate is "remotely majoritarian"—that is, that the high bar that prevents many bills from being passed is the result of choices by a simple majority to keep the traditional rules in place. Importantly, however, there is also
a class of procedures that makes the Senate actively majoritarian, preventing
filibusters on particular bills. By preventing one form of obstruction, these

procedures, which I call "majoritarian exceptions," increase the number of senators who must go on record as opposing a bill to stop it from passing. In the presence of the filibuster, if forty-one senators wish to see a measure fail, they can vote down a cloture motion. With majoritarian exceptions, however, the coalition opposing the bill must be larger (fifty-one) to ensure defeat.

The earliest examples of these procedures date to the early twentieth century—the Reorganization Act of 1939, for example, contained special rules for considering proposals by the president to reorganize the executive branch—but they have become a more common force in Senate politics since the 1970s, with Congress enacting more than one hundred since 1969. They cover a wide range of policy areas, including defense matters (such as procedures for closing military bases); the federal budget (including the process for passing the congressional budget resolution); and health care (such as the provisions governing the adoption of proposed cuts in Medicare spending). One majoritarian exception—the budget reconciliation process—has been at the center of a range of important changes to both taxes and entitlement spending since the early 1980s (Mann et al. 2010). As we see at the end of the chapter, moreover, two recent major policy objectives in Congress—the nuclear agreement with Iran and the twelve-nation trade deal known as the Trans-Pacific Partnership (TPP)—have involved these special rules.

What Are Majoritarian Exceptions?

For our purposes, we define a "majoritarian exception" as a provision, included in statutory law, that exempts some future piece of legislation from a filibuster by limiting debate on that measure. To understand how exactly this works, let us consider an illustrative example. In 1970, Congress passed the Federal Pay Comparability Act of 1970, which made permanent a system of annual pay adjustments for federal employees so that Congress did not need to consider whether to increase federal salaries each year but could still ensure that federal and private-sector salaries were comparable.[1] Rather than keep that responsibility for itself, it gave actors in the executive branch the power to develop recommendations on the size of the increase;[2] the president would then either act on those recommendations or submit an alternative plan to Congress. If he chose the latter option, Congress could disapprove of the proposal, using special, expedited procedures—the "majoritarian exception." Specifically, the bill stated, "Debate on the resolution is limited to not more than two hours, to be divided equally between those favoring and those opposing the resolution."[3] While the exact length of allowable debate varies across majoritarian exceptions, it is this strict cap on debate that prevents the measure from being filibustered.

This specific limitation on debate is the defining characteristic of a majoritarian exception. There are two additional provisions that majoritarian exceptions often contain, but a set of legislative procedures need not include either of them in order to be considered a majoritarian exception. First, the legislation may contain the following: "an amendment to, or motion to recommit, the resolution is not in order."[4] This clause prevents the filibuster-proof bill from being amended on the Senate floor; roughly 85 percent of majoritarian exceptions prevent any amendments, while an additional 5 percent or so permit only germane amendments. Both of these restrictions represent a significant departure from the Senate's usual procedures, which permit amendments to bills regardless of whether they are related to the legislation being considered.[5]

In addition, many majoritarian exceptions provide a way to prevent the filibuster-proof bill from being obstructed off the Senate floor by the committee with jurisdiction over the measure. In some cases, the time the panel can spend deliberating over the legislation is limited to a set number of days. After that, the bill is either automatically placed on the Senate Calendar or can be forcibly discharged from the committee by a nondebatable, filibuster-proof motion. Other instances, moreover, stipulate that the protected measure be reported directly to the floor.[6]

Majoritarian exceptions are changes to the Senate's rules made through statutory legislation approved by both houses of Congress and signed by the president. In this way, they are different from, for example, the 2013 modification to the Senate's rules for judicial and executive branch nominations (Peters 2013), which involved what Gregory Koger (2010) calls "reform by ruling." In the nominations case, the Senate's presiding officer made a ruling on a question about how the chamber's rules were to be implemented. A series of subsequent votes, each requiring only a simple majority to pass, sustained that ruling. This kind of "reform by ruling" is easier to achieve from a coalition-building perspective than is enacting majoritarian exceptions. Because the latter are contained in regular legislation, their supporters must overcome any threats from their colleagues to filibuster now, so that the bill can prevent a filibuster later. Additionally, they must also gain the support of a majority in the House of Representatives and the signature of the president. The bar to creating a majoritarian exception, therefore, is quite high.

Despite these obstacles, Congress created over one hundred majoritarian exceptions between 1969 and 2014. In general, they can be divided into two groups, which we will call "oversight" and "delegation." Oversight exceptions—described on the left side of figure 12.1—make a particular presidential

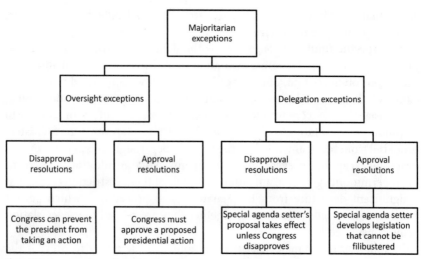

FIGURE 12.1.
Types of majoritarian exceptions.

action subject to legislative review. In general, once the president has taken the specified action, a measure accepting or rejecting the executive's decision comes to Congress. Because these exceptions increase Congress's opportunities to weigh in on a given topic, Congress generally turns to them when it is at an institutional disadvantage. Often, this occurs in policy areas where the president has a significant first-mover advantage—that is, when, if the president wants to make a change, he can so do so "quickly, forcefully, and (if [he] like[s]) with no advance notice" (Moe and Howell 1999). Previous work has found this benefit to be especially present in the foreign policy arena (Canes-Wrone, Howell, and Lewis 2008). One example of an oversight exception comes from the International Security Assistance and Arms Control Export Act of 1976, which allows Congress the opportunity to disapprove of sales of major defense equipment, with debate on the disapproval resolution capped at ten hours. Prior to the creation of these procedures, arms sales could be handled entirely within the executive branch. The president had to certify that the sale would "strengthen the security of the United States and promote world peace," but that determination was made for all proposed transactions by both Presidents Lyndon Johnson and Richard Nixon (U.S. Congress 1975, 14–15).

Like oversight exceptions, the policy questions addressed by delegation exceptions (described on the right side of figure 12.1) also tend to share a defining feature: answering them involves imposing concentrated costs in exchange for diffuse benefits. Reform in these policy areas, then, represents a classic collective action problem (Olson 1971). Collective action problems are situations in which all members of a group would be better off if they cooperated to solve a problem, but each individual has an incentive to avoid contributing to the group effort. In the case of Congress, this can arise when addressing a policy problem, like the growth in federal spending on Medicare, is in the interest of the country as a whole. Individual legislators, however, wanting to avoid blame from their constituents (Weaver 1987), are unlikely to invest the time in developing a solution or to vote for one when it comes to the floor. To address these kinds of problems, Congress will occasionally delegate some of its power to one or more actors, either within or outside the chamber. The actor or actors to whom this power is delegated will draft a new policy, and that proposal comes to the floor of the Senate under expedited legislative procedures. The process used for closing military bases since the 1980s is a well-known case of this kind of exception. An independent Base Realignment and Closing (BRAC) Commission was authorized by Congress to select bases for closure, and the legislation rejecting those selections cannot be filibustered or amended.

Both oversight and delegation exceptions designate a particular piece of legislation that is protected from a filibuster in the future, and that bill can take two forms: an approval resolution or a disapproval resolution. For oversight exceptions, if the protected bill is an approval resolution, the president cannot take the designated action unless Congress affirmatively approves. These often involve restrictions on appropriations, limiting the president's broad powers to direct the executive branch to spend appropriated money as he sees fit. Take, for example, a provision in the fiscal year 2001 Department of Defense appropriations bill. To ensure increased oversight over U.S. military actions to combat Colombian drug cartels, Congress prohibited the president from deploying military personnel to Colombia unless he delivered regular reports to Congress and Congress responded by enacting a joint resolution approving the requested funds.[7]

When an oversight exception protects a disapproval resolution, meanwhile, Congress has the chance to prevent the president from taking some action. The Congressional Review Act, for example, allows Congress to overturn executive branch regulations. Thanks to the Supreme Court's 1983 decision in *INS v. Chadha* (462 US 919), however, the president must sign the resolution that rejects the regulations,[8] so these kinds of oversight exceptions require a veto-proof majority in both houses of Congress to effectively check the president.

When a delegation exception protects an approval resolution, meanwhile, the measure looks much like a regular piece of legislation, except that it cannot be filibustered. Take, for example, the annual congressional budget resolution (see chapter 5). In 1974, the Congressional Budget Act created a special agenda setter (new standing committees in both chambers) to develop an annual measure setting out broad guidelines for spending and revenue. Debate on the resolution is limited to fifty hours, and if Congress does not approve it, it does not take effect. Indeed, Congress has often struggled with this in recent years, completing a budget resolution only eight times since 2000 (Heniff 2014). By comparison, when a delegation exception protects a disapproval resolution, the underlying proposal takes effect unless the disapproval legislation passes. This, for example, is the model under which Congress reviewed the BRAC Commission recommendations in 1988, 1991, 1993, 1995, and 2001. In each case, Congress set up a special commission to decide which military installations should be closed or realigned. The commissions delivered their recommendations to Congress, which could disapprove of the proposal in its entirety, without amendment. If the president signed that measure, only then would the work of the special agenda setter be rejected (Davis 2015).

When Will Congress Change the Rules?

As we saw above, majoritarian exceptions are prevalent in the Senate, spanning a wide range of issue areas. If we compare the number of times that Congress has created these procedures to the number of times they have been proposed, however, we see that successful enactment is relatively uncommon; of those formally proposed in Congress (that is, included in an introduced bill) since 1969, only approximately 17 percent have been enacted.[9] Members of Congress, then, often propose changing the rules but only sometimes succeed. What, then, predicts when a proposal to change the rules will be successful?

Majoritarian exceptions are narrowly tailored but, at their core, are limitations of minority rights in the Senate. Work on other instances of this kind of procedural change, such as the evolution of the filibuster, highlights how procedures are changed in response to short-term political forces. One prominent account of the creation of the cloture rule (Rule XXII) in 1917, for example, examines the political circumstances surrounding the measure whose passage was made possible by new procedures. Senate (majority) Democrats and President Woodrow Wilson framed that bill, which permitted the arming of merchant ships during World War I, as a "national security measure," portraying the procedural question as a matter of policy. The new rules, they argued, were needed if the Senate was going to enact a popular and salient policy change. Senators, then, responded to "pragmatic and (legitimate) political considerations" in choosing to create a mechanism for ending debate (Binder and Smith 1997, 194).[10] In a nineteenth-century case, the ability to table an amendment without killing the underlying bill was, argues Sarah A. Binder (1997, 183), the result of "senators' frustration over their inability to pass an appropriations bill to fund western expansion."

The policy-specific nature of majoritarian exceptions complicates this story somewhat. If current senators are seeking a rule change because they want to ease the passage of some future bill, they must believe that future is nigh. Put differently, the new procedures are of little value to the current Senate if the measure they protect does not appear on the agenda in the near future. An examination of the circumstances surrounding the enacted majoritarian exceptions, however, suggests that this assumption is often valid. In some cases, the legislation creating the rules contains a firm deadline; the last time special procedures were created to consider military base closings, for example, the statute required that the recommendations be transmitted to Congress by September 8, 2005.[11] In other instances, it is possible to identify how quickly the special rules were first used after they were created. The provision allowing Congress to disapprove of a proposed arms sale, for example, was first invoked less than three months after the oversight exception was enacted in 1976.[12]

In other circumstances, we can isolate the first time Congress could have deployed the procedures but chose not to. In 1980, Congress extended the oversight exception allowing it to disapprove of export licenses for weapons sales to include wholly private transactions. The first deal eligible to be reviewed by Congress under these rules occurred in 1982, but the legislature let the sale proceed unimpeded (Campbell 1982). On the whole, the majority of majoritarian exceptions become relevant within two years of enactment (Reynolds 2015), suggesting that the Senate may be considering its current political challenges in creating these special rules.

Oversight Exceptions

These general dynamics should apply to both kinds of majoritarian exceptions, oversight and delegation. At the same time, there are important differences between the two kinds of procedures; as a result, there are additional factors that should predict when each type is created. First, let us consider oversight exceptions, where Congress has a protected opportunity to weigh in on an action by the executive branch. In general, the president has substantial authority to act unilaterally, without consulting Congress (Cooper 2005). Much of this authority is drawn from the "executive powers" clause in Article

II of the Constitution, where the president is directed to "take care that the laws be faithfully executed." Congress, through explicit delegations of responsibility to the president, has also fed this well of power over time. Regardless of how the president establishes discretion in a policy area, once he has done so, it is difficult for Congress to claw back that power (Volden 2002). Because members of Congress must run for reelection every two or six years, they are generally more concerned about short-term, personal political consequences than long-term, institutional ones (Howell 2003).

If individual members of Congress have little appetite for institutional maintenance, then they must be motivated to pursue oversight exceptions for reasons beyond principles. Prior research on other successful attempts to check the president's power reveals a strong role for partisanship. Restrictions on the president's war powers, for example, are more frequent when Congress and the presidency are controlled by opposite parties (Kriner 2010), as are limitation riders, which restrict the executive branch's ability to promulgate particular regulations (MacDonald 2010, 2013).

Should we expect the same for oversight exceptions? Because the rules are fundamentally a tool to facilitate policy change—and often on a short time horizon—we should expect to see them created when both Congress and the president prefer what they can enact with the new rules in place to what they can do with the current ones. Let us start by considering a hypothetical world where no special rules exist, following the basic logic of William G. Howell's (2003) theory of presidential unilateral action in which the president has wide latitude to act on his own; we call this "regular order." In policy areas in which the president enjoys significant first-mover advantages—such as foreign and military affairs—his ability to change current policy unilaterally is constrained by the possibility that Congress, tipped off by his actions, will step in to overturn the policy choice he's just made. Since the president must sign any legislation passed by Congress before it can take effect, this limit is relatively weak; to explicitly revise an executive action, congressional leaders would need a veto-proof majority in both chambers. Still, knowing that this kind of congressional response is a possibility, we should expect the president to take into account the policy preferences of members of Congress when deciding what new policy to craft.

Given the need for a veto-proof majority to revise executive actions, in many cases Congress's preferences will not bind what the president can do. Under unified partisan control of Congress and the presidency, the president's most preferred policy will often be popular enough that congressional leaders would not be able to muster enough votes to change it. When Congress and the presidency are controlled by different parties, meanwhile, the president may not be able to implement his most preferred policy, but as long as his action is preferred to existing policy by at least one-third of both chambers, he can avoid a congressional response.

There is, however, a particular set of circumstances in which the president may be concerned about the consequences of his unilateral actions: when current policy is extreme on his own side of the political spectrum (i.e., if policy is very liberal and the president is a Democrat, or if policy is very conservative and the president is a Republican). Here, any action preferred by the president could conceivably be overturned by a veto-proof majority in Congress—and in doing so, Congress would create a much more moderate policy than the president wants.

An illustrative example of this phenomenon involves arms sales to Iran by the executive branch in the early to mid-1970s. Beginning in 1972, President Richard Nixon adopted a policy that Iranian requests to purchase arms from the United States "should not be second-guessed" (U.S. Congress 1983, 43). This extremely conservative position on the part of Nixon meant that the United States would "'sell Iran virtually any conventional weapons it wanted' [and was] locked . . . into a policy whereby sales levels could not be reduced 'without precipitating a major crisis in U.S.-Iranian relations.'" ("Congress Declines to Block Arms Sales" 1976, 254). In 1976, then, President Gerald Ford was between a rock and a hard place. On one hand, there were likely veto-proof majorities in both Democratically-controlled chambers that would respond with legislation placing conditions on those sales or halting them outright. On the other hand, not pursuing the policy might have deleterious effects on U.S. foreign relations.

Now, imagine a different procedural world, one where after the president takes a unilateral action, it automatically comes to Congress for review. That review involves an oversight exception: a review resolution cannot get stuck in committee, cannot be amended during floor consideration, and cannot be filibustered in the Senate. In many situations, these rules would dramatically limit what the president could do as compared to in the "regular order" world; this is especially true when the oversight exception takes the form of an approval resolution. The president must sign the law creating the special rules, and the procedures are generally created with an eye toward proximate policy problems. We would expect, then, that the president would anticipate Congress's future actions and simply not sign the bill changing the rules.

In other situations, such as when the status quo policy is relatively moderate and the oversight exception takes the form of a disapproval resolution, the special rules do not affect the final policy outcome because the measure passed under the expedited procedures must still be signed by the president. The president would never take a unilateral action for which he would sign a resolution of disapproval, so as long as one-third of the House or Senate prefers the new policy initiated by the president to the current status quo, the existence of the expedited procedures neither limits nor enhances the president's power.

Recall, however, those situations in which the president is concerned about possible successful reprisals from Congress in the "regular order" world—that is, when policy is currently relatively extreme on his side of the ideological spectrum. Here, the special rules actually benefit the president. Why? Congress's preferences still must be accommodated, but the limitations on the review resolution—such as protecting it from amendment and limiting the time Congress can spend considering the bill—mean that Congress is limited in how much it can revise the president's action. Thus, the president can ensure policy is closer to his most preferred outcome without being concerned that Congress will respond with a substantially more moderate policy. Congress, meanwhile, also prefers the new outcome, which better reflects its preferences than the extreme policy. By granting the president the ability to make a protected proposal and ensuring that the measure is actually taken up by preventing a filibuster, Congress incentivizes the president to act. From a policy perspective, both branches are better off in the presence of the new special rules.

We can see these dynamics at play in the Ford administration's ultimate approach to arms sales to Iran in 1976. In 1975, a Democratically-controlled Congress had demonstrated a willingness to take on the president on the issue of large weapons sales to Middle Eastern countries, threatening to block the sale of fourteen batteries of Hawk ground-to-air missiles and eight Vulcan antiaircraft guns to Jordan. Ford was forced to change strategy midstream when it became clear that legislation preventing the deal was likely to pass. To avoid a congressional response, Ford eventually agreed that the weapons would only be used for "defensive and non-mobile anti-aircraft" ("Congress Weighs New Controls on Arms Sales" 1975, 359) purposes. By the time he wanted to sell F-16 jet fighters to Iran in mid-1976, however, Congress had passed, and Ford had signed, legislation that included an oversight exception with a disapproval resolution for sales of defense articles or services over $25 million and sales of defense equipment over $7 million.[13] Early indications were that Iran wanted to purchase as many as 300 F-16s and 250 F-18s, but by the time the offer was transmitted to Congress for its review, the proposal was for only 160 F-16s (U.S. Congress 1976, 120). While Congress did hold hearings on the sale, it did not formally threaten to overturn it legislatively, as it had with the Jordanian proposal the year prior. Both sides, then, were better off: Democrats in Congress had some input on the president's action, but the review structure put in place by the oversight exception meant that uncertainty was reduced for the president.

When current policy in an area where the president has a lot of discretion is quite liberal (under Democratic presidents) or conservative (under Republican presidents), we should see more oversight exceptions created. Partisan control of Congress, moreover, should also matter. In the situations where the president is willing to sign off on the legislation creating new rules, congressional majorities of the opposite party are always better off. After all, they would prefer policies that are substantially more liberal (in the case of a Republican president) or conservative (in the case of a Democratic one) than what the president is willing to offer even with the protections of an amendment restriction.

When Congress and the presidency are controlled by the same party, however, this is not necessarily always the case. If the congressional majority is exceptionally liberal (under a Democratic president) or conservative (under a Republican president), it may actually prefer the more extreme policy that remains in place under regular order to the one the president could implement in the presence of the oversight exception. Since the review resolution cannot be filibustered or bottled up in committee, the congressional majority is better off not approving the legislation containing the special rules in the first place. In sum, then, we should also expect to see more oversight exceptions enacted under divided government than unified government.

Delegation Exceptions

Now, consider the conditions that give rise to delegation exceptions, where special rules protect a proposal that has been developed by a special agenda setter designated by Congress. Whereas oversight exceptions help Congress and the president enact mutually beneficial policy changes by adjusting the usual balance of power between the two branches, delegation exceptions serve a different purpose, helping Congress address policy problems whose solutions impose concentrated costs in exchange for diffuse benefits.

To understand why delegation exceptions are particularly attractive tools in these situations, it is helpful to turn to R. Douglas Arnold's (1990) work on how voters reward or punish incumbents for previous actions in office. For a given policy choice to affect a future election, argues Arnold, that decision must be "traceable," with three conditions necessary for traceability. First, voters must perceive the effect of a policy choice in their daily lives. Second, they must be able to connect those consequences to an identifiable action taken by the government. Third, their representatives must have made a visible contribution to that action. If voters recognize positive effects of a specific governmental action to which a representative clearly contributed, the account goes, they can reward the incumbent with reelection; if the traceable consequences are negative, however, the incumbent is apt to be punished.

For the kinds of issues covered by delegation exceptions, if voters are able to trace a policy choice, the electoral effects are likely to be, on average, negative. Take, for example, the decision to close military bases. Chances are that only voters hurt by the decision will notice; evidence suggests that the communities in which shuttered bases are located may experience less overall economic activity, spillover job losses, and/or decreased government revenue as a result of the closures (Cowan 2012). The benefits of closing bases—such as overall budget savings and increased efficiency of military operations—are much less likely to be noted by individual citizens. It is in the interest of individual, reelection-minded members, then, to minimize the traceability of the kinds of policy changes with which delegation exceptions generally deal. These incentives, argues Arnold, are exactly what motivate coalition leaders to use procedural strategies—like granting the ability to make a protected proposal to a special agenda setter—in pursuit of the underlying policy change.

Delegation exceptions reduce traceability mainly by affecting the third link in Arnold's chain. They make it harder for voters to connect their individual representatives to a policy choice, and they do so in two key ways. First, by giving a special agenda setter the ability to develop the reform proposal, the delegation exception reduces the number of legislators who can be identified as having had a hand in the development of the proposal, such as having been the original sponsor or a cosponsor of the proposal. Empirical evidence suggests that these kinds of visible actions are used by interest groups to tie legislators to policy proposals (Rocca and Gordon 2010), and delegation exceptions make these connections more difficult to make, especially when the agenda setter is outside the chamber.

Second, by protecting the proposal from amendments and filibusters on the floor of the Senate, delegation exceptions eliminate the expectation that individual members will exploit their various procedural rights to the benefit of their constituents. The presumption that senators are obligated to use all the procedural tools at their disposal has only grown in the Senate over the course of the twentieth century (Binder and Smith 1997; Smith 2014). If legislators are limited in their ability to change or obstruct the proposal, they cannot make visible contributions to its passage or its defeat. In the case of disapproval resolutions, moreover, the possibility that constituents will detect individual contributions by their representatives is reduced even more.

If delegation exceptions minimize traceability, then, we should expect the chances that these special rules are created to be highest when individual members most want to hide their actions or avoid blame (Weaver 1987). We have already explored how issue content can encourage the creation of expedited procedures; when policy reforms involve imposing specific costs in exchange for diffuse benefits, delegation exceptions are especially attractive.

Other factors likely matter as well, including voter preferences. If the policy change facilitated by the special rules is unpopular with constituents, minimizing traceability should be more attractive as legislators seek to avoid being tagged with the decision. Take, for example, the choice to create the Independent Payment Advisory Board (IPAB), as part of the 2010 Patient Protection and Affordable Care Act, to address the persistent growth in Medicare spending. Under the law, if average growth in Medicare spending is projected to exceed a specified target, the IPAB is charged with developing a proposal to reduce spending. Legislation implementing the board's proposal is then protected in Congress by a delegation exception; the IPAB's expedited procedures prevent a filibuster but permit amendments as long as the total reductions approved by Congress are equal to those proposed by the board. The board's recommendations take effect automatically unless Congress is able to pass such an equivalent bill (Hahn and Davis 2013).

Unsurprisingly, cuts to Medicare are extremely unpopular. A March 2010 Quinnipiac poll found that 76 percent of respondents agree that "cutting the growth of spending on Medicare benefits . . . should not be a main part of any government approach to the deficit" (Quinnipiac University Polling Institute 2010), while in a similarly timed Democracy Corps poll, 67 percent of respondents somewhat or strongly opposed "reduc[ing] future spending on entitlements such as Social Security and Medicare" as a way of addressing the federal budget deficit (Democracy Corps 2010). Reducing the traceability of the cuts, then, is an attractive way to solve the underlying policy problem while also, hopefully, avoiding electoral punishment.

Conversely, if the underlying measure is popular, members of Congress will want to claim credit for their actions on it. Richard L. Hall (1996) has argued that, for members to be seen as credible when they tout accomplishments, they need to be able to point to actual contributions they made to those decisions. When tackling popular legislation, then, legislators will want as many opportunities as possible to put their fingerprints on the decision. There is no reason to minimize traceability, and members of Congress will want to use the regular legislative process.

Creating an Oversight Exception: The Case of Iran Sanctions, 2014–2015

To explore how these dynamics have played out in practice, let us now consider the first of two case studies of majoritarian exceptions that were at the center of recent high-profile legislative initiatives. Among the most significant foreign policy debates of President Obama's second term was the debate over a deal reached between Iran and the so-called P5+1 (the United States, United Kingdom, France, Russia, China, and Germany) that sought to limit Iran's ability to obtain a nuclear weapon. The seven countries had been negotiating in some form or another about Iran's nuclear program since 2006, and these talks accelerated after the 2013 election of Iranian president Hassan Rouhani. In April 2015, the parties agreed on a framework for a Joint Comprehensive Plan of Action (JCPOA), which was finalized in July 2015. Key provisions of the JCPOA include specific constraints on how much uranium Iran may enrich over ten- and fifteen-year periods, a requirement that Iran redesign a key reactor so that it cannot produce weapons-grade plutonium, and various inspection protocols. In exchange for Iran's implementing these limits, the United States, the European Union, and the United Nations will lift many of the sanctions each has imposed against that country (Katzman and Kerr 2015).

Congressional opposition became more active in late 2013, after the parties reached an interim agreement that would guide the rest of the talks. Among the opponents' major goals was to guarantee that Congress would have formal input on the agreement. In December 2013, a bipartisan group of senators, led by Robert Menendez (D-NJ) and Mark Kirk (R-IL), introduced legislation that would both impose additional sanctions on Iran and limit the president's ability to waive existing sanctions as part of any final agreement that came out of the multiparty talks.[14] Their efforts and similar ones in the House of Representatives failed in the face of substantial pressure from the White House (Bruck 2014).

In the summer of 2014, as negotiations between Iran and the P5+1 continued, Senator Bob Corker (R-TN) and four Republican cosponsors took a more streamlined approach, introducing legislation that would create a straightforward oversight exception for reviewing a final agreement with Iran. Once a deal was reached and transmitted to Congress, relevant committees would have fifteen days to consider a review resolution, after which it would be automatically reported to the floor. Once on the floor, the motion to proceed to consideration of the resolution could not be filibustered, and the measure itself could not be amended or filibustered. When Corker and colleague Lindsey Graham (R-SC) attempted to bring the bill to the floor of the Senate in November 2014, their efforts were thwarted by Democrats (Zengerle 2014).

By the spring of 2015, as the parties made more progress toward a final agreement, Corker and eleven cosponsors from both parties attempted one additional time to guarantee Congress the ability to review the deal. This time, however, the bill—which would be enacted into law as the Iran Nuclear

Agreement Review Act—looked different. It did not contain an oversight exception for a measure that would disapprove of an agreement with Iran, but it did include expedited procedures for so-called snapback sanctions. This "snapback" provision ensured that if, after its implementation, Iran was found to be in violation of the deal, the president would be able to reimpose sanctions, subject to congressional approval. The approval resolution would be handled as an oversight exception, complete with automatic report from committee and protections from amendments and a filibuster.[15]

To understand why Congress did not create an oversight exception for the disapproval resolution on the deal itself but did include one for a potential snapback measure, let us return to the logic sketched out above. First, throughout the complicated pre-JCPOA Iran sanctions regime, the president enjoyed a first-mover advantage in being able to waive sanctions against Iran (Rennack 2015)—one of the key factors that can encourage Congress to create an oversight exception. The negotiations that culminated in the JCPOA were carried out in the shadow of that sanctions regime, so when Congress was considering a new oversight exception for the purpose of reviewing the deal, it knew that the president had the kind of significant latitude to change policy on his own.

Second, recall also that oversight exceptions should be more likely under divided government. This condition, too, was clearly satisfied, with President Obama in the White House and the Republicans holding fifty-four seats in the Senate. What about policy toward Iran going into the negotiations? Determining the extent to which a policy is more liberal or conservative than what a given actor prefers is notoriously difficult, but we have little reason to expect that it was more liberal than President Obama's own preferences. After all, most of the opposition to the final agreement came from Republicans who found the deal too lax toward to the Iranians; a few of the more moderate Democrats also opposed the deal (Steinhauer 2015).

If current policy on Iran was moderate to conservative before the deal was negotiated, then the logic sketched out above tells us that an oversight exception would have made no difference to the final policy outcome. Because at least one-third of either the House or Senate agreed with the president in supporting the agreement (Fritze 2015), a resolution of disapproval would never have been enacted into law. The only effects of an oversight exception, then, would have been political. Special rules would have made it easier for Republicans and moderate Democrats who opposed the deal to go on record with their opposition, potentially generating position-taking benefits for those individual members (Mayhew 1974) in future elections. A Senate-passed resolution of disapproval might have also helped the Republicans, who were unified in their opposition, build their party brand for the next election (Cox and McCubbins 1993, 2005). Given that it was in the interest of Senate Democrats as a party team to deny Republicans even this small victory (Lee 2009), it is likely that even the moderate Democrats who opposed the underlying deal would have opposed a proposed oversight exception.

Now, let us consider the decision by Congress to include an oversight exception for snapback sanctions. Recall that in policy areas where the president has a first-mover advantage, when policy reflects his preferences reasonably well but is unpopular with a congressional majority of the opposite party, the president is likely to be concerned about provoking an aggressive congressional response with any actions. This scenario could easily arise in the near future in the context of Iran under the JCPOA if Republicans continue to control the Senate and a Democrat remains in the White House. Given that Congress is ill equipped to monitor Iranian compliance itself, the executive branch will clearly have an advantage in terms of knowing whether action is appropriate.

Suppose, then, that the president learns of even a small breach of the agreement. In the presence of the oversight exception, he can propose reintroducing exactly the same sanctions in place prior to the JCPOA with the knowledge that the expedited procedures will ease their passage and protect them from amendment. A congressional majority of the opposition party, meanwhile, is better off knowing that the president has an incentive, in the form of procedural protections, to keep it apprised of Iranian compliance. Without the special rules, however, the president might be concerned that, if he drew congressional attention to a small violation by proposing a response, Congress would respond more aggressively, with severer sanctions than existed before the agreement. Should these hypothetical circumstances come to pass, then Congress and the president are both potentially helped by having the expedited procedures in place.

Creating a Delegation Exception: The Case of Fast-Track Trade Authority, 2014–2015

The role of the president in oversight exceptions, like the one involving the reimposition of sanctions against Iran, is straightforward: the procedures are meant to ensure Congress has input on certain executive actions while also preventing that involvement from producing policy outcomes that make the president significantly worse off. The executive branch also, however, may be an important player in the creation of a delegation exception. After all, the president may be the special agenda setter to whom power for developing a protected proposal is delegated.

An important example of such a delegation exception emerged on the agenda in early 2014, when it appeared that Congress was on track for another year of record-low productivity (DeSilver 2013). Early on, however, one bright spot for potential bipartisanship emerged: the possible renewal of the president's lapsed fast-track trade authority, which would allow him to bring trade deals—including the Trans-Pacific Partnership, a deal involving Asia and Latin America that was nearing completion—to the Senate floor for approval ineligible for amendment and exempt from the possibility of a filibuster.[16] Obama had repeatedly articulated his support for the renewal, and Senate Finance Committee chairman Max Baucus (D-MT) was among the measure's original sponsors. It was hugely popular with the business community, and Kevin McCarthy (R-CA), then House Republican whip, even suggested that Obama's first call to Congress should be about trade (Lowrey 2014). But barely four weeks into the year, the legislation was dead on arrival, thanks in large part to opposition from the president's own congressional co-partisans, especially Senate Majority Leader Harry Reid (D-NV). Following a mention of the proposal by Obama in his State of the Union address, Reid announced that he would prevent the legislation from coming to the floor of the Senate, saying "Everyone would be well-advised to not push this right now" (Bradner and Raju 2014). His House Democratic leadership counterpart, Minority Leader Nancy Pelosi (D-CA), expressed similar opposition, saying the plan was "out of the question" (Babington 2014).

Fast-forward to April 2015, when key congressional leaders—Senate Finance Committee chair Orrin Hatch (R-UT), Finance Committee ranking member Ron Wyden (D-OR), and House Ways and Means chair Paul Ryan (R-WI)—announced they had reached a deal on legislation granting fast-track authority to the president for six years (Weisman 2015a). After roughly two months of additional haggling between the chambers (Weisman 2015e), the measure was signed into law by President Obama in June (Weisman 2015d).

Why was Congress successful at creating the delegation exception in 2015 but not in 2014? First of all, it is worth noting that trade policymaking is ripe with collective action problems. The benefits of protectionist policies are concentrated in the hands of a few firms, while the costs are widely dispersed across the consumer population (Alt and Gilligan 1994). Relaxing these policies through free trade agreements, then, has the opposite effect: the benefits are diffuse, but the costs are felt deeply by those companies now competing with cheaper imported goods. Because electorally minded legislators from areas likely to be hit hard by free trade will attempt to undo any bargain reached to deliver the broad-based benefits, the regular legislative process is ill equipped to implement free trade agreements. Members of Congress are better off giving more power to a special agenda setter—here, the executive branch—and then protecting that actor's proposal procedurally.

In explaining the changing fortunes of the TPP, many congressional observers would point to the preferences of the interest groups loyal to the two parties. Previous research suggests that Democrats are less likely to support free trade agreements in part because of the strong opposition of labor unions to the pacts, while Republicans, thanks to their alliance with business groups, tend to support them (Bailey and Brady 1998; Baldwin and Magee 2000). Certainly, these group coalitions likely played a role, but a look at polling data on the issue from 2014 and 2015 complicates this account. In February 2014, when a Senate controlled by the Democrats might have taken up the delegation exception, 59 percent of Democrats indicated in a Pew Research Center/ Bertelsmann Foundation poll that they thought the TPP would be a "good thing" for the United States (Pew Research Center 2014). By June 2015, when the now Republican-controlled chamber was debating the measure, only 43 percent of Republican poll respondents agreed (Pew Research Center 2015). Support for the underlying policy among the Senate majority party's key constituents, then, had dropped sixteen points in just fifteen months.

In light of our theory, however, pushing for fast-track authority in the face of higher public opposition is unsurprising. The chances that the majority party will ask some of its members to give up some of their influence should increase when the policy is unpopular. The fact that the TPP was supported by only a minority of Republican voters meant that the Republican majority leadership had a greater incentive to change the rules in order to minimize the traceability of the eventual decision to approve the underlying trade agreement. In addition to facing lower levels of support for the underlying policy, the Republican majority was also operating on a decidedly different timetable than the Democrats had been in the previous year—a difference that our theory suggests should matter. In early 2014, observers of the negotiations noted that there was much work left to be done ("No End in Sight" 2014). By March 2015, however, various negotiators had met eight additional times (Organization of American States 2015), with nine of the agreement's estimated thirty chapters completed and several more nearing completion ("Australian Official" 2015). As we saw in the descriptive data at the beginning of this chapter, majoritarian exceptions tend to be created to meet proximate political needs. The closer negotiators got to completing the TPP, then, the more relevant were expedited ratification procedures to the Senate's majority party.

Of course, these factors do not operate independently of one another. Indeed, the accelerated timetable for Republicans in 2015 may have interacted with their constituents' opposition to the deal. Because President Obama was the special agenda setter who would get to make a procedurally protected proposal, the ultimate congressional endorsement of the TPP would hand him a major political victory. Public opinion research tells us that policies can become less popular with voters of one party merely because they are associated with a president of the opposite party (Nicholson 2012). If Senate Republicans reasonably believed that the TPP would be completed and approved under President Obama, their incentive to minimize the traceability of that decision was likely greater than it would have been otherwise. Indeed, when asked about their support for fast-track legislation in a way that explicitly referenced the president's role in the process, support among Republicans was even lower; in May 2015, only 27 percent of Republican respondents approved of "giving the president authority to negotiate international trade deals that Congress can only approve or disapprove, but not change" (CBS News/*New York Times* 2015). Indeed, at the time of this writing, the TPP itself remained under congressional consideration, with increasing opposition from individual Republican legislators worried about their role in a potential high-profile achievement by a Democratic president (Swanson and Cusack 2015).

Obstruction, often in the form of the filibuster, undoubtedly shapes much of the Senate's deliberation. Indeed, of the four major legislative initiatives highlighted by the media as possible filibuster targets in the opening weeks of the 114th Congress (2015–2016), only one—the measure approving the Keystone XL Pipeline—managed to clear the sixty-vote threshold on the Senate floor, after which it was promptly vetoed by President Obama (Davenport 2015). At the same time, as illustrated here, simply asserting that the Senate has become a uniformly supermajoritarian chamber obscures important exceptions to that overall trend. Certainly, majoritarian exceptions are not likely to be wholesale solutions to the problems of obstruction in the Senate—the success rate of proposed rule changes cited above suggests that conditions for creating them are, after all, relatively rare. In addition, as the TPP case illustrates well, the rules often shepherd to passage policies that could enhance the electoral standing of the current majority party, making it more difficult to attract the often necessary partners from the other party for enacting the rule change. At the same time, as we have seen here, when the circumstances are right, we can and do see special, targeted procedures that exempt specific bills from a filibuster in the Senate playing an important role in policymaking in a range of important policy areas.

Notes

1. This system and the accompanying majoritarian exception were replaced by a new arrangement under the Federal Employees Pay Comparability Act of 1990.

2. Specifically, the authority was given to a Federal Employee Pay Council (comprised of representatives from the major federal employee unions) and the Advisory Committee on Federal Pay (consisting of three nonfederal employees).

3. See P.L. 91-656, §3(i).

4. See P.L. 91-656, §3(i).

5. See Senate Rule XVI.

6. For an example of a day limitation, see P.L. 91-656, §3(e), and P.L. 91–656, §3(f). For an example of a provision that sends the bill directly to the floor, see P.L. 100-119, §105.

7. See P.L. 106-246, §3204.

8. Specifically, *INS v. Chadha*, 462 U.S. 919 (1983), declared the legislative veto, defined as a provision requiring "congressional review, deferral, approval, or disapproval of proposed executive actions" (Norton 1976, 1), by a single chamber of Congress unconstitutional.

9. For details on how proposed and enacted majoritarian exceptions were identified from the historical record, see Reynolds (2015, ch. 2).

10. See Wawro and Schickler (2006) for a competing account of how short-term political considerations shape choices about procedural change that deemphasizes public opinion.

11. See P.L. 107-107.

12. See S. Con. Res. 150 (94th Congress). See also companion legislation in the House: H. Con. Res. 740, H. Con. Res. 757, H. Con. Res. 766, H. Con. Res. 770, and H. Con. Res. 777 (94th Congress).

13. See P.L. 94-329, §211. It is worth noting that Ford vetoed earlier legislation that would have extended the oversight exception to commercial arms sales, though such a requirement was eventually added in 1980 (Tompa 1986).

14. See S. 1881, Nuclear Weapon Free Iran Act of 2013 (113th Congress).

15. See P.L. 114-17, especially §2(d).

16. A second deal, the Transatlantic Trade and Investment Partnership (T-TIP), was also mentioned as a forthcoming beneficiary of fast-track authority, but that agreement was unlikely to be completed until after a new president took office in 2017 (Kanter 2014).

References

Adler, E. Scott, and John Wilkerson. 2012. *Congress and the Politics of Problem-Solving*. New York: Cambridge University Press.

Alt, James E., and Michael Gilligan. 1994. "The Political Economy of Trading States: Factor Specificity Problems and Domestic Political Institutions." *Journal of Political Philosophy* 2: 165–92.

Arnold, R. Douglas. 1990. *The Logic of Congressional Action*. New Haven, CT: Yale University Press.

"Australian Official Says Nine TPP Chapters Closed, Others Nearing Conclusion." 2015. *Inside U.S. Trade* 33, no. 10: March 13.

Babington, Charles. 2014. "Pelosi Rejects Obama Bid for Fast-Track Trade." Associated Press, February 12.

Bailey, Michael, and David W. Brady. 1998. "Heterogeneity and Representation: The Senate and Free Trade." *American Journal of Political Science* 42: 524–44.

Baldwin, Robert E., and Christopher S. Magee. 2000. "Is Trade Policy for Sale? Congressional Voting on Recent Trade Bills." *Public Choice* 105: 79–101.

Binder, Sarah A. 1997. *Minority Rights, Majority Rule: Partisanship and the Development of Congress*. New York: Cambridge University Press.

Binder, Sarah A., and Steven S. Smith. 1997. *Politics or Principle? Filibustering in the United States Senate*. Washington, DC: Brookings Institution Press.

Bradner, Eric, and Manu Raju. 2014. "Harry Reid Rejects President Obama's Trade Push." *Politico*, January 29.

Bruck, Connie. 2014. "Friends of Israel." *New Yorker*, September 1.

Campbell, Colin. 1982. "Indonesia Seeks to Keep Pace in Arms." *New York Times*, July 30.

Canes-Wrone, Brandice, William G. Howell, and David E. Lewis. 2008. "Toward a Broader Understanding of Presidential Power: A Reevaluation of the Two Presidencies Thesis." *Journal of Politics* 70: 1–16.

CBS News/*New York Times*. 2015. "Americans' Views on the Workplace and Income Inequality." May.

"Congress Declines to Block Arms Sales." 1976. *CQ Almanac 1976*, 253–56. 32nd ed. Washington, DC: Congressional Quarterly.

"Congress Weighs New Controls on Arms Sales." 1975. *CQ Almanac 1975*, 356–60. 31st ed. Washington, DC: Congressional Quarterly.

Cooper, Phillip J. 2005. "George W. Bush, Edgar Allan Poe, and the Use and Abuse of Presidential Signing Statements." *Presidential Studies Quarterly* 35, no. 3: 515–32.

Cowan, Tadlock. 2012. "Military Base Closures: Socioeconomic Impacts." Congressional Research Service. Washington, DC: Library of Congress.

Cox, Gary W., and Mathew D. McCubbins. 1993. *Legislative Leviathan*. Berkeley: University of California Press.

———. 2005. *Setting the Agenda: Responsible Party Government in the U.S. House of Representatives*. New York: Cambridge University Press.

Davenport, Coral. 2015. "Senate Fails to Override Obama's Keystone Pipeline Veto." *New York Times*, March 4.

Davis, Christopher M. 2015. "'Fast Track' Legislative Procedures Governing Congressional Consideration of a Defense Base Closure and Realignment (BRAC) Commission Report." Congressional Research Service. Washington, DC: Library of Congress.

Democracy Corps. 2010. "Democracy Corps Poll." March. USGREEN.10DCMAR31. R72. Greenberg Quinlan Rosner Research. Storrs, CT: Roper Center for Public Opinion Research, iPOLL.

DeSilver, Drew. 2013. "Congress Ends Least-Productive Year in Recent History." Pew Research Center, December 23, http://www.pewresearch.org/fact-tank/2013/12/23/congress-ends-least-productive-year-in-recent-history.

Fritze, John. 2015. "Mikulski Hands Obama Victory on Iran Deal." *Baltimore Sun*, September 2.

Hahn, Jim, and Christopher M. Davis. 2013. "The Independent Payment Advisory Board." Congressional Research Service. Washington, DC: Library of Congress.

Hall, Richard L. 1996. *Participation in Congress*. New Haven, CT: Yale University Press.

Heniff, William, Jr. 2014. "Congressional Budget Resolutions: Historical Information." Congressional Research Service. Washington, DC: Library of Congress.

Howell, William G. 2003. *Power without Persuasion: The Politics of Direct Presidential Action*. Princeton, NJ: Princeton University Press.

Kanter, James. 2014. "Major Hurdles Still Remain in Trans-Atlantic Trade Talks." *New York Times*, June 2.

Katzman, Kenneth, and Paul K. Kerr. 2015. "Iran Nuclear Agreement." Congressional Research Service. Washington, DC: Library of Congress.

Koger, Gregory. 2010. *Filibustering: A Political History of Obstruction in the House and Senate*. Chicago: University of Chicago Press.

Krehbiel, Keith. 1991. *Information and Legislative Organization*. Ann Arbor: University of Michigan Press.

Kriner, Douglas L. 2010. *After the Rubicon: Congress, Presidents, and the Politics of Waging War*. Chicago: University of Chicago Press.

Lee, Frances E. 2009. *Beyond Ideology: Politics, Principles, and Partisanship in the U.S. Senate*. Chicago: University of Chicago Press.

Lowrey, Annie. 2014. "Obama and G.O.P. Facing Opposition to Trade Pacts." *New York Times*, January 30.

MacDonald, Jason A. 2010. "Limitation Riders and Congressional Influence over Bureaucratic Policy Decisions." *American Political Science Review* 104: 766–82.

———. 2013. "Congressional Power over Executive Branch Policy Making: Limitations on Bureaucratic Regulations, 1989–2009." *Presidential Studies Quarterly* 43: 523–37.

Mann, Thomas, Norman J. Ornstein, Raffaela Wakeman, and Fogelson-Lubliner. 2010. "Reconciling with the Past." *New York Times*, March 6.

Mayhew, David R. 1974. *Congress: The Electoral Connection*. New Haven, CT: Yale University Press.

Moe, Terry M., and William M. Howell. 1999. "Unilateral Action and Presidential Power: A Theory." *Presidential Studies Quarterly* 29: 850–73.

Nicholson, Sean. 2012. "Polarizing Cues." *American Journal of Political Science* 56: 52–66.

"No End in Sight." 2014. *Banyan* (blog), *Economist*, February 25, http://www.economist.com/blogs/banyan/2014/02/trans-pacific-partnership-0.

Norton, Clark F. 1976. "Congressional Review, Deferral and Disapproval of Executive Actions: A Summary and an Inventory of Statutory Authority." Congressional Research Service. Washington, DC: Library of Congress.

O'Keefe, Ed. 2015. "Immigration Maneuver Advances in the House." *Washington Post*, January 15.

Olson, Mancur. 1971. *The Logic of Collective Action: Public Goods and the Theory of Groups*. Cambridge, MA: Harvard University Press.

Organization of American States. 2015. "Trans Pacific Partnership Agreement (TPP)—Australia, Brunei Darussalam, Canada, Chile, Japan, Malaysia, Mexico, New Zealand, Peru, Singapore, the United States, and Vietnam: Background and Negotiations." Foreign Trade Information System, http://www.sice.oas.org/TPD/TPP/TPP_e.ASP.

Peters, Jeremy. 2013. "In Landmark Vote, Senate Limits Use of the Filibuster." *New York Times*, November 21.

Pew Research Center. 2014. "Support in Principle for U.S.-EU Trade Pact." April, http://www.pewglobal.org/files/2014/04/Pew-Research-Center-Bertelsmann-Foundation-U.S.-Germany-Trade-Report-FINAL-Wednesday-April-9-20142.pdf.

———. 2015. "Global Publics Push Back on U.S. Fighting ISIS, but Are Critical of Post-9/11 Torture." June, http://www.pewglobal.org/files/2015/06/Balance-of-Power-Report-FINAL-June-23-20151.pdf.

Quinnipiac University Polling Institute. 2010. "Quinnipiac University Poll." March. USQUINN.032910.R53. Quinnipiac University Polling Institute. Storrs, CT: Roper Center for Public Opinion Research, iPOLL.

Rennack, Dianne E. 2015. "Iran: U.S. Economic Sanctions and the Authority to Lift Restrictions." Congressional Research Service. Washington, DC: Library of Congress.

Reynolds, Molly E. 2015. "Exceptions to the Rule: Majoritarian Procedures and Majority Party Power in the United States Senate." PhD diss., University of Michigan.

Rocca, Michael S., and Stacy B. Gordon. 2010. "The Position-Taking Value of Bill Sponsorship in Congress." *Political Research Quarterly* 63: 387–97.

Schumer, Chuck. 2005. "Rules of the Senate." *Congressional Record*, Senate, 151, pt. 7 (May 10): 8987–88.

Smith, Steven S. 2014. *The Senate Syndrome: The Evolution of Procedural Warfare in the Modern U.S. Senate*. Norman: University of Oklahoma Press.

Steinhauer, Jennifer. 2015. "Democrats Hand Victory to Obama on Iran Nuclear Deal." *New York Times*, September 10.

Sullivan, Sean. 2015. "Keystone Pipeline Hits Bump in Senate." *Washington Post*, January 27.

Swanson, Ian, and Bob Cusack. 2015. "Obama's Trade Deal Is in Trouble." *Hill*, November 17.

Tompa, Peter K. 1986. "The Arms Export Control Act and Congressional Codetermination over Arms Sales." *American University International Law Review* 1, no. 1: 291–330.

U.S. Congress, Senate, Committee on Foreign Relations. 1975. *Foreign Assistance Authorization: Arms Sales Issues*. Hearings before the Subcommittee on Foreign Assistance, 94th Cong., 1st sess., June 17 and 18, November 19 and 21, and December 4 and 5.

———. 1976. *U.S. Arms Sales Policy*. Hearings before the Committee on Foreign Relations and the Subcommittee on Foreign Assistance on Proposed Sales of Arms to Iran and Saudi Arabia, 94th Cong., 2nd sess., September 16, 21, and 24.

———. 1983. *Legislative Veto: Arms Export Control Act.* Hearing before the Committee on Foreign Relations, 98th Cong., 1st sess., July 28.

Volden, Craig. 2002. "A Formal Model of the Politics of Delegation in a Separation of Powers System." *American Journal of Political Science* 46: 111–33.

Wawro, Gregory J., and Eric Schickler. 2006. *Filibuster: Obstruction and Lawmaking in the U.S. Senate.* Princeton, NJ: Princeton University Press.

Weaver, R. Kent. 1987. *The Politics of Blame Avoidance.* Washington, DC: Brookings Institution Press.

Weisman, Jonathan. 2015a. "Deal Reached on Fast-Track Authority for Obama Trade Accord." *New York Times,* April 16.

———. 2015b. "House Fires Shot at Health Care Law, Seeking to Alter Critical Coverage Rule." *New York Times,* January 9.

———. 2015c. "House Passes Legislation to Ease Some Dodd-Frank Financial Rules." *New York Times,* January 15.

———. 2015d. "House Rejects Trade Measure, Rebuffing Obama's Dramatic Appeal." *New York Times,* June 12.

———. 2015e. "Trade Accord, Once Blocked, Nears Passage." *New York Times,* June 23.

Zengerle, Patricia. 2014. "Lawmakers Try, but Fail, to Force Vote on Iran Sanctions Bill." Reuters, November 13.

IV

INTERCHAMBER
ANALYSIS AND NEGOTIATION

13

Intraparty Caucus Formation in the U.S. Congress

James Wallner

A T ITS MOST BASIC LEVEL, the term "congressional caucus" simply denotes a group of members who share similar positions on an issue or issues and meet periodically to coordinate action in pursuit of their common legislative agenda. The number of congressional caucuses in the House of Representatives and the Senate has increased dramatically over the last four decades. Today, caucuses reflect a diversity of interests and perform a variety of functions in Congress. This chapter explores how these caucuses relate to the larger theoretical debate on legislative organization.

Specifically, I consider the implications of one particular type of caucus, the *intraparty caucus*, for our understanding of partisan models of legislative organization. Doing so requires that we better understand why such caucuses are formed in the first place. In short, intraparty caucuses form because they help their members capture gains from cooperation, and thus achieve their goals, in a way that the formal party organizations in Congress do not. While this finding is not new, the literature on congressional caucuses to date has not sufficiently pursued its implications for partisan models of legislative organization more generally. In an effort to fill this void, this chapter represents a first step toward understanding the role played by intraparty caucuses in the legislative process and the constraints they impose on congressional parties in the contemporary Congress.

To this end, I explore here the pressures and opportunities driving the creation and early institutionalization of the Republican Study Committee (RSC) in the House and the Senate Steering Committee (SSC) in the mid-1970s. The RSC and SSC represent two prominent examples of intraparty caucuses in

Congress. They have both influenced the legislative process in significant ways and precipitated important institutional changes in the House and Senate. An examination of the dynamics surrounding their formation illustrates the challenges associated with forming congressional caucuses and the benefits such organizations provide their members once fully institutionalized. Additionally, recent events associated with the RSC and the creation of the House Freedom Caucus (HFC) illustrate the consequences for intraparty caucuses when they no longer serve the purposes for which they were originally created.

I first review the literature on partisan models of legislative organization. I then situate the congressional caucus within this literature before turning to the two case studies. Using firsthand accounts from the period in which the RSC and SSC were formed, I analyze the formation of both caucuses in the House and Senate. The RSC's recent decline as an intraparty caucus is also examined in order to capture the limitations faced by such caucuses when they fail to perform the function for which they were originally formed. I conclude with a broader discussion of the implications of the RSC and SSC for our understanding of strong parties in the contemporary Congress and outline avenues for future research.

Partisan Theories of Legislative Organization

Partisan theories of legislative organization view the Democratic and Republican parties in Congress as "teams" or "cartels" that pursue policy objectives commonly held by their members (Rohde 1991; Cox and McCubbins 1993, 2005). These approaches do not generally consider internal constraints on legislative parties beyond ideological homogeneity. For example, the theory of conditional party government developed by David W. Rohde (1991) posits that congressional decision-making will become more centralized and partisan as cohesive majority parties seek to exert control over the legislative process in an effort to enact their agendas over the objections of minority parties.

Similarly, Gary W. Cox and Mathew D. McCubbins (1993, 2005) present a theory of legislative cartels to account for the behavior of majority parties in Congress. According to their approach, majorities seek to structure the decision-making process in a way that advantages policy outcomes favored by their members. Legislation with which the party disagrees faces considerable barriers to enactment and is typically blocked from floor consideration. As a consequence, the majority party exercises nearly exclusive control over the agenda.

Yet intraparty caucuses have some impact on the extent to which majority parities can exercise such control in the first place. As such, it makes sense to peel back the layers and look inside legislative parties. Doing so helps us better understand what makes them tick by bringing the internal constraints on their actions into sharper focus. Examining the role played by intraparty caucuses in the maintenance of these cartels helps inform our understanding of the internal dynamics that are ultimately reflected in the congressional agenda as well as policy outcomes. Such an approach also allows us to acknowledge the extent to which these cartels are limited by internal disagreements over policy, strategy, and tactics.

It is important to also note that partisan theories of legislative organization have been primarily applied to the House and have largely neglected the Senate. Several differences between the two institutions complicate the applicability of House-based theories of legislative organization to the Senate. Specifically, the majority party's inability to easily alter formal procedures in its favor, the diverse nature of constituencies that compose entire states, and the considerable power of individual members to participate in the legislative process all serve to dilute the level of partisanship in the Senate vis-à-vis the House. As a result, the majority party does not exert the same control over the legislative process as its counterpart in the House (Gailmard and Jenkins 2007).

Nevertheless, it would be a mistake to then infer that majority parties are weak or powerless in the Senate. As in the House, partisanship, as well as the ideological cohesiveness of the two parties, has increased over the past several decades. Intraparty caucuses are also present in the Senate and thus may attenuate the ability of majority parties to control the legislative process even to the limited extent possible in the institution. Therefore, they can be added to the factors listed above that weaken party control in the Senate.

Congressional Caucuses

What is a congressional caucus? According to Susan Webb Hammond, Daniel P. Mulhollan, and Arthur G. Stevens Jr. (1985, 583), caucuses are "voluntary associations of members of Congress, without recognition in chamber rules or line item appropriations, which seek to have a role in the policy process." They share common features such as a name, membership list, designated leaders, or chairs, and staff. Congressional caucuses have been referred to as informal groups, informal member organizations, legislative service organizations (LSOs), and congressional member organizations (CMOs). LSOs and CMOs refer only to House caucuses that are required to register with the Committee on Administration; they do not include informal groups in the House that are not required to register or to Senate caucuses. In this chapter, I use the term "caucus" in the broader sense.

Offering a more general definition that draws our focus to the specific dynamics examined here, Hammond (1998, 7–9) defines caucuses as "informal member groups, outside of the formal system." The important point here is that caucuses exist *outside*, or separate and apart from, the committee system and party organizations. This observation tells us something important about the factors precipitating caucus formation. Put simply, caucuses are less likely to form outside existing structures if those structures are adequately serving member needs. According to Hammond (1998, 8), "Members have used congressional caucuses to do what they could not otherwise accomplish." Acknowledging this *outside-ness* aspect of caucuses draws our focus to the primary reason for the creation and endurance of the RSC and SSC.

Caucus Types and General Activities

Why is a caucus formed in the first place? While caucuses come in a variety of forms and perform many different functions, they all seek to influence the policy process in some way. Reflecting this, all caucuses have electoral and/or policy objectives. Six types of caucuses have been identified based on these objectives (Hammond, Mulhollan, and Stevens 1985; Hammond 1998). A caucus may be based on party, personal-interest, national-constituency, regional-interest, state/district, or industry concerns. Due to recent significant increases in their formation, Robert Jay Dilger and Jessica C. Gerrity (2013) have added a seventh type: caucuses based on diplomatic interests.

These caucuses exist to affect policy directly through the legislative process or indirectly through the electoral process by increasing the voting public's knowledge of and attention to their policy priorities. Caucuses seek to influence the agenda, the alternatives considered, and the final shape of legislation through a variety of activities. These include research and policy development, information exchange, agenda setting, and coalition building. The more active caucuses serve an important function by providing a forum for member socialization apart from the official party organizations. They also help coordinate member activity with allied advocacy groups outside Congress. This role has been largely overlooked by the literature. A caucus's outside game is particularly important in compensating for the lack of formal resources enjoyed by committees and party organizations. For example, caucuses may educate outside groups about the consideration of particular policies in the House and Senate. These groups may, in turn, help educate the constituencies of individual representatives and senators about the upcoming consideration of a bill or amendment on the House or Senate floor. This process may be utilized to help persuade noncaucus members to oppose particular policies. Outside groups may be similarly utilized to draw attention to and generate support for policies proposed by caucus members inside Congress. Such outside support enables caucus members to overcome the institutional and procedural barriers to placing their policy proposals on the congressional agenda.

House-Senate Differences

Caucuses exist in both the House and Senate. Yet, as with other aspects of Congress, their particular characteristics and activities vary between the two chambers. As such, an analysis of congressional caucuses should take these differences into account. The literature captures some of these differences. Hammond (1998, 29) observes that Senate caucuses are generally "less active" than their House counterparts. Similarly, Arthur G. Stevens Jr., Daniel P. Mulhollan, and Paul S. Rundquist (1981) observe that House caucuses tend to place more emphasis on developing a research capability at the staff level. This is needed to compensate for the informational asymmetry between rank-and-file caucus members and the committee and/or party leaders.

In contrast, Senate caucuses are typically tasked with solving a different coordination problem for their members. The informational asymmetries confronting House members are not as large in the Senate because members there serve on more committees than their counterparts in the House. In addition, individual senators have a greater ability to participate in the legislative process on the Senate floor. This allows members to engage in position-taking and credit-claiming activities independent of committee membership. As a consequence, caucus activities may assume a more operational focus in the Senate and are focused on coordinating the activities of individual members on and off the Senate floor.

Intraparty Caucuses

I am concerned here with party, or intraparty, caucuses. Hammond (1998, 31) defines intraparty caucuses as those that are "formed to articulate and advance the policy views of an intraparty group." Intraparty caucuses are typically based on "attitudinal" or ideological differences between caucus members and nonmembers (Stevens, Mulhollan, and Rundquist 1981, 427). Intraparty caucuses form because the committee system and official party organizations no longer help members achieve a particular goal.

In short, they form because the party establishment in Congress fails to provide leadership on an issue important to members, impedes consideration of that issue, or effectively blocks consideration of it altogether. The key point here is that unresolved differences over both substantive and tactical questions between prospective caucus members and party leaders precipitate the formation of intraparty caucuses.

In the broader sense, the research and information-exchange activities of caucuses supplement the information provided by the committees and party leadership (Stevens, Mulhollan, and Rundquist 1981). Yet this dynamic only pertains to specialized caucuses focused on a specific, often overlooked issue. In contrast, the information provided by *intraparty* caucuses, as well as the agenda-setting and coalition-building activities in which such caucuses typically engage, is more likely to bring them into competition with the formal party organizations, either directly or indirectly (Hammond 1998).

For example, the Democratic Study Group (DSG) is considered to be the first modern caucus. Liberal rank-and-file House members created the DSG in 1959 to serve as a counterweight to the more conservative southern Democrats who played an influential role in the legislative process as a result of their control of many of the most important committees. Similarly, liberal House Republicans formed the Wednesday Group in 1963 to provide a forum for like-minded members to discuss issues outside the regular party meetings.

The DSG and Wednesday Group were formed when the formal committee system and party organizations no longer served as reliable structures through which certain ideological subsets of members in both parties could achieve their goals. The DSG's information activities represented an effort to compensate for the structural biases in the House at the time that privileged the committee system (Stevens, Mulhollan, and Rundquist 1981, 427). According to Hammond (1998, 13), "Many caucuses are established precisely because the party system has failed in various ways, including addressing issues important to members and providing needed legislative information or coordination regarding legislation." Thus caucuses are formed when the committee system and party leaders do not facilitate the achievement of member goals.

While intraparty caucuses are technically party-based coalitions and are thus consistent with the broader claims of partisan theories of legislative organization, they are party-based coalitions that form in response to the failures of the existing structures to address the needs of their members. As a result, intraparty caucuses potentially tell us something important about the inner workings of the partisan model and the constraints faced by parties in government.

Once formed, intraparty caucuses may compete with party leaders in a variety of ways. They can seek to place issues on the agenda, modify issues already on the agenda, or keep issues off of the agenda altogether. They may also work to defeat legislation favored by the broader party organization on the House and Senate floors. While intraparty caucuses seek to influence policy without dividing their party, it is important to note that they potentially compete with party leaders to shape the party's position and plan legislative strategy if the two are in disagreement on substance and/or tactics. For example, intraparty caucuses may influence the content of bills taken up by the leadership. A member of the United Democrats of Congress (UDC), an intraparty caucus of moderate Democrats, described the dynamic: "Let's say the leadership of the UDC . . . feels strongly about a piece of legislation. Very quietly they go to the Speaker, or invite the Speaker down for a very candid, off-the-record discussion of what membership is willing to do. . . . I think that perhaps the UDC is most influential in continuing to remind the leadership that there are Democrats who may not share their same views on all issues" (quoted in Hammond 1991, 288).

Thus, intraparty caucuses should not necessarily be viewed as alternatives to the formal party organizations. Rather, they represent an additional way to impact the calculations of party leaders and, by extension, the overall direction of the party.

Republican Study Committee

The Republican Study Committee was formed in 1973 to serve as an "ideological rallying point" where conservative Republicans in the House could coordinate their activities, thereby enabling "a minority of committed men and women without years of seniority or formal leadership positions" to affect policy change.[1] An "ideological rallying point" was needed because the Republican Conference was not solving the coordination problems faced by House conservatives in a way that helped them achieve their goals in the institution. According to the RSC's first executive director, "In the early 1970s a group of conservative congressmen concluded that successful pursuit of their goals required a new approach. Republican differences over policy questions, the use of staff resources, and legislative strategy forced them to admit that their purposes could not be adequately served by the existing formal structure in the House of Representatives" (Feulner 1983, 1). Put simply, the RSC was formed to provide a conservative alternative to the information circulated by the House Republican Conference and as a forum in which like-minded members could coordinate legislative strategy (Malbin 1977, 56–58).

Disagreement over policy and legislative strategy between future RSC members and the party leadership was the most important precipitating factor driving the formation of the intraparty caucus. The relative absence of such disagreement prior to the 1970s helps explain why the RSC did not form earlier. As noted, similar intraparty dynamics influenced the formation of the

DSG in 1959, fourteen years prior to the creation of the RSC. Yet by 1973, the differences between the Republican Conference and House conservatives had grown too large to ignore. From the perspective of the founding RSC members, the Republican leadership and senior members had essentially drifted away from their conservative views.

Whether the abandonment of conservative principles by party leaders or the conservatism of new members was responsible for this widening gulf between the party leadership and the rank and file is not important. What is important here is that a subset of the House Republicans no longer viewed the Republican Conference as an organization through which they could achieve some of their goals. This widening difference was both substantive (i.e., dissatisfaction with the Richard M. Nixon administration and the policy positions of the party establishment more generally) and tactical (i.e., dissatisfaction with the leadership strategy to cooperate with congressional Democrats in order to get as much of Nixon's agenda through Congress as possible). Reflecting this, one RSC founder, Edward J. Derwinski (R-IL), observed, "A Republican Study Committee was not formed earlier because we Republicans were united under President Lyndon Johnson, largely tolerated during the first Nixon Administration, the Democrats hadn't been radicalized by McGovern yet, and Nixon was just starting to take non-conservative positions" (Feulner 1983, 4). Thus, the RSC finally formed to "promote conservative views on legislative issues" because no other organization was performing this function in the House to the satisfaction of its founding members (Feulner 1983, 81).

Activities

The RSC engaged in agenda-setting and coalition-building activities that periodically placed the caucus in competition with the Republican Conference. Staff responsibilities included providing information to RSC members regarding legislation being considered in committee and on the House floor. Staff also kept RSC members apprised of the caucus's legislative initiatives, helped coordinate member activities, and generally encouraged members "to be more aggressive in legislative battles" (Feulner 1983, 6). A staff of approximately eleven, primarily researchers and subject-matter experts, was employed to fulfill these responsibilities.

The RSC's staff structure was specifically modeled on the DSG. The liberal intraparty caucus also emphasized research and information-exchange activities during its formative years. This common emphasis underscores the fact that House intraparty caucuses are formed primarily to address the informational asymmetries between caucus members and nonmembers.

The RSC staff also supported caucus members in coordinating legislative activity, developing an agenda for electoral outreach, and forming a relationship with the Nixon administration. The RSC's early success can be largely attributed to the nature of the congressional agenda, an influx of new members, and the involvement of more experienced, entrepreneurially minded members and their staffs.

First, the nature of the legislative agenda played an important role in allowing House conservatives to overcome the significant collective action problems to forming the RSC. Put simply, the Nixon administration's agenda, particularly legislative initiatives such as the Family Assistance Plan and the Child Development Act, exerted a centripetal influence on House conservatives, bringing them together in opposition to what they considered bad policy.

Yet, despite the polarizing effect of the Nixon agenda on House conservatives, RSC members were still a relatively small minority within the Republican Party. New members would be needed in order to support an intraparty caucus based entirely on their concerns. Luckily, the freshman class of 1972 included approximately thirty self-identified conservative Republicans. These new members were important in building support for the RSC.

Finally, the participation of experienced, entrepreneurially minded members and staff was critical in supplying a sense of legitimacy and vision for the nascent organization. The participation and leadership of several more senior members of the Republican Conference provided the RSC with experience and knowledge of House operations. The drive of key entrepreneurial staff played an important role in making sure that the more routine tasks were handled in a satisfactory manner.

Limitations

The RSC has increased dramatically in recent years. Membership has been on a voluntary basis; the only requirement is that members contribute a specified amount of money to support RSC staff. In the 104th Congress (1995–1996), the RSC consisted of 15 out of 228 House Republicans (approximately 6.5 percent). By the 113th Congress (2013–2014), the RSC had grown to include 171 out of 234 House Republicans (approximately 73 percent). This dramatic increase in membership has prompted vocal complaints from some of the RSC's more conservative members about the organization's direction. For example, Representative Justin Amash (R-MI) commented in January 2014, "There are a lot of conservative Republicans who feel the RSC has gotten too big" (Alberta 2014). In response, Amash started an informal lunch group in 2013 called the House Liberty Caucus, which originally counted only "five or six" members who regularly participated in its meetings. However, frustration with the RSC helped increase this number to approximately twenty-four members in 2014. Reflecting these concerns, Representative Mick Mulvaney (R-SC) observed, "The RSC today covers a fairly broad philosophical swath of the party. It's no longer just the hard-core right-wingers. . . . If you want to pay dues, you can get in" (Alberta 2014).

In short, the RSC's burgeoning membership increasingly mirrored the larger Republican Conference in the House. As a consequence, the influence of House conservatives in an organization that was originally created to serve as an "ideological rallying point" for like-minded members was diluted. This development, more than any other, undermined the RSC's original role in providing a forum for member socialization apart from the official party organization. It also reduced the ability of the RSC to coordinate member activity with allied advocacy groups outside Congress.

Reflecting these developments is the fact that the RSC's membership elected members to chair the organization over more conservative challengers in the 113th (2013–2014) and 114th (2015–2016) Congresses. Representative Steve Scalise (R-LA) defeated the conservative-backed candidate, Tom Graves (R-GA), in the 113th Congress. Scalise subsequently "made a concerted effort to restore [the RSC's] profile as a 'member-driven organization' that welcomes wide-ranging dialogue in hopes of producing organic policy solutions the caucus can rally around" (Alberta 2014). Similarly, Representative Bill Flores (R-TX), who prevailed over several more conservative challengers in the 114th Congress (2015–2016), informed his colleagues at the time that "he [did] not believe the RSC's core mission should be to put pressure on leadership" (Newhauser 2015).

As a consequence, House conservatives formed a new intraparty caucus, the House Freedom Caucus, at the beginning of the 114th Congress (2015–2016) (Gehrke 2015; Fuller 2015). This new caucus was formed in direct response to the failures of the existing structure, the RSC, to address the needs of its membership. A former RSC chairman, Jim Jordan (R-OH), was chosen as the HFC's first chairman. Conservative members felt that a new "ideological rallying point" was needed because the RSC was no longer capable of solving the coordination problems they faced in achieving their goals in the institution. As with the creation of the RSC in the first place, the impetus behind the formation of the HFC was the realization that a conservative alternative to the RSC was needed in which like-minded members could coordinate legislative efforts on both policy and procedure.

Senate Steering Committee

The Senate Steering Committee was formed in 1974, one year after the RSC, to help coordinate "the activities and policies of conservative senators"

(Weyrich 1974a). The one-year lag between the formation of the RSC and the SSC was due more to the individualism inherent in the Senate's institutional structure than to any larger satisfaction with the committee system and party organization among senators. Indeed, Senate conservatives had long "talked of forming such a group to fight more effectively for conservative and against liberal programs. In the past the natural individualism of conservatives and the inevitable independence of senators combined to abort each proposal" ("The Right Report" 1974).

The SSC and RSC were both formed to advance conservative policy. The unique institutional characteristics of the Senate now led the SSC to assume a different form and to engage in different activities to achieve that goal. Despite these differences, it is important not to lose sight of the fundamental point driving the SSC's formation in the first place: to solve coordination problems for conservatives in a variety of areas. These included policy, legislative strategy and tactics, and presidential appointments.

Several areas in which Senate conservatives were in need of improved co-ordination were discussed at the first meetings of the SSC. First and foremost, members were concerned that conservative policies and alternatives were not being developed through the existing committee system. For example, issues discussed at an early meeting included "legal services, government control of private business, land use, and a variety of issues related to budget control" ("Minutes" 1974a). These echo similar concerns expressed by RSC members in the House.

From the beginning, the SSC had a much more operational focus than the RSC, reflecting the procedural autonomy possessed by individual senators and the primacy of the Senate floor as an arena for decision-making during this period. According to a former executive director, the SSC's "sole purpose was to allow the conservatives . . . to gather and talk about what was happening on the floor. It was totally floor focused" (West 2002). As a consequence, members spent considerable time discussing legislative strategy and floor tactics.

Coordinating member behavior on the floor fell into two areas. First, there was a need to coordinate obstructive behavior since the Republicans were in the minority at the time. In particular, SSC members were concerned with developing a floor watch system separate from the Republican Conference floor staff and party leaders in order to monitor the Senate floor and protect their rights. This was needed to ensure that the party leaders would not propound objectionable unanimous consent requests in their absence. The members also discussed ways in which they could coordinate their efforts to offer amendments. These amendments "would put the liberals on the defensive and give conservative candidates issues upon which they could run in November" (Weyrich 1974b).

Finally, the early meetings of the SSC were concerned with presidential appointments. Members wanted to influence Nixon's selection before they were officially nominated. An early member, Strom Thurmond (R-SC), suggested that SSC members "contact the White House insisting that major presidential appointments be discussed with Republican members" ("Minutes" 1974b).

The need for improved coordination outside the formal party organizations presented unique challenges in the Senate. First, the overall institutional environment at the time was much more inhospitable to collective action than in the House. The Senate in the 1970s was a highly individualistic institution, and even the committees and political parties experienced difficulty coordinating the behavior of their members (Sinclair 1989; Smith 1989).

Second, the SSC was not a strictly partisan organization when it was formed. According to an early chairman, the SSC had "never held itself out to be an official body of either the Republicans or the Democrats and, therefore, ha[d] not sought to have such a partisan designation" (McClure 1979, 5928). Conservative Democrats were even invited to join the group's early meetings. James Allen (D-AL) and Harry F. Byrd, Jr. (I-VA) were the first two non-Republicans that SSC members discussed inviting at an early meeting.

Other membership questions confronting the first members included size, the addition of new members, and formality. Twelve members were invited to the first meeting in April 1974. Ten members regularly participated. There was a consensus to gradually enlarge the group with the arrival of new conservatives in the Senate.

The question of formality was more difficult to resolve. Yet most of the members wanted the SSC "to be a sort of loose-knit group with a floating membership" (Thompson 1974). This preference eventually prevailed. In a meeting with White House staff several months after the group's formation, the first SSC chairman, Senator Carl T. Curtis (R-NE), described his caucus as "a group of conservative senators who believed in the free market system and who were organizing themselves for strategy on an issue basis. . . . [M]embership was floating and could grow or decline depending on the issue on the floor" (Cantrell 1974). This view persists. Today, unlike the RSC, the SSC still has no formal list of members (West 2002).

Finally, there was considerable discussion over whether the SSC should be a secret or public organization. By the end of April, the general consensus was not to publicize the SSC's formation. Instead, the members were content to "let people just gradually find out" ("Minutes" 1974a). In May, the members agreed that press queries regarding membership should be "answered by saying that the membership 'floats' from time to time according to the issues before the Senate, that it is a casual group meeting informally" ("Minutes" 1974b). SSC members did not decide to notify the Nixon administration of the group's existence until May 28, 1974.

Activities

The Steering Committee engaged in a two-pronged approach in order to advance its agenda in the 1970s. First, an obstructionist approach was needed in order to prevent passage of what conservatives' deemed bad policy. According to a former SSC executive director, the members were primarily engaged in "general strategic floor planning" (West 2002). As previously mentioned, one of the first activities discussed was the need to cover the floor and object to unanimous consent requests. The members went so far as to create a temporary floor watch system separate from the existing Republican operation until something more systematic could be established. As stated in SSC meeting minutes, "Until a floor watch system is developed, Senator [Jesse] Helms [R-NC] was asked to 'keep an eye' open for anything which might be of importance to the Committee. The Committee generally agreed that the members should individually approach the Republican leadership about agreeing to unanimous consent requests for bills not yet on the Calendar or which might have just been placed on it" ("Minutes" 1974b).

Second, a policy approach was needed. One of the important purposes of the SSC in the first place was to propose conservative policy alternatives. One form this took was urging President Nixon to nominate conservatives and to support other conservatives in the Senate. For example, members discussed how best to get conservatives assigned to the new budget committee during the summer of 1974. Their goal was to offset the liberal slate of members who would serve under the panel's new chairman, Edmund Muskie (D-ME). The SSC members were also actively working to offer messaging amendments on the Senate floor. Their goal was to put Democrats on the defensive.

As with the RSC, staff played a critical role in the formation and early institutionalization of the SSC. The primary concern from the beginning was how to pay staffers under the existing Senate rules. The solution was to rotate salaries month by month. According to a former executive director, "The complicated method was you were on a senator's payroll for a month or two, and then you shifted to another senator's payroll for a month or two" (West 2002). This eventually changed when the Senate's rules were amended to permit shared staff. Once SSC staffers were designated as "shared staff," multiple members could contribute to the salary of each.

The informal nature of SSC staff and the administrative difficulties associated with paying staff presented several difficulties. According to the caucus's executive director, "One of the unique things about the Steering Committee is that the executive director had traditionally not worked for the chairman specifically, but for the membership, and was on call to the membership at any time, although the chairman was clearly the dominant force. Trying to keep twenty members happy all at the same time was not an easy task" (West 2002).

The staff had several responsibilities. They were charged with monitoring committee hearings and markups and the Senate floor. On the floor, they were responsible for managing what has come to be known as the Steering Committee hold. First implemented by Chairman James A. McClure (R-ID), the hold process became the central staff responsibility of the Steering Committee by the late 1970s. As former SSC executive director Jade West mentioned in her oral history with the Senate historian's office, "If a member or members of the Steering Committee wanted to put a hold on a nomination or a bill, the chairman did it on behalf of them. . . . A Steering Committee hold gave cover to individual members to be able to maneuver a little bit more freely. We could never put a Steering Committee hold on a bill for a parochial reason, never a state issue, never a parochial member issue, never a personal hold" (West 2002). The staff was also charged with researching legislation and producing fact sheets on bills and issues.

The RSC has experienced important opportunities and challenges over the last four decades. As a consequence, its original mission to provide a conservative alternative to information circulated by the party leadership and committees and to serve as a forum for like-minded members to coordinate legislative strategy and tactics has changed. For example, the membership of the RSC increased dramatically as the result of the House Republican Conference's becoming more conservative in the 1990s and early 2000s. The elevation of RSC members to important committee chairmanships and into the party leadership that resulted from this change has meant that the caucus's policy products have frequently served as a supplement, instead of an alternative, to the information circulated by the more traditional institutional structures in the House.

Yet a larger membership also complicated the RSC's ability to perform its original operational mission. In short, it became more difficult for the RSC to serve as an effective forum for its members to coordinate legislative strategy and tactics as the sheer size of the organization increased. Additionally, the policy cohesiveness of the RSC's membership has not translated into procedural cohesiveness in debating legislative strategy. As noted, the RSC's inability to perform its operational role to the satisfaction of a subset of its members led to the formation of the House Freedom Caucus in 2015.

In contrast, the SSC has changed less over the past four decades. Specifically, the organization has maintained its mission to advance conservative policy and to help solve the coordination problems of its members. The SSC's original focus on operational issues has also persisted. This reflects the continued procedural autonomy of individual senators and the importance of the Senate floor in the institution's decision-making process.

The SSC also continues to be less institutionalized than the RSC. Its membership has grown as the Senate Republican Conference has become more conservative. Yet, despite this fact, the SSC's informal structure persists to this day. Similarly, the SSC remains outside the official party structure in the Senate. To this end, it continues to serve as an independent organization focused on achieving the goals of its members. While the SSC's membership is comprised of only Republicans today, this is the result of partisan polarization more broadly and the disappearance of conservative Democrats in the Senate rather than a conscious desire to transform the organization into a strictly partisan entity.

Conclusion

Intraparty caucuses may serve an informational purpose or distribute benefits to their members in some other way. But at their most basic level, their existence is best understood as a response to the failure of existing party organizations in the House and Senate to solve coordination problems for their members and allow them to achieve their goals in Congress. This presents an interesting dilemma. On one hand, the partisan model of legislative organization suggests that parties are "solutions to collective dilemmas that their members face" (Cox and McCubbins 1993, 124). On the other hand, intraparty caucuses represent "both a response to leadership failure and a challenge to current leadership style" (Hammond 1991, 293). Put simply, legislative parties form and persist to facilitate the goal achievement of their members, and intraparty caucuses form and persist when legislative parties are unable to serve that purpose for a significant subset of their members. The dilemma arises when these two occur simultaneously.

How do we reconcile these two competing views of legislative parties and intraparty caucuses? Perhaps the answer lies in the fact that differences between RSC and SSC members and nonmembers in the early 1970s centered on policy disagreements. In contrast, partisan models are typically focused on collective dilemmas that present "electoral inefficiencies" instead of "policy inefficiencies." Yet partisan models generally acknowledge that policy inefficiencies will eventually lead to electoral inefficiencies. As a result, majority parties attempt to control the agenda in order to prevent policy disagreements that divide their members from reaching the House and Senate floors. The difference between the two inefficiencies is thus "inconsequential" (Cox and McCubbins 1993, 124–25).

The reconciliation of these two views depends on acknowledging that while legislative parties and intraparty caucuses are in competition with one another, this competition is not zero-sum. In short, intraparty caucuses are not inconsistent with strong congressional parties even though they form in direct response to failures of the existing party organizations to address their members' needs. Rather, intraparty caucuses serve as pressure valves. They allow members to express disagreement within the formal party organization without jeopardizing the overall cartel. While such disagreement may undermine the ability of parties to control the agenda or enforce voting discipline on the House and Senate floors in the near term, it does not represent an existential threat to the party establishment over the medium to long term. Paradoxically, intraparty caucuses may actually provide an unexpected source of stability that reinforces legislative parties in that they empower frustrated members to act independently of the party organization when needed without having to leave the party altogether. Avoiding such an all-or-nothing situation may make legislative majorities more resistant to internal pressures in the long run.

Intraparty caucuses should not be viewed as an alternative to the formal party organizations in the House and Senate. On their own, they are incapable of solving all of the coordination problems faced by their members. The broader party organization is still needed, if only to maintain (or regain) the majority. As Cox and McCubbins (1993, 125) astutely observe, "Nearly everyone in the party prefers that there be *some* agreed-upon leadership team rather than that there be *no* agreed-upon leadership team, even if they disagree on which team would be best." Intraparty caucuses are useful tools with which to influence the selection of that leadership team as well as the direction of party strategy once it is in place.

The preceding analysis represents a needed first step to situate intraparty caucuses within the larger theoretical debate on legislative organization. Further theoretical development and empirical research are needed. Two caveats in particular are in order at this stage.

First, partisan models acknowledge the link between ideological heterogeneity and decentralization in Congress and the amount of power that is delegated to party leaders to plan and implement legislative strategy (Rohde 1991). The political parties were much more heterogeneous in the 1970s than they are in the contemporary era. Thus, it should be no surprise that intraparty caucuses formed based on ideological differences between subsets of party members. Yet, notwithstanding this consideration, the RSC and SSC have persisted over the past four decades despite the increasing ideological homogenization of the Republican Party in Congress and nationally. The relationship between ideological cohesiveness and the formation and institutionalization of intraparty caucuses warrants additional detailed examination.

Second, more research is needed to understand the distinction between minority and majority parties and their relationship to the formation of intraparty caucuses. Both the RSC and the SSC formed when the Republican Party was in the minority. As a result, their members did not experience the pressures of being in the majority party. However, the SSC persisted throughout the first six years of the Reagan administration, when the Republicans controlled the Senate. In addition, both the RSC and SSC persist to this day after multiple periods of Republican control of the House and Senate. Further research is needed to better understand how majority and minority status influences the formation of intraparty caucuses and the activities in which they engage.

Note

1. The Republican Study Committee website is available at http://rsc.flores.house. gov.

References

Alberta, Tim. 2014. "Conservatives Form Their Own Caucus Because the RSC Isn't 'Hard-Core' Enough." *National Journal*, January 15.

Caldwell, Charles F. 1989. "Government by Caucus: Informal Legislative Groups in an Era of Congressional Reform." *Journal of Law & Politics* 5: 625–55.

Cantrell, Tom. 1974. "Memorandum for the Files." Senate Steering Committee, July 1.

Cox, Gary W., and Mathew D. McCubbins. 1993. *Legislative Leviathan: Party Government in the House*. New York: Cambridge University Press.

———. 2005. *Setting the Agenda: Responsible Party Government in the U.S. House of Representatives*. New York: Cambridge University Press.

Dilger, Robert Jay, and Jessica C. Gerrity. 2013. "Congressional Member Organizations: Their Purpose and Activities, History and Formation." Congressional Research Service. Washington, DC: Library of Congress.

Feulner, Edwin J., Jr. 1983. *Conservatives Stalk the House: The Story of the Republican Study Committee*. Ottawa, IL: Green Hill Publishers.

Fuller, Matt. 2015. "Rival Conservative Group Might Present Challenges to RSC." *Congressional Quarterly*, January 26.

Gailmard, Sean, and Jeffrey A. Jenkins. 2007. "Negative Agenda Control in the Senate and House: Fingerprints of Majority Party Power." *Journal of Politics* 69: 689–700.

Gehrke, Joel. 2015. "Meet the Freedom Caucus." *National Review Online*, January 26.

Hammond, Susan Webb. 1991. "Congressional Caucuses and Party Leaders in the House of Representatives." *Political Science Quarterly* 106: 277–94.

———. 1998. *Congressional Caucuses in National Policy Making*. Baltimore: Johns Hopkins University Press.

Hammond, Susan Webb, Daniel P. Mulhollan, and Arthur G. Stevens Jr. 1985. "Informal Congressional Caucuses and Agenda Setting." *Western Political Quarterly* 38: 583–605.

Malbin, Michael J. 1977. "Where There's a Cause There's a Caucus." *National Journal,* January 8.

McClure, James A. 1979. "The So-Called 'Senate Steering Committee.'" *Congressional Record,* Senate, 125, pt. 5 (March 22): 5928.

"Minutes." 1974a. Senate Steering Committee, April 30.

"Minutes." 1974b. Senate Steering Committee, May 7.

Newhauser, Daniel. 2015. "Conservative Revolt Splits House GOP Group." *National Journal,* January 13.

"The Right Report: A Newsletter That Tells You What Is Happening on the American Right." 1974. June 3, 3.

Rohde, David W. 1991. *Parties and Leaders in the Postreform House.* Chicago: University of Chicago Press.

Sinclair, Barbara. 1989. *The Transformation of the U.S. Senate.* Baltimore: Johns Hopkins University Press.

Smith, Steven S. 1989. *Call to Order: Floor Politics in the House and Senate.* Washington, DC: Brookings Institution Press.

Stevens, Arthur G., Jr., Daniel P. Mulhollan, and Paul S. Rundquist. 1981. "U.S. Congressional Structure and Representation: The Role of Informal Groups." *Legislative Studies Quarterly* 6: 415–37.

Thompson, Dick. 1974. "Memorandum for the Files." Senate Steering Committee, May 9.

West, Jade. 2002. "Executive Director of the Senate Steering Committee (1982–1996) and Staff Director of the Republican Policy Committee (1996–2002)." *Oral History Interviews,* Washington, DC: Senate Historical Office.

Weyrich, Paul. 1974a. "Memorandum for the Files." Senate Steering Committee, April 3.

———. 1974b. "Memorandum for the Files." Senate Steering Committee, May 16.

14

Gender and Party
Politics in a Polarized Era

Michele L. Swers

IT STARTED WITH A SERIES OF STING videos implying that Planned Parenthood mishandled the procurement and sale of aborted fetal tissue. In
response, the Republican-controlled Congress sought to eliminate federal
funding for the organization, raising the political stakes by attaching defunding provisions to must-pass budget bills. Since Planned Parenthood is also
a major provider of cancer screenings and preventive health care to low-
income women, Democrats denounced Republican efforts as jeopardizing
women's health. In one contentious floor debate on a continuing resolution
to avert a government shutdown, Democratic (minority) leader Nancy Pelosi
(D-CA) declared, "Tonight, 151 Republicans voted to shut down government
rather than allow women to access affordable family planning and life-saving
preventative health care. One-hundred and fifty-one Republicans decided
their obsession with women's health was more important than the thousands
of disabled veterans, disadvantaged children and working families who would
pay the price of another government shutdown" (quoted in Dumain 2015).

Pelosi's condemnation of Republican policies as harmful to women highlights the elevation of women's rights as a key fault line in today's polarized
politics. In this chapter, I examine the role that women in Congress and
women's issues play in contemporary partisan politics. Women are drastically
underrepresented in Congress compared to their proportion of the population. Their entrance into the institution, however, coincided with accelerated
polarization between the parties. Women in Congress and issues related to
women's rights, particularly abortion, are a key component of the party wars.
With women voters and women's organizations constituting a central pillar

in the Democratic electoral coalition, female Democrats aggressively pursue policies to advance women's place in the economy and society. To sharpen the gender gap and mobilize their voters and donors, Democratic women also work to burnish the image of Democrats as the party of women's rights, while portraying Republicans as engaged in a war on women that threatens the well-being of women and their families.

Republicans, in turn, aggressively pursue initiatives to restrict abortion in order to appeal to the social conservatives who are critical to the party's electoral coalition. Republicans, however, do not want to be portrayed as antiwomen. To combat the Democratic narrative that Republicans are threatening women's health, the party deploys Republican women to advocate for these bills and defend the party against accusations that Republicans are hurting women. This complicated dance mobilizes each party's voters, activists, and donors and furthers the polarized politics and brinksmanship that characterize the contemporary Congress.

Breaking into the Institution

Historically, Congress is an institution dominated by men. Today women remain woefully underrepresented, holding only 19 percent of the seats in the House of Representatives and constituting 20 percent of senators (Center for American Women and Politics 2015). With the exception of Nancy Pelosi, who served as Speaker of the House from 2007 to 2010 and remains party leader, no woman has ever held the top leadership posts of party leader or party whip. As late as 1991, there had never been more than two women serving in the Senate at the same time. Indeed, in the 1992 election, then candidate Dianne Feinstein (2006) highlighted women's underrepresentation in her campaign, declaring that "2% might be good for the fat content in milk, but it's not good enough for women's representation in the United States Senate."

In the early years, many women elected to Congress were widows of congressmen, chosen as placeholders to keep the seat in party control until the party elite could coalesce around a candidate. By the 1970s and 1980s, when the feminist movement opened more of the careers that lead to politics to women, more women entered Congress as professional politicians (Gertzog 1995). The largest increase in women's representation came after the election in 1992, dubbed the "Year of the Woman," when the number of women in Congress jumped from thirty-two to fifty-four (see figure 14.1). To date, this remains the greatest increase in women's representation in a single election. However, the 1992 Year of the Woman elections were really the year of

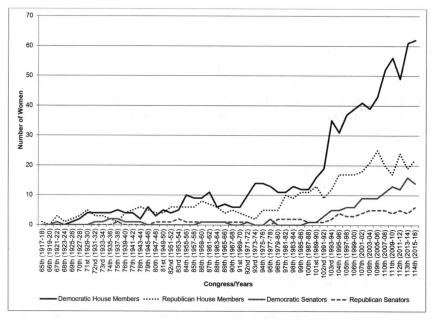

FIGURE 14.1.
Women in the House and Senate by party, 1917–2016.
Source: Center for American Women and Politics 2015.

the Democratic woman, as the number of Democratic women in Congress jumped from twenty-two to forty, while only four new Republican women were elected, increasing the presence of Republican women in Congress from ten to fourteen (Center for American Women and Politics 2015).

Since 1992, the partisan gap has grown, with representation of Democratic women far outpacing that of Republican women. Indeed, Republican women have not significantly benefitted from their party's recent dramatic victories, including the 1994 Republican revolution, when Republicans won fifty-four House seats and retook the majority after forty years in the minority, or the more recent 2010 wave election, when Republicans gained a historic sixty-three seats and recaptured majority control. Of the 104 women in the current 114th Congress (2015–2016), 76 are Democrats, and only 28 are Republicans (Center for American Women and Politics 2015).

Explaining the Party Gap in Women's Representation

The growing partisan gap in women's representation stems from a divergence in the nature of the parties' electoral coalitions. The emergence of the civil rights movement and the adoption of the Civil Rights Act of 1964 precipitated a movement of southern white Democrats to the Republican Party. The formerly solid Democratic South is now a Republican stronghold, and historically this region is also less likely to elect women. As the South moved to the Republican Party, northeastern states and urban areas became Democratic bastions. Over time, the districts that elect women have tended to be more urban and more racially and ethnically diverse, with a higher median income. In contemporary politics, these districts lean Democratic (Palmer and Simon 2008; Pearson and McGhee 2013).

In addition to these regional shifts in the parties' voters, the creation of majority/minority districts in the 1990s also changed the demographics of the legislators elected. To guarantee that minorities could elect a representative of their choice, minority populations were concentrated into districts that are more urban and strongly Democratic. The surrounding suburban districts became whiter and more Republican (Jacobson 2013). The adoption of majority/minority districts expanded the representation of minority men and women in the House, and these legislators, who represent some of the most Democratic districts in the country, anchor the liberal end of the ideological spectrum. While the Republican caucus remains overwhelmingly white and male, by the 113th Congress (2013–2014), minorities and women constituted a majority of the Democratic caucus. In the current 114th Congress (2015–2016), only 42 percent of Democratic House members are white men (Strauss 2015). Although the caucus is the most diverse in history, the number of seats held by Democrats is at a low point, with Republicans maintaining their largest majority since the Herbert Hoover administration (Davidson et al. 2015). Since Republicans also control the Senate, although by a smaller margin, the partisan disparity in women's representation means most women in Congress are currently in the minority party.

Finally, comparing the activists, donors, and voters who form the base of the Democratic and Republican parties reinforces the fact that women are more likely to be elected as Democrats. Since the late 1960s and early 1970s, women's groups, civil rights organizations, environmentalists, and other liberal groups have become increasingly central to the Democratic base (Sanbonmatsu 2002). These groups prioritize increasing representation of women and minorities in elective office. Women's groups, most notably EMILY's List, which supports pro-choice Democratic women, have developed operations to identify and recruit women candidates and support them with fund-raising networks and campaign services (Burrell 2014; Elder 2014). Moreover, polarization among elites and party sorting among the public, in which voters' ideological views and party affiliations are increasingly aligned, means that the donors and voters who support Democratic candidates in the primary and general elections are increasingly liberal (Abramowitz 2011). Liberals are most responsive to messages about the importance of group representation in Congress, and these voters are more likely to embrace positive stereotypes about female candidates, such as the idea that women are more knowledgeable about social welfare issues (K. Dolan 2014; Sanbonmatsu and Dolan 2009; Burrell 2014; Elder 2014).

Meanwhile, the Republican Party eschews identity politics, focusing instead on the ideological conservatism of the candidate. Furthermore, with the election of Ronald Reagan in 1980, social conservatives became an increasingly important part of the Republican coalition as the party mobilized white evangelical Christians. These voters hold more traditional views about gender roles and prioritize policies aimed at restricting abortion (Burrell 2014; Sanbonmatsu 2002). Thus, there is not a natural constituency of donors and voters within the Republican Party that is responsive to explicit calls to expand women's representation. Recently the party has increased its efforts to recruit women, establishing Project GROW (Growing Opportunities for Republican Women) (Newton-Small 2014). Party-aligned activists have also formed donor networks to help female candidates, such as SHE PAC and Maggie's List. However, these organizations do not have the presence and donor connections that groups allied with Democrats have developed (Political Parity 2015; Elder 2014).

Therefore, to get elected, today's Republican women need to be strong conservatives who can appeal to an increasingly conservative primary electorate of social conservatives, Tea Party activists, business conservatives, and libertarians. These activists and donors do not respond to calls to expand diversity in representation. They do not prioritize women's issues beyond abortion. Instead, women's issues are increasingly viewed as Democratic issues (Burrell 2014; Swers 2013).

In sum, the evolving contours of the parties' electoral coalitions influence the types of women who can get elected—pro-choice Democrats and conservative Republicans—and the issues they emphasize. The concentration of women in the Democratic Party, the status of abortion as a major fault line between the parties, and the increasing association of women's issues beyond abortion with the Democratic Party exacerbate the partisan divide, contributing to the gridlock and acrimony that characterize modern polarized politics.

Democrats, Republicans, and the Politics of Women's Issues

The rising number of Democratic women elected since 1992 and the centrality of feminist organizations and pro-choice groups to the Democratic coalition have elevated the importance of women's issues as a driver of the Democratic coalition. The party appeals to women voters, particularly college-educated women, single women, and minority women, by highlighting its commitment to the social safety net and promoting reproductive rights, equal pay, and expansion of family leave and child-care initiatives (Dolan, Deckman, and Swers 2016).

For Democratic women, championing policies on a range of women's issues allows them to pursue their policy priorities while helping the party build support with pivotal groups of voters, donors, and activist groups. Their status as women advocating for women's interests gives them additional moral authority with colleagues and credibility as spokespersons in the party's media outreach. Given the alignment of their policy priorities and the electoral interests of the party, female Democrats are often the most aggressive advocates for women's issue initiatives (Swers 2002, 2013). During the early 1990s, women played pivotal roles in developing the Family and Medical Leave Act. Patricia Schroeder (D-CO), a leading proponent of the legislation, spent ten years advocating for family leave. Compromising to make the leave unpaid and place other limitations on eligibility for leave, Schroeder saw the bill through two presidential vetoes before Democrat Bill Clinton was elected president and made the Family and Medical Leave Act his first signature piece of legislation. Democratic women were also prime drivers of legislation to expand research on women's health issues and create an Office of Women's Health at the National Institutes of Health (Swers 2002). They aggressively advocated for the Violence against Women Act and its inclusion in the Clinton administration's omnibus crime bill (Dodson 2006).

By the time Barack Obama was elected president and Democrats again had unified control of Congress and the presidency, women had attained the seniority necessary to advance to committee and subcommittee chairmanships in the House and Senate, and Nancy Pelosi was now Speaker of the House. Therefore, women had more clout to pursue their vision of legislating in women's interest. Pelosi helped convince President Obama to pass the Lilly Ledbetter Fair Pay Act as the first major policy initiative of his administration, and she pushed through an expansion of the State Children's Health Insurance Program, which provides health insurance to poor children whose families' incomes are above the threshold to qualify for Medicaid (Halloran 2009; Pear 2009).

The defining legislation of Obama's presidency is the Affordable Care Act, a comprehensive overhaul of health insurance coverage. ObamaCare, as it is more commonly known, both fulfilled a Democratic policy aspiration to provide national health insurance that dated back to the Harry S. Truman administration and fueled the anger that birthed the Tea Party movement and propelled Republicans back into the majority. Among Obama's advisers in the White House and the party leaders in Congress, Nancy Pelosi was most strongly committed to passing comprehensive reform. The bill was almost derailed after Republican Scott Brown (R-MA) won the seat of the late liberal lion and health-reform champion Ted Kennedy (D-MA) in a special election in which he promised to oppose ObamaCare. Brown's victory eliminated Democrats' filibuster-proof Senate majority and convinced Senate leader Harry Reid (D-NV) and high-ranking White House officials, including Chief of Staff Rahm Emanuel, that the party should scale back its health proposals and pass something more incremental. Pelosi insisted on a large-scale reform. She lobbied for the votes to pass it and brokered deals to overcome obstacles, including a revolt by some pro-life Democrats who wanted to ensure that no federal funds could be utilized for abortion before granting their support (Bzdek 2010; Peters and Rosenthal 2010).

Democratic women in the House and Senate played key roles in propelling the legislation forward and expanding provisions related to women's health. Democratic women focused on the fact that insurance companies charged women higher premiums than they did men because of the likelihood that women will utilize more medical care, for instance, potentially becoming pregnant and incurring costs related to prenatal care and possibly a C-section. As Speaker Pelosi said when the bill reached the House floor, "After we pass this bill, being a woman will no longer be a preexisting medical condition" (Bzdek 2010).

Democratic women were particularly interested in ensuring that women's health needs were included in a package of benefits that all employers are required to provide. Republicans opposed creating mandates concerning what services must be included in employer coverage because it would drive up premium costs and force some individuals to pay for policies that cover services they would not need. During a contentious Senate Finance Committee markup session, Senator John Kyl (R-AZ) offered an amendment to prohibit the government from defining the specific health services that insurers must cover. In response, Senator Debbie Stabenow (D-MI) defended the need for a minimum benefit package, explaining that many insurance companies do not cover basic services like maternity care. Kyl maintained, "I don't need maternity care," and Stabenow asserted, "Your Mom probably did" (Slajda 2009). The exchange highlights the fact that Democratic women like Stabenow, who held a seat on the coveted Finance Committee that played a key role in drafting the bill, utilized their positions to press for their vision of women's interests (Swers 2013).

Similarly, the Democratic women were the most aggressive advocates for inclusion of free contraceptive coverage as part of a package of preventive health benefits. When the Obama administration drafted the rule regarding implementation of this coverage, Democratic women lobbied for the contraceptive coverage to be broad and to limit employer exemptions. The administration originally issued a rule that limited exemptions to the contraception mandate to employers that were houses of worship and did not include religiously affiliated institutions such as Catholic hospitals and universities. The rule set off a firestorm in which Republicans denounced the administration for violating religious liberty. Left-leaning Catholic groups and Catholic political figures, including Vice President Joe Biden and Obama's former chief of staff Bill Daley, urged Obama to broaden the rule (Brownstein 2012). Meanwhile, Democratic women and women's groups strongly pressured the administration to keep the coverage broad, arguing that women who work for religiously affiliated institutions should have access to care and should not be burdened with the exorbitant cost of many contraceptives. Ultimately the administration adopted a compromise that required the health insurance companies to cover the services without participation of the employer and at no cost to the employee (Swers 2013). The Supreme Court extended eligibility for this work-around to privately held corporations in the *Hobby Lobby* case, but some religious institutions are still challenging the rule in court, maintaining it violates religious liberty (J. Fuller 2014). Thus, when women's health concerns conflict with other deeply held convictions, Democratic women are the most tenacious advocates for an expansive view of women's rights.

Republicans and Abortion Politics

At the same time that feminist and pro-choice groups gained prominence in the Democratic Party, social conservatives, particularly Christian evangelicals, became pivotal members of the Republican coalition seeking to protect traditional family values. Abortion and same-sex marriage are especially important issues for these voters and activists. Mobilizing voters through their churches, social conservatives were an important part of President George W. Bush's electoral coalition (Williams 2010; Layman 2001). Starting in 2006, Focus on the Family and other evangelical groups began holding an annual Values Voter Conference. The conference is now a required stop for Republican presidential aspirants. Senator Ted Cruz (R-TX), a favorite of evangelical voters and Tea Party supporters, won the conference's straw poll in 2013, 2014, and 2015 (Kamisar, Easley, and Swan 2015).

For social conservatives, reversing *Roe v. Wade* is a long-standing goal. Abortion opponents achieved a major policy victory in 1976 when Congress passed the Hyde Amendment, which prohibits federal funding for abortion in Medicaid. The Supreme Court upheld the constitutionality of this limit and opened the door to legislative efforts to restrict abortion even further in the *Webster v. Reproductive Health Services* and *Planned Parenthood v. Casey* decisions. The *Casey* decision created the "undue burden" standard, allowing states to place restrictions on abortion as long as they do not place an undue burden on a woman's ability to obtain an abortion. The ruling set off a flurry of activity in the states as pro-life groups lobbied for various restrictions, from waiting periods to parental consent. Republican presidents utilized their executive authority to further curtail abortion. For example, the Mexico City policy first adopted by Ronald Reagan and reinstated by Republican presidents George H. W. Bush and George W. Bush, prohibits federal funding for family-planning programs from going to international organizations that also provide abortions or lobby their governments in favor of access to abortion (Ainsworth and Hall 2010; Shimabukuro 2014).

Throughout the 1980s and early 1990s, a coalition of conservative Democrats and Republicans passed additional restrictions banning federal funding for abortion in a range of programs that provide health services or insurance benefits to military personnel, federal employees, Peace Corps volunteers, and federal prisoners. In 1992, after Bill Clinton won the presidency, ending Republicans' twelve-year hold on the oval office, and Democratic women expanded their numbers, Democrats pursued a limited abortion-rights agenda. They passed a bill to protect women from harassment by protesters as they tried to enter abortion clinics. However, a bill to codify *Roe v. Wade*, the Freedom of Choice Act, and efforts to repeal the Hyde Amendment failed (Swers 2002; Dodson 2006).

When Republicans gained the majority in the 1994 Republican Revolution, they aggressively used the appropriations process to maintain and expand policy riders restricting funding for abortion in various federal health programs. However, with Democrat Bill Clinton in the White House, Republicans could not push through legislation placing further limitations on abortion, such as a proposal barring the transport of minors across state lines to obtain an abortion without parental consent or a ban on late-term abortions titled the Partial Birth Abortion Act. With the election of George W. Bush and unified control of Congress, Republicans finally passed the Partial Birth Abortion Act, the first major federal ban on an abortion procedure. However, the loss of their congressional majority in 2006 stymied further efforts to curtail abortion. Even after Barack Obama won the presidency, Democrats did not actively work to expand abortion rights, recognizing that the small remaining number of pro-life Democrats would collaborate with Republicans to block such efforts. Instead they tried to keep the issue off the agenda and focused on other women's health causes, such as the expansion of access to contraception. Still, abortion remained one of the final sticking points in negotiation of the Affordable Care Act (Swers 2013; Shimabukuro 2014).

Since the Tea Party wave swept in a new Republican majority in 2010, Republicans have pursued abortion restrictions with renewed vigor. Raising the political stakes, Republicans used must-pass budget legislation as a vehicle to defund Planned Parenthood. The confrontation almost led to a government shutdown in 2011 and again in 2015. To preempt a high-stakes budget confrontation over Planned Parenthood funding in 2015, Speaker John Boehner (R-OH) resigned to mollify conservatives in the House Freedom Caucus, a group of about forty strongly conservative members (Kliff 2015).

In an effort to respond to the groundswell of anger among conservative activists and media generated by the Planned Parenthood sting videos, Republican leadership in the House passed a one-year moratorium on federal funding for Planned Parenthood and a bill to allow states to exclude medical providers who perform abortions from their Medicaid contracts. They also created a special committee to investigate the subject of the sting videos: Planned Parenthood's handling of procurement and distribution of fetal tissue (Ferris 2015). Beyond targeting Planned Parenthood funding, since 2011 House leaders have brought other abortion-related proposals to the floor, including an effort to ban abortions after twenty weeks, titled the Pain Capable Unborn Child Protection Act. Republicans are also pursuing a measure to alter the federal tax code to permanently prohibit all types of federal funding for abortion, obviating the need to add policy riders to the various annual appropriations bills (Shimabukuro 2014). With a Democrat in the White House and Democrats controlling the Senate or wielding the filibuster when in the minority, Republicans know that these bills cannot pass, but they continue to pursue these policies to demonstrate their commitment to the social conservatives in their electoral base.

Democrats, Republicans, and the War on Women

Throughout the 1990s and early 2000s, conservative Democrats who espoused pro-life positions and moderate Republicans who held liberal views on social issues retired or lost their reelection bids, leaving a more uniformly liberal Democratic caucus with an increasing number of women and a more strongly conservative and largely male Republican contingent. Looking to energize their liberal base and mobilize women voters, especially single women, minority women, and college-educated women, the Democratic caucus, and Democratic women in particular, pursue policies that burnish the reputation of the Democratic Party as the party of women's rights. They also utilize these policy proposals to draw sharp contrasts with Republicans, portraying Republicans as engaged in a war on women that threatens women's economic and social well-being. Meanwhile, the increasingly conservative Republican caucus continues to prioritize legislation to restrict abortion. However, seeking to compete for the votes of key groups of women, such as married suburban women, the party urgently works to counter the Democrats' war-on-women narrative.

During the 1990s moderate Republican women often cast votes in favor of abortion rights. These moderate women, including Connie Morella (R-MD), Olympia Snowe (R-ME), Marge Roukema (R-NJ), and Nancy Johnson (R-CT), also collaborated with majority-party Democrats on bills related to women, children, and families, including the Family and Medical Leave Act, the Violence against Women Act, and an initiative expanding women's health research and creating an Office of Women's Health at the National Institutes of Health (Swers 2002; Dodson 2006). When Republicans took over the majority and passed a major overhaul of welfare, moderate Republican women with seats on the committee of jurisdiction, Ways and Means, including Nancy Johnson (R-CT) and Jennifer Dunn (R-WA), convinced the Republican leadership to include child-care subsidies and child-support enforcement provisions in the legislation (Swers 2002; Dodson 2006).

By the time Democrats regained control of the House in the 2006 election, almost all of the moderate Republican women were gone, replaced by conservative women from the Republican strongholds of the South and West. Indeed, DW-NOMINATE scores[1] tracking the ideological leanings of members' voting records indicate that the voting patterns of Republican men and women in the House had converged by the 108th Congress (2003–2004), while the small contingent of Republican women in the Senate remain more moderate than their male counterparts (Frederick 2009, 2010).

With current levels of polarization, opportunities to collaborate across party lines on proposals to advance women's rights are relatively rare. Instead women's issues are a staple of the partisan divide, and Democrats use these issues to build enthusiasm with their base of women's groups and abortion-rights supporters and to undermine Republican support among women. For example, the Supreme Court's 2007 ruling against Lilly Ledbetter's pay-discrimination case prompted Democrats to draft legislation that would make it easier for women to file pay-discrimination suits. For years Ledbetter was paid less than her male counterparts at Goodyear Tire and Rubber Company, but she did not know about the discrimination until she received an anonymous letter alerting her to the disparity. Despite these circumstances, the Supreme Court ruled that she could not pursue a case because the time frame for filing a complaint had expired. In response, the Democrats pursued legislation to restart the clock after each discriminatory paycheck (Barmes 2007; Swers 2013).

Committed to the principle of pay equity, Democrats also sought to utilize the bill to help their 2008 presidential primary candidates, Barack Obama (D-IL) and Hillary Clinton (D-NY), showcase their support for women's rights in contrast to Republican opposition to the bill. Introducing their bill in the Senate on Equal Pay Day, a date that marks how far into the next year a woman must work for her pay to catch up to a man's, Democrats extended the time for floor debate so that Obama and Clinton could return from the campaign trail. This allowed Obama and Clinton to trumpet their support for pay equity in contrast the Republican nominee, John McCain (R-AZ), who was absent from the Senate and, like other Republicans, opposed the legislation on the grounds that it would subject employers to unlimited litigation. After Republicans blocked cloture on the bill, Democrats launched a public campaign to build support for the legislation, with many Democratic women appearing at press conferences, on the House and Senate floor, and in the media to denounce Republicans as blocking equal pay for women. Lilly Ledbetter herself campaigned for Barack Obama once he became the 2008 Democratic nominee, and the Ledbetter Act became the first piece of legislation passed by the new Obama administration. In his 2012 reelection campaign, President Obama cited the bill as a key piece of evidence of his commitment to women's rights (Swers 2013).

By 2012 Democrats rolled out a campaign theme that characterized Republicans as engaged in a "war on women." Democratic National Committee chair Debbie Wasserman Schultz (D-FL), Minority Leader Nancy Pelosi, and Democratic Senate Campaign Committee chair Patty Murray (D-WA) aggressively promoted this theme, highlighting Democrats' and President Obama's support for women's rights, from equal pay to women's health, including abortion rights and contraception coverage in the Affordable Care Act (ACA, or ObamaCare) health plan. Interest group allies, including Planned Parenthood and EMILY's List, echoed the theme in the ubiquitous ads they financed to promote Democratic candidates (Swers 2013).

To flesh out the war-on-women theme, Democrats trumpeted incidents when Republican candidates made inflammatory statements, such as the declaration by a Republican Senate candidate in a key competitive race that a "legitimate rape" rarely results in pregnancy because "the female body has ways to try to shut that whole thing down" (Sullivan 2014). They also focused attention on Republican legislative actions that would harm women, including efforts to defund Planned Parenthood. Democrats painted a picture of Republicans' disregard for women's health by highlighting the fact that the majority of services provided by the organization are not related to abortion; rather, Planned Parenthood provides a range of preventive health services, such as screenings for breast cancer and access to contraception.

In another case, the House Government and Oversight Committee held a hearing to highlight Republican criticisms of ObamaCare and focus on the concern that the requirement to provide contraception was a government mandate that tramples religious freedom. However, the hearing turned into a public relations bonanza and a fund-raising tool for Democrats and women's groups when the Republican chairman, Darrell Issa (R-CA), featured an all-male panel to talk about the contraception mandate and refused to hear testimony from Sandra Fluke, a Georgetown law student who did not have contraceptive coverage because the health plan of the Catholic school she attended did not provide it. Incensed by the chairman's refusal to allow Fluke to testify, two female committee members—Democrats Carolyn Maloney (NY) and Eleanor Holmes Norton (DC)—walked out of the hearing. Minority Leader Nancy Pelosi followed up by convening a special hearing with Fluke as the only witness. Democrats and their interest group allies then utilized the photo of the all-male panel in their fund-raising appeals (Swers 2013; Bravender 2012). This pattern of highlighting Democratic policies that help women and characterizing Republican policies as an attack on women's well-being is now a mainstay in the Democrats' political arsenal.

Republicans Fight Back

Not wanting to be seen as antiwomen, Republicans push back on this Democratic narrative by deploying Republican women as surrogates to defend the party against Democratic attacks and help the party reach out to women voters by framing the Republican message of lowering taxes and reducing burdensome regulations in a way that appeals to women voters. Indeed, two women have served as Republican Conference chair, the third-ranking leadership post in the House and the highest level of leadership attained by women in the Republican Conference. The conference chair plays a key role in framing the Republicans' media message. Both Deborah Pryce (R-OH) and current conference chair Cathy McMorris Rodgers (R-WA) cited expanding the party's outreach to women as one of their primary goals for the post (Swers and Larson 2005; Ferraro 2012; Dumain 2014).

For moderate Republican women, the imperative to defend the party requires a careful balance of their own policy views on women's issues and their desire to help the party. The moderate Republican women serving in the House in the late 1990s and early 2000s and the few remaining moderates, such as Senators Susan Collins (R-ME), Lisa Murkowski (R-AK), and Shelly Moore Capito (R-WV), vote their policy beliefs but try not to draw negative attention to the party by criticizing Republican policies in the media or participating in press conferences and floor debates organized by Democrats. Thus, when the Lilly Ledbetter Fair Pay Act was passed, three of the four Republican women serving in the Senate first voted in favor of a Republican alternative to the Democratic legislation sponsored by Kay Bailey Hutchison (R-TX). Not wanting to be portrayed as women opposing equal pay for women, Hutchison, Collins, and Murkowski then joined Republican Olympia Snowe (R-ME) in voting for the Democratic bill (Swers 2013).

Conservative women, who generally support the party's position on women's issues, take a more active role, providing a female voice of authority to refute Democratic assertions that Republican policies are harmful to women. For example, during the conflict over the Obama administration's rule guiding employer coverage of contraceptives, Republican Senator Kelly Ayotte (R-NH) was a key spokesperson pushing back against the Democratic narrative that Republicans wanted to deny women access to contraception, which would jeopardize their health. As a woman, Ayotte spoke with moral authority when she insisted that Republicans are committed to women's health and that the real issue was protecting the religious freedom of employers. Ayotte, along with Marco Rubio (R-FL), was a primary cosponsor of an amendment sponsored by Republican Conference vice chair Roy Blunt (R-MO) that would create a broad conscience exemption to allow employers to deny coverage of contraceptives if it violated their religious beliefs. She made floor speeches, issued press releases, and appeared on television to drive home the message that Republicans were protecting religious freedom and not attacking women's health. Ayotte also took her message on the presidential campaign trail, serving as a frequent surrogate for 2012 Republican nominee Mitt Romney, helping him appeal to women voters and refute assertions that he would bring women's rights back to the 1950s (Ayotte 2012a, 2012b; Swers 2013).

As more conservative women have been elected since 2010, some of these Republican women are prioritizing socially conservative goals and taking leadership roles in promoting Republican efforts to protect life and restrict abortion. Responding to the Planned Parenthood sting videos, Republican leaders developed a two-pronged strategy that would demonstrate Republicans' commitment to protecting life but avoid the threat of the government shutdown that would result from tying the issue to a must-pass spending bill. First, leaders tapped Diane Black (R-TN), the conference vice chair, to sponsor legislation that would prohibit funding of Planned Parenthood for one year while Congress investigated the organization's practices regarding procurement of fetal tissue and its distribution for research (M. Fuller 2015a).

Then Republicans created a select subcommittee of the House Energy and Commerce committee to investigate Planned Parenthood's actions and appointed Marsha Blackburn (R-TN), a conservative woman with ties to the Tea Party, to chair the committee. The select investigative panel to investigate Planned Parenthood is the second special committee created since Republicans gained the majority in 2010. The other, the Select Committee on Benghazi, was created to investigate the terrorist attack against American diplomats in Benghazi, Libya. It yielded political dividends when it uncovered the fact that former secretary of state and 2016 Democratic presidential candidate Hillary Clinton had utilized a private e-mail server, rather than the secure government server, to conduct official business. Just like the Benghazi committee, the special committee to investigate Planned Parenthood has subpoena power and is tasked with investigating a wide range of practices related to abortion and fetal tissue procurement (DeBonis 2015).

To drive home the message that Republicans are protecting women and unborn children, Republican leaders titled the panel the Select Investigative Panel on Infant Lives and appointed an equal number of women and men to the committee. In addition to Blackburn, conference vice chair Diane Black (R-TN), Vicki Hartzler (R-MO), and Mia Love (R-UT), the first Republican African American woman in Congress, all serve on the committee (Blackburn 2015; Marcos 2015). The inclusion of equal numbers of Republican men and women showcases conservative Republican women and helps insulate Republicans from Democratic attacks that the panel is a partisan witch hunt and part of the Republicans' continuing war on women. Meanwhile, Democrats have worked to reframe the debate as another attack on women's health, renaming the committee the Select Committee to Attack Women's Health and appointing five women and one man to represent the party on the committee (Pelosi 2015; Marcos and Ferris 2015). The creation of the committee and the composition of its membership elevate abortion politics for the 2016 election and place women at the center of party efforts to energize the parties' respective bases of activists and donors and to mobilize key voting groups, including religious conservatives for Republicans and single women for Democrats.

Whither Bipartisanship?

The increasing polarization on women's issues and the emergence of more conservative Republican women as champions of socially conservative causes means even formerly bipartisan women's issues are now caught up in the party wars. For example, the Violence against Women Act, a bill to help victims of domestic violence and sexual assault, was first passed in 1994, then reauthorized in 2000 at the end of Bill Clinton's presidency and in 2005 with Republican President George W. Bush in the White House and Republicans controlling Congress (Helderman 2012). However, efforts by Senate Democrats to reauthorize the bill in 2012 became entangled in presidential election politics. House Republicans objected to provisions of the bill that would extend benefits to individuals in same-sex relationships, expand the number of visas for illegal immigrants who are the victims of domestic violence, and address high levels of violence against Native American women by giving tribal courts more authority to prosecute non–Native American offenders. To defend the party, a group of conservative women led by Sandy Adams (R-FL), herself a victim of domestic violence and a former law enforcement official, sponsored an alternative bill that passed the House (Bolduan 2012).

Seeking to deflect Democratic attacks, Republicans, led by House Majority Leader Eric Cantor (R-VA), engaged in high-level negotiations with Vice President Biden, a lead author of the first Violence against Women Act. To pressure Republicans and highlight the party's indifference to the plight of victims of domestic violence, the twelve Democratic women in the Senate penned a letter to the twenty-five Republican women in the House, asking them to unite as women to convince their leadership to pass the reauthorization: "As mothers, daughters, grandmothers, and women intent on protecting the inclusive and bipartisan history of the Violence Against Women Act (VAWA), we are reaching out to you to ask for your help. . . . With your leadership on this issue we will resolve this matter in a way that puts the safety of all women ahead of partisan politics" (quoted in Bendery 2012). Still, at the close of the 112th Congress (2011–2012), the issue remained unresolved.

With a newly reelected President Obama, Democrats made reauthorization of the Violence against Women Act a top priority. The party also hoped the bill would help them turn out women voters in the upcoming 2014 midterms, when Democratic control of the Senate was at risk. Twenty-three Republican senators, including the four Republican women, joined with Democrats to pass the bill, a bipartisan demonstration that pressured House Republicans to bring the legislation to the floor. Once again Republicans turned to their conservative women members for help. Concern over the party's poor performance with women voters in the 2012 election led Republican House leaders to schedule the Senate bill.

First, conference vice chair Cathy McMorris Rodgers (R-WA) offered the Republican alternative. When that bill failed, the House passed the Senate proposal (Nocera 2013). Republican leaders were so concerned about protecting the party's image with women voters that the Violence against Women Act reauthorization was one of the only nonbudget bills passed that violated the Hastert Rule of passing legislation with a majority of the majority. For the vast majority of votes that thwarted the Hastert Rule, Republican leaders were forced to rely on Democratic votes in order to avoid the economic catastrophe that would result from missing important budget deadlines or failing to raise the debt ceiling. In the end, the bill passed with 87 Republicans voting with all the Democrats, while 138 Republicans opposed the bill (Bettelheim 2014).

Like domestic violence, breast cancer research, a longtime bastion of bipartisanship, was recently caught up in party warfare over abortion and Planned Parenthood. Democrat Carolyn Maloney (NY) and Republican Pete Sessions (TX), chair of the Rules Committee and former chair of the National Republican Campaign Committee, sponsored a bill to create a commemorative coin that would raise funds for breast cancer research. The bill had 309 cosponsors and was scheduled to pass under suspension of the rules, a procedure used for noncontroversial bills. The money raised from the coin would be divided equally between the Breast Cancer Foundation headquartered in Maloney's New York and the Susan G. Komen for a Cure foundation headquartered in Sessions's Texas. In more fallout from the Planned Parenthood videos, conservatives objected to the fact that Susan G. Komen had financed breast cancer services at some local Planned Parenthood clinics. As a result, the influential conservative group Heritage Action for America came out against the bill and said it would score the vote. In response, twenty-six Republican members went to the floor to withdraw their names as cosponsors, including seven of the twelve Republican women who cosponsored the bill. House leaders then had to pull the legislation from the floor and drop Komen as a recipient of funds before the bill could move forward (M. Fuller 2015b, 2015c).

Conclusion

As we move toward the 2016 presidential election, the frontrunner for the Democratic nomination, Hillary Clinton, is more fully embracing her gender and her status as the first female major-party nominee than she did in her 2008 run. On the campaign trail Clinton emphasizes equal pay for women, paid family leave, and help for middle-class families trying to afford child care or pay for their kids' college education (Karni 2015). Clinton is working to build up the Democrats' electoral coalition of women, youth, and minorities. Democratic women in Congress and the women's groups that support the Democratic Party will reinforce these themes and contrast Democrats' policies on women's issues in a way that appeals to target groups of women, particularly single and minority women voters. They will also try to mobilize women voters by contrasting Democratic support for women's issues with Republican policies that harm women's rights and ignore women's needs.

Anticipating these attacks, Republicans now have a small but growing group of conservative Republican women who take to the campaign trail and the media airwaves to defend the party and promote Republican policies as better suited to help women and their families. As more conservative women get elected from the Republican strongholds of the South and West with support from core party constituencies, including social conservatives and Tea Party activists, these women are eager to champion conservative causes, particularly protecting the unborn. As a result we will see Republican women more forcefully pushing back on the Democratic narrative that Republicans are engaged in a war on women, and these Republican women will also take more prominent leadership roles in crafting conservative initiatives to restrict abortion. With increasing polarization between the parties and women's issues occupying a pivotal position in partisan warfare and electoral outreach, there will be little room for bipartisan collaboration among women. Instead we should expect more instances of confrontation, with women playing key roles as policy leaders, defenders of their parties, and symbols of what women truly want.

Note

1. DW-NOMINATE scores utilize all roll call votes cast in a congressional session to place members on a scale from most liberal to most conservative. See the Voteview website (http://www.voteview.com) for more information.

References

Abramowitz, Alan. 2011. *The Disappearing Center: Engaged Citizens, Polarization, and American Democracy*. New Haven, CT: Yale University Press.

Ainsworth, Scott, and Thad Hall. 2010. *Abortion Politics in Congress: Strategic Incrementalism and Policy Change*. New York: Cambridge University Press.

Ayotte, Kelly. 2012a. "Ayotte: Health Care Mandate Is Affront to Religious Freedom." Kelly Ayotte, February 7, http://www.ayotte.senate.gov/?p=video&id=423.

———. 2012b. "Ayotte: We Must Respect Conscience Rights for All Religions." Kelly Ayotte, February 8, http://www.ayotte.senate.gov/?p=video&id=426.

Barnes, Robert. 2007. "Over Ginsburg's Dissent, Court Limits Bias Suits." *Washington Post*, May 30.

Bendery, Jennifer. 2012. "Violence against Women Act: House Republican Women Emerge as Key to Possible Action." *Huffington Post*, December 12.

Bettelheim, Adriel. 2014. "Key House Vote of 2013: Violence against Women Act." *CQ Weekly*, February 3.

Blackburn, Marsha. 2015. "An Investigation in Defense of Life." *US News & World Report*, November 10.

Bolduan, Kate. 2012. "House Passes GOP Version of Violence against Women Act Renewal." CNN, May 16.

Bravender, Robin. 2012. "Birth Control Battle Brings in Bucks." *Politico*, March 18.

Brownstein, Ronald. 2012. "Why Contraceptives Is the Latest Wedge Issue Dividing Democrats and Republicans." *National Journal*, February 17.

Burrell, Barbara. 2014. *Gender in Campaigns for the U.S. House of Representatives.* Ann Arbor: University of Michigan Press.

Bzdek, Vince. 2010. "Why Did Health-Care Reform Pass? Nancy Pelosi Was in Charge." *Washington Post*, March 28.

Center for American Women and Politics. 2015. "Fact Sheet: Women in the U.S. Congress 2015." New Brunswick, NJ: Center for American Women and Politics, Rutgers, State University of New Jersey.

Davidson, Roger H., Walter J. Oleszek, Frances E. Lee, and Eric Schickler. 2015. *Congress and Its Members*, 15th ed. Washington, DC: CQ Press.

DeBonis, Mike. 2015. "Special Committee Will Investigate Planned Parenthood, Abortion Issues." *Washington Post*, October 7.

Dodson, Debra L. 2006. *The Impact of Women in Congress.* New York: Oxford University Press.

Dolan, Julie, Melissa Deckman, and Michele Swers. 2016. *Women and Politics: Paths to Power and Political Influence*, 3rd ed. Lanham, MD: Rowman & Littlefield.

Dolan, Kathleen. 2014. *When Does Gender Matter? Women Candidates and Gender Stereotypes in American Elections.* New York: Oxford University Press.

Dumain, Emma. 2014. "McMorris Rodgers Works to Rebuild, Rebrand Party Image One Republican at a Time." *Roll Call*, March 6.

——. 2015. "Breaking Down the CR Vote." *Roll Call*, September 30.

Elder, Laurel. 2014. "Women and the Parties: An Analysis of Republican and Democratic Strategists for Recruiting Women Candidates." Paper presented at the annual meeting of the American Political Science Association Conference, Washington, DC, August 28–31.

Feinstein, Dianne. 2006. "Women in Politics and Business." Dianne Feinstein, http://www.feinstein.senate.gov/public/index.cfm/speeches?ID=5aceabe1-7e9c-9af9-7152-0a03ca4a9fe6 (accessed June 3, 2015).

Ferraro, Thomas. 2012. "Top Republican Woman in Congress Becomes a Force." Reuters, May 18.

Ferris, Sarah. 2015. "House Creates Panel to Investigate Planned Parenthood." *Hill*, October 7.

Frederick, Brian. 2009. "Are Female House Members Still More Liberal in a Polarized Era? The Conditional Nature of the Relationship between Descriptive and Substantive Representation." *Congress and the Presidency* 36: 181–202.

——. 2010. "Gender and Patterns of Roll Call Voting in the U.S. Senate." *Congress and the Presidency* 37: 103–24.

Fuller, Jamie. 2014. "After Hobby Lobby: The Next Fronts in the Contraception Fight." *Washington Post*, July 1.

Fuller, Matt. 2015a. "Ahead of Planned Parenthood Battle, House to Vote on Abortion Bills." *Roll Call*, September 14.

——. 2015b. "Breast Cancer Bill Pulled amid Abortion Funding Concerns." *Roll Call*, July 14.

——. 2015c. "Breast Cancer Coin Bill Back on Floor Schedule." *Roll Call*, July 15.

Gertzog, Irwin. 1995. *Congressional Women: Their Recruitment, Integration, and Behavior*, 2nd ed. Westport, CT: Praeger Publishers.

Halloran, Liz. 2009. "House Approves Bills to Fight Gender Wage Gap." NPR, January 9.

Helderman, Rosalind S. 2012. "Violence against Women Act Reauthorization Bill Passed by Senate." *Washington Post*, April 26.

Jacobson, Gary. 2013. *The Politics of Congressional Elections*, 8th ed. New York: Pearson.

Kamisar, Ben, Jonathan Easley, and Jonathan Swan. 2015. "Cruz Wins Values Voter Summit Straw Poll for Third Straight Year." *Hill*, September 26.

Karni, Annie. 2015. "This Time Hillary Embraces 'Gender Card.'" *Politico*, July 21.

Kliff, Sarah. 2015. "A Government Shutdown Fight Is Brewing. This One Is over Planned Parenthood." *Vox*, September 10.

Layman, Geoffrey. 2001. *The Great Divide: Religious and Cultural Conflict in American Party Politics*. New York: Oxford University Press.

Marcos, Cristina. 2015. "Boehner Appoints Woman to Lead Planned Parenthood Investigation." *Hill*, October 23.

Marcos, Cristina, and Sarah Ferris. 2015. "Party Leaders Send Women into Committee Brawl over Abortion." *Hill*, November 7.

Newton-Small, Jay. 2014. "Republicans Struggle to GROW Women in Recruitment Drive." *Time*, February 27.

Nocera, Kate. 2013. "House Passes Violence against Women Act." *Politico*, February 28.

Palmer, Barbara, and Dennis Simon. 2008. *Breaking the Political Glass Ceiling: Women and Congressional Elections*. New York: Routledge.

Pear, Robert. 2009. "House Votes to Expand Children's Health Care." *New York Times*, January 15.

Pearson, Kathryn, and Eric McGhee. 2013. "What It Takes to Win: Questioning 'Gender Neutral' Outcomes in U.S. House Elections." *Politics & Gender* 9: 439–62.

Pelosi, Nancy. 2015. "Pelosi Statement on Republicans' Select Committee to Attack Women's Health." Nancy Pelosi, Democratic Leader, September 26, http://www.democraticleader.gov/newsroom/pelosi-statement-on-republicans-select-committee-to-attack-womens-health (accessed November 12, 2015).

Peters, Ronald M., Jr., and Cindy Simon Rosenthal. 2010. *Speaker Nancy Pelosi and the New American Politics*. New York: Oxford University Press.

Political Parity. 2015. "Right the Ratio: Clearing the Primary Hurdle for Republican Women." Cambridge, MA: Hunt Alternatives, https://www.politicalparity.org/wp-content/uploads/2015/01/primary-hurdles-full-report.pdf (accessed October 28, 2015).

Reinhard, Beth. 2013. "The Democrats' War to Win Women Voters." *National Journal*, February 4.

Sanbonmatsu, Kira. 2002. *Gender Equality, Political Parties, and the Politics of Women's Place*. Ann Arbor: University of Michigan Press.

Sanbonmatsu, Kira, and Kathleen Dolan. 2009. "Do Gender Stereotypes Transcend Party?" *Political Research Quarterly* 62: 485–94.

Shimabukuro, Jon O. 2014. "Abortion: Judicial History and Legislative Response." Congressional Research Service. Washington, DC: Library of Congress.

Slajda, Rachel. 2009. "Kyl: 'I Don't Need Maternity Care.' Stabenow: 'Your Mom Probably Did.'" *Talking Points Memo*, September 25.

Strauss, Daniel. 2015. "Chart: Actually Most of the Diversity in Congress Comes from Democrats." *Talking Points Memo*, January 6.

Sullivan, Sean. 2014. "Todd Akin Takes Back Apology for 'Legitimate Rape' Comment." *Washington Post*, July 10.

Swers, Michele L. 2002. *The Difference Women Make: The Policy Impact of Women in Congress*. Chicago: University of Chicago Press.

———. 2013. *Women in the Club: Gender and Policy Making in the Senate*. Chicago: University of Chicago Press.

Swers, Michele L., and Carin Larson. 2005. "Women and Congress: Do They Act as Advocates for Women's Issues?" In *Women and Elective Office: Past, Present, and Future*, edited by Sue Thomas and Clyde Wilcox, 110–28. New York: Oxford University Press.

Williams, Daniel K. 2010. *God's Own Party: The Making of the Christian Right*. New York: Oxford University Press.

15

The Government Shutdown of 2013

A Perspective

Walter J. Oleszek

"DEADLINES HERE, DEADLINES THERE. But always deadlines. Management by crisis" is how Senate Minority Leader Harry Reid (D-NV) characterized governance in the GOP-controlled 114th Congress (2015–2016) (Sherman and Everett 2015, 11). Deadline lawmaking on major issues is commonplace regardless of which party is in control of the House, Senate, or White House. Deadlines are established in various ways. Some are imposed by the majority-party leadership, as these classic examples illustrate. Consider Speaker Newt Gingrich's 1995 "Contract with America" agenda, which he promised the nation that the new Republican House majority (previously in the minority for forty consecutive years) would vote on within the first one hundred days of the 104th Congress (1995–1996). Republicans accomplished the deed in less than one hundred days. Not to be outdone, when Democrats reclaimed control of the House in the November 2006 elections, Speaker Nancy Pelosi (D-CA) won rapid chamber adoption of her party's six-point "100-legislative hours" agenda, such as raising the minimum wage and expanding stem cell research.

There are many other types of deadlines. Crises can provoke legislative deadlines. In September 2008, as the stock market plummeted and financial institutions collapsed, Treasury Secretary Hank Paulson recognized that the nation faced an economic crisis of major proportions. Unless Congress acted quickly, there could be another Great Depression in the country. Mindful that economic conditions were deteriorating, Speaker Pelosi, on September 18, telephoned Paulson and requested that he and other officials come to

Capitol Hill the next morning to brief the bipartisan and bicameral congressional leadership about the financial turmoil. Paulson responded, "Madam
Speaker, it cannot wait until tomorrow morning. We have to come today. We
need legislation passed quickly. We need to send a strong signal to the market
now" (Kaiser 2013, 6).[1] Within fifteen days, Congress responded by passing
a major financial reform bill (the Troubled Asset Relief Program), which the
president signed into law.[2]

There are also statutory deadlines that Congress imposes on itself. Two are
especially important to the well-being of the nation because failure to win
their enactment into law by a specific deadline can produce severe negative
consequences for the country.[3] One such deadline is the requirement that
each of the dozen annual appropriations measures be enacted into law by
the September 30 fiscal year deadline referenced in the 1974 Congressional
Budget and Impoundment Control Act. (The fiscal year begins on October 1
and ends at midnight on September 30.) Appropriations bills fund much of
the federal government, such as every cabinet department. Congress's failure
to enact into law one or more of the spending bills during the twelve-month
fiscal year can lead to a partial shutdown of the government. This happened
in October 2013 and is the principal focus of this chapter.

Another must-pass measure is raising the statutory debt ceiling. It became
intertwined with the October 2013 effort to open the government. These laws
restrict the amount of debt that may be outstanding at any given time. If the
government cannot continue to borrow money when it hits the statutory debt
ceiling, as determined by the Treasury Department, it will be unable to pay its
bills. This outcome would trigger serious economic consequences nationally
and globally. Both must-pass measures—appropriation bills and debt-ceiling
hikes—may also attract policy riders that are sometimes so toxic to one political party or the White House that they provoke a government shutdown or
threaten a debt default. Moreover, there are many lawmakers who willingly
use the threat or reality of a government shutdown (or oppose raising the debt
ceiling) as leverage to try to extract concessions from the White House and
the opposition party. As one legislative budget expert stated, "Threatening a
government shutdown is [viewed] as an appropriate, even desirable legislative
strategy. Refusing to make a decision on an appropriation until the very last
minute and creating the agony of heartburn along the way is thought of as a
proper negotiating tool" (Collender 2011, 46).

An analysis of the politics and procedures associated with the October 2013
shutdown—what happened, why, and how it ended—provides a window
onto the policymaking difficulties today's polarized Congress encounters
in enacting even must-pass legislation. Since the midterm elections of 2010
produced divided government (split party control of the House and Senate, or

Congress and the White House), governance by brinksmanship and partisan position taking have often been the new normal in policymaking.

Numerous analyses and studies illuminate factors that explain why lawmaking on Capitol Hill is so contentious, such as the marked differences—geographic, demographic, racial, policy, and ideological, for example—between the two congressional parties (Persily 2015). Simply put, the political center of gravity of the two parties has evolved to where the two parties are fundamentally dissimilar across various dimensions (racial composition, party unity, and so on). Democrats are more liberal (an activist role for the federal government) and Republicans are even more conservative (a reduced role and reach for national government) than they were three decades ago. Centrist lawmakers are in short supply on Capitol Hill.

An examination of the October 2013 shutdown of the federal government reveals many of the actors, forces, and factors that shape and suffuse contemporary legislating. This chapter is organized into six sections. It begins with general background on the differences between gaps (lapses) in funding the government and closing down the government. Second, the chapter focuses on the origins of the GOP's strategy of using the appropriations process to undermine President Barack Obama's signature policy achievement—the Affordable Care Act (ObamaCare). The GOP's objective: force the president to sign appropriations legislation that would deny funds for ObamaCare or be blamed for closing major parts of the government.

The third section identifies some of the key advocates and opponents of the defund-shutdown strategy. Fourth, the chapter examines the legislative back-and-forth between the House and Senate prior to the government's shutting down. The fifth section reviews a selected number of procedural maneuvers employed in the House and Senate during the shutdown. Among the purposes of these maneuvers was to encourage capitulation by one chamber to the other. Sixth, the chapter closes with a few observations about fiscal brinksmanship.

General Background: Gaps and Shutdown

There is no constitutional requirement for the enactment of annual appropriations measures, but this has been the practice since the 1st Congress (1789–1791). By custom, the House also originates the annual appropriations measures, no doubt based on its constitutional prerogative to initiate revenue-raising measures. Add Congress's constitutional borrowing authority, and this trio—appropriating, taxing, and borrowing—are the fundamentals of the legislature's "power of the purse." Little surprise that presidents, lawmakers, and agency officials, among others, pay close attention to the appropriations process and the various elements (House and Senate rules and fiscal laws, for example) that influence the funding of federal programs and agencies to the tune today of over $1 trillion.

Length of time, or duration, constitutes the fundamental difference between funding gaps (also called "lapses") and government shutdowns (Brass 2014). Lapses are commonly brief (a day or two) and involve little or no interruption of government services. Funding gaps are also more common than shutdowns. Gaps occur when appropriations measures are not enacted in a timely manner. The result: agencies lack the legal authority to spend money and are required to begin a shutdown process. The funding lapse remains until Congress passes either an agencies' appropriations measure or some form of interim or stopgap funding. Stopgap funding is often provided through what are called continuing resolutions (CRs). Congress often employs short-term CRs to provide House and Senate negotiators additional time to determine whether negotiators can resolve their differences and enact one or more of the outstanding appropriations measures. If the negotiations fail, CRs (sometimes lasting a full year) are the main way to keep the government operating, usually at the previous year's spending level. Members of the House and Senate Appropriations Committees dislike CRs because they negate "the work that we've done," said Hal Rogers (R-KY), chair of the House panel. "And at the end of the fiscal year, it's either shut down or CR—and obviously a CR is better" (Bade 2015, 1).[4] To be sure, federal agencies detest CRs, which disrupt operations and impede the fulfillment of their responsibilities (Samuelsohn 2015, 1).

Government shutdowns, by contrast, can start as funding gaps and morph into shutdowns. Shutdowns disrupt government services, last several days or weeks, and involve furloughing numerous government employees. The 2013 shutdown lasted sixteen days, furloughed eight hundred thousand federal employees, and closed scores of national parks and federal facilities. It also negatively impacted various sectors of the economy. As one account noted, the "16-day shutdown has . . . led to the biggest plunge in consumer confidence since the collapse of Lehman Brothers in 2008." The chief executive of Family Dollar Stores said that "his customers, most with modest incomes, had pulled back on spending" during the government shutdown (Lowrey, Popper, and Schwartz 2013, A19).

Unlike Family Dollar Store customers, congressional Republicans have not pulled back from trying to repeal, modify, or weaken the Affordable Care Act. Since its enactment in 2010, the GOP House has tried nearly sixty times to repeal, replace, or weaken the overall health law. The attempts have basically failed. Nonetheless, the zeal among numerous Republicans inside and outside

Congress to terminate the health law or block its effective implementation has not waned. They have been relentless in trying to disable the health law through such means as legislative fights, procedural tactics, and budgetary maneuvers (Gerson 2013, A15).[5] In 2013, they embarked on a bold course: congressional Republicans decided to use the strategy of defunding Obama-Care by shutting down most of the federal government unless President Obama acceded to their demands to kill the health law.

Planning the Government Shutdown

The Plan

At the start of President Obama's second term, press accounts indicated that a network of conservative activists, led by Edwin Meese (former attorney general for President Ronald Reagan), had begun organizing for a government shutdown months in advance of its occurrence. Frustrated by Congress's inability to "repeal and replace" ObamaCare, as Republicans had long promised, the Meese-led group devised a "blueprint to defunding Obamacare."[6] Their strategy, as noted, was to use the appropriations process to defund the president's health law by deliberately provoking a government shutdown. Their blueprint "articulated a take-no-prisoners legislative strategy that had long percolated in conservative circles: that Republicans could derail the health care overhaul if conservative lawmakers were willing to push fellow Republicans—including their cautious leaders—into cutting off financing for the entire federal government" (Stolberg and McIntire 2013, S7254).

The appropriations process is employed by lawmakers of both parties to oversee executive agencies and hold them accountable for their actions, as well as to eliminate, restrict, or undermine specific federal programs lawmakers dislike. To employ the appropriations process to force a government shutdown was a high-stakes decision by GOP leaders and their outside allies. In anticipation of the sharp criticism against the Republican plan, "A defunding 'tool kit' created in early September [2013] included talking points for the question, 'What happens when you shut down the government and you are blamed for it?' The suggested answer was the one House Republicans [used]: 'We are simply calling to fund the entire government except for the Affordable Care Act/Obama Care'" (Stolberg and McIntire 2013, S7254).

To be sure, both opponents and proponents of the Affordable Care Act waged public messaging wars, with one side urging the law's demise and the other encouraging citizens to support and sign up for the health insurance provided under the health law. How to characterize the "shutdown" was also part of the public relations battle. Senator Ted Cruz (R-TX) emphasized, "The term 'shutdown' is a misnomer. It's actually a partial, temporary shutdown" (Zeller 2013, 1632). GOP lawmakers preferred using words and phrases like "keeping the government open," "slowdown," "slimdown," and "lapse in government operations." Democrats and the media constantly used the word "shutdown," said a political scientist, "because it grabs your attention" (Zeller 2013, 1632).

The Pressure of Time

Timing was critical for opponents of ObamaCare because the health plan's public enrollment period via the Internet would open on October 1, 2013, the start of the new fiscal year. As Edwin Meese said, "I think people realized that with the imminent beginning of Obamacare, that this was a critical time" to put an end to the law (Stolberg and McIntire 2013, S7255). Although the initial Internet rollout of the sign-up period turned out to be a debacle, conservative activists and lawmakers recognized that it would be difficult to defund ObamaCare once millions of people began to receive the health benefits of the law. Many people would become "addicted" to the health law and the subsidies provided to many enrollees. "We either stand for principle now," declared Senator Cruz, a vociferous critic of the president and his health law, "or I believe we surrender to Obamacare permanently" (Newhauser and Ethridge 2013, 1550). Little surprise that the pressure of time motivated hard-right conservatives to go all out to defund ObamaCare, even if a shutdown occurred.

The Shutdown Backdrop: Advocates and Opponents

Shutdown Advocates

Numerous conservative groups—the Tea Party, Heritage Action for America, the Club for Growth, Freedom Works, and more, with financial aid provided by the billionaire Koch brothers—participated in pressuring congressional Republicans to derail ObamaCare with a "take-no-prisoners legislative strategy." Conservative groups orchestrated a campaign to sway congressional on-the-fence and electorally vulnerable Republicans. They used various techniques to win their support, including social media posts, telephone messages to GOP offices, sample letters to newspaper editors in lawmakers' districts, a "Defund Obamacare Town Hall Tour," and radio and television advertisements against the health law (Stolberg and McIntire 2013, S7254).

Many GOP lawmakers also worked hard to defund ObamaCare. Notable in the House was Mark Meadows (R-NC). He delivered a letter signed by eighty House Republicans to Speaker John Boehner (R-OH), urging him to support the defund-shutdown approach to eviscerating ObamaCare. In the Senate, Ted Cruz and Mike Lee (R-UT)[7] strongly supported the defund-shutdown strategy (Cottle 2015, 18). Senator Cruz in particular enjoyed large influence with a small group of Tea Party members of the House, in part because of his communication skills and unyielding campaign against ObamaCare. "Senator Cruz is now joint Speaker with Boehner in leading House Republicans," exclaimed Senator Harry Reid (Bolton 2013b, 10).

Periodically, hard-right House conservatives would meet with Senator Cruz in various locales (in Cruz's office, in the House, or at Tortilla Coast, a restaurant popular with Cruz's House allies) to plan tactics and strategy on a variety of topics, including ObamaCare (Fuller 2014, 1; Bolton 2014, 1). Their broad strategy was to use "their influence in the House majority to steer leadership toward conservative goals like defunding Obamacare in spending bills while right-wing all-stars like Cruz use[d] the Senate floor as a national press platform" (Everett 2013, 17). The judgment of conservative lawmakers was that intense public dislike of ObamaCare would mean that Democrats who supported the Affordable Care Act would get blamed for any shutdown. The public outcry against a shutdown might encourage enough Democrats to vote to reopen the government and, if unwilling to defund ObamaCare, at least agree to a year's delay in the law's implementation, a GOP fallback position.

Shutdown Opponents

Senior Republican lawmakers, including Speaker Boehner and Senate GOP leader Mitch McConnell (R-KY), business trade associations, and the defense industry, among others, opposed the defund-shutdown approach. They reminded their party colleagues of what happened in 1995 and 1996 when House Republicans twice shut down the government in their attempt to shrink the federal role through spending cuts and other means. As an ABC News/*Washington Post* poll found after the 1995 and 1996 shutdowns, "81 percent of the public disapproved of the shutdown and 53 percent blamed Republicans for it" (Zeller and Hallerman 2013, 21). In short, the two 1990s shutdowns were public relations disasters for Republicans.

During the 1990s closures, various GOP lawmakers vociferously urged the two government shutdowns on the grounds that the public would never notice. They were wrong. For example, Americans throughout the nation soon learned to their dismay that they could not visit national parks, the Statue of Liberty, or the Washington Monument. Senate Majority Leader Bob Dole

(R-KS) worked successfully to win legislative support for reopening the government because the public was focusing more on the shutdowns than on the GOP's budget and policy initiatives. "Somewhere along the way, we've gotten off message," he said (Wayne 1997, B11).

In 2013, many House Republicans simply ignored the historical record and proceeded once more to use the shutdown strategy. Their animus toward ObamaCare was so intense that they would risk public damage to the party's reputation for governance and policymaking. Even so, Republicans recognized the imperative of satisfying their conservative political base. Many Republicans understood that attempts at pragmatic compromise with President Obama or the Democratic Senate could attract something they did not want: hard-right primary opponents. To be sure, Senator Cruz urged the GOP House to delete health-care funding from any CR. "I will do everything necessary and anything possible to defund Obamacare," remarked Senator Cruz. "[Senator] Mike Lee and I will use every procedural means available" (Hook and Peterson 2013, A5).

Procedural Actions Prior to the Shutdown

The GOP House

Speaker Boehner, Majority Leader Eric Cantor (R-VA), and Majority Whip Kevin McCarthy (R-CA) wanted to avoid a government shutdown to prevent public damage to the Republican brand. They recognized that neither the Democratic Senate nor President Obama would agree to legislation that undermined the president's signature health-care overhaul law. Thus, for the first two weeks or so of September 2013, GOP leaders devised ways to try to accommodate the demands of their right-leaning members—for example, granting the hard-liners a largely symbolic vote to defund ObamaCare—without provoking a government shutdown in the process.

Majority Leader Cantor proposed a "two-measures" approach to oblige his most conservative lawmakers. First, the House would pass a "clean" CR to keep the government open through mid-December 2013. However, before the clean CR was sent to the Senate, that chamber would first vote to accept or reject the second House measure: a concurrent resolution to defund the health law. (Concurrent resolutions do not have the force of law and are not transmitted to the White House for presidential consideration.) If the concurrent resolution was adopted, language in that measure authorized the House clerk to change the text of the clean CR to defund ObamaCare. House GOP leaders realized that the Senate would be unlikely adopt the concurrent resolution. Nonetheless, it appeared evident that the Senate would support a clean CR, and its enactment would send the measure directly to the president for his signature.

The two-measures approach gave House conservatives the opportunity to vent and vote for a concurrent resolution that would defund ObamaCare; contemporaneously, the House would also pass a clean CR to keep the government open. As for the Senate's expected reaction to this plan, a House GOP leadership aide stated that Cantor's plan ostensibly "forces the Senate to vote on defund before they are allowed to vote on a CR. It puts the onus back on Senate Democrats—that they are responsible for funding ObamaCare" (Berman, Hooper, and Wasson 2013, 6). Cantor's plan was not executed, however. Tea Party–aligned Republicans opposed Cantor's plan "as a watered-down version of the policy that conservatives wanted: a single spending bill that would withhold funds for the healthcare law" (Berman, Hooper, and Wasson 2013, 7). Senators Cruz and Lee also opposed Cantor's proposal (Cruz called it "procedural chicanery"), which "caused a rebellion among House conservatives" (Sherman and Bresnahan 2013a, 25). Cantor's plan failed to receive sufficient GOP support; hence, it was not voted upon by the House. This result underscored both the intraparty influence of the Tea Party conservatives and the challenge they posed for GOP leaders in mobilizing enough votes from within their own party to pass legislation (the requirement of the informal Hastert Rule).[8]

Speaker Boehner broached another way that might keep the government open: use the debt limit as a bargaining chip. House Republicans could refuse to raise the debt ceiling unless Democrats agreed to reduce funding for ObamaCare in a CR. As a follow-on to that approach, Majority Leader Cantor suggested adding to legislation increasing the debt ceiling a one-year delay in implementing ObamaCare, as well as adding other matters (tax reform, for instance) to that legislation (Fuller 2013). GOP leaders at the time were unsure whether they had the votes to even pass a hike in the debt ceiling (Sherman and Bresnahan 2013b, 1, 19). President Obama vowed to oppose efforts by congressional Republicans to extort concessions from the White House in exchange for increasing the debt limit.

Finally, in mid-September 2013, House Republican leaders included the defund provision in the CR and sent the legislation to the Senate. House GOP leaders had resisted the shutdown approach because it could promote an unwanted government shutdown and was unlikely to achieve the GOP's goal of defunding the Affordable Care Act. Speaker Boehner explained, "We're going to put Obamacare defunding directly in the CR. And then we're going to send it over to the Senate so our conservative allies over there can continue the fight" (Fuller 2013). For instance, Senator Cruz, with the aid of Senator Lee, launched a twenty-one-hour talkathon (September 24–25) about the perils of ObamaCare.

The Democratic Senate

Led by Majority Leader Harry Reid of Nevada, Senate Democrats supported a clean CR. Senator Reid adamantly opposed the House GOP's defund strategy and refused any attempt to compromise with House Republicans. Throughout the pre- and post-shutdown period, Senator Reid held fast to his no-negotiation position, which angered House Republicans. Part of the reason for Senator Reid's no-negotiation stance was to dissuade House Tea Party conservatives "from demanding major concessions in exchange for passing future bills essential to the smooth functioning of government" (Bolton 2013b, 10), such as appropriation and debt-ceiling measures. Moreover, Reid viewed the House's repeated attempts to add a "defund ObamaCare" provision to the CR as wasted efforts because it was not going to pass the Senate.

Yet, with the Senate divided 54–46, Senator Reid was mindful that he would need to keep his party unified and secure the votes of six Republicans if it was necessary to bring a filibuster (prolonged debate) to an end. Cloture, or closure of debate, requires sixty votes to invoke. It is the Senate's only formal procedure (Rule XXII) to bring debate to a close. Senator Reid had little difficulty winning sufficient support from Senate Republicans to invoke cloture. They viewed the House GOP's defund-shutdown strategy as unwise, unworkable, unachievable, and unhelpful to the public image of the party. Senator Richard Burr (R-NC), for example, called the House GOP's defund plan the "dumbest idea I've ever heard" (Bolton 2013a, 6). Senator John McCain (R-AZ), declared, "In the United States Senate, we will not repeal or defund Obamacare. We will not. And to think we can is not rational" (Kane and O'Keefe 2013, A4). Senator Bob Corker (R-TN) considered the House shutdown effort as simply pointless. "Box canyon, here we come," was how he viewed the matter (Kane and O'Keefe 2013, A4). GOP Senator Susan Collins of Maine said, "I voted against Obamacare and have repeatedly voted to repeal, reform, and replace it, but I disagree with the strategy of linking Obamacare with the continuing function of government—a strategy that cannot possibly work" (Dinan 2013, A6).

Interestingly, after Speaker Boehner announced in mid-September that he would include the defund provision in the CR, Senator Cruz—the key legislator vehemently opposed to the health law—indicated that there was little chance that the Senate would pass the House's CR. Senator Cruz knew that with sixty votes in hand to invoke cloture, Senator Reid could break the Senate's oft-used "double filibuster": one on the procedural motion to bring a measure to the floor and the other on the substantive measure itself. Unsurprisingly, Senator Reid offered amendments to strike from the CR the House's defund provision without fear that a filibuster could frustrate that objective.

Worth brief mention is that once cloture is invoked, the Senate does not immediately vote on the clotured item. Rule XXII provides an additional thirty hours of consideration of the matter. Some of that time was used for debate by opponents of Reid's amendment to strike the defund provision from the CR (H. J. Res. 59); however, his repeated exhortations that "each day that goes by . . . we are that much closer to a government shutdown" were heeded by his colleagues. It was usual for senators to agree that "all time postcloture [the thirty hours] be yielded back" (Reid 2013b, S6937).

Senator Reid used a parliamentary device—filling the amendment tree—to help ensure that the Senate could strip the defund rider from the House-passed CR (H. J. Res. 59). The so-called tree is a chart depicted in the Senate's book of precedents that determines the maximum number and type of amendments to a measure that may be offered and pending at the same time (Riddick and Frumin 1992, 74–89). Filling the tree allows the majority leader—who receives priority of recognition by the presiding officer—to offer to legislation a series of back-to-back amendments that "freezes" the amending process. With the tree filled, no senator can propose an amendment until one of the pending amendments is disposed of. There are various reasons why the majority leader might fill the tree, such as maintaining control of the floor, expediting action, or preventing opposition senators from offering and debating unwanted amendments. These three factors contributed to Senator Reid's decision to fill the tree on the continuing appropriations resolution.

On September 24, 2013, Majority Leader Reid filled the tree on his amendment to strike the defund language from H. J. Res. 59, much to the chagrin of Senator Cruz. Cruz (2013, S6777) exclaimed that there was only one real amendment offered by Senator Reid, and its purpose was "to gut [strike] the defunding language" from the continuing resolution. The other amendments offered by Reid were placeholders—merely changing a date, for example—to prevent senators like Cruz from offering troublesome amendments. Senator Cruz recommended two options for dealing with the House-passed CR. He urged Senate Democrats to vote up or down on the House's CR with the defund provision or, alternatively, to permit an open amendment process so senators could offer and debate numerous amendments to the CR. Reid did not accept either suggestion. He filed two cloture motions, one to close debate on the motion to call up the House's CR and the other on his amendment to strike the defund provision from H. J. Res. 59.

Both cloture motions were adopted by the Senate: the first by a 100–0 vote and the second by a 79–19 vote (Cruz 2013, S6777). Some senators were confused by the 100–0 vote. As Senator Corker (2013, S6938) remarked, "I do not think ever in the history of the Senate have we had a 21-hour filibuster and then the persons [mainly Senators Cruz and Lee] carrying out the filibuster voted for the issue they were filibustering." Senator Cruz quickly responded that he supported cloture on the motion to proceed and even recommended that the vote be unanimous so the Senate could "get on the bill."

Once the Senate was "on the bill," Friday, September 27, became the decision day on the clotured matter. Texas Senator John Cornyn, the GOP majority whip, emphasized the significance of the critical vote. He said, "A 'yes' vote [on Reid's strike amendment] will be a vote to fund ObamaCare because it will take out of the underlying continuing resolution the House position that Republicans have universally supported to defund ObamaCare" (Cornyn 2013, S6992). First, the Senate voted 54–44 for the Reid amendment. (Senator Reid's amendment also deleted a House GOP debt-limit provision that prioritized debt payments first to nations, such as China, and then to people in the United States.) Then, the Senate passed H. J. Res. 59, as amended, by a 54–44 vote.

Bicameral "Ping-Pong" Accelerates

On Saturday, September 28, divided House Republicans met to determine their next policy and procedural moves. Some wanted to pass a seven-day CR, which would allow time to determine if the GOP could unite behind a plan that the Senate might accept. Others suggested that the House pass a CR with a one-year delay in implementing the health overhaul law. GOP Representative Richard Hudson (R-NC) recommended that House leaders engage in hard bargaining with the Senate and use a "carrot or stick" strategy. "Do we try to do something bad enough to force Harry Reid to negotiate with us, or do we do something that we think he can't refuse?" (Weisman and Parker 2013a, A11). One approach, while technically available, was suggested to Speaker Boehner by moderate Republicans: bring the Senate's clean CR to the floor and pass it with a bipartisan coalition of Democrats and moderate Republicans. This option, however, would further divide the GOP and threaten Boehner's hold on the Speakership, provoke bitter partisan debate, and even prompt GOP actions to weaken or remove him as Speaker.

With time running out before the government shut down on September 30, House Republicans decided to end their effort to defund ObamaCare. Instead, they adopted two key amendments to the Senate amendment (the clean CR) to H. J. Res. 59 (the continuing appropriations measure). The first House amendment repealed a tax on medical devices that was included in Obama-Care, a proposal supported by many Democrats. The second amendment delayed implementation of ObamaCare for one year. Both amendments were adopted ("Continuing Appropriations Resolution, 2014," 2013, H6008-9) early on Sunday morning (12:17 a.m.); the bill and the amendments thereto were messaged to the Senate.

Much to the chagrin of House Republicans, Senate Majority Leader Reid had deliberately not scheduled a Sunday session for the Senate. His decision was "a calculated move to stall action on the House measure until Monday afternoon, just hours before the government's spending authority [ran] out at midnight" (Peters and Weisman 2013, A1). The objective: to pressure the GOP House to enact a clean CR and, if not, be blamed for closing the government. The Senate convened on Monday at 2 p.m. and in less than twenty-five minutes rejected the House's amendments and returned a clean CR (H. J. Res. 59) to that chamber. During the Senate's Monday session, Majority Whip Richard Durbin (D-IL), informed senators that the ping-pong process might not be over. He cited a House e-mail circulating in that chamber that said, "After the Senate tables [kills] the House amendments to the CR later this [Monday] afternoon, and the papers [H. J. Res. 59 and pertinent bicameral messages] come back to the House, we will send it [the CR] back to the Senate with another amendment delaying the individual mandate and ObamaCare for a year and affect the Members' health subsidy as well" (Durbin 2013a, S7016).

The House's e-mail was correct. In the early evening of September 30, a frustrated Hal Rogers, chair of the Appropriations Committee and floor manager of the House's new offer to the Senate, pointed out that his chamber had sent three or four compromises to the Senate. The Senators "simply ignore us, throw [each compromise] in the trash can." This time, he said, the revised CR (H. J. Res. 59) "delays for 1 year ObamaCare's individual mandate, and eliminates the employer subsidy for the health insurance plans of Members of Congress and our staffs and for political appointees at the White House" (Rogers 2013a, H6033–34). New York Representative Nita Lowey (2013, H6034), the ranking Democrat on the Appropriations Committee, responded, "Here we go again. Republicans insist on including riders that do not belong in an appropriations bill. Both the Senate and the President already made clear they will not accept these provisions."

At around 9:00 p.m., the House adopted the revised measure by a vote of 228–201 and transmitted it to the Senate. "But 57 minutes later, and with almost no debate, the Senate killed the House health care provisions and sent the stopgap spending bill right back [to the House] free of policy prescriptions" (Peters and Peters 2013, A1). The clock struck midnight before the House could ping-pong another version of H. J. Res. 59 to the Senate. The government shut down. On October 1, at around 1:15 a.m., the House requested that the Senate join it in creating a conference committee to resolve their bicameral differences. When the Senate reconvened later that morning at 9:30 a.m., it required only a few minutes to table the House's request for a conference by a party-line vote of 54–46 ("Making Continuing Appropriations for Fiscal Year 2014," 2013, S7065).[9] The federal government shut down, except for essential services (air-traffic controllers, for instance). With Congress gridlocked over defunding the health law, it is somewhat ironic that "about 15 percent of the population [on October 1] could begin enrolling in the state-based insurance marketplaces, known as exchanges, created by the 2010 law" (Calmes and Peters 2013, A1).[10]

The Sixteen-Day Shutdown: House and Senate Actions

House-Senate Procedural Background

Before discussing the procedural state of play on ObamaCare in the House and Senate, it is useful to note a stark procedural characteristic that distinguishes decision-making in each chamber. "Majority rule" is the procedural principle that guides House decision-making; "minority rule" is the hallmark of the Senate. House rules and precedents are designed to allow a unified majority, however constructed (partisan or bipartisan), to achieve its procedural and policy preferences. Because the defund-shutdown strategy was a top GOP priority, Speaker Boehner knew that a cohesive majority (218 if all 435 members voted) of Republicans would vote to eliminate funding for ObamaCare or for other legislative options to weaken the law. Moreover, the House Rules Committee, known as the "Speaker's Committee," would bring health-care overhaul legislation to the floor under procedural rules that support and advantage the majority party's preferences. These procedural rules are approved by the full House, but they are party-line votes. The procedural rules are rarely rejected and usually only when the majority party is internally divided.

In contrast, the Senate is a "minority rule" institution. Individual senators, regardless of party affiliation or seniority, have awesome procedural prerogatives to accomplish their objectives. For example, nearly everything in the Senate is subject to unlimited debate, which sometimes arises several times on the same measure. Any senator can speak at great length—Senator Cruz's earlier mentioned twenty-one-hour talkathon, for instance. Recall that sixty votes—a high threshold in today's polarized Senate—are required to invoke cloture to bring extended debate to a close. Without sixty votes—the "new normal" in the Senate for adopting many bills or amendments—the odds are against passing measures. To advance legislation, majority-party leaders strive to craft unanimous consent agreements to limit the number of amendments, the length of debate on each one, and dilatory motions. However, two words—"I object"—can foil the best-laid plans of the majority leader. The

Senate, in short, is an institution that often functions at three speeds—slow, slower, and slowest—where every member has the capacity to stall and block decision-making.

House

House actions to reopen the government are examined first because that chamber initiates appropriations measures. House Republicans, advised by Senator Cruz, came up with a strategy: reopen specific parts of the government. This strategy aimed to mute Democratic criticism of the GOP-made shutdown and to woo conservative-leaning Democratic senators to vote for reopening, on a piecemeal basis, federal agencies and programs recognized as popular and important to the populace. Republicans believed that President Obama directed the closure of popular federal entities, such as national parks and Washington's monuments, to arouse the public to pressure GOP lawmakers to reopen the government and to drop their attempt to defund the health law.

Republicans relied on two principal procedural approaches to reopen parts of the government: suspension of the rules, which was a short-lived approach, or a "rule" from the Rules Committee. Suspension procedure was relatively short-lived because of its features: no amendments are allowed by members, only forty minutes of debate are permitted, and a two-thirds vote is required for passage of the legislation. For example, on the first day (October 1) of the shutdown, a GOP appropriations subcommittee chair (Michael Simpson of Idaho) moved to suspend the House rules and pass a continuing appropriations resolution that would fund many of the most popular—nationally and internationally—parts of the federal government: the National Park Service, the Smithsonian Institution, the National Gallery of Art, and the United States Holocaust Memorial Museum. As Chairman Simpson (2013, H6071) stated, "Tourists yesterday [September 30] raced from one museum to another, trying to see as many sights [as] they could with the government shutdown looming."

In response, Democratic Representative from Virginia Jim Moran (2013, H6072), a member of the Appropriations Committee, exclaimed that trying to open these popular institutions was "an act of political desperation. It's evidence, really, of how politically bankrupt this position of shutting down the government has become—degenerating down to picking winners and losers among Federal workers, just so as to dissipate the political heat," with television stations around the country showing "closed" signs on national museums and visitors being turned away from Yosemite, Yellowstone, and other national parks.

Unable to secure the required two-thirds vote on this bill, along with two additional failed suspension procedures that day aimed at providing funds for the District of Columbia and veterans' benefits, House GOP leaders turned the next day (October 2) to using procedural rules from the Rules Committee to pass the three continuing resolutions.[11] Recall that these procedural rules require a majority vote for adoption and that the voting is nearly always along party lines. Once adopted, the procedural rules make in order for chamber consideration one or more bills and establish the conditions for debating and amending them. Thus, all three continuing appropriations bills rejected the previous day under suspension procedure were adopted on October 2, with debate limited to one hour on each and no amendments permitted to any of the three.

House Democrats lacked the votes to stymie the GOP's strategy, so they castigated the GOP's plan and employed a number of procedural tactics. Used regularly by Democrats was the motion to recommit. Under House rules, just before a measure is voted upon for passage (or rejection), the minority party is afforded an opportunity to offer a motion to recommit the bill to the committee that reported it. Embedded in this motion is the minority party's policy alternative.

Numerous times on a single-agency continuing appropriations bill, a Democratic lawmaker would include in the motion to recommit a policy provision that, if adopted, would fund and reopen the entire federal government. On each of these occasions, a GOP member would make a point of order that the Democratic motion to recommit contained a nongermane matter—reopening the federal government—and was not in order. The presiding officer would uphold the point of order; a Democratic member would then appeal the chair's ruling; a GOP member would move to table (kill) the appeal; a recorded vote was demanded by Democrats; and on a party-line vote, the appeal was killed and the chair's ruling upheld.[12] This pattern was repeated over and over with the same result, but it served Democratic message purposes: blame Republicans for the shutdown and the hardship it was causing many Americans.

The GOP strategy to open parts of the government continued throughout the shutdown period. The House enacted numerous continuing appropriations bills to fund various programs and parts of the federal government, each designed to attract Democratic support in both chambers, encourage bicameral negotiations, and minimize adverse effects of the shutdown. For example, Republicans took up specific CRs to fund, among other entities, the supplemental nutrition program for women, infants, and children; the Federal Emergency Management Agency (FEMA); the Food and Drug Administration; the Head Start program; the Border Security and Enforcement program; the Federal Aviation Administration; and the National Institutes of Health. These piecemeal measures passed the House but not the Senate.

Senate

For its part, the Democratic Senate ignored the House-passed legislation funding certain federal agencies. The Democratic Senate vowed to block such piecemeal measures, and President Obama promised to veto any that might reach his desk. When the House-passed measures arrived in the Senate, they were placed on the Senate's legislative calendar and received no further action. The two Senate parties were stalemated as each blamed the other for the shutdown. On a daily basis, senators from each party went to the chamber to highlight the adverse effects of the shutdown and to urge negotiations between and among the relevant actors. For example, GOP Senator Dan Coats (2013b, S7200) of Indiana exclaimed, "Nine times the Senate has had the opportunity to pass legislation to reopen our government and fund essential services, but the Senate majority leader chose not to do so and the President refuses even to engage" with congressional Republicans. He also asked unanimous consent that the Federal Emergency Management Agency be funded because of its important role in responding to manmade and natural disasters. So many FEMA employees "have been furloughed," Coats (2013a, S7331) said, that they are not available to respond when a disaster hits.

Majority Whip Durbin agreed with Coats about FEMA's importance in responding to disasters but said that this role is not exclusive to that agency. He then pointed out the many other federal agencies "that are a critical part of responding to natural disasters." Durbin (2013b, S7331) elaborated, "The Small Business Administration, they are usually the first on the scene with the Red Cross. Sadly, they are closed down because of the Republican shutdown of the government, and the Senator doesn't include them in his natural disaster request; DOT—the Department of Transportation—and the need for emergency highways in the midst of hurricanes and tornadoes is not included in the request of the Senator from Indiana; the Corps of Engineers, the National Guard and Reserve, the Public Health Service, none of these are included." Selecting which federal agencies should and should not remain open during a government shutdown is difficult.

The Senate took up other business, such as presidential nominations, but much of the chamber's activities consisted of rhetorical volleys between the two parties, each blaming the other for the shutdown. The Senate also practiced an internal form of "ping-pong," with each party proposing alternative unanimous consent agreements to reopen the government. For example, Minority Whip Cornyn asked for "unanimous consent that the Senate proceed

to the immediate consideration of H. J. Res. 70, making continuing appropriations for National Park Service operations, which was received from the
House; that the measure be read three times and passed." Majority Leader
Reid (2013d, S7146) quickly objected to Cornyn's request and proposed an
alternative to it: "I ask unanimous consent that [the GOP] request be modified as follows: That an amendment [the clean CR], which is at the desk, be
agreed to; that the [House] joint resolution, as amended, be read a third time
and passed." Senator Cornyn objected to Reid's request. As the two parties
wrangled over who was to blame for the shutdown, another imminent crisis
loomed large: the potential for the United States to default on its debt.

A Hike in the Debt Ceiling

In addition to the defund-shutdown controversy concerning the health-
care law, there was the added complexity of Congress's enacting an increase
in the debt ceiling by October 17, 2013. President Obama and congressional
Democrats insisted that Republicans in both houses support passage of a
clean debt-ceiling measure. Their "no-negotiation" strategy was similar to
their steadfastness in advocating passage of a clean CR to open the government without any change to ObamaCare. Speaker Boehner and many GOP
lawmakers rejected that approach. As the Speaker said, "We're not going to
pass a clean debt limit increase. I told the president, there's no way we're
going to pass one. The votes are not in the House to pass a clean debt limit.
And the president is risking default by not having a conversation with us"
(Epstein 2013, 3).[13] Part of that conversation was shaped by GOP actions
undertaken two years earlier.

In 2011, House Republicans successfully employed the strategy of winning
large spending cuts in exchange for raising the debt ceiling. The 2011 strategy,
dubbed the Boehner Rule, called for a dollar in spending cuts for every dollar
of additional borrowing authority. Two years later, as Representative Kevin
Brady (R-TX) remarked in what might have been a bargaining ploy, "It's very
much in play, the dollar-for-dollar approach" (Schroeder 2013, 8). Little surprise after the controversies surrounding the 2011 debt fight, which included
a downgrade by Standard & Poor's in the federal government's creditworthi-
ness, that President Obama in 2013 exclaimed that the administration would
pay no "ransom" to raise the debt ceiling. Nonetheless, the president and both
parties and chambers recognized that hiking the debt ceiling was now paired
with ending the government shutdown.[14] Negotiations to resolve both would
have to occur on simultaneous tracks. And that conversation started when a
bipartisan group of senators joined forces to suggest ideas to end the partisan
and policy standoff. Importantly, they were backed by the chamber's two

party leaders, who subsequently produced the compromise that reopened the government and prevented a debt default.

The Impasse Ends

On October 5, 2013, Senator Susan Collins (R-ME) gave a speech in the chamber urging her colleagues to work collaboratively to resolve the difficult issues that were before the Senate. Thirteen other senators heard her request, and on a bipartisan basis they came together to do just that, forming the so-called Gang of 14. In addition to Collins, the GOP side included John McCain (R-AZ), John Johannes (R-SD), Mark Kirk (R-IL), Jeff Flake (R-AZ), Lisa Murkowski (R-AK), and Kelly Ayotte (R-NH). In addition to Independent Angus King of Maine, the six Democratic senators were Joe Manchin (D-WV), Mark Begich (D-AK), Jeanne Shaheen (D-NH), Joe Donnelly (D-IN), Heidi Heitkamp (D-ND), and Mark Pryor (D-AR).[15]

The gang's ideas for a compromise plan—for example, repealing or delaying a medical-device tax, a provision in the health-care law—were funneled to the two party leaders (Senators Reid and McConnell), who on October 12 began talks on how to open the government and avert a default. "I hope everyone understands how positive this is," said Senator Reid (2013c, S7430). "It is the first discussions we have had here, period, during the whole pendency of this artificially driven government shutdown and not raising the debt limit when we should." Four days later, the bipartisan leadership plan was taken up by the Senate. Among the major features of the Reid-McConnell plan were these two: (1) the government would be reopened by extending the CR through January 15, 2014, with ObamaCare funded; and (2) the statutory debt limit would be suspended through February 7, 2014, averting any default.[16]

Because the Reid-McConnell compromise enjoyed broad support, no senator blocked its swift passage, not even such vehement opponents as Senator Cruz. Asked if he would filibuster the compromise, Senator Cruz responded, "Of course not; never had any intention to delay this vote. . . . Delaying this vote would not accomplish anything" (Mascaro, Memoli, and Bennett 2013). The two leaders' plan completely replaced the text in H.R. 2775, the No Subsidies without Verification Act, which was pending on the Senate's legislative calendar. Majority Leader Reid asked and received unanimous consent to expedite passage of the compromise. Specifically, under the unanimous consent agreement, various procedural steps would occur in rapid succession: the Senate would proceed (without debate) to consider H.R. 2775; the Reid-McConnell substitute amendment (the bipartisan plan) to H.R. 2775 would be agreed to; the Senate would vote on a motion to invoke cloture on the bill, as amended; if cloture was invoked, all postcloture debate time would be yielded back; and the Senate would proceed to vote on final passage of the bill, as amended by the Reid-McConnell compromise plan. Cloture was adopted (83–16), followed immediately by the vote (81–18) to pass H.R. 2775. The eighteen negative votes were all cast by Republican senators.[17] The Senate transmitted H.R. 2775, as amended, to the House on October 16.

Speaker Boehner, aware of the Reid-McConnell compromise plan, tried on October 15 to craft a GOP bill to send to the Senate. He presented it to his GOP colleagues as a way "to give the House a coherent position from which to negotiate with the Senate and to avoid being 'jammed' to accept the McConnell-Reid deal as the Oct. 17 deadline for lifting the debt ceiling bore down" (McManus 2013). Speaker Boehner failed to win the backing of many Republicans, and his proposal was shelved. Part of the reason was that Boehner's plan was not tough enough in blocking ObamaCare. Two prominent conservative groups, the Club for Growth and Heritage Action, also "announced that they would consider as betrayals any lawmaker's vote to accept half-measures" rather than the repeal of the health law (Marcos and Krawzak 2013, 1757).[18] In a major reversal, Speaker Boehner subsequently told his GOP colleagues that the House would vote on the Senate's package to reopen the government and raise the debt ceiling with no strings attached to either. As Speaker Boehner said in a radio interview a few hours before the climactic vote, "We fought the good fight. We just didn't win" (Mascaro, Memoli, and Bennett 2013).

When the House called up the Reid-McConnell compromise on Wednesday, October 16, at around 9:30 p.m., it took less than an hour for the chamber to approve the legislation. The vote was 285–144, with all 198 Democrats voting yes, joined by 87 Republicans; 144 Republicans, however, voted no. The measure was quickly sent to the White House, and President Obama signed it into law on Thursday, October 17, at around 12:30 a.m. Federal agencies reopened that day, and the statutory debt limit was suspended until February 7, 2014. Suspension meant that the government could spend (borrow money) to meet its financial obligations through February 7, when the issue of lifting the debt ceiling returned to Congress.

Concluding Observations

After a shutdown of sixteen days, the government was opened and a debt crisis avoided, but only for several weeks—until January 15, 2014, for funding the government and February 7, 2014, when the statutory borrowing limit would be reached. In fact, the next major funding battles were already being anticipated. As one conservative House Republican stated after the October shutdown ended, "See, we're going to start this all over again" (Weisman and Parker 2013a, A1). The pattern for "all over again" typically means that each party will use confrontational rhetoric, outside groups, and the media to blame "the other's intransigence for a lack of progress" in averting an impending fiscal crisis ("Cleaning the Barn" 2015, 25). A few months later, Congress avoided a government shutdown and debt default.

Noteworthy is that after four bitter years (2011–2015) of pitched fiscal battles, it appears that party clashes over closing the government or forcing a debt default might be abating for a time. This outcome seems likely because of an October 2015 two-year spending/debt-ceiling package that was signed into law. Congressional leaders and President Obama reached a two-part agreement: (1) providing more money for defense and domestic programs— exceeding the spending caps in the Budget Control Act of 2011 but with offsetting cuts in other areas (for example, eligibility requirements for Social Security disability payments)—and (2) suspending the debt ceiling until March 15, 2017, or even later in the year, given the Treasury secretary's legal authority to use "extraordinary measures" (postponing payments to various federal trust funds, for instance) to permit the government to pay its debts.

Unusual circumstances produced the spending/debt-ceiling accord. On September 25, 2015, to the surprise of many, Speaker Boehner announced that he would both resign the Speakership pending the election of a new Speaker and resign from the House at the end of the following month. Boehner's resignation as Speaker was welcomed by many conservative House Republicans and celebrated by outside conservative activists. Before he departed the House, Speaker Boehner said, he would try to "clean the barn" so the next Speaker (GOP Representative Paul Ryan of Wisconsin) and the Congress could "fund governmental activities without 'fiscal cliffs' that could interfere with [2016] election-year campaigning" (Hallerman 2015a, 138). The two-year budget agreement was Boehner's parting gift to incoming Speaker Ryan so he would not have to deal with these controversial topics soon after taking office.

The agreement lessens the chance of government shutdowns (or gaps in funding) because spending is increased for both defense and domestic programs. Nonetheless, they still might occur for at least one key reason: attempts to add divisive policy riders (defund Planned Parenthood, for example) to the must-pass appropriations bills. Showdown clashes over hiking the debt ceiling—partisan demands that any hike in the debt ceiling must be combined with equivalent spending reductions—are off the table until 2017.

The reality of the 2013 government shutdown was not without public, private, and personal costs. Publicly, the country lost trust and confidence in the governing capacity of the Congress. Privately, according to some accounts, the 2013 shutdown resulted in 6.6 million lost workdays; back pay to furloughed federal employees cost $2 billion; 120,000 private-sector jobs were lost; and the gross domestic product lost an estimated $3.1 billion (Lowrey 2013, A16; Lowrey and Shear 2013, A12; McCrimmon and Krawzak 2015, 19). Personally, many individuals faced some degree of hardship because of absent paychecks and inadequate savings to meet financial obligations.

Political costs were temporary as shutdown effects receded and other events took center stage. Public opinion polls showed that Republicans were blamed for both the 1995–1996 and 2013 government shutdowns. Yet they suffered little damage to the party's brand (image) and scant electoral fallout. As former GOP Speaker Newt Gingrich, the architect of the 1995 and 1996 shutdowns, stated, "We closed the government twice in 1995 and '96 and became the first re-elected House Republican majority since 1928. . . . The Republicans closed the government in 2013 and won a big election in 2014" (Thomas 2015, B4; Balz and Clement 2013, A1). Thus, the likelihood remains that various lawmakers and partisan factions will use crucial deadlines "to hold out until the other side caves" as leverage to win their political and policy demands. "The more you do something like this [governing by brinksmanship]," said a political historian, "the more comfortable you get to do it again" (Chaddock 2011, 16).

Today's fiscal battles reflect the sharply divergent views of Democrats and Republicans over the role and reach of the national government—an argument that has been going on since 1789. Democrats believe that an activist federal government can produce policies and programs that benefit the collective good and public well-being. Republicans want to shrink the government, especially entitlements (Social Security and Medicare, for instance) and other domestic programs; they emphasize tax cuts, regulatory reform, and individual reliance. Understandably, the two parties provide different answers to a key question, posed by former Democratic Representative from Massachusetts Barney Frank (2002, 13146): "What is the appropriate level of public [government] activity in our society?" Former Speaker Boehner suggested this answer: "I came here to fight for a smaller, less costly and more accountable government. But I began to realize over the years that there's no winning this fight. It's going to be this constant struggle [between the two parties] over how big the government should be" (Mascaro and Parsons 2015).

Notes

This chapter reflects the views of the author and does not reflect the views of the Congressional Research Service or the Library of Congress.

1. Kaiser recounts the story of the enactment of a major reform measure that transformed the country's financial sector.

2. When Franklin Roosevelt was first elected president, he took office during the 1930s Great Depression. There were thousands of bank failures. As one of his first actions, President Roosevelt sent to Congress an emergency banking act. The president wanted fast action—a deadline of immediacy—to meet the crisis in banking, and Congress responded. As David Kennedy (2005, 136) wrote, "The [banking] bill was read to the House at 1:00 P.M., while some new representatives were still trying to locate their seats. Printed copies were not ready for the members. A rolled-up newspaper symbolically served [as the bill]. After thirty-eight minutes of 'debate,' the chamber passed the bill, sight unseen, with a unanimous shout."

3. There are many laws that expire on a certain date. They may be renewed or not. There are laws that might be enacted to avert automatic spending cuts required by deadlines in other statutes. Some laws, or legal provisions thereof, are not enforced because they reflect lofty aspirations difficult to meet. The statutory timetable in the 1974 Budget Act (P.L. 93-344) is an example. It obligates the House and Senate to adopt an annual concurrent budget resolution—Congress's fiscal blueprint outlining, for instance, aggregate spending for different policy categories—on or before April 15 of each year. This requirement is not always met. Why? The concurrent budget resolution reflects the fiscal priorities of the majority party in each chamber. Because the fiscal priorities of each party diverge, the concurrent budget resolution often provokes bitter battles between the parties and chambers. Neither chamber suffers any legal penalty for its inability to adopt a budget resolution since enforcement rests with the legislative branch itself. There may be political penalties, however. The minority party in each chamber and the media typically castigate the majority party for its failure to fulfill its governing responsibility.

4. Under CRs, federal agencies usually operate under the previous year's funding levels, which hinders their ability to end programs or initiate new ones. Heightened polarization in the Congress has meant that since 1977, "there have been only four Congresses that have not needed a CR—the most recent was almost two decades ago, in 1997—and lawmakers have sent the president an average of six CRs per year to avoid shutdowns" (Hallerman 2015b).

5. In the judgment of Michael Gerson (2013), a former speechwriter for President George W. Bush, "The Republican Party is the only institution capable of reversing Obamacare. Here is an actual iron rule: A measure passed by a Democratic president, House and Senate (and approved by the Supreme Court) can be reversed only by a Republican president, House and Senate."

6. This part of the chapter draws from an excellent journalistic account of the planning for the shutdown: Sheryl Gay Stolberg and Mike McIntire, "A Federal Budget Crisis Months in the Planning," *New York Times*, October 5, 2013, A1. This detailed article was reprinted in the *Congressional Record*, October 7, 2013, S7253–55. Footnotes relevant to this article will use page numbers from the *Congressional Record*.

7. According to one account, Senator Lee was a central player in the battle to defund ObamaCare. While Senator Cruz "became the face of the fight, Lee labored behind the scenes to coordinate support from grassroots groups."

8. The so-called Hastert Rule is named after Dennis Hastert (R-IL), the longest serving (1999–2007) Speaker in GOP history. He articulated his namesake "rule" at a 2003 Congressional Research Service conference honoring the hundred-year anniversary of Speaker Joe Cannon's ascension to that high post in 1903. Simply put, the Hastert Rule says that only measures that have the support of the majority of the majority party should reach the floor, even if those bills could attract a bipartisan majority of the House membership. During his Speakership, according to one account, John Boehner violated the Hastert Rule nine times, which, among other factors, no doubt contributed to his decision to resign from that post and retire from the 114th Congress on October 30, 2015 (Zeller and Hallerman 2013, 18).

9. House Appropriations chair Hal Rogers was upset by the Senate's refusal to convene a conference committee. He said, "I was so disappointed this morning when the U.S. Senate declared that they didn't want to meet with us to talk about how to end this shutdown. We offered to sit down and talk in a conference committee. The Senate at 9:30 a.m. brusquely says, No way. We don't want to talk to you. I thought that's what Congress was all about, was working out differences from this body across to the Senate, but, apparently, I am wrong" (Rogers 2013b, H6083).

10. Public use of the federal exchange websites proved to be a public relations disaster for the Obama administration. People encountered large technical challenges in purchasing health coverage (Reichard 2013, 1793–94).

11. Suspension procedure was used successfully to fund programs supported by a large bipartisan majority. For example, by a vote of 425 to 0, the House passed a mini continuing appropriations measure to provide without delay death gratuity benefits (burial services, for instance) to the families of military troops killed serving the nation. As Rodney Frelinghuysen, the Defense Appropriations subcommittee chair, stated, "Our government has no greater responsibility . . . than to take care of the families of our brave men and women who have fought and died for our country." Since October 1, 2013, seventeen military personnel had been killed (Frelinghuysen 2013, H6431).

12. See, e.g., "Special Supplemental Nutrition Program for Women, Infants, and Children Continuing Appropriations Resolution, 2014" (2013).

13. Senate Majority Leader Reid introduced a bill (S. 1569) focused solely on raising the debt ceiling and introduced a cloture motion to end debate on the "clean" debt legislation. On October 12, the Senate failed to invoke cloture.

14. Overlaid on the shutdown and debt ceiling fights were two other partisan controversies. One involved adoption of the concurrent budget resolution as stated in the 1974 Budget Act. The Senate and House adopted their respective concurrent budget resolutions in March 2013. These resolutions serve as the fiscal blueprint for Congress's tax and spending decisions. However, a number of GOP senators blocked the procedure to convene a conference with the House so the two chambers could resolve their fiscal differences. Why? GOP senators worried that the conference would authorize the Senate to use a filibuster-proof procedure called "reconciliation" to raise the debt ceiling. These senators wanted a hike in the debt ceiling brought to the Senate floor as a stand-alone bill, which they could castigate and use as leverage to win concessions from the White House. The other controversy concerned the Bud-

get Control Act (BCA) of 2011, enacted as part of the "Boehner Rule" controversy: Congress raised the debt ceiling but only in exchange for deep spending cuts. The BCA imposed strict (unrealistic to many lawmakers) spending caps on defense and domestic spending. If the caps were not adhered to, then automatic spending cuts (called "sequestration") would occur. Many Democratic and GOP lawmakers wanted to raise the spending caps (which occurred temporarily in 2013 for a two-year period) to accommodate the demands and pressures for new spending. GOP lawmakers emphasized increasing the caps for defense; Democratic lawmakers, also supportive of defense hikes, wanted increases in spending for domestic programs; and other Republicans, such as Senate GOP leader Mitch McConnell (R-KY), touted "the BCA as one of the GOP's biggest fiscal accomplishments of the past decade" (Bolton 2015, 8).

It is worth mentioning that Senator McConnell included in the Reid-McConnell 2013 compromise an artful procedure to have the president and not Congress take responsibility for raising the debt ceiling. Debt ceiling hikes are difficult votes for majority-party lawmakers because minority-party members typically will not provide any votes for debt hikes. Challengers can then run campaign ads castigating majority-party incumbents as irresponsible spenders. Under Senator McConnell's proposal, which was included in the BCA of 2011, the president would certify to Congress that the debt ceiling would be increased unless Congress passed a joint resolution of disapproval. No doubt the president would veto the disapproval legislation to avoid an economic crisis, Congress would be unable to override the veto, the debt ceiling increase would go into effect, and the president would get blamed as a spendthrift.

15. For more information on the "Gang of 14," see "Default Prevention Act of 2013—Motion to Proceed," S7511.

16. Other matters were also included in the compromise plan, such as retroactive pay for the furloughed federal employees and a verification process for individuals to determine their eligibility for health-care income subsidies (recall the original title of H.R. 2775).

17. The House, by long-standing custom, initiates appropriations measures. To adhere to this custom, the Senate amended the title of H.R. 2775 per Senate precedent after the bill was passed. The original title of H.R. 2775, as mentioned, was the No Subsidies without Verification Act. The new title, reflecting the general style of appropriations titles, was An Act Making Continuing Appropriations for the Fiscal Year Ending September 30, 2014, and for Other Purposes. For an interesting critique of the GOP's shutdown strategy, see Lowry (2013, 4).

18. Senate Majority Leader Reid viewed Boehner's October 15 draft proposal as an attempt "to torpedo" the Senate's bipartisan compromise plan (Reid 2013a, S7481).

References

Bade, Rachel. 2015. "Funding Battle Could Get Punted into Election Year." *Politico*, July 13.

Balz, Dan, and Scott Clement. 2013. "Poll Finds Major Damage to GOP after Shutdown." *Washington Post*, October 22.

Berman, Russell, Molly K. Hooper, and Erik Wasson. 2013. "GOP Tries to Finesse Vote on ObamaCare." *Hill*, September 10.

Bolton, Alexander. 2013a. "GOP Fight Spreads to the Senate." *Hill*, September 19.

———. 2013b. "Smash-Mouth Reid." *Hill*, October 7.

———. 2014. "Cruz Warns House Colleagues: Don't Let Democrats Fool You." *Hill*, July 24.

———. 2015. "McConnell Wary of Murry-Ryan 2.0." *Hill*, September 14.

Brass, Clinton T. 2014. "Shutdown of the Federal Government: Causes, Processes, and Effects." Congressional Research Service. Washington, DC: Library of Congress.

Calmes, Jackie, and Jeremy W. Peters. 2013. "President Tells Republicans to 'Reopen the Government.'" *New York Times*, October 2.

Chaddock, Gail Russell. 2011. "The Politics of Playing Chicken." *Christian Science Monitor*, October 11.

"Cleaning the Barn." 2015. *Economist*, October 31.

Coats, Dan. 2013a. "Continuing Appropriations." *Congressional Record*, Senate (daily edition), 159 (October 9).

———. 2013b. "Extension of Morning Business." *Congressional Record*, Senate (daily edition), 159 (October 4).

Collender, Stan. 2011. "Agony, 'Agita' and Anguish over Appropriations." *Roll Call*, October 4.

"Continuing Appropriations Resolution, 2014." 2013. *Congressional Record*, House of Representatives (daily edition), 159 (September 28): H6008–9.

Corker, Bob. 2013. "Making Continuing Appropriations for Fiscal Year 2014—Continued." *Congressional Record*, Senate (daily edition), 159 (September 26): S6938.

Cornyn, John. 2013. "Making Continuing Appropriations for Fiscal Year 2014." *Congressional Record*, Senate (daily edition), 159 (September 27): S6992.

Cottle, Michelle. 2015. "Mike Lee's Idea Factory." *National Journal*, May 2.

Cruz, Ted. 2013. "Making Continuing Appropriations for Fiscal Year 2014—Motion to Proceed—Continued." *Congressional Record*, Senate (daily edition), 159 (September 24): S6775–79.

"Default Prevention Act of 2013—Motion to Proceed." 2013. *Congressional Record*, Senate (daily edition), 159 (October 16): S7503–31.

Dinan, Stephen. 2013. "Winning the Blame Game for Shutdown: It's All in the Timing." *Washington Times*, September 30.

Durbin, Richard. 2013a. "Continuing Appropriations." *Congressional Record*, Senate (daily edition), 159 (September 30).

———. 2013b. "Continuing Appropriations." *Congressional Record*, Senate (daily edition), 159 (October 9).

Epstein, Jennifer. 2013. "Dems, GOP Exchange Fire from Entrenched Positions." *Politico*, October 7.

Everett, Burgess. 2013. "House-Senate GOP 'Caucus' Takes Root." *Politico*, October 28.

Frank, Barney. 2002. "Department of the Interior and Related Agencies Appropriations Act, 2003." *Congressional Record*, House of Representatives, 148, pt. 10 (July 16).

Frelinghuysen, Rodney. 2013. "Department of Defense Survivor Benefits Continuing Appropriations Resolution, 2014." *Congressional Record*, House of Representatives (daily edition), 159 (October 9): H6431–35.

Fuller, Matt. 2013. "Boehner Puts Obamacare Defunding in the CR." *Roll Call*, September 18.

———. 2014. "Cruz Hosts Secret Meeting with Select House Members." *Roll Call*, April 30.

Gerson, Michael. 2013. "A Custer for Our Time." *Washington Post*, August 2.

Hallerman, Tamar. 2015a. "Barn Is Cleared for the New Speaker." *CQ Weekly*, November 2.

———. 2015b. "Why a Stopgap Spending Bill Might Not Be So Bad After All." *CQ News*, September 15.

Hook, Janet, and Kristina Peterson. 2013. "Spending Bill Set for the Senate." *Wall Street Journal*, September 20.

Kaiser, Robert G. 2013. *Act of Congress*. New York: Alfred A. Knopf.

Kane, Paul, and Ed O'Keefe. 2013. "Republican Divisions on Funding Bill Deepen." *Washington Post*, September 20.

Kennedy, David M. 2005. *Freedom from Fear*. New York: Oxford University Press.

Lowey, Nita. 2013. "Continuing Appropriations Resolution, 2014." *Congressional Record*, House of Representatives (daily edition), 159 (September 30).

Lowrey, Annie. 2013. "White House Puts Price on Government Shutdown." *New York Times*, November 8.

Lowrey, Annie, Nathaniel Popper, and Nelson D. Schwartz. 2013. "Gridlock Has Cost U.S. Billions, and the Meter Is Still Running." *New York Times*, October 17.

Lowrey, Annie, and Michael D. Shear. 2013. "Shutdown to Cost U.S. Billions, Analysts Say, While Eroding Confidence." *New York Times*, October 19.

Lowry, Rich. 2013. "The Defunding Debacle." *Politico*, October 17.

"Making Continuing Appropriations for Fiscal Year 2014." 2013. *Congressional Record*, Senate (daily edition), 159 (October 1): S7065.

Marcos, Christina, and Paul M. Krawzak. 2013. "Battle Over, but 'War' Continues." *CQ Weekly*, October 21.

Mascaro, Lisa, Michael A. Memoli, and Brian Bennett. 2013. "Government Crisis Is Averted—for Now." *Los Angeles Times*, October 16.

Mascaro, Lisa, and Christi Parsons. 2015. "A Key Moment in Talks." *Los Angeles Times*, October 31.

McCrimmon, Ryan, and Paul M. Krawzak. 2015. "2013 Shutdown Revisited." *CQ Weekly*, September 21.

McManus, Doyle. 2013. "McConnell Delivers; Boehner Can't." *Los Angeles Times*, October 16.

Moran, Jim. 2013. "National Park Service Operations, Smithsonian Institution, National Gallery of Art, and United States Holocaust Memorial Museum Continuing Appropriations Resolution, 2014." *Congressional Record*, House of Representatives (daily edition), 159 (October 1).

Newhauser, Daniel, and Emily Ethridge. 2013. "Shutdown Showdown." *CQ Weekly*, September 23.

Persily, Nathaniel. 2015. *Solutions to Political Polarization in America*. New York: Cambridge University Press.

Peters, Jeremy W., and Jonathan Weisman. 2013. "Senate to Act at the Brink of Shutdown." *New York Times*, September 30.

Peters, Jonathan, and Jeremy W. Peters. 2013. "U.S. Government Is Shutting Down in Fiscal Impasse." *New York Times*, October 1.

Reichard, John. 2013. "Secretive Style May Have Undermined Rollout." *CQ Weekly*, October 28.

Reid, Harry. 2013a. "Default Prevention Act of 2013—Motion to Proceed." *Congressional Record*, Senate (daily edition), 159 (October 15).

———. 2013b. "Making Continuing Appropriations for Fiscal Year 2014—Continued." *Congressional Record*, Senate (daily edition), 159 (September 26): S6937.

———. 2013c. "Preliminary Talks." *Congressional Record*, Senate (daily edition), 159 (October 12).

———. 2013d. "Unanimous Consent Request—H.J.Res. 72." *Congressional Record*, Senate (daily edition), 159 (October 3).

Riddick, Floyd M., and Alan S. Frumin. 1992. *Senate Procedure: Precedents and Practices*. Washington, DC: Government Printing Office.

Rogers, Hal. 2013a. "Continuing Appropriations Resolution, 2014." *Congressional Record*, House of Representatives (daily edition), 159 (September 30).

———. 2013b. "Veterans Benefits Continuing Appropriations Resolution, 2014." *Congressional Record*, House of Representatives (daily edition), 159 (October 1).

Samuelsohn, Darren. 2015. "Welcome to CR Hell." *Politico*, October 22.

Schroeder, Peter. 2013. "GOP Puts New Price on Debt Hike." *Hill*, October 3.

Sherman, Jake, and John Bresnahan. 2013a. "Shutdown Possible as GOP Divisions Sharpen." *Politico*, September 12.

———. 2013b. "Shutdown Showdown Looms amid Gridlock." *Politico*, September 16.

Sherman, Jake, and Burgess Everett. 2015. "Congress Faces a Fall from Hell." *Politico*, July 29.

Simpson, Michael K. 2013. "National Park Service Operations, Smithsonian Institution, National Gallery of Art, and United States Holocaust Memorial Museum Continuing Appropriations Resolution, 2014." *Congressional Record*, House of Representatives (daily edition), 159 (October 1).

"Special Supplemental Nutrition Program for Women." 2013. *Congressional Record*, House (daily edition) 159 (October 4): H6270–71.

Stolberg, Sheryl Gay, and Mike McIntire. 2013. "A Federal Budget Crisis Months in the Planning." *New York Times*. In *Congressional Record*, Senate (daily edition), 159 (October 7): S7253–55.

Thomas, Cal. 2015. "John Boehner, Then and Now." *Washington Times*, September 29.

Wayne, Leslie. 1997. "Lobbyists' Gifts to Politicians Reap Benefits, Study Shows." *New York Times*, January 23.

Weisman, Jonathan, and Ashley Parker. 2013a. "Shutdown Is Over." *New York Times*, October 17.

———. 2013b. "Shutdown Looms as Senate Passes Budget Bill." *New York Times*, September 28.

Zeller, Shawn. 2013. "Shutdown Is Open to Interpretation." *CQ Weekly*, October 7.

Zeller, Shawn, and Tamar Hallerman. 2013. *CQ Weekly*, September 21.

Index

About the Contributors

Briana Bee is pursuing a bachelor of arts and sciences in political science at the Catholic University of America. Hailing from Longport, New Jersey, Bee plans to pursue policy work in Washington, DC, after graduation.

Jennifer Hayes Clark is Pauline Yelderman Chair and associate professor of political science at the University of Houston, where she has taught since 2007. She received her PhD from Indiana University. In 2009, she served as an American Political Science Association congressional fellow working on health-care reform and education policy. Her book *Minority Parties in U.S. Legislatures: Conditions of Influence* was published in 2015.

Matthew E. Glassman is an analyst with the Congressional Research Service (CRS), where he focuses on congressional operations and administration, judicial branch appropriations, and congressional history. His research interests include institutional design and nineteenth-century American political development. He earned his PhD from Yale University.

Matthew Green is associate professor of politics at the Catholic University of America. He is author of *Underdog Politics: The Minority Party in the U.S. House of Representatives* (2015) and *The Speaker of the House: A Study of Leadership* (2010) and coauthor of *Washington 101: An Introduction to the Nation's Capital* (2014). He has also authored or coauthored several articles and book chapters on Congress, American elections, and public policy.

Aaron S. King is assistant professor in the Department of Public and International Affairs at the University of North Carolina, Wilmington. His research focuses on congressional procedure and elections, ambition and representation, political parties, and public opinion.

Gregory Koger is associate professor of political science at the University of Miami. He specializes in legislative politics and political parties. His is author of *Filibustering: A Political History of Obstruction in the House and Senate* (2010), which won the 2011 Fenno Prize for best book on legislative studies. Koger's research has been featured in the *Washington Post* and on *Fresh Air* with Terry Gross. He has also testified before the Senate Rules Committee. Koger has also published research articles on parties, lobbying, and Congress in *American Journal of Political Science, Journal of Politics, Legislative Studies Quarterly, American Political Research, British Journal of Political Science, PS: Political Science & Politics,* and *Journal of Theoretical Politics.* He earned his PhD from the University of California, Los Angeles.

Scott Levy is a student at Yale Law School and a former health-care staffer for the Senate Finance Committee. On the committee, he served as the lead staffer for Medicare Part A issues.

Michael S. Lynch is assistant professor of political science at the University of Georgia. He received his PhD in political science from Washington University in St. Louis in 2007. His research interests include political methodology, congressional politics, the presidency, and separation of powers. His work has appeared in such journals as *Journal of Politics, Political Analysis, Legislative Studies Quarterly, Journal of Public Policy,* and *Political Research Quarterly.*

Anthony J. Madonna is associate professor of political science at the University of Georgia. He received his PhD in political science from Washington University in St. Louis in 2008. His research interests include American political institutions and development, with an emphasis on U.S. congressional politics and procedure. His work has appeared in such journals as *American Journal of Political Science, Political Research Quarterly, Journal of Politics, Legislative Studies Quarterly,* and *Illinois Law Review.*

Mark J. Oleszek is an analyst on Congress at the Congressional Research Service. Before coming to CRS he taught courses in American politics as assistant professor of political science at Albright College, and he has worked as a staff aide in two Senate offices. He received his PhD in political science from the University of California, Berkeley, with a dissertation that examined the importance of member-to-member collaboration to the Senate's lawmaking process. He has published a number of articles and book chapters on topics that include congressional-presidential relations, the regulation of conflicts of interest in the United States, and passage of the Affordable Care Act, and he is a coauthor (with Walter Oleszek, Elizabeth Rybicki, and Bill Heniff Jr.) of *Congressional Procedures and the Policy Process* (2015).

Walter J. Oleszek is a senior specialist on Congress at the Congressional Research Service. He has been at CRS since 1968 and worked closely with many lawmakers and on many House and Senate committee reform initiatives. The author or coauthor of several books on the Congress, he is a longtime adjunct faculty member at the American University. He received his PhD from the State University of New York, Albany.

Frank J. Orlando is instructor of political science in the Department of Social Sciences at Saint Leo University. His research interests include national institutions, and he serves as the politics expert for the Saint Leo Polling Institute.

Molly E. Reynolds is a fellow in governance studies at the Brookings Institution. She studies Congress, with an emphasis on the congressional budget process and how congressional rules and procedure affect domestic policymaking. She received a PhD in political science and public policy from the University of Michigan.

David W. Rohde is Ernestine Friedl Professor of Political Science at Duke University and director of the Political Institutions and Public Choice Program. He has researched various aspects of American national politics, including Congress, the presidency, the Supreme Court, and presidential and congressional elections.

James V. Saturno is a specialist on Congress and the legislative process at the Congressional Research Service. His work has appeared in *The Encyclopedia of Congress*, *Legislative Studies Quarterly*, and *Public Budgeting and Finance*. During the 103rd Congress, he was detailed to the Joint Committee on the Organization of Congress as a consultant on the budget process. He has taught courses on Congress as an adjunct professor at American University and the Boston University Washington Center. He earned a bachelor's in history from the State University of New York, Albany, and a master's in history from the University of Rochester.

Colleen J. Shogan is a senior executive at the Library of Congress and an adjunct professor of government at Georgetown. She is a former Senate staffer and former deputy director of the Congressional Research Service.

Joel Sievert is a postdoctoral fellow in the Political Institutions and Public Choice Program in the Department of Political Science at Duke University. His research interests include congressional politics and elections, interbranch relations, and American political development. His previous research has appeared in *Political Research Quarterly* and *Legislative Studies Quarterly*.

Jacob R. Straus is an analyst with the Congressional Research Service at the Library of Congress. He earned his bachelor's degree from the University of Maryland, College Park, and his master's and doctorate from the University of Florida. He was an assistant professor of political science at Frostburg State University in Maryland and currently is adjunct professor of political science at the Johns Hopkins University and the University of Maryland, Baltimore County's Shady Grove campus. He is editor of *Party and Procedure in the United States Congress* (2012), and his previous research has appeared in *PS: Political Science & Politics*, *Journal of Legislative Studies*, and *Presidential Studies Quarterly*.

Rachel Surminsky is completing her bachelor's degree in political science and international affairs at the University of Georgia, where she is a member of the Honors Program. She plans to attend graduate school in the fall of 2016 with a focus on American political institutions. She presented research on presidential politics at the 2015 Center for Undergraduate Research annual symposium and has coauthored an article on separation of powers that appeared on the *Washington Post*'s *Monkey Cage* blog.

Michele L. Swers is professor of American government in the Department of Government at Georgetown University. Her research interests include congressional elections and policymaking and women and politics. She has written two books examining the policy behavior of women in Congress, including *The Difference Women Make: The Policy Impact of Women in Congress* (2002) and *Women in the Club: Gender and Policy Making in the Senate* (2013). She is also coauthor of *Women and Politics: Paths to Power and Political Influence*, 3rd ed. (2016), with Julie Dolan and Melissa Deckman. Dr. Swers has written numerous articles and book chapters on women in Congress and women in elections as candidates and voters.

James Wallner is executive director of the Senate Steering Committee. Prior to this, he served as legislative director to two U.S. senators. He is also an adjunct professor in the Department of Politics and the Congressional and Presidential Studies Program at the Catholic University of America. He is author of *The Death of Deliberation: Partisanship and Polarization in the United States Senate* (2013). He has a master's of science from the University of Edinburgh in Scotland and received his doctorate in politics from Catholic University.